D1273390

Journals of the
Council of the State of
Virginia

JOURNALS

OF THE

Council of the State of
Virginia
Vol. V

(13 November 1788–29 November 1791)

Edited by

SANDRA GIOIA TREADWAY

Virginia State Library

RICHMOND

1982

Standard Book Number 0–88490–093–2

Contents

PREFACE

This fifth volume of the journals of Virginia's Council of State contains the proceedings of the Council from Governor Edmund Randolph's resignation on 12 November 1788 through the end of Governor Beverley Randolph's three-year administration on 30 November 1791. It concludes the series of revolutionary-era Council journals published by the Virginia State Library, and contains short biographical sketches of all members of the Committee of Safety and the Council of State from 1776 through November 1791. Microfilm copies of the original journals from 1791 to 1852 are readily available to researchers in the Archives Branch of the State Library.

The Council of State served as an advisory board to Virginia's governors from July 1776 until January 1852, when the Constitution of 1851 took effect. Article 5 of this document abolished the Council in favor of a single, popularly elected executive. Although prompted by a desire to strengthen the power and prestige of the office of governor, this constitutional change also reflected how insignificant the Council of State had become by the mid-nineteenth century. The framers of the Constitution of 1776 never intended their privy council to wield as much power as the colonial governors' Council had, but they did expect the postrevolutionary body to be an equal partner with the governor in the administration of the state's affairs. The Council initially fulfilled this expectation, and the proceedings of its first fifteen years provide valuable insights into the establishment of republican government in Virginia and the workings of a plural executive during war and peacetime. Not long after the Revolution, however, the Council and its members declined in power and importance. By 1852, many of the Council's original functions were performed by other executive departments, and governors sought and heeded their councillors' advice less frequently.

The text of this volume has been taken from the pertinent parts of four manuscript journals in the Virginia State Library: pages 383–409 and 500–626 of the Council journal for 1 October 1787 through 28 March 1789 (pages 410–499 of this manuscript are blank); pages 1–513 of the journal for 1 April 1789 through 15 October 1791; pages 1–42 of the journal for 17 October 1791 through 31 October 1793; and, pages 3–4 and 93–130 of the additional journal of the Council, a supplementary record book that covers the period 20 March 1789 through 2 October 1802. Previously published volumes of the Council journals also drew upon a series of minute books kept by the executive body; however, no Council minute books are known to be extant for the period covered in this volume.

In editing the journal text for publication, superior letters have been brought down to the line; conventional signs, like the ampersand, have been replaced by the appropriate word or abbreviation; and abbreviated or contracted words, except titles and proper names, have been expanded without comment. Proper names have been reproduced exactly as the clerk wrote them; titles before such names have been made uniform (Colo. has become Col., Revd. has become Rev., and so on).

Accepted eighteenth-century spellings have not been changed; inadvertent misspellings and slips of the quill have been corrected and are noted in the Textual Notes, which begin on page 369. Missing words or letters have been inserted in square brackets. Capitalization conforms to the clerk's usage, with the exception that all lowercase words beginning a sentence have been capitalized. Punctuation has been supplied when necessary for good sense; the clerk's frequent dash has been interpreted as a comma, a period, a semicolon, or a colon— whichever seemed most fitting to the context.

A uniform arrangement has been adopted for the journal heading before each session of the Council and for the signatures of members after the journal entry for the day. As the clerk usually began each line at the left side of the page, paragraphs follow his intentions, as shown by his indentation or by his marginal markings. The marginal note "issued," which the clerk wrote beside most entries after an order or instruction had been carried out, has been disregarded. All other marginal notations are transcribed in the footnotes.

Each of the manuscript journals contains an index in the front of the book. The indexes are incomplete and difficult to use, and often contain variant spellings of proper names. The footnotes indicate discrepencies between the text and the index and clarify the clerk's occasional cross-references to the governor's letter book or the additional journal, but they are not meant to explain or identify facts or persons mentioned in the text.

SANDRA GIOIA TREADWAY

A List of Manuscript and Printed Journals of the Committee of Safety and Council of State 1776–1852

JOURNALS OF THE COMMITTEE OF SAFETY

7 February 1776–4 June 1776

Printed in H. R. McIlwaine, ed., *Journals of the Council of the State of Virginia*, vol. 2, *October 6, 1777–November 30, 1781* (Richmond, 1932), 405–516.

June 1776–5 July 1776

Printed in H. R. McIlwaine, ed., *Journals of the Council of the State of Virginia*, vol. 1, *July 12, 1776–October 2, 1777* (Richmond, 1931), 1–66.

JOURNALS OF THE COUNCIL OF STATE

12 July 1776–30 May 1777

Printed in H. R. McIlwaine, ed., *Journals of the Council of the State of Virginia*, vol. 1, *July 12, 1776–October 2, 1777* (Richmond, 1931), 67–420.

[2] June 1777–31 December 1778

Printed in ibid., 421–503 and H. R. McIlwaine, ed., *Journals of the Council of the State of Virginia*, vol. 2, *October 6, 1777–November 30, 1781* (Richmond, 1932), 1–249.

1 January 1781–30 November 1781

Printed in McIlwaine, ed., *Journals of the Council*, 2:268–404.

1 December 1781–16 November 1782

Printed in Wilmer L. Hall, ed., *Journals of the Council of the State of Virginia*, vol. 3, *December 1, 1781–November 29, 1786* (Richmond, 1952), 1–177.

10 November 1782–30 October 1783
3 November 1783–29 December 1785
2 January 1786–28 August 1787

Printed in ibid., 178–303.
Printed in ibid., 304–507.
Printed in ibid., 507–599 and George H. Reese, ed., *Journals of the Council of the State of Virginia*, vol. 4, *December 1, 1786–November 10, 1788* (Richmond, 1967), 1–146.

1 October 1787–28 March 1789	Printed in Reese, ed., *Journals of the Council,* 147–310 and Sandra Gioia Treadway, ed., *Journals of the Council of the State of Virginia,* vol. 5, *13 November 1788–29 November 1791* (Richmond, 1982), 1–66.
20 March 1787–2 October 1802	Portions of this manuscript, the additional journal of the Council, are printed in volumes 3, 4, and 5 of this series.
1 April 1789–15 October 1791	Printed in Treadway, ed., *Journals of the Council,* 66–322.
17 October 1791–31 October 1793	Through 29 November 1791 printed in ibid., 322–340.

2 November 1793–30 June 1795
2 July 1795–27 April 1797
4 May 1797–30 October 1798
1 November 1798–29 October 1799
1 November 1799–7 February 1801
14 February 1801–9 July 1803
23 July 1803–1 December 1806
3 December 1806–4 December 1807
7 December 1807–1 December 1808
5 December 1808–11 December 1809
12 December 1809–7 December 1810
10 December 1810–5 December 1811
6 December 1811–2 December 1812
3 December 1812–4 December 1813
9 December 1813–12 October 1814
13 October 1814–8 December 1815
9 December 1815–9 November 1816
12 November 1816-8 December 1817
9 December 1817–16 December 1818
17 December 1818–16 December 1819
14 December 1819–7 December 1820
19 December 1820–6 December 1821
7 December 1821–9 December 1822
19 December 1822–9 December1823
12 December 1823–10 December 1824
14 December 1824–9 December 1825
13 December 1825–8 December 1826
12 December 1826–8 December 1827
13 December 1827–9 December 1828
12 December 1828–16 December 1829
22 December 1829–30 March 1831
31 March 1831–31 March 1832
3 April 1832–30 March 1833
2 April 1833–29 March 1834
31 March 1834–28 March 1835

1 April 1835–30 March 1836
31 March 1836-30 March 1837
31 March 1837–30 March 1838
31 March 1838–29 March 1839
1 April 1839–30 March 1840
1 April 1840–30 March 1841
31 March 1841–30 March 1842
31 March 1842–30 March 1843
1 April 1843–30 March 1844
3 April 1844–29 March 1845
31 March 1845–30 March 1846
31 March 1846–30 March 1847
31 March 1847–30 March 1848
31 March 1848–29 March 1849
31 March 1849–30 March 1850
1 April 1850–29 March 1851
31 March 1851–15 January 1852

MINUTE BOOKS OF THE COUNCIL OF STATE

23 October 1776–1 March 1777
22 March 1779–8 July 1780

Printed in H. R. McIlwaine, ed., *Journals of the Council of the State of Virginia*, vol. 2, *October 6, 1777–November 30, 1781* (Richmond, 1932), 250–268.

1 January 1781–31 August 1782
10 February 1785–16 January 1786
5 December 1787–2 October 1788
2 December 1793–4 October 1794
25 May 1797–25 January 1798
5 July 1800–31 December 1800
7 June 1806–22 January 1807
24 February 1810–22 June 1811
9 November 1816–21 June 1818
22 April 1820–18 January 1822
22 January 1822–2 September 1823
5 September 1823–11 March 1825
15 March 1825–21 April 1827
21 April 1827–10 June 1830
11 June 1830–12 November 1832
16 March 1832–24 June 1833
13 November 1832–30 March 1837
31 March 1837–1 January 1841
2 January 1841–22 November 1845
26 November 1845–31 May 1849
1 June 1849–15 January 1852

Journal *of the* Council *of the* State *of* Virginia

Thursday November 13th 1788

Present

The President, who presides as Lieutenant Governor,
the Governor having resigned

Mr. Wood   Mr. Heth
Mr. Braxton   Mr. Moore
                Mr. Goode

The Lieutenant Governor informed the board that William Crittendon, who lately absconded from the labor assigned him, by consequence of his conditional pardon, had been retaken and committed to the public Jail; and referred to their consideration what ought to be done with the said Crittendon, and what allowance should be made the person who apprehended him; Whereupon it is advised, that William Crittendon remain in Jail until the attorney general can have an opportunity of submitting to the general court at their next session, "whether the malefactors having conditional pardons can be legally retained in service" And that a warrant issue on the contingent fund, for six pounds, to John Smith for apprehending the said Crittendon.

It appearing that Patrick Bremegen and Lieutenant James Campbell come within the requisitions of the pension law; It is advised, they be continued on the List of pensioners, the former with an allowance of twelve pounds, and the latter thirty pounds per annum from the 1st of January 1786.

On consideration of the petition of Pheebe Conway[1] on behalf of her husband who has been condemned in the State of Maryland to seven years labour, for negro stealing; It is advised that the same be rejected.

It is advised that the payroll of the rangers enployed in the County of Madison, be referred to the Auditor for settlement in the usual way.

Absent Mr. Moore.

The Lieutenant Governor laid before the board an account of Mr. Moores expences, incurred in consequence of his late mission, to the Indian treaty to be held at Tugalo, amounting to twenty seven pounds

---

1. "Phebe Conway" in the clerk's index.

seventeen shillings and three pence. Whereupon it is advised, that the Auditor issue a warrant on the Contingent fund for the amount of the said account, to be paid. And the board further advise that it be referred to the general Assembly to make Mr. Moore a suitable allowance for his services.

Present Mr. Moore.

Upon good cause Shewn, It is advised that the Solicitor be instructed to suspend the execution against William Call as Sheriff of Prince George for the revenue taxes of 1786, until the 12th Day of March next.

The Lieutenant Governor laid before the board an account amounting to sixty five pounds nine shillings and eight pence for the treasury office expences. Whereupon it is advised that the same be referred to the Auditor for settlement and a warrant on the Contingent fund for what shall appear due (to be paid).

It is advised that Mr. William Rose be authorized to contract with some person on the best terms he can for putting up the railings about the Jail which were lately blown down by the gust.

All which matters so advised the Lieutenant Governor orders accordingly.

James Wood
Carter Braxton
Will Heth
A. W. Moore
Robt. Goode

Friday November 14th 1788

Present

The Lieutenant Governor

Mr. Wood	Mr. Heth
Mr. McClurg	Mr. Moore
Mr. Braxton	Mr. Goode

On recommendations, It is advised that commissions issue appointing Richard Buckner Sheriff of Westmoreland, and James McCorkle Sheriff of Montgomery.

The Lieutenant Governor laid before the board a resolution of the general assembly of the 11th instant, referring to the Executive for settlement an Account of Major Richard Call for sundry sums of money disbursed by him in recruiting the third regiment of Dragoons. Whereupon it is advised that the Auditor be directed to allow Major Call a credit for all the items of his account except the charge of ninety thousand dollars said to have been paid to forty five recruits in part of their bounty, which sum the board do not mean absolutely to reject but wish that it may lay open to give Major Call an opportunity of collecting the best proof which the nature of the case will admit. It is further advised that the Auditor be directed to furnish Mr. Dunscomb with the amount of the credit which he shall allow Major Call in order to its being made a charge against the United States.

All which matters so advised, the Lieutenant Governor orders accordingly.

James Wood
James McClurg
Carter Braxton
Will Heth
A. W. Moore
Robt. Goode

Monday November 17th 1788

Present

The Lieutenant Governor

Mr. Wood
Mr. McClurg
Mr. Braxton

Mr. Heth
Mr. Moore
Mr. Goode

It is advised that a warrant issue on the Contingent fund for thirty pounds, to the Solicitor upon account, to defray expences in giving notices. (to be paid).

It appearing that Mary Brooks comes within the requisitions of the pension law; It is advised that She be put on the List of pensioners with an allowance of ten pounds per annum from the first of January last.

Present Mr. Jones.

The board resumed the consideration of Mr. John H. Nortons claim against the public. Whereupon it is advised, that the decision thereon be postponed, until satisfactory proof be produced, that the merchandize sold to the public in June 1780, were to have been paid for in upper James river tobacco.

The Lieutenant Governor laid before the board a payroll of a company of Rangers employed in greenbriar, and a letter from Col. George Clendennin, representing that from the peculiar situation of that country provisions could not be procured under 7½ d. per ration. Whereupon it is advised that the said payroll be referred to the Auditor for settlement, and that seven pence half penny be allowed for the ration.

It is advised that the application for placing on the aggregate fund, a warrant, granted to William Payne Junr. on the 25th of June 1782, for seventy four pounds, thirteen shillings and nine pence, for his services as a Captain of a Volunteer Troop of horse, be rejected.

On consideration of a memorial of Joseph Latil, agent of Mr. Caron De Beaumarchais, complaining of the method pursued by the Solicitor in calculating the interest on the Debt due to foreign creditors; and a report from the Solicitor of the mode he has always pursued, It is advised that no alteration can with propriety be made, in the mode which has been uniformly practiced by the Solicitor in calculating the interest on the Debts due to foreigners.

All which matters so advised, the Lieutenant Governor orders accordingly.

> James Wood
> James McClurg
> Jos. Jones
> Carter Braxton
> Will Heth
> A. W. Moore
> Robt. Goode

Thursday November 20th 1788

Present

The Lieutenant Governor

Mr. Wood	Mr. Braxton
Mr. McClurg	Mr. Heth
Mr. Jones	Mr. Moore
Mr. Goode	

The Lieutenant Governor informed the board that during the recess he issued a register for the Ship Rappahannock; satisfactory proof having been made in due form of law. The board approve thereof.

On recommendation, It is advised that a commission issue appointing William Lumpkin an Inspector at Todds Warehouse in King and Queen County.

It appearing that Abram. Field comes within the requisitions of the pension law, It is advised that he be continued on the List of pensioners with an allowance of ten pounds per annum, from the first of January 1786.

The Lieutenant Governor laid before the board an account of Messrs. Loyall and Wilson, which appears on the commercial books for the Charter of the Schooner Matilda. Whereupon it is advised that the Auditor be directed to settle the said Account; allowing at the rate of twenty one shillings per hundred for the tobacco; and grant a warrant on the aggregate fund for what shall appear due.

The board took under consideration the Auditors report on Mr. John Stringers Account, as an Agent of Thomas Smith, late State Agent, which was referred to him by the Lieutenant Governor to compare with the books and papers of the said Smith. Whereupon it is advised that the Auditor be directed to settle the said Account; allowing a credit for the balance of four thousand three hundred and sixty pounds seventeen shillings and a penny paper money which is to be returned to the treasury and destroyed, on Mr. Stringers making oath that it is the same money which he received on public account, and that he never applied any part thereof to his own use: and that the Auditor grant him a warrant on the aggregate fund for sixty pounds as a compensation for his services.

The Treasurer having suggested that it would be more advantageous to the public to employ a confidential person to go to the different warehouses and collect the money for which the inspectors sold the transfer tobacco belonging to the state agreeably to the tobacco law, The Lieutenant Governor desired the opinion of the board upon the subject. Whereupon it is advised that the treasurer be directed not to offer for sale any of the transfer tobacco now in the treasury; and that he be requested to employ some proper person or persons to receive from the respective Inspectors the money in their hands arising from the Sale of the said tobacco. And the board, having reason to believe that the quantity of such Warrants as will be received in payment for the public tobacco now in circulation is so small as will probably reduce the amount of the sales of the said tobacco: Advise, that the Treasurer be directed to allow a credit until the 15th of January next for the Warrants so to be received; taking care to retain in his hands a deposit sufficient to secure punctual payment.

In consideration of the particular situation of the rangers of Greenbriar County, it is advised that the Auditor be directed to allow serjeants pay to Francis Watkins who appears by the payroll to be a supernumerary serjeant; he having been necessarily employed in issuing provisions to the rangers.

All which matters so advised the Lieutenant Governor orders accordingly.

> James Wood
> James McClurg
> Jos. Jones
> Carter Braxton
> Will Heth
> A. W. Moore
> Robt. Goode

Friday November 21st 1788

Present

The Lieutenant Governor

| Mr. Wood | Mr. Jones |
| Mr. McClurg | Mr. Braxton |

The Lieutenant Governor laid before the board an account of Francis Spencer for the hire of a negro waterman employed two months at the Point of Fork in the year 1781 as appears by a Certificate from Natt. Anderson, Deputy Quartermaster. Whereupon it is advised that the said Account be referred to the Auditor for settlement and a warrant for what shall appear due.

The Lieutenant Governor laid before the board the accounts of John Scott as a District Commissioner under the arrangement of the 27th of March 1782. Whereupon it is advised, that Captain Coleman be directed to examine the said accounts, and report a state thereof to this board as soon as may be.

It is advised that the Auditor be directed to settle the claim of Mr. John McMillian as a Deputy Commissioner of the provision law under Messrs. Brown and Pierce from the 8th of May 1781 to the 14th of January 1782, and make him the usual allowance for his Services; taking care to cancel the funded Certificate for the sum of nineteen thousand five hundred and thirty seven pounds ten shillings paper money which was intended to have been returned to the treasury, but was funded through mistake of the person employed by Mr. McMillian[2] to bring it down, as appears by the certificate of Mr. Pierce.

On consideration of the petition of George Brown and James Cuningham praying for the remission of ten pounds imposed by the Court of Botetourt on each of them as securities for Thomas Pitcher who forfeited his recognizance to keep the peace twelve months and a day; It is advised that the said petition be rejected.

All which matters so advised, the Lieutenant Governor orders accordingly.

James Wood
James McClurg
Jos. Jones
Carter Braxton
Robt. Goode

Monday November 24th 1788

Present

The Lieutenant Governor

Mr. Wood   Mr. Braxton
Mr. McClurg   Mr. Heth
Mr. Jones   Mr. Moore
Mr. Goode

The Lieutenant Governor informed the board that during the recess, He issued a register for the Sloop Rebecca and Ann, satisfactory

2. "Jno. McMillan" in the clerk's index.

proofs having been made in due form of law; and a Commission appointing Robert Townshend Hoos Sheriff of Fairfax County, he having been recommended according to law. Approved.

It being suggested that a great proportion of the tobacco at Deacon's neck warehouses which has been paid into the treasury for public taxes, was considerably damaged by the gust in July last; It is advised that the treasurer be directed to withhold from sale the whole of the tobacco at the said warehouses; and that he engage Mr. Matthew Anderson or some other person to have the said tobacco picked and reprized on the best terms he can; giving assurance that the expences shall be punctually paid.

For reasons appearing to the board, it is advised that a pardon issue to David Lock, who was condemned by the general court in April last to be burnt in the hand and to remain in prison twelve months.

It is advised that the application for putting on the aggregate fund, a Warrant issued the 24th of October 1788, for thirty three pounds eighteen shillings and five pence, to Simion Walton for his services as Clerk to the Commissioners of Amelia County appointed under an act of the general assembly, of the October Session 1780, be rejected; the said Warrant having been issued since the establishment of the said fund.

The Lieutenant Governor laid before the board an account of Mr. Harry Heth, in part, for his services in settling the Westham Foundery accounts. Whereupon it is advised, that a Warrant issue on the Contingent fund, to Mr. Heth, for twelve pounds, upon account. And It is further advised that he be instructed to make report without delay, of his progress in the settlement of the said accounts, and of the obstacles, if any, to the final settlement thereof.

On consideration of the petition of Duncan McLauchlan, attorney in fact for the representatives of Andrew Sprowle Deceased, It is advised that the Auditor be directed to grant Warrants for what shall appear to be due for the hire of Mr. Sprowles Negroes, from December 1783, to the 28th of August 1787.

The Lieutenant Governor laid before the board a payroll of Bladen Ashbys company of Rangers employed in the County of Nelson, and the accounts of the Scouts of the said County; also the Account of John Farris as a Scout belonging to Lincoln County, and the Account of Elijah Farris as a Scout of Mercer County. Whereupon it is advised that the said payroll and accounts be referred to the Auditor for settlement in the usual way.

On consideration of Mr. Vivion Brookings request, that the Solicitors mode of calculating interest on the Debts due to the commonwealth may be changed, It is advised that the said request be rejected; the board not chusing to interfere with the established rules of the Solicitors office.

All which matters so advised, the Lieutenant Governor orders accordingly.

> James Wood
> James McClurg
> Jos. Jones
> Carter Braxton
> Will Heth
> A. W. Moore
> Robt. Goode

Tuesday November 25th 1788

Present

The Lieutenant Governor

Mr. Wood	Mr. Braxton
Mr. McClurg	Mr. Heth
Mr. Jones	Mr. Moore

The Board, conceiving that the State would derive great advantage by extending the time of Credit given for the Warrants receiveable for the public tobacco, Advise, that Credit be given for the said Warrants until the last day of January next.

The Committee appointed to examine the Sinking fund, having reported a state thereof up to the 30th Day of October last. It is advised that the same be entered in the additional journal;[3] and that a copy of the said report be transmitted to the general assembly.

The Lieutenant Governor laid before the board a payroll of Ensign Vallendighams company of rangers employed in Jefferson County; Whereupon It is advised that the same be referred to the Auditor for settlement in the usual way.

Pursuant to the resolution of the general assembly of the 19th and 22[d] of this present month; it is advised, that a proclamation issue making known the times and places for appointing Electors to choose a president, and for choosing representatives to serve this state in Congress; that Col. Meriwether be instructed to treat with the several printers in Richmond for printing 500 copies of the Act intituled "An Act for the appointment of Electors pursuant to the Constitution of Government of the United States" and 500 copies of the Act intituled "An Act for the election of representatives pursuant to the Constitution of government of the United States" and report their terms tomorrow: and that the said Acts, when printed, be transmitted by express to the Sheriffs of the several counties, within this commonwealth.

---

3. *See* page 359 for the sinking fund dated 19 July–30 Oct. 1788.

All which matters so advised the Lieutenant Governor orders accordingly.

James Wood
James McClurg
Jos. Jones
Carter Braxton
Will Heth
A. W. Moore

Thursday November 27th 1788

Present

The Lieutenant Governor

Mr. Wood	Mr. Braxton
Mr. McClurg	Mr. Heth
Mr. Jones	Mr. Moore

It being suggested that the State would be greatly benefitted, were the Agent of the Sinking fund permitted to lay out part of the money in his hands in the purchase of public tobacco, as the same is selling exceeding[ly] low; It is advised that the said Agent be authorized, at his discretion, to purchase of the said tobacco, to the amount of three or four hundred pounds specie on account of the Sinking fund.

It is advised that a register issue for the Sloop Nancy, satisfactory proofs having been made in due form of law.

All which matters so advised the Lieutenant Governor orders accordingly.

James Wood
James McClurg
Jos. Jones
Carter Braxton
Will Heth
A. W. Moore

Saturday November 29th 1788

Present

The Lieutenant Governor

Mr. Wood	Mr. Braxton
Mr. McClurg	Mr. Heth
Mr. Jones	Mr. Moore

The Lieutenant Governor laid before the board a resolution of the general assembly of the 28th instant, requesting the Executive to procure the usual number of copies of the Laws of the present Session of assembly, to be printed with all possible dispatch. Also a resolution, of the same date, requesting the Executive to lay before the Legislature a general statement of the public arms, ammunition, military stores, etc. etc. Whereupon it is advised, that the Clerk of the house of Delegates be desired to furnish this board with the several acts, from time to time, as they pass; that, on their being received, they be immediately distributed among the different printers in order that the usual number be printed pursuant to the 1st resolution: that Col. Meriwether be directed to make out a general statement of the arms, ammunition, military stores, etc. etc. and that the same be transmitted to the Legislature pursuant to the 2d resolution. Upon good cause shewn, It is advised that the Solicitor be directed to take measures according to law, for the further suspension of the execution against Thomas Flornoy as Sheriff of Prince Edward, for the revenue taxes of 1786, until the 20th of December 1788.

It is advised that a commission issue appointing Mr. Stage Davis searcher at Urbanna in the room of Mr. George Davis who hath resigned.

Mr. William McGuire having, by letter dated the 21st of October last, resigned the office of Land Searcher at Winchester; it is advised that his resignation be accepted according to the date thereof.

The Lieutenant Governor laid before the board an account of Archibald Richardson as an assistant of Thomas Smith and Benja. Day late State agents. Whereupon it is advised that the said Account be referred to the Auditor for examination and report.

It appearing that John Laman comes within the requisitions of the pension law It is advised that he be put on the List of pensioners with an allowance of five pounds per annum from the 1st of January last.

The Lieutenant Governor laid before the board an account of the costs which the several searchers are to pay on account of appeals from the court of admiralty on certain Quitam actions,[4] amounting to 8800 lbs. of tobacco at 12/6 per hundred. Whereupon it is advised, that the Auditor be directed to issue a warrant on the Contingent fund, to the Clerk of appeals, for one half of the said costs, to be refunded by the searchers interested, in case the judgments shall be affirmed.

All which matters so advised, the Lieutenant Governor orders accordingly.

> James Wood
> James McClurg
> Jos. Jones
> Carter Braxton
> Will Heth
> A. W. Moore

---

4. A *qui tam* action is a legal action taken to recover a penalty under a statute that gives part of the penalty to the individual initiating the action and the rest to the state or public body.

Monday December 1st 1788

Present

The Lieutenant Governor

Mr. Wood   Mr. Braxton
Mr. McClurg   Mr. Heth
Mr. Jones   Mr. Moore

The Lieutenant Governor laid before the board the accounts of William Fulton, William Graham and James Vanbibber, three additional Scouts ordered into service for the County of Greenbriar by Col. Ward, on a particular occasion. Whereupon it is advised that, in consideration of the circumstances stated in a letter from Col Clendinnin of the 16th ultimo, the said three Scouts be paid in the usual way.

It is advised that a Warrant issue on the Contingent fund, to Joseph Leiplong, for Eight pounds in part for going express with public Dispatches to North Carolina.

On recommendation, It is advised that Commissions issue appointing Edward Spencer an Inspector at Shepherd warehouses in the room of Richard Bray deceased and Christopher Stedman additional inspector at said warehouse in the room of the said Spencer.

It is advised that Levi Smith, William Wallace, James Scott and James Irvine, who are condemned to die on friday next, be reprieved until friday the 12th instant, they having requested a week longer.

All which matters so advised the Lieutenant Governor orders accordingly.

James Wood
James McClurg
Jos. Jones
Carter Braxton
Will Heth
A. W. Moore

Tuesday December 2d 1788

Present

The Lieutenant Governor

Mr. Wood   Mr. Jones
Mr. McClurg   Mr. Heth
                Mr. Goode

It is advised that a warrant issue on the Contingent fund to John Dixon for four pounds ten shillings for printing 500 copies of the two Acts of Assembly concerning the new Constitution.

The Lieutenant Governor laid before the board the claim of Tarlton Woodson, which has been referred to the Executive for settlement by a resolution of the general assembly of the 24th ultimo. Whereupon it is advised, that the Auditor be directed to issue a Warrant, on the aggregate fund, for fifty three pounds two shillings, to Mr. Woodson, in lieu of the Donation allowed him by the Assembly, when a prisoner on Long Island; the said Woodson having returned the notes for five thousand three hundred and ten pounds of tobacco which was not to be found in the warehouses.

It is advised that the application for putting on some fund, a Warrant issued the 17th of June 1782, for one hundred and fifty pounds, to Joshua Campbell, for pork furnished the troops marching through North Carolina, be rejected.

On recommendation, It is advised that Commissions issue appointing Johnny Scott and Catlett Conway Coroners for the County of Orange.

The Lieutenant Governor laid before the board a resolution of the General Assembly requiring the Executive to transmit with out delay, copies of the Letter to Governor Clinton and of the Circular Letter to the several States, inclosing copies of the application agreed to by the General Assembly, to be made to the Congress of the united States. Whereupon it is advised that the said Dispatches be transmitted to the several States by post.

The Lieutenant Governor laid before the board a recommendation from the Court of Goochland of William Radford as Colonel of the Militia of the said county; and Letters from Col. Guerrant and Major Saunders remonstrating against the said Radford (who is only a private) being placed over all the officers of the battalion. Whereupon it is advised that the said recommendation be rejected; and that Col. Meriwether be directed to write to the commanding officer of the said county, to procure a recommendation to be made by a full court.

All which matters so advised, the Lieutenant Governor orders accordingly.

James Wood
James McClurg
Jos. Jones
Will Heth
Robt. Goode

Thursday December 4th 1788

Present

The Lieutenant Governor

Mr. Wood   Mr. Braxton
Mr. McClurg   Mr. Heth
Mr. Jones   Mr. Moore
Mr. Goode

It is advised that a pardon issue to James Irvine who stands condemned for horsestealing, he appearing to be a proper object of mercy.

On consideration of a letter from Captain Taylor of the 24th ultimo, It is advised that he be informed that the board consider the sale of the flat taken by Capt. Baron, before legal condemnation, notwithstanding the consent of parties, as improper, and the like should not be done in future, that he ought to account with the public for half the prize money, that the application of the hogshead of rum to the use of the boats is approved; and that provisions for the boats should be purchased only in small quantities as occasion require, from time to time.

It appearing from the certificate of the Clerk of James City County Court, that the Depositions, of Mr. Charles Hunt and Mr. Matthew Anderson, complaining of certain Acts of misconduct in William James Lewis as an Inspector at the College landing warehouse, were taken according to law before Samuel Griffin and Dudley Digges gentlemen, justices of the peace for the said county, (the said Lewis being present). The board resumed the consideration of the said Depositions, and, upon mature deliberation thereon, are of opinion that the said William James Lewis is guilty of a breach of his duty as an Inspector. Whereupon it is advised that the said William James Lewis be removed from his office; and that commissions issue appointing William Wilkinson senr. Inspector at the College landing warehouse, in the room of the said Lewis, and Edmund Cowles additional inspector in the room of the said Wilkinson.

The board took under consideration the Auditors report on the accounts of Archibald Richardson to him referred, whereby it appears that there is a balance of one hundred and twenty one pounds twelve shillings and three pence due to the said Richardson on account of disbursements; and that he acted as an assistant of Benjamin Day from the 16th of April 1779 to the 17th of March 1780, for which time he has received no compensation. Whereupon it is advised, that the Auditor be directed to settle with Mr. Richardson for his services from the 16th of April 1779 to the 17th of March 1780, at the rate of one hundred pounds per annum, according to the scale at the time he entered as an assistant to Thomas Smith late State agent; and to grant him Warrants on the aggregate fund for the sum due including the above balance of one hundred and twenty one pounds twelve shillings and three pence.

It is advised that a warrant issue on the aggregate fund in lieu of one issued the 23d of June 1783, pursuant to a resolution of the assembly of the 14th of June 1783, for sixty pounds, to George Watkins, for pay and compensation for his sufferings while in captivity.

It appearing that Mary Kellar and Jane Barns[5] come within the

---

5. "Jane Barnes" in the clerk's index.

requisitions of the pension law; It is advised that the first be put on the List of pensioners with an allowance of fifteen pounds per annum, from the first of January 1788, and the last continued on the said List with ten pounds per annum from January 1786.

All which matters so advised the Lieutenant Governor orders accordingly.

James Wood
James McClurg
Jos. Jones
Carter Braxton
Will Heth
A. W. Moore

Saturday December 6th 1788

Present

The Lieutenant Governor

Mr. Wood   Mr. Braxton
Mr. McClurg   Mr. Heth
Mr. Jones   Mr. Moore
              Mr. Goode

Beverley Randolph esquire having been elected Governor of this Commonwealth, he produced a Certificate of his qualification before John Pendleton gentleman a justice of the peace for the County of Henrico, and took his seat at the board.

The Board proceeded to the election of a President in the room of Mr. Randolph, and Mr. Wood, being proposed, was unanimously elected.

Moses Hinkle having been appointed Surveyor of Pendleton County; It is advised that he be required to give bond in the penalty of one thousand pounds.

The Governor laid before the board an account of Joseph Leiplong for going express to North Carolina making a balance of five pounds sixteen shillings as certified by Col. Meriwether. Whereupon it is advised that the said account be referred to the Auditor for a warrant on the contingent fund for the sum due (to be paid).

On recommendations It is advised that Commissions issue appointing John Curd Coroner for Goochland; David Crews and John South inspectors and William Jones additional inspector at Boonsborough and Collier warehouses in Madison County.

It is advised that the Claims of Leonard Cooper, Charles McClung, David Robinson, and John Young as Scouts for Greenbriar County, be referred to the Auditor for settlement in the usual way.

The Governor laid before the board a resolution of the General

Assembly of the 3d instant referring to the Executive for settlement, the Claim of Thomas Harris for his services whilst an armourer in the City of Williamsburg, during the late war; and a Certificate from the Honble. John Page of the services of the said Harris. Whereupon it is advised that the auditor be directed to issue a warrant on the Contingent fund to the said Thomas Harris, for twenty pounds, as a full compensation for his services (to be paid).

All which matters so advised the Governor orders accordingly.

The Governor notified to the board his intention to be absent which is ordered to be entered on the journal.

> James Wood
> James McClurg
> Jos. Jones
> Carter Braxton
> Will Heth
> A. W. Moore
> Robt. Goode

Monday December 8th 1788

Present

The Lieutenant Governor

Mr. McClurg	Mr. Heth
Mr. Jones	Mr. Moore
Mr. Braxton	Mr. Goode

It appearing that there was a mistake made in the register issued the 18th Day of November by calling the Vessel the *Ship* Rappahannock instead of the *Brigantine,* It is advised that a new register issue with the necessary alterations.

It is advised that Commissions issue appointing Thomas Marshall senr., John Craig senr., Richard Young, Robert Johnson, James Wilkinson, John Watkins, William Cave, George Blackburn, John Finney, John Fowler, William Trotter and William Steel gentlemen Justices of the peace for the new County of Woodford, Richard Young gentleman Sheriff of the said county, Charles Scott Lieutenant and Robert Johnson Colonel of the Militia of the said county, the said commissions to take effect from and after the 1st Day of May next.

All which matters so advised, the Lieutenant Governor orders accordingly.

> James McClurg
> Jos. Jones
> Carter Braxton
> Will Heth
> A. W. Moore
> Robt. Goode

Tuesday December 9th 1788

Present

The Lieutenant Governor

Mr. Jones   Mr. Moore
Mr. Heth   Mr. Goode

The Lieutenant Governor laid before the board the applications of the following persons for arrearages of pensions, to wit, Captain John Stokes, Lieutenant Willis Wilson, William Peake, William McClintock and John Conner. Whereupon it is advised that the consideration of the said applications be postponed.

Pursuant to a resolution of the General Assembly of the 3d and 8th instants it is advised that a Warrant issue on the Contingent fund to Col. William Heth, for two hundred and forty four pounds two shillings as a further consideration for his services in the settlement of the claim of this State against the United States for the Northwestern Territory ceded to Congress.

On recommendation, It is advised that an additional commission issue appointing Sterling Niblett, Joseph Yarbrough, Peter Lamkin jr., John Pettus, Frederick Nance, junr., and William Betts, gentlemen Justices of the peace for the County of Lunenburg.

Joseph Prentis esquire, an additional Judge of the General Court appeared and took the oath of office.

All which matters so advised the Lieutenant Governor orders accordingly.

Jos. Jones
Will Heth
A. W. Moore
Robt. Goode

Thursday December 11th 1788

Present

The Lieutenant Governor

Mr. Jones   Mr. Heth
Mr. Braxton   Mr. Moore
Mr. Goode

The Lieutenant Governor informed the board, that during their recess, and on the tenth instant, he had issued a commission to Edmund Winston Esquire, in lieu of one formerly issued, but accidentally lost or mislaid, appointing him a judge of the General Court: that on recommendation he had also issued a Commission appointing Charles Gwatkins sheriff for the County of Bedford: that he had issued a register for the Brigantine Kitty and Nancy, satisfactory proof having been made according to law: And that he had ordered a Warrant to issue in favour of Daniel Morin[6] for seventy two pounds, eighteen shillings and seven pence due him for building a magazine at the Point of Fork pursuant to contract as certified by Colonel Meriwether: of which several matters, so done, the board approve.

On recommendation, it is advised, that a Commission issue, appointing Charles Conner gentleman, sheriff for the county of Norfolk, in the room of Daniel Sanford, who it is certified is unable to procure Security.

For good cause shewn, it is advised, that the execution against Sir John Peyton as Sheriff of Gloucester for the arrearages of taxes for the years 1782 and 1783; and that the execution against John Dixon as sheriff for the county of Gloucester for arrearages of taxes for the year 1784, be suspended until the first day of February next.

The administrators of John Robinson esquire, having requested, that the Executive would resume the consideration of their late memorial and direct the money for the rent due from the public for the Lead mines to be paid, one third part to Mr. Charles Lynch and the remaining two third parts to the said Administrators, subject to the decree of the High court of chancery; and Mr. Charles Lynch having agreed to the same, It is advised, that no monies for the rent of the said mines ought to be paid until the high court of chancery shall have first ascertained the rent and the title thereto.

The board, taking into consideration the situation of the public cannon near the Court house in the county of Hanover, advise, that Colonel Meriwether be instructed to have the same removed to Taylor's ferry and put under cover upon the best terms he can.

Present Mr. McClurg.

Pursuant to a resolution of the General Assembly, it is advised, that the Auditor be directed to issue a Warrant upon the contingent fund for fifty pounds in favour of the honourable Andrew Moore esquire, allowed him for his services attending a late treaty with the Cherokee Indians.

All which matters, so advised, the Lieutenant Governor orders accordingly.

> James McClurg
> Jos. Jones
> Carter Braxton
> Will Heth
> A. W. Moore
> Robt. Goode

---

6. "Daniel Morrin" in the clerk's index.

Saturday December 13th 1788

Present

The Lieutenant Governor

Mr. McClurg   Mr. Heth
Mr. Jones   Mr. Moore
Mr. Braxton   Mr. Goode

The Lieutenant Governor laid before the board an account of Josiah Davison as a Scout for 31 Days, Whereupon it is advised, that the said account be referred to the Auditor for settlement in the usual way.
Which the Lieutenant Governor orders accordingly.

James McClurg
Jos. Jones
Carter Braxton
Will Heth
A. W. Moore
Robt. Goode

Monday December 15th 1788

Present

The Lieutenant Governor

Mr. McClurg   Mr. Heth
Mr. Jones   Mr. Moore
Mr. Braxton   Mr. Goode

It is advised, that registers issue to the Brigantines Mary and Favourite Betsey, satisfactory proof having been made according to law.
The Lieutenant Governor laid before the board two bills of exchange drawn by William Shannon[7] on the Treasurer of this Commonwealth in favour of messrs. Applegate and Company; one for £37500 paper money, the other for £18.6 specie. Whereupon it is advised, that the said bills be referred to the Auditor for settlement in the usual Way.
The board according to their former order of which the parties were notified resumed the further consideration of the charges exhibited by Captain William Helm against Jesse Ewell esquire Lieutenant of the county of Prince William, and having duly considered the same, together with sundry depositions taken on the part of the said Jesse Ewell in presence of the said Captain Helm, are of opinion that the

7. "Wm. Shanan" in the clerk's index.

complaint is frivolous and groundless and advise that the same be dismissed.

All which matters so advised the Lieutenant Governor orders accordingly.

> James McClurg
> Jos. Jones
> Carter Braxton
> Will Heth
> A. W. Moore
> Robt. Goode

Thursday December 18th 1788

Present

The Lieutenant Governor

Mr. McClurg	Mr. Heth
Mr. Jones	Mr. Moore
Mr. Braxton	Mr. Goode

It appearing that James Simmons comes within the requisitions of the pension law, It is advised that he be continued on the pension List with an allowance of fifteen pounds per annum commencing the first day of January 1786.

It is advised, that the Auditor be directed to issue the following Warrants on the contingent fund, to wit: to the reverend Mr. Blagrove[8] for fifteen pounds being a quarter's salary due him the 14th instant as Ordinary to the public Jail; to Joseph Clarke as Express per account certified by Colonel Meriwether for twelve pounds fifteen shillings; to Robert Rawlings as an Express per account certified as above for ten pounds ten shillings; and to Alexander Drumgold as express employed by Andrew Moore esquire to go to the Cherokee Nation, for nine pounds: the Warrants to be said Expresses to be paid out of any money in the Treasury.

On recommendation it is advised, that Commissions issue appointing Henry Collier Foster and Drury Beale Inspectors and Jeremiah Drake as additional Inspector of Tobacco at Brownes Warehouse in the County of Southampton.

The Lieutenant Governor informed the board, he received yesterday sundry depositions taken on the part of William Helm, in support of the charges exhibited against Jesse Ewell esquire Lieutenant of the county of Prince William, and the same being read and considered, It is advised, that, in as much as the decision on the 15th instant (the day assigned for hearing the parties) was founded on a

---

8. "Ben. Blagrave" in the clerk's index.

consideration of the testimony on one side only and not of the whole of the proofs in the case, the said charge be reconsidered by the board and that they resume the reconsideration thereof on the 22d day of January next; and that the parties have notice of this determination.

The Lieutenant Governor laid before the board an Information exhibited by Edward Booker esquire county Lieutenant of Amelia against Paulin Anderson Colonel of the first Battalion of militia of the said county, charging him "with endeavouring to prevail on Charles Hodges to take a false oath in order to screen him from paying a fine, for which he was presented by the Grand Jury of Amelia County." On consideration whereof it is advised, that a court martial be appointed for the trial of the said Paulin Anderson, to consist of the following officers to wit; Gabriel Fowlkes Colonel of the 2d Battalion as president, a field officer from each battalion in the said county, the two senior Captains and the three senior Lieutenants from the said battalions, provided they be not Witnesses, that a copy of the charge be forwarded to the President, and that a special state of the evidence and facts together with the sentence of the court martial be transmitted to the Governor as soon as possible.

All which matters, so advised, the Lieutenant Governor Order's accordingly.

> James McClurg
> Jos. Jones
> Carter Braxton
> Will Heth
> A. W. Moore
> Robt. Goode

Saturday December 20th 1788

Present

The Lieutenant Governor

Mr. McClurg	Mr. Heth
Mr. Jones	Mr. Moore
	Mr. Braxton

It is advised, that a register issue for the ship Dauphin satisfactory proof having been made according to law.

On recommendation of the Judges of the General Court it is advised, that a pardon issue to Arthur Farley, who stands condemned for murder he appearing to be a proper object of mercy.

It is advised that the Auditor be directed to settle the following accounts and issue warrants thereon upon the contingent fund accordingly; the said accounts being for articles furnished the public Jail etc. as certified by the clerk of the general Court viz: An account of

Turner Southall for straw 15/., of William Rose for sundry services rendered by Samuel Bennett £7.7, of John Roper for Wood £6.12, of Hugh Patton for Ruggs etc. £10.7.7, of Doctor William Carter for medecine £5.16.3 and of William Rose for cleaning the court house £1.7.6; It is also advised, that the Auditor be directed to settle the following accounts and issue Warrants thereon for what shall appear due viz. The Payroll of a company of rangers for the county of Ohio commanded by Capt. McMachan amounting to £417, the accounts of Isaac Greathouse and Joseph Edgington as Scouts for the said county amounting each to £23.10, of John Vanbuskirk employed in the same manner £55.5, of William McCollock and Jacob Whitsle, the same each £24, of Vechil Dickenson the same £20.15, of Robert McClure for 15435 rations furnished the aforesaid company of rangers for the County of Ohio at 6d. per ration, And of Thomas Allsberry junr. as a ranger from the first of April to the first of October 1788 in the County of Greenbriar he having been omitted in the payroll formerly settled, as certified by Colonel George Clendinen.

It is advised, that Commissions issue appointing Edmund Lyne, Thomas Worring, Henry Lee, Miles Weathers Conway, Alexander Dalrimple Orr, Robert Rankin, John Macker, Arthur Fox, William Lamb, George Stocton, and Jacob Edwards gentlemen Justices of the peace; Thomas Worring, gentleman, Sheriff; Henry Lee, County Lieutenant; Robert Rankin, Colonel; and Alexander Dalrimple Orr, Lieutenant Colonel, for the County of Mason to take effect from and after the 1st day of May next.

All which matters, so advised, the Lieutenant Governor orders accordingly.

> James McClurg
> Jos. Jones
> Carter Braxton
> Will Heth
> A. W. Moore

Monday December 22d 1788

Present

The Lieutenant Governor

Mr. McClurg	Mr. Heth
Mr. Braxton	Mr. Moore
	Mr. Goode

It is advised, that the Auditor be directed to issue the following Warrants on the contingent fund, to wit; to Reuben Slaughter[9] as Express per Account certified by Col. Meriwether for eleven pounds

---

9. "Reubin Slaughter" in the clerk's index.

five shillings to be paid out of any money in the Treasury; and to Mr. John Dixon for sundry extra printing per account amounting to Six pounds.

The Lieutenant Governor laid before the board a pay roll for a company of cavalry commanded by Capt. Ballard Smith in the county of Jefferson ordered into actual service by the county Lieutenant; Whereupon it is advised, that the application for payment of the said payroll be rejected; this board not having authorized the calling of the said company into service. (Pay roll returned)

Pursuant to a resolution of the General Assembly of the 17th instant, it is advised, that the Auditor be directed to issue a Warrant in lieu of one formerly issued to Charles Moorman[10] for £7449.12.6 paper money upon the said Moorman's complying with directions of the laws heretofore in force in like cases.

It appearing that Robert Clendinen[11] comes within the requisitions of the Pension law, it is advised, that he be continued on the Pension List with an allowance of ten pounds per Annum to commence the first day of January 1786.

All which matters so advised the Lieutenant Governor orders accordingly.

> James McClurg
> Carter Braxton
> Will Heth
> A. W. Moore
> Robt. Goode

Wednesday December 24th 1788

Present

The Lieutenant Governor

Mr. McClurg	Mr. Heth
Mr. Braxton	Mr. Moore

Mr. Goode

The Lieutenant Governor informed the board, that he had yesterday issued Commissions appointing Thomas Threildkeld and Ezekiel Kennedy, Inspectors, and William Armstrong additional Inspector of Tobacco at Harrod's Landing Warehouse in the County of Mercer pursuant to a recommendation from the Court of the said county of which the board approve.

The Lieutenant Governor laid before the board an account of Moses Shepherd for transporting Arms and Ammunition from

---

10. "Charles Mooreman" in the clerk's index.
11. "Robt. Clendinnen" in the clerk's index.

Morgan town to Ohio County. Whereupon it is advised that the said Account be rejected as being a county charge.

For good cause shewn, it is advised, that the execution against Patrick Lockhart, late sheriff of Botetourt, for the arrears of taxes for the years 1784 and 1785, be suspended until the 10th of April next.

It is advised, that the Auditor be directed to issue the following Warrants on the Contingent fund, to wit; to John Nevins as express per account certified by Col. Meriwether for £17.5 to be paid out of any money in the Treasury, and to Colonel George Clendenen[12] for 200 lbs. powder and 100 lbs. Lead purchased for the use of the County of Greenbriar as per account amounting to thirty pounds.

On recommendation, it is advised, that Commissions issue appointing Thomas Smith and Elisha Lawrence Ballard Gentlemen, Coroners for the County of Isle of Wight.

It is advised, that a register issue for the schooner Nancey, satisfactory proof having been made in due form of law.

All which matters so advised the Lieutenant Governor orders accordingly.

> James McClurg
> Carter Braxton
> Will Heth
> A. W. Moore
> Robt. Goode

Friday December 26th 1788

Present

The Lieutenant Governor

| Mr. McClurg | Mr. Heth |
| Mr. Braxton | Mr. Moore |

It is advised, that Commissions issue appointing Peter Lamkin, Samuel Sherwin, Raleigh Carter, William Cryer, William Cross Cradock, Peter Randolph, William Greenhill, Freeman Eppes, Abner Osborne, William Yates and Stephen Cocke, gentlemen, Justices of the peace; Peter Lamkin, Sheriff; and Gabriel Fowlkes, gentleman, County Lieutenant, for the County of Nottoway to take effect from and after the first day of May next.

The Lieutenant Governor laid before the board a recommendation of the county court of Dinwiddie of Field officers of the militia of said county, when information was given to the board, that Peterson Goodwin, at present Lieutenant Colonel in said county and one of the persons so recommended, stands publicly accused of peculation, while acting as deputy sheriff in the said county; in support of which, a

---

12 "Clendinnen" in the clerk's index.

narrative of the circumstances touching said peculation published by Doctor James Greenway in the month of July last, together with copies of sundry records of the said county court of Dinwiddie were duly read: Whereupon it is advised, to suspend the issuing of the Commission of Colonel to the said Peterson Goodwin, unless it shall be certified to this board by a full court on or before the first day of May next, that in their opinion, he the said Goodwin is innocent of the aforesaid charge.

All which matters so advised the Lieutenant Governor orders accordingly.

James McClurg
Will Heth

Saturday December 27th 1788

Present

The Lieutenant Governor

Mr. McClurg	Mr. Heth
Mr. Braxton	Mr. Moore
	Mr. Goode

The Lieutenant Governor laid before the Board a payroll of Francis Watkins's company of rangers employed in Green Briar, and an account of Shedrick Henemon for 976 rations furnished the said rangers at seven pence half penny, as certified by the County Lieutenant of the said County. Whereupon it is advised that the said Payroll and account be referred to the Auditor for settlement in the usual way.

It appearing that Mary Dorton comes within the requisitions of the pension law; It is advised that She be put on the List of pensioners with an allowance of eight pounds per annum from the first of January last.

The Lieutenant Governor laid before the board a resolution of the General Assembly of the 22d and 24th instant, authorizing and empowering the Executive to cause accounts to be made of all Sums of money or other things for which this commonwealth is intitled to credit on account of the requisitions of Congress from the 30th day of October 1781, to the twentieth day of August 1788, inclusive and for which no such credit hath yet been obtained; and requiring that they cause the said Accounts together with the necessary Vouchers to be presented at the Treasury of the United States and there settled so as to be duly placed to the Credit of this Commonwealth against the said requisitions. Whereupon it is advised that the said resolution be referred to the Solicitor with an instruction that he cause accounts to be made up of all monies and other things for which this commonwealth is still intitled to a credit on account of the requisitions of Congress mentioned in the said resolution, and transmit the same together with the necessary Vouchers to this board as soon as may be in order to their being presented to the treasury of the United States for settlement.

All which matters so advised the Lieutenant Governor orders accordingly.

James McClurg
Will Heth
Robt. Goode

Monday December 29th 1788

Present

The Governor

Mr. Wood	Mr. Heth
Mr. McClurg	Mr. Moore
Mr. Braxton	Mr. Goode

The Governor reported that he had issued a Commission to Williams Dabbs junr. as Surveyor of Charlotte County and required him to give bond in the penalty of one thousand pounds; the said Dabbs having been recommended according to law. Approved.

It is advised that a commission issue appointing Corbin Griffin gentleman, Sheriff of York, in the room of James Shield who hath not been able to give security according to Law.

On consideration of the petition of the Commissioners for the defence of Chesapeake Bay, It is advised that the Solicitor be directed to take measures for suspending the Execution against the said Bay Commissioners for four hundred and five pounds fourteen shillings and five pence half penny, until the first of June next: It is further advised that so much of the said petition as prays for leave to discharge the said execution in Loan office Certificates or warrants be rejected.

In pursuance of the resolution of the General assembly of the 25th and 26th instant, It is advised that the Clerk "advertize all persons who, during the late War, acted as commanding Officers of Counties, Commissioners of provisions, Commissaries, Quarter Masters, or in any other character chargeable with the reception or distribution of supplies, or with the raising of men for the army, that they for[th]with prepare for adjustment of their accounts and Vouchers of delivery and distribution of the same, as persons will speedily be appointed for the special purpose of calling upon and settling with them: It is also advised that circular letters be written to the Justices and county Lieutenants of the several counties on the same subject. (See letter book)[13]

It is advised that the Jailor be authorized to procure, on the best

---

13. Circular to the Justices of the several counties, 29 Dec. 1788, Letter Book 1788–1792, Governor's Office, Executive Department, Archives Branch, Virginia State Library, Richmond, Va. (hereafter cited as Letter Book 1788–1792, Governor's Office).

terms he can, a Nurse for the child of Catherine Crull,[14] one of the culprits under condemnation, the expences of which Nurse shall be paid by warrants on the contingent fund.

It is advised that a Commission issue appointing Wm. Croghan[15] principal Surveyor of the lands reserved by law for the Officers and Soldiers of the late Virginia State Line and Navy, in the room of George Rogers Clark who hath resigned; and that the said Wm. Croghan be required to give bond in the penalty of three thousand pounds.

It is advised that Commissions issue appointing John Guerrant junr. Colonel and Robert Saunders Lieutenant Colonel of the Militia of Goochland County; the Court of the said County having refused to make any further recommendation of a Colonel; and Col. Meriwether is directed to write to the County Lieutenant desiring him to procure recommendations for supplying the Vacanc[i]es in the said Militia.

In pursuance of a resolution of the General Assembly of the 13th and 16th instant, It is advised that the Auditor be directed to make out, as soon as possible, an account of the expences incurred by this State for protecting and defending her frontier Inhabitants from the cruelties and depredations of the Indians since the Cession of the Lands west of the Ohio river made by this Commonwealth to the United States; and transmit the same, with the Vouchers, to this board, in order that a credit may be obtained from the United States therefor.

It is advised, That the Clerk of the house of Delegates be required to deliver to Col. Davies, from time to time, pursuant to an order of that house of the 25th instant, such returns and other documents, as may be useful in founding and supporting the claims of this State against the United States.

It is advised that a warrant issue on the contingent fund to William Galt for eighteen shillings for tongs, shovel and poker furnished for the use of the Council chamber (to be paid).

The Governor laid before the board a recommendation from the Court of Culpeper of sundry persons to be added to the commission of the peace for the said County, and there appearing to be twenty nine now in commission, It is advised that the said recommendation be rejected; and that the Clerk write for a full State of the commission.

All which matters so advised the Governor orders accordingly.

> James Wood
> James McClurg
> Will Heth
> Robt. Goode

---

14. "C. Cralle" in the clerk's index.
15. "Wm. Craghan" in the clerk's index.

Tuesday December 30th 1788

Present

The Governor

| Mr. Wood | Mr. Braxton |
| Mr. McClurg | Mr. Heth |

Mr. Moore

It is advised that a Warrant issue on the Contingent fund for seven pounds ten shillings to Richard Adams for the rent of an office for the High Court of Chancery up to the 25th instant agreeably to contract. (To be paid)

On recommendation, It is advised that a commission issue appointing John Cowan Sheriff of Mercer County.

It is advised that Lieutenant Col. George Jackson of Harrison and Major Zac. Sprigg of Ohio, be appointed to take command of the several detachments of militia ordered from the counties of Monongalia, Harrison, Randolph and Ohio, so soon as they shall assemble at the place of rendezvous which may be appointed by Governor St. Clair agreeable to the orders of this board of the 15th of October last.

For reasons appearing to the board, It is advised that the commission, issued on the 26th instant, appointing Gabriel Foulks, County Lieutenant of Notaway County, which is to take place the first of may next, be cancilled.

All which matters so advised the Governor Orders accordingly.

James Wood
James McClurg
Will Heth

Wednesday December 31st 1788

Present

The Governor

Mr. Wood	Mr. Heth
Mr. McClurg	Mr. Moore
Mr. Braxton	Mr. Goode

In pursuance of a resolution of the present Session of Assembly, It is advised, that a Duplicate Loan Office Certificate, for three hundred and eighty six pounds be issued to Thomas Matthews,[16] esquire, as Guardian of John Johnson; in lieu of the original certificate which appears to the satisfaction of the board to have been destroyed: but the said Matthews is required to give the usual security.

---

16. "Tos. Mathews" in the clerk's index.

It is advised that pardons issue in favor of Negro Billy, belonging to Elizabeth river parish, and negro Ben, the property of Thomas Baker, under sentence of Death by the Judgment of the Court of Norfolk Borough, for felony; they appearing to be proper objects of mercy.

It is advised that Col. John Hardin and Maj. Williams Whitley be appointed to take the command of the Militia ordered from the District of Kentucky to join Governor St. Clair, so soon as they shall assemble at the place of rendezvous to be appointed by the said Governor.

The Governor laid before the board a resolution of the General Assembly empowering the Executive to take effectual measures for settling the accounts of this State against the United States. And it being suggested that it is not decided whether Col. Davies or Mr. Dunscombe had authority to controul all proceedings in the settlement of the said Accounts, The Board advise that Mr. Dunscombe be directed to give to Col. Davies every information in his power respecting the demands of this State against the United States, and take his advice and directions in preparing and stating the same; and that he suffer him at all times to have access to any books, papers or Vouchers in his possession. The board further advise that a Committee of their body be appointed to enquire into the State of Mr. Dunscombs office and report how far it may be proper to reduce the expences of the said office And Mr. Braxton and Mr. Heth are accordingly appointed a Committee for that purpose.

The board took under consideration the providing for the defence of the Western Country, and thereupon advise, that the counties of Monongalia, Randolph, Montgomery and Washington Shall not be allowed either Scouts or rangers; and that Madison, Lincoln and Mercer have Scouts only:

That four Scouts and fifty rangers be ordered to be ready for service for the county of Ohio, Two Scouts and thirty rangers for Harrison, four Scouts and fifty rangers for Greenbriar, four Scouts and fifty rangers for Russell, four Scouts and thirty rangers for Fayette, two Scouts and forty rangers for Bourbon, four Scouts and forty rangers for Nelson, four Scouts and forty rangers for Jefferson, two Scouts for Mercer, two for Madison and two for Lincoln: the Scouts to be appointed by the field officers and captains of the aforesaid Counties respectively, and the Rangers to have the proper proportion of officers allotted to them.

That the pay of the Scouts be five shillings per day:

That the pay of the Rangers be as for militia and that the number of rations be according to the act intituled "An Act to amend and reduce into one act the several laws for regulating and disciplining the militia and guarding against invasions and insurrections" and consist of one pound of fresh beef or pork, three quarters pounds of salt pork, one pound wheat bread or flour or one and a quarter pounds of corn meal, one gill of spirits; and to every hundred rations one one quart of salt.

That it is however to be understood that no greater number than one half of the said Rangers to be employed in the said counties whether in Kentucky or other parts of the Western frontier, be drawn into actual Service until further instructions be received from this board; unless in cases of great and pressing emergency; and whenever such emergency shall cease, the respective county Lieutenants will consider it as their duty immediately to discharge the whole or such parts of the said rangers as shall not be indispensably necessary for the defence of their counties.

That for the supplying of rations whensoever, under the regulations aforesaid, or the further order of the Executive, any party of rangers shall be called into actual service, a contract shall be made by the commanding officer of the counties respectively, on the funds provided by law. But all accounts shall be settled according to the number of rations actually furnished agreeable to the allowances aforesaid: and the price of a ration shall not exceed six pence.

It is advised that commissions issue to Edmund Pendleton, John Blair, Peter Lyons, Paul Carrington, and William Fleming, esquires as Judges of the Court of appeals; and to Richard Cary, John Tyler, James Henry and Cuthbert Bullit esquires as Judges of the General Court, they having been appointed by joint ballot of the General Assembly.

Mr. Bullit appeared, and took the oath prescribed by law to be taken by a Judge of the General Court.

All which matters so advised, the Governor orders accordingly.

James Wood
James McClurg
Will Heth
Robt. Goode

Friday January 2d 1789

Present

The Governor

| Mr. Wood | Mr. Braxton |
| Mr. McClurg | Mr. Moore |

It is advised that the Auditor be directed to issue a warrant on the Contingent fund, for a Quarters Salary due to Col. Davies, as Council to Mr. Dunscombe, twenty pounds thereof, to be paid out of any money in the treasury.

On consideration of a letter from Col. Davies; it is advised, that the Governor write to the several late Quarter Masters, in the continental department requesting them to forward to this board by as early a day as possible, accounts of all supplies furnished by this State for the use of the Continent; assuring them that full compensation shall be made them in proportion to their trouble and expence.

Pursuant to the 19th section of the Act "establishing District Courts, and for regulating the General Court." It is advised that the second Monday in February be appointed the day on which the Judges of the general Court are to assemble for the purpose of appointing a Clerk for each district court; and that each of the said Judges be notified thereof.

The Governor informed the Council that he had received applications from several persons for payment of the debts due to the Scouts and rangers on the western frontier; and it appearing from a Statement made by the Treasurer that there cannot at present be spared from appropriations which are by law indispensably necessary to be complied with, a sufficient Sum of money to discharge the whole of the debt due to the said Scouts and rangers; and that there is no money in the treasury belonging to the fund especially appropriated to that purpose, The board advise that the Treasurer be directed to borrow from any other fund the Sum of fifteen hundred pounds to be applied to the present relief of this class of creditors, and in order that the aforesaid sum may be justly distributed among the respective Claimants, it is further advised that the Auditor be directed to furnish the treasurer with the amount of the warrants which have been heretofore issued to each county respectively for the pay of Scouts and rangers or for rations supplied them and that he pay a just apportionment of the said Sum of fifteen hundred pounds to the Lieutenants of the several counties on the western frontier or to such persons as have been intrusted by them to settle the claims of their counties. But it is to be understood that where any payments have been already made to any particular County, the sums so paid shall be considered as a part of the present apportionment.

It appearing that there is no money now in the Treasury belonging to the funds appropriated to the payment of the Salaries of the Judges and other officers of civil Government. It is advised that the Treasurer be directed to borrow from any other funds such a sum of money as will be sufficient to discharge the warrants which shall be issued for the last Quarters salary to the said Judges and other officers of civil government.

The Governor informed the board that he yesterday issued a commission appointing William Nutt Sheriff of Northumberland County in the room of John Hull deceased. Also a Commission appointing William Alivey an Inspector at Fraziers and Mantapike warehouses, in the room of Joseph Fox deceased. Approved.

All which matters so advised, the Governor orders accordingly.

James Wood
James McClurg

Thursday January 8th 1789

Present

The Governor

Mr. Wood　　　　　　Mr. Heth
Mr. McClurg　　　　　Mr. Goode

The Governor informed the board that during the recess he referred to the Auditor for settlement in the usual way, the account of William Rose for supplies furnished the public Jail agre[e]ably to Contract.

That he directed Warrants to issue to Capt. Langham for one hundred and fifty five pounds six shillings and seven pence, as the balance due the Superintendant and Artificers at the Point of Fork; for seventy two pounds twelve shillings balance due the Guard; for twenty five pounds fifteen shillings for so much advanced by him for repairs etc. at the said post, and for twelve pounds upon account to enable him to complete the purchase of corn for the said post; for the payment of which Warrants he directed the treasurer to borrow from other funds, there being no money in the Treasury belonging to the funds appropriated for the Support of the said post:

That he examined and certified for payment the account of the Auditor for his last quarters salary: and

That he inclosed to congress the report of the Superintendants who met on the 15th ultimo, and of the Register and Col. Meriwether relative to the Lands northwest of the Ohio: Approved.

The Governor laid before the board a resolution of the General Assembly authorizing the Directors of the public buildings to sell to the Executive such public securities as they may have in their hands. Whereupon it is advised that the Agent for the Sinking fund be directed to negotiate with the Directors for the purchase of the said Securities.

It is advised that a Warrant issue for fifty pounds to Captain Singleton for a quarters salary due to him as agent for the sinking fund.

It appearing that Mary Minton comes within the requisitions of the pension law, It is advised that She be put on the pension List, with an allowance of five pounds per annum from the first January 1788.

On consideration of a Letter from Hezekiah Davisson, Charles Martin and Thomas Laidley relative to the road from the North fork of Potowmack to the Monongalia river, It is advised that the Governor write to Mr. Joseph Neville inclosing to him a copy of the said Letter (see Letter book).[17]

---

17. Beverley Randolph to Joseph Neville, 9 Jan. 1789, Letter Book 1788–1792, Governor's Office.

All which matters so advised, the Governor orders accordingly.

> James Wood
> James McClurg
> Will Heth
> Robt. Goode

Monday January 12th 1789

Present

The Governor

Mr. Wood	Mr. Jones
Mr. McClurg	Mr. Heth

Mr. Goode

The Governor laid before the board a resolution of the general assembly empowering the Executive to dispose of the public tobacco. Whereupon it is advised, that a Committee of this board be appointed to confer with any person who may be willing to purchase the whole of the said tobacco, and report the terms which may be had: and Mr. McClurg and Mr. Jones are accordingly appointed a committee for that purpose.

The board proceeded further to consider the cases of the malefactors who were condemned to die at the last session of the General Court. Whereupon it is advised, That William Jenkins, who stands condemned for horsestealing, be pardoned; he appearing to be a proper object of mercy.

On consideration of a petition of William Frazier praying for the remission of a fine of fifteen pounds imposed on him by the General Court for an assault; It is advised that the said fine be remitted.

Present Mr. Braxton.

All which matters so advised, the Governor orders accordingly.

> James McClurg
> Jos. Jones
> Carter Braxton
> Will Heth
> Robt. Goode

Thursday January 15th 1789

Present

The Governor

Mr. Wood   Mr. Braxton
Mr. McClurg   Mr. Heth
Mr. Jones   Mr. Goode

The Governor laid before the board a resolution of the General assembly of the 1st and 4th of December last referring to the Executive a report of the board of Treasury of the 4th of September last comprehending a letter from the said board to Oliver Walcot esqr.; Comptroller of accounts for the State of Massachusetts-bay, to be acted upon according to the constructions therein contained and in conformity to such explanations as may be received hereafter from Congress or the board of treasury. Whereupon it is advised, that the Clerk of this board do advertize in the public Gazettes that it will be necessary for all officers or soldiers whether regulars or militia who may be upon the list of pensioners and have any claim to arrearages of pensions to produce to the Executive satisfactory proof of the time when their pay in the Service of the United States ceased, and that they have not received any certificates for commutation of half pay, or that, if they have ever received any such Certificates, they have returned them to the proper office to be cancelled: And it is further advised that the acts of Congress of the 26th of August 1776, 7th of June 1785, and 11th of June 1788, the report of the board of treasury, the letter addressed to Oliver Walcot Esqr.; and the aforesaid resolution of the General Assembly of the 1st of December last, on the subject of pensioners, be entered in the additional Journal.[18]

The Governor laid before the board an application of the representatives of William McClentock for arrearages of pension. Whereupon it is advised that the said application be rejected; as it does not appear that the said McClentock was ever put on the List of pensioners.

All which matters so advised the Governor orders accordingly.

James Wood
James McClurg
Jos. Jones
Carter Braxton
Robt. Goode

---

18. *See* page 341 for the additional journal entry dated 15 Jan. 1789.

Saturday January 17th 1789

Present

The Governor

Mr. Wood	Mr. Braxton
Mr. McClurg	Mr. Heth
Mr. Jones	Mr. Goode

At the request of Thomas Williamson and Matthew Farley two of the malefactors under sentence of death; It is advised that they be reprieved until friday the 30th of this present month.

The Governor laid before the board the accounts of Messrs. Davis and Nicolson for printing the laws of the last Session of assembly; Whereupon it is advised, That they be allowed the Sum of two hundred and seven pounds ten shilling according to their respective charges for printing the said laws: to be paid, one half out of the quarters salary which shall be due the public printer in march next, and the other half, out of the quarters salary which shall be due the said Printer in June next.

It is advised that Warrants issue on the Contingent fund, to Archibald Blair, for twenty five pounds being for four months salary due him the 4th instant as Keeper of the public Seal; and to John Dixon for two pounds eight shillings for printing 200 copies of the Governors circular letter concerning supplies furnished the United States. (This last to be paid).

On recommendations, It is advised that a commission issue appointing William Herring, Sheriff of Rockingham; and an additional commission appointing Bennedict Crump, Burwell Bassett junr., John Hockaday, William Armistead junr., George Wilkinson (son of George), and William Chamberlayne Gentlemen Justices of the peace of New Kent County.

The Governor laid before the board Col. Meriwethers report of Delinquents under the Militia laws. Whereupon it is advised that the same be referred to the Solicitor, with instructions to confer with the Attorney General on the subject, and prepare notices in order that motions may be made thereupon in the most speedy manners.

All which matters so advised, the Governor orders accordingly.

James Wood
James McClurg
Jos. Jones
Carter Braxton
Robt. Goode

Monday January 19th 1789

Present

The Governor

Mr. Wood	Mr. Braxton
Mr. McClurg	Mr. Heth
Mr. Jones	Mr. Goode

On reconsideration of the case of Timothy OConner[19] It is advised that his pension be augmented to twelve pounds per annum from the 1st of this present month.

It is advised that Catherine Crulle[20] who is under sentence of Death, be reprieved until Friday the 30th of this month.

It is advised that a register issue for the Ship Sally; satisfactory proof having been made in due form of law.

It is advised that a warrant issue on the Contingent fund to Francis Pearce for eighteen pounds being the amount of his account for express hire, as certified by Col. Meriwether (to be paid).

All which matters so advised the Governor orders accordingly.

James Wood
Jos. Jones
Carter Braxton
Robt. Goode

Thursday January 22d 1789

Present

The Governor

Mr. Wood	Mr. Braxton
Mr. Jones	Mr. Heth
	Mr. Goode

The board resumed the consideration of the recommendation from Culpeper, of fit persons to be added to the Commissi[on] of the peace, the Clerk of the Court of the said County having certified, that of the persons named in the present Commission, John Strother and John Slaughter have resigned, Robert Alcock and Cadwallader Slaughter have removed; John Green, Elijah Kirlley and Joseph Roberts have failed to qualify, John Wharton and Walter Compton have refused to qualify: Whereupon it is advised, that an additional Commission issue appointing David Jameson, John Thompson, Philip Slaughter, William Madison, Robert Cowne, Mordecai Barbour, Wil-

---

19. "Timothy Oconner" in the clerk's index.
20. "C. Cralle" in the clerk's index.

liam Gray, Henry Ward and William Stanton Gentlemen Justices of the peace of the said County.

It is advised that a register issue for the Schooner charming Betsey; satisfactory proof having been made in due form of law.

In pursuance of a resolution of the general assembly of the 5th and 18th ultimo, and on satisfactory proofs being produced; It is advised that the Auditor be directed to issue duplicate Certificates to Lewis Jones for three hundred and seventeen pounds seven shillings and eleven pence in lieu of those which appear to have been destroyed; on the usual Security being given by the said Jones.

On consideration of the report of the Committee appointed to confer with such persons as might be willing to purchase the public tobacco, It is advised that an Agent be appointed on Saturday next to sell the said tobacco.

The Board resumed the consideration of the case of William Crittendon one of the labouring criminals now in the public Jail. Whereupon it is advised that he be delivered to Mr. Harris for the purpose of performing labour according to the terms of his conditional pardon.

In pursuance of a resolution of the general assembly of the 3d and 8th december, It is advised, that the Auditor be directed to issue a warrant on the aggregate fund to Richard Brooke, for one hundred and one pounds fifteen shillings and eight pence, with interest thereon from the 1st of November 1775, in paiment for a piece of land Purchased from him by the Commissioners of the gun factory at Fredericksburg for public use.

Mr. Dunscombe[21] having reported that he found among the papers taken to his office a sum of paper money to the amount of £85936.11.0. and desired to Know what ought to be done with the same. It is advised that the Auditor be directed to give Credits in his books for the said money as far as any documents in Mr. Dunscombes office, or elsewhere, will authorize it; and to order the money so credited, to be returned to the Treasurer and that report of the proceedings herein be made to this board.

On consideration of the petition of Thomas Allen late Sheriff of Shenandoah, It is advised that the same be referred to the Solicitor to examine and report the truth of the allegations stated therein.

On recommendation, It is advised that an additional commission issue appointing Jeremiah McCoy, Joseph Strickler, Peter Ironberger, John Croudson, George Travell, Archibald Wilson, John Grove (at New Markett) and Locklan McIntosh Gentlemen Justices of the peace of Shenandoah County.

On consideration of Col. Meriwethers report concerning certain books and papers of Captain Young, the Successor of the commercial

---

21. "A. Dunscomb" in the clerk's index.

agent, which are required by Col. Davies as Vouchers in support of the Claims of this State against the united States; It is advised that the said books and papers be sent to the Auditor, with instructions that he cause the proper credits and debits to be immediately made for and against individuals, and report to the Solicitor any balances that shall appear in favor of the State, in order for the recovery thereof; and that he withold any of the said books and papers, which, in his opinion ought not to be possessed by Col. Davies.

This being the day appointed for the further consideration of the complaint exhibited by William Helm against Jesse Ewell as County Lieutenant of Prince William: But the board, not having time to go through the depositions, advise, that the consideration of the said complaint be postponed until Saturday next.

All which matters so advised the Governor orders accordingly.

James Wood
Jos. Jones
Carter Braxton
Will Heth
Robt. Goode

Saturday January 24th 1789

Present

The Governor

Mr. Wood	Mr. Braxton
Mr. McClurg	Mr. Heth
Mr. Jones	Mr. Goode

It is advised that a Commission issue appointing Henry Thweat junr. inspector at Robert Bollings Warehouse in the room of Samuel Hinton deceased. The said Thweat appeared and took the oath of office before the Governor.

It is advised that the Account of Samuel Swann, amounting to six pounds six shillings, for repairs of the furniture belonging to the Governors house be referred to the Auditor for a Warrant on the Contingent fund for the sum due. (to be paid)

Absent Mr. Heth.

The board resumed the consideration of the resolution of the general assembly empowering the Executive to dispose of the public tobacco and thereupon it is advised

1. that Harry Heth be appointed an agent for the purpose of disposing of such tobacco, as now is, or hereafter may be in the hands of the treasurer, in discharge of taxes, according to such Instructions as he shall receive from time to time from the Executive.

2. that the Auditor be instructed to grant to the said Agent, an

Order on the treasurer for such proportions of the said tobacco, as the said Agent may from time to time require, debiting him therewith;

3. that the said Agent, settle with the Auditor for the sales of the tobacco so put into his hands, and obtain from him an order on the treasurer to receive the amount of Such sales, and on the treasurer's receipt there for, the Auditor shall give him a quietus.

4th. that proper Instructions be prepared for the said Agent:

5th. that he be required to give bond with two or more sufficient Securities in ten thousand pounds for the faithful discharge of his office; and

6th. that, as he has submitted his allowance to the discretion of the board, He be assured that such reasonable compensation shall be made him for his trouble and expences as the nature of his services may be justly intitled to.

Present Mr. Heth.

On recommendation, it is advised, that an additional commission issue appointing Matthew Hanna gentleman, a Justice of the peace for the County of Rockbridge.

The board took under consideration the appropriations made by the last assembly for the Sinking fund, and thereupon advise,

That the treasurer be directed to furnish the Agent for the Sinking fund, with an authenticated State of the amount of the military Certificates which heretofore have, by any means, come into the treasury;

That the Auditor be directed to issue Warrants to the said agent, "for the interest accruing on all military certificates which have heretofore by any means come into the treasury;" to be applied to the purposes of the sinking fund, at the discretion of the Agent: and

that, in order to distinguish, in case of loss, the Certificates belonging to the Sinking fund, the Agent be directed to punch a hole through each certificate purchased by him.

It is advised that the consideration of the charges against Col. Ewell be further postponed till monday next.

All which matters so advised the Governor orders accordingly.

James Wood
James McClurg
Jos. Jones
Carter Braxton
Will Heth
Robt. Goode

Monday January 26th 1789

Present

The Governor

Mr. Wood	Mr. Braxton
Mr. McClurg	Mr. Heth
Mr. Jones	Mr. Goode

It appearing that Captain Joseph Scott comes within the requisitions of the pension law It is advised that he be continued on the List of pensioners with full pay pursuant to the Act of Assembly passed in 1786, intituled "an act concerning the claims to full pay of certain officers, and to half pay of the widows and orphans of officers that died in the service."

The board resumed the further consideration of the charges exhibited by Captain Wm. Helm against Jesse Ewell esquire Lieutenant of the County of Prince William. Whereupon it is advised,

That, in order to give Col. Ewell the best opportunity of vindicating his character from the charges aforesaid, and at the same time to quiet the minds of such officers as think themselves injured by his conduct, a Court martial be appointed for the trial of the said Jesse Ewell, to be composed of the following officers: Col. John Fitzgerald as President, one Major and two Captains from the militia of the County of Fairfax; one Colonel, one Lieutenant Colonel, one Major and two Captains from the County of Fauquier; one Lieutenant Colonel, one Major and two Captains from the County of Stafford;

That a copy of the charges be transmitted to the said President;

That the President appoint a time and place within the said County of Prince William for holding the said court martial, giving notice thereof to the parties; and that he call upon the Lieutenants or commanding officers of the militia of the said counties to order the number of officers required from each to attend at the time and place appointed to serve as members of the said court martial; and that a special state of the Evidence and facts, together with the sentence of the Court be transmitted to the Governor as soon as possible.

It is advised, that the Clerk advertize in the public gazette, the names of the persons who have been returned Electors to Vote for a President in conformity to the constitution of Government for the United States.

All which matters so advised, the Governor orders accordingly.

James Wood
James McClurg
Jos. Jones
Carter Braxton
Will Heth
Robt. Goode

Tuesday January 27th 1789

Present

The Governor

Mr. Wood   Mr. Braxton
Mr. McClurg   Mr. Heth
Mr. Jones   Mr. Goode

It is advised that a Commission issue appointing Nathl. Fox an additional inspector at Mantapike and Fraziers warehouse, in the room of William Alvey who hath been appointed a principal inspector.

Mr. Harry Heth produced his bond as agent for Selling the public tobacco, with John T. Griffin, Benja. Harrison, jr. and Thomas M. Randolph Securities thereto, which is approved and ordered to be filed. And Mr. Heth received his Instructions.

The Committee appointed to examine the state of Mr. Dunscombs office having made their report and the same being read and considered, it is thereupon advised,

That Mr. Dunscombs Salary be reduced to two hundred pounds per annum as, by the advice of this board of the 31st Day of December last a considerable portion of the labour of his office and all responsibility was taken from him, it can be no longer proper to continue the high Salary he at present enjoys;

That Col. Davies be required to report as soon as may be whether any and what reduction of the Clerks of the said office may be made and,

That he prepare and report proper Instructions for the persons to be appointed to collect Vouchers pursuant to the advice of the 29th of December last.

The Governor is requested to write to Mr. Dunscomb informing him, as to what is expected by the board to be his future duty. (See Letter book)[22]

All which matters so advised the Governor orders accordingly.

James Wood
James McClurg
Jos. Jones
Carter Braxton
Will Heth
Robt. Goode

---

22. Beverley Randolph to Andrew Dunscomb, 27 Jan. 1789, Letter Book 1788–1792, Governor's Office.

Thursday January 29th 1789

Present

The Governor

Mr. Wood	Mr. Braxton
Mr. McClurg	Mr. Heth
Mr. Jones	Mr. Goode

On consideration of a letter from the Attorney General concerning Catharine Cruelle[23] who is under sentence of death for murder, It is advised that She be reprieved until Friday the 6th of next month: And, it being suggested that the said Catherine is disordered in mind, it is further advised that the Governor write to the Rev. John Buchanan, John Marshall and William Foushee esqrs. requesting them to examine and report to this board their opinion as to the present state of her intellects.

It appearing that Stephen Terry comes within the requisitions of the pension law It is advised that he be continued on the pension list with twelve pounds per annum.

The Governor laid before the board a state of the delinquent inspectors, and Clerks of the County courts. Whereupon it is advised, that the Solicitor be called upon for information as to the Steps which have been taken by him for the recovery of the balances due from the said inspectors and Clerks.

It is advised that Col. Meriwether be desired to visit the Post at the Point of Fork and report a state of the arms, etc., there deposited, in order that the Executive may be able to judge of the propriety of reducing the said post.

The Governor laid before the board a letter from Andrew Limozine, at Havre de Grace, inclosing a bill of lading for the Bust of the Marquis Fayette, to be delivered at the Port of Baltimore. Whereupon it is advised, that the Governor take measures for bringing the said bust here; and draw upon the Treasurer for the freight, and expences thereof.

It is advised that the board proceed, on Saturday the 28th of February, to appoint Public Jailors for the several Districts, in pursuance of the 96th Section of the Act of the general assembly, "Establishing District Courts and for regulating the general court;" and that the Clerk give notive thereof in the public gazette.

All which matters so advised, the Governor orders accordingly.

James Wood
James McClurg
Jos. Jones
Carter Braxton
Will Heth

---

23. "C. Cralle" in the clerk's index.

Saturday January 31st 1789

Present

The Governor

Mr. Wood   Mr. Braxton
Mr. McClurg   Mr. Heth
Mr. Jones   Mr. Goode

It appearing that Judah Levi comes within the requisitions of the pension law; It is advised that he be continued on the List of pensioners with an allowance of fifteen pounds per annum from the 1st of January 1786.

It is advised that registers issue for the Sloop Metampkin, Schooner Antelope and Sloop Betsey; Satisfactory proofs having been made in due form of law.

Martin Oster, Esquire, Vice Consul of France having certified to the Executive in due form of law, that he had taken cognizance of a certain controversy arising between Henry Cagneau and Jean Alexis Subercaseaux, merchants and subjects of his most Christian Majesty, and Jean Cauvy, another Merchant and subject of his most Christian Majesty, all residing in Petersburg and on the 26th instant had determined the same by condemning the said Jean Cauvy to pay to the said Henry Cugneau and Jean Alexis Subercaseaux in the space of 24 hours the sum of forty one pounds fifteen shillings and 4d. with interest from the day of the demand and 15/. costs: Also that he had taken cognizance of a certain controversy arising between Pierre Barthis a Merchant and subject of his most Christian Majesty and the said Jean Cauvy, and on the 12th instant, had determined the same by condemning the said Jean Cauvy to pay to the said Pierre Barthis the sum of eighty five pounds thirteen shillings and eleven pence half penny, and the said Martin Oster Esquire having required aid for executing the said determinations. It is advised, that orders issue to the Sheriff of Dinwiddie to execute or aid and assist in executing such determinations according to the act of the general assembly in that case made and provided.

It is advised that the following persons be appointed, in pursuance of the advice of the 29th Ultimo, to collect Vouchers in support of the Claims of this State against the United States to wit:

Alexander Parker, or in the case of his refusal, Thomas Parker, for the counties of Prince William, Loudon, Fairfax, Stafford, Fauquier, King George, Westmoreland, Richmond, Northumberland and Lancaster:

Thomas Buckner, or in case of his refusal, Lawrence Butler, for the counties of Gloster, Middlesex, Essex, King and Queen, Caroline, King William and Hanover:

Charles Russell; or in case of his refusal, Richd. Yarborough, for the counties of Norfolk, Accomack, Northampton, Princess Anne, Nansemond, Isle of Wight and Surry:

John Langhorne for the counties of Chesterfield, Henrico, New Kent, Charles City, James City, York, Warwick and Elizabeth City:

William Price for the counties of Albemarle, Amherst, Fluvanna, Goochland, Louisa, Spotsylvania, Orange and Culpeper:

Mayo Carrington, for the counties of Brunswick, Sussex, Greenesville, Prince George, Dinwiddie, Mecklenburg, Lunenburg, Amelia, Cumberland, and Powhatan:

Capt. Thomas Holt, or in case of his refusal, Tunstal Quarles, for the Counties of Campbell, Charlotte, Buckingham, Bedford, Prince Edward, Franklin, Henry, Pittsylvania and Halifax:

Robert Porterfield, for the Counties of Russell, Washington, Montgomery, Botetourt, Rockbridge, Green Briar and Augusta.

William Eskridge, for the Counties of Rockingham, Shenandoah, Pendleton, Hardy, Hampshire, Berkeley, Frederick, Ohio, Monongalia, Harrison and Randolph.

All which matters so advised, the Governor orders accordingly.

> James Wood
> James McClurg
> Jos. Jones
> Carter Braxton
> Will Heth
> Robt. Goode

Tuesday February 3d 1789

Present

The Governor

Mr. Wood	Mr. Jones
Mr. McClurg	Mr. Braxton
	Mr. Goode

The Governor informed the board that he yesterday directed a Warrant to issue on the Contingent fund in favor of James Vaughan for three pounds sixteen shillings and ten pence half penny due him for express hire; as certified by Col. Meriwether. Approved.

Henry Dade Hooe having been appointed Surveyor of Prince William County; It is advised that he be required to give bond in penalty of one thousand pounds.

The Governor laid before the board strong recommendations of John Crump as a fit person to serve as Public Jailor for the James City District. Whereupon it is advised, that the said John Crump be appointed Public Jailor for the said District.

On consideration of the memorial of William Winder representing that there is a considera[b]l[e] Sum due from the United States for the pay and Expences of his office as Commissioner for receiving etc. the Claims of this State and the State of North Carolina against the United States; and requesting that a Sum may be advanced by this State for the purpose, and charged to the United States, It is advised, that the same be rejected; the appropriations made by the assembly having put it out of the power of the Executive to comply with Mr. Windors request.

The Governor laid before the board a letter from the honorable Edmund Pendleton suggesting that no provision had been made for the payment of salaries to the Judges of the Court of appeals. Whereupon it is advised, That the Auditor be directed to issue quarterly to each of the Judges of the new Court of appeals who may qualify to their appointments the usual Warrants for seventy five pounds, and that a letter be written to each of the said Judges respectively informing them of this Order and assuring them that the matter will be represented to the general assembly at their next Session.

The Governor laid before the board the proceedings of Fairfax Court in January last denying the power of County Courts to lay levies. Whereupon it is advised that the said proceedings be referred to the attorney general for his opinion thereon.

All which matters so advised, the Governor orders accordingly.

James Wood
James McClurg
Jos. Jones
Carter Braxton
Robt. Goode

Thursday February 5th 1789

Present

The Governor

Mr. Wood   Mr. Jones
Mr. McClurg   Mr. Braxton
Mr. Goode

The Governor laid before the board an account of Wm. Geddy amounting to six pounds seventeen Shillings and eight pence for Grates, etc., for the Governors house. Whereupon it is advised, that the same be referred to the Auditor for settlement and a warrant on the Contingent fund for the sum due (to be paid).

It appearing that James Chambers comes within the requisitions of the pension law; It is advised that he be continued on the List of pensioners with eighteen pounds per annum.

The board having received satisfactory proofs of the fitness of

James Dougherty to serve as a public Jailor; It is advised that the said James Dougherty be appointed Public Jailor for the District of Harrison.

On consideration of Col. Meriwethers report concerning the Militia, It is advised that Col. Meriwether be desired to write to the Lieutenants of those counties from which no recommendations have been received of Officers for the cavalry, requiring them forthwith to transmit the proper recommendations.

The Governor laid before the board the report of the Rev. John Buchanan, John Marshall, and William Foushee esquires concerning Catherine Crull,[24] in the following words viz "In obedience to the request of your Excellency We have visited Catherine Crull: She appears to us to be almost in a State of entire ideotcy. Her mind seems so much disordered that we think her totally incapable of distinguishing right from wrong, or even of knowing what is said to her." Whereupon it is advised, That the said Catherine Crull be pardoned; and that the Jailor be directed to have her examined and forwarded to the hospital in Williamsburg, according to law.

The Governor laid before the board a letter from William McCleary esquire of Monongalia County Stating that the Militia of that County as well as the Counties of Harrison and Randolph are alarmed at so great a proportion of their militia being embodied and directed to march on the order of Governor St. Clair. On consideration of the exposed situation of the Inhabitants of the said Counties in case of a general Indian war, The board advise that so much of the advice of the 15th of October last as directs the Counties of Ohio, Harrison, Monongalia and Randolph to embody certain proportions of their Militia, be rescinded, and that Instructions be immediately given to the Lieutenants of the Counties of Ohio, Monongalia, Harrison, Randolph, Hardy, Pendleton, Hampshire, Frederick and Rockingham to embody on the requisition of his Excellency Arthur St. Clair Governor of the Western Territory the following proportions of their respective Militias that is to say the County of Ohio one Captain and 45 non commissioned and privates; Monongalia, one Lieutenant and 30 non commissioned and privates; Harrison one Ensign and 30 non commissioned and privates; Randolph, two Serjeants and 20 privates; Frederick, one Captain, two Lieutenants, one ensign and 96 non commissioned and privates; Hampshire, one Captain, one Lieutenant, one ensign and 52 non commissioned and privates; Hardy, one Captain, one Lieutenant, one ensign and 50 non commissioned and privates; Rockingham, one Captain, one Lieutenant, one ensign and 52, noncommissioned and privates; Pendleton, one Captain, one Lieutenant, one Ensign and 50 non commissioned and privates.

It is further advised that a copy of the foregoing advice be sent to Governor St. Clair.

---

24. "C. Cralle" in the clerk's index.

All which matters so advised, the Governor orders accordingly.

James Wood
James McClurg
Jos. Jones
Carter Braxton
Robt. Goode

Monday February 9th 1789

Present

The Governor

Mr. Wood   Mr. Braxton
Mr. Jones   Mr. Heth
                   Mr. Goode

The Governor informed the board that, on Saturday last, he referred to the Auditor for settlement in the usual way the Account of Christopher Roane, Searcher at City point, amounting to twenty nine pounds Seven shillings and eight pence for the expences of a boat for the use of his office. Approved.

Richard Cary esqr. appeared and took the oath prescribed by law to be taken by a Judge of the General Court.

It is advised that John Richards be appointed Public Jailor for the District which includes the County of Spotsylvania.

The Governor laid before the board a letter from Gabriel Fawlks esquire appointed President of a General Court martial for the trial of Col. Pauling Anderson, stating that one of the Field Officers appointed to serve as a member had failed to attend. It is advised that the said Gabriel Fawlks be continued President, that the County Lieutenant be directed to cause two field officers, six Captains and four Lieutenants, not being Witnesses, to be summoned and required to attend, at such time and place as the President may appoint, to serve as members of a General Court martial for the trial of the said Pauling Anderson, now under arrest and charged with "endeavouring to prevail on Charles Hodges to take a false Oath in order to screen him from paying a fine for which he was presented by the grand Jury of Amelia County." The facts to be stated specially together with the sentence of the Court Martial and forwarded to the Governor as soon as possible.

Present Mr. McClurg.

It appearing that the Sheriff failed to give bond for the collection of the taxes of the year 1787 in the County of Pittsylvania; It is advised that John Buckley, gentleman, be appointed a Collector in the said County for the year aforesaid; pursuant [to] the Act of Assembly "for granting relief to Sheriffs and Collectors of the public revenue in certain cases."

It is advised that the Auditor be directed to settle the accounts of Jonathan Clarke[25] "for the disbursement of several considerable Sums of paper money, received by him for the purpose of recruiting and re enlisting Soldiers during the late war," pursuant to a resolution of the general assembly of the 30th of November 1786.

The Governor laid before the board a memorial of Joseph Latil, in behalf of himself and other foreign creditors, concerning the appropriations for the discharge of the Debts due to such creditors. Whereupon it is advised that the said memorial be referred to the Attorney General for his opinion thereon.

All which matters so advised the Governor orders accordingly.

> James Wood
> James McClurg
> Jos. Jones
> Carter Braxton
> Will Heth
> Robt. Goode

Thursday February 12th 1789

Present

The Governor

Mr. Wood	Mr. Braxton
Mr. McClurg	Mr. Heth
Mr. Jones	Mr. Goode

The Governor reported that on the 10th, he referred to the Auditor for settlement in the usual way, the Accounts of Samuel McDonald amounting to One hundred and twenty five pounds eighteen shillings and nine pence, for supplies furnished at the Point of Fork to the 31st of January 1789, agreeably to Contract, as certified by Col. Meriwether: and that on the 11th he directed a warrant to issue on the Contingent Fund for fifteen shillings to Joseph Leplong for riding express to Peter Lyons esqr. at the instance of the Judges of the general court. Approved.

It is advised that the Auditor be directed to issue a Warrant on the contingent fund, for thirty pounds to Col. William Finnie for services rendered in furnishing Vouchers in support of the Claims of this State against the United States, as appears by Certificate from Col. Davies. (To be paid)

The Governor laid before the board an account of Col. Finnie for additional pay, as Quarter master General, at twenty five Dollars per month from April 1779 to the 15th of February 1780. Whereupon it is

---

25. "Jonathan Clark" in the clerk's index.

advised that the said Account be rejected, the door being shut against the Settlement of Such claims.

It is advised that a warrant issue, on the contingent fund, for six pounds, payable to [. . .][26] Kevan, for conveying to the public Jail John Fowler, who escaped from labor (to be paid).

It appearing that James Askew[27] comes within the requisitions of the pension law; It is advised that he be continued on the List of pensioners, with an allowance of eight pounds per annum from the 1st of January last.

Major Call having produced certain papers as Vouchers concerning the charge of Ninety thousand Dollars excepted against in his claim presented to the Executive, on the 14th of November last, for settlement, It is advised that the Auditor be directed to settle with Major Call for the said Ninety thousand Dollars, so far as he shall produce satisfactory proofs.

It is advised, that Thomas Marshall senr. be appointed a Receiver for the District of Kentucky, pursuant to an act of assembly "for further amending" an Act for establishing a District Court on the Western waters."

The Governor laid before the board the opinion of the Attorney General on the proceedings of the Court of Fairfax referred to him the 3d instant. Whereupon it is advised that the same be transmitted to the Clerk of the said Court.

It is advised that Edward Powers be appointed public Jailor for the District which includes the County of Berkeley.

The Governor laid before the board a memorial of Mr. John Cauvy, stating that at the time of the decision of the Consul of France on the controversy between Messrs. Cagneau and Subercaseaux and himself, there was a suit depending in the county court of Dinwiddie on the same subject, as appears by the Certificate of the Clerk of the said County; and praying that the Order of the 31st Ultimo to the Sheriff of Dinwiddie to aid and assist in the Execution of the Consuls decree may be suspended. Whereupon it is advised that the Order of the 31st of January last directing the Sheriff of Dinwiddie to aid in Executing the Determination of the Consul of France in the controversy between the said Cauvy and Messrs. Cagneau and Subercaseaux, be suspended until further orders.

It is advised that the Auditor be directed to issue a Warrant on the Contingent Fund, for thirty pounds to John Coke, for the purchase of Negro Timothy in order to his being emancipated, pursuant to a resolution of the General Assembly of the 20th of December last. (To be paid)

---

26. Blank in the journal.
27. The name appears to be "Jas. Askey" in the clerk's index.

All which matters so advised, the Governor orders accordingly.

James Wood
James McClurg
Jos. Jones
Carter Braxton
Robt. Goode
Will Heth

Monday February 16th 1789

Present

The Governor

Mr. Wood   Mr. Jones
Mr. McClurg   Mr. Braxton
                    Mr. Goode

The Governor informed the board that he took the opportunity by Mr. Beckley who was going to new York, of forwarding the several matters directed by the assembly to be transmitted to the representatives of this State in Congress. Approved.

It is advised that Jedediah Johnson be appointed a Collector of the Taxes due for the years 1785 and 1786 in the County of Fluvanna, the late Sheriff of the said County having removed to Kentucky.

The Governor laid before the board an account of William Graves Searcher at Norfolk, amounting to thirty pounds four Shillings for the expences of the boat allowed for the use of his office. Also an account of Joseph Clark amounting to fifteen shillings for riding Express to Judge Fleming, at the instance of the Judges of the general Court. Whereupon it is advised That the said Accounts be referred to the auditor for settlement, and Warrants on the Contingent fund for the sums due. (To be paid)

The Governor laid before the board a letter from the Solicitor on the Subject of the Account directed to be made up of all monies and other things for which this Commonwealth is still entitled to a credit on Account of the requisitions of Congress. Whereupon it is advised, That the said letter be referred to Col. Davies, and he be requested to report by Wednesday next, whether the necessary Documents for making out the aforesaid Account are in his office.

On the Solicitors report, It is advised that a warrant issue on the Aggregate fund, to Marsdens Executors, for the amount of five thousand one hundred and ten pounds of tobacco, at 20/. per hundred, in full, for the rest of the Governors-house, from the 20th of April 1780, to the 15th of August following.

The Governor laid before the board an account of Messrs. Marsden Maxwell and Company making a balance of 18,403 lbs. [of]

tobacco, said to be *"due Marsden and Smith and my* (Mr. Armisteads) *Certificate to James Marsden."* Whereupon it is advised, That the said account be rejected for the want of the aforesaid Certificate.

All which matters so advised the governor orders accordingly.

> James Wood
> James McClurg
> Jos. Jones
> Robt. Goode

Thursday February 19th 1789

Present

The Governor

Mr. Wood	Mr. Braxton
Mr. McClurg	Mr. Heth
Mr. Jones	Mr. Goode

The board having called for and taken into consideration the reports of the Treasurer, Auditor, and Solicitor, respecting the returns of Bonds, settlements, and payments made by the Inspectors of tobacco and Clerks of Courts, and finding several neglects and omissions in performing the duties required of them by law, are of Opinion and do advise That the Solicitor be directed to proceed against all Delinquent Inspectors of tobacco, Clerks of Courts and Notaries Public for such penalties and forfeitures as they have incurred under any of the Acts of Assembly for neglecting to give and transmit to the proper office the bonds required of them by law, or for failing to settle and account for all public monies coming into their hands as public officers and Collectors of fines, taxes, or duties, and that he also proceed against the defaulters in the most effectual way authorised by law to enforce the payment of the balances now due from them to the public; That in all instances where the Solicitor shall have doubts respecting the most proper and effectual course of proceeding against the delinquents he have recourse to the Attorney General for his advice and directions; That He communicate from time to time to the Executive those cases wherein their interposition may be necessary for carrying into effect the "Act for the more speedy recovery of debts due to the Commonwealth;" That he acquaint the Executive where he shall have reason to believe the postponement of an execution to the 1st of June next may put the Debt in danger, of the particular cases wherein he shall have reason to apprehend danger that he may receive their directions for issuing executions.

For the more effectually checking the Accounts of tobacco Shipped, rendered by the different Inspectors, It is advised that the Auditor be directed, in no case in settling the said Accounts, to omit comparing them with the quarterly returns of the naval officers.

It is advised that registers issue for the Ship Two Brothers, and Schooner Mary; Satisfactory proofs having been made in due form of law.

It appearing that William Turvy and David Lyon come within the requisitions of the pension law; It is advised that the former be continued on the List of pensioners with eighteen pounds, and the latter put on the List with fifteen pounds per annum, from the first of January last.

On consideration of a letter from the Auditor, It is advised that he be authorized to employ some person on the best terms he can, to copy the report of the Commissioners appointed by the general Assembly to adjust the Claims for two expeditions against the Wabash and Shawanese Indians, as a Voucher to support the Claim of this State against the United States for the expences of the said expeditions.

On the Solicitors report It is advised that he cause the Execution against Thomas Allen, as Sheriff of Shenandoah, for the taxes of 1785, to be superceded; it appearing that the judgment against the said Allen was wrongfully obtained.

A letter to Col. Davies on the subject of the resolutions of Assembly of the 13 and 22d December last: (See Letter book).[28]

All which matters so advised, the Governor orders accordingly.

James Wood
Robt. Goode
Carter Braxton
Will Heth
Jos. Jones

Saturday February 21st 1789

Present

The Governor

Mr. Wood	Mr. Braxton
Mr. Jones	Mr. Heth

The Governor laid before the Board the payrolls of the Public Boats for the last quarter. Whereupon it is advised, That the said payrolls be referred to the Auditor for settlement in the usual way.

It is advised That the returns of the representatives of this State in Congress, be forwarded by the mail to the President of Congress.

On consideration of a Certificate from the Court of Goochland County; It is advised that the Solicitor be directed to allow credit for fifty three pounds ten shillings and ten pence with interest from the time it became due, on the judgment obtained against Nathaniel G. Morris as County Lieutenant of the said County for the one eighth per

---

28. Beverley Randolph to William Davies, 19 Feb. 1789, Letter Book 1788–1792, Governor's Office.

Cent Tax for the year, one thousand seven hundred and eighty two.

On consideration of the Petition of John Greenlee, and the Solicitors statement of the judgement obtained against the said Greenlee as Sheriff of Rockbridge for the revenue taxes of 1783; It is advised that the interest on the said Judgment from March 1784 to March 1786, be remitted.

All which matters so advised, the Governor orders accordingly.

James Wood
Jos. Jones
Carter Braxton
Will Heth

Monday February 23d 1789

Present

The Governor

Mr. Wood	Mr. Braxton
Mr. Jones	Mr. Heth

Mr. Goode

In pursuance of a resolution of the General Assembly of the 13th of December last, It is advised that Col. Meriwether be directed to make up an account of all arms and military Stores which have been at any Time since the Cession of Western Territory to the United States furnished to the Inhabitants of the Western frontier for their defence and that he procure from the Superintendent at the Point of Fork all receipts or other proper Vouchers for the delivery of them. It is also further advised that Col. Meriwether report to the board as soon as may be whether there are in his office, Documents which will serve to establish any Claim of this State against the United States for expences incurred in defending and protecting the Frontier Inhabitants from the Depredations of the Indians.

In pursuance of a resolution of the General Assembly of the 22d of December last, It is advised that the Treasurer be desired to have made out and forwarded to this board, authenticated Copies of the receipts in his office for all Sums of money or other things for which this Commonwealth is intitled to a Credit on Account of the requisitions of Congress from the 30th of October 1781 to the 20th of August 1788 inclusive and for which no such Credit hath yet been obtained.

The Governor laid before the board an account of James Marsden deceased for Nailrods furnished the public in 1779 and 1780. Whereupon It is advised that the Auditor be directed to settle the said account according to Vouchers produced; disallowing interest; and grant a Warrant for what shall appear due.

The Solicitor having communicated to the board that in April

1786, he obtained a judgment against George Stubblefield Sheriff of Spotsylvania for two thousand three hundred and thirty six pounds one shilling and nine pence, the balance due from him for the revenue taxes of 1784; that Execution had issued upon the said Judgment and had been levied upon the Estate of the said Stubblefield, and that in August 1788 a Writ of Venditioni exponas[29] issued which has been returned with the following indorsement viz "By virtue of this Writ to me directed I have exposed to Sale the Goods and Chattles of George Stubblefield which still remain on hand for want of buyers." Whereupon it is advised that the Officer to whom any subsequent Process may be directed (provided the said Property cannot be sold agreeable to the direction of such subsequent process) cause the same to be removed to the Court house of Culpeper County and there exposed to Sale by as early a Day as possible allowing reasonable time to give notice of the Day and place of Sale; and that payment may be made for the said Property in money or such Warrants or other government Securities of this State as were receivable in the revenue taxes of 1784.

Absent Mr. Heth.

Mr. John Heth having for some time past done the duties and received the pay of a Lieutenant on board the public boats, and no Commission has yet been made out to him, It is advised, that a Commission now issue to the said Heth giving him rank as Lieutenant from the 2d Day of July last.

Present Mr. Heth.

It is advised, that a register issue for the Sloop Polly, satisfactory proof having been made in due form of law.

On recommendation, It is advised that a Commission issue appointing Henry Vaughan additional Inspector at Robert Bollings warehouse in Dinwiddie.

On consideration of Col. Meriwethers report concerning the Point of Fork, It is advised that the Public Negroes belonging to that Post be sold at Albemarle Court in March next, for ready cash or tobacco; or on three months credit, if Capt. Langham shall think such credit will be for the benefit of the State; That all old Anvills and other useless articles at the said Post be sold, for Cash, on the spot, and report made of such sales to the Executive: and That the further consideration of Col. Meriwethers report be postponed.

It is advised that the Auditor be directed to issue a warrant on the Contingent fund for two pounds ten shillings, to Col. Meriwether, for the expences of his visit to the Point of Fork (to be paid).

It is advised that the Auditor be directed to issue a Warrant on the Aggregate fund in lieu of one issued the 7th of July 1783, to John Thornburn for thirty eight pounds two shillings and six pence for

29. *Venditioni exponas* is the name of a writ of execution requiring a sheriff to sell the goods of a defendant to render satisfaction on a judgment, when he has already levied against those goods and returned that they remained unsold for want of buyers.

making soldiers cloths in 1780 as per Certificate from Wm. Armistead, former State Agent.

The board resumed the consideration of Col. Meriwethers report concerning the Militia, Whereupon it is advised, that Commissions issue appointing Miles Selden Colonel and John Mayo Lieutenant Colonel of the second Regiment of Henrico Militia.

It is advised that William Lindsay be appointed Naval Officer for the District of Elizabeth river in the room of Josiah Parker who hath resigned.

All which matters so advised the Governor orders accordingly.

> James Wood
> Jos. Jones
> Carter Braxton
> Robt. Goode

Saturday February 28th 1789

Present

The Governor

Mr. Wood	Mr. Jones
Mr. McClurg	Mr. Braxton

Mr. Goode

The Governor informed the board that in the recess, Mr. Lindsay gave bond and qualified to his commission as Naval Officer according to law: and That he issued commissions appointing Benja. Bramham inspector and Daniel Lawson additional inspector at Totuskey warehouses in Richmond county; agreeably to recommendation. Approved.

It is advised, in pursuance of the 96th section of the act of assembly, "Establishing District Courts and for regulating the General Court" that the following persons be appointed Public Jailors viz: William Rose, for the District including Henrico County; Christopher Harwood, for the District including Essex County; Thomas Roads, for the District including Augusta County; George Bruce, for the District including Albemarle County; Colin Campbell, for the District including Fairfax County; Charles Moss for the District including Norfolk County; and Robert Armistead, for the District including Prince George County. The farther appointments Postponed for want of information as to persons fit for the office.

It is advised that payment of a Warrant, to John Carter, for five pounds, upon account, to purchase stationary for the Auditors office, be directed out of the Contingent fund.

The board resumed the consideration of Col. Meriwethers report concerning the Point of Fork, and thereupon Advise, That Col.

Meriwether report to this board as soon as may be, an Estimate of the Expences of erecting a strong picketing around the Ars[e]nol and Magazine.

The Governor laid before the board a Claim of William Armistead for the hire of three Negroes to Philip Moody as superintendant of the Public Artificers; Whereupon it is advised, that the Auditor be directed to settle the said Claim, disallowing interest, and to grant a Warrant on the Aggregate fund for the sum due.

It is advised that a commission issue appointing Richard Randolph Major of the 2d regiment of Henrico Militia, the court having failed to recommend.

It appearing that Holt Richeson hath been prevented, by sickness, from giving bond for the collection of the taxes due in the County of King William for the year 1787, as required by the Act in that case made; It is advised that the said Holt Richeson be appointed a Collector of the taxes due in the said County for the year 1787, pursuant to an act "for granting relief to Sheriffs and Collectors of the public revenue in certain cases," and that he be required to give bond, to be approved as to the sum and sufficiency of the Securities by the next Court to be held for the said County.

All which matters so advised the governor orders accordingly.

> James Wood
> James McClurg
> Jos. Jones
> Carter Braxton
> Robt. Goode

Tuesday March 3d 1789

Present

The Governor

Mr. Wood   Mr. Braxton
Mr. McClurg   Mr. Jones
                    Mr. Goode

Edmund Pendleton and John Blair esquires having resigned their offices as Judges of the High Court of Chancery, It is advised that George Wythe esqr. the Chancillor be notified thereof.

It is advised that John Foulkes be appointed Public Jailor for the District including the County of Prince Edward.

The Governor laid before the board an application for putting on the aggregate fund a Warrant issued to William Whitehead the 20th November 1788, for twenty six pounds five shillings for his pay as a private in the Illinois regiment from 1st January 82 to 1st of August following and as a corporal from 1st of August to the 29th December

1782. Whereupon it is advised that the said application be rejected.

The Governor laid before the board a letter from Col. Davies inclosing an abstract of such laws as will serve as a guide to the persons appointed to collect vouchers and proofs of advances for the service of the United States. Whereupon it is advised that the said abstract be returned to Colonel Davies with a List of the Districts and persons appointed to collect in each the necessary Vouchers and proofs aforesaid; and that he be instructed to prepare and send out to the said persons, as soon as possible, the proper instructions.

Satisfactory proof having been produced that the pay of Lieutenant Willis Wilson in the service of the United States ceased on the 1st Day of January 1783, and that he has returned to the office of the Continental Commissioner of Loans to be cancilled his Certificate for commutation of half pay; It is advised that the auditor be directed to issue Warrants for the arrearages of pension due him from the said 1st Day of January 1783 to the 1st Day of January 1788; and that he be continued on the List of pensioners with an allowance of forty pounds per annum.

The Governor laid before the board a letter from the attorney general on the subject of Mr. Latils memorial to him referred, giving it as his opinion, "that the Solicitor under the last revenue law, is bound to receive, indiscriminately, in discharge of Duties, the Warrants which have been heretofore granted to foreign creditors by order of the Executive, in the years 1786, 1787, 1788." Whereupon it is advised that the Solicitor and Mr. Latil be furnished with copies of the said opinion.

Upon reconsideration of the Solicitors letter of the 23d of February last containing a State of the Situation of a balance due from George Stubblefield late Sheriff of Spotsylvania for the revenue taxes of 1784, whereby it appears that the property of the said Stubblefield in the hands of the present Sheriff of Spotsylvania is of a perishable nature and may be easily removed in case it shall be released, And the Attorney General having declared his opinion upon this case referred to him in the following words viz:

"I consider the Act "for granting relief to Sheriffs, and Collectors of the public Revenue in certain Cases," as a remedial law, and therefore ought to be so liberally construed, as to extend the remedy as far as possible. The objects to be benefitted by the Indulgence held forth in this law, are *Sheriffs collectors* and *their Securities, indebted to the Commonwealth, for taxes prior to November 1788;* levying an Execution, taking Effects, and returning that they are unsold, does not operate a discharge of the debt, until the Execution is returned satisfied; the Sheriff or Collector, against whom it is issued, is still considered as *indebted* to the public, and as such, comes within the express words of the above recited act. I am therefore of opinion, that the Sheriff of Spotsylvania is within the meaning of the law alluded to. If however the Executive, fearing the loss of the Debt, shall think proper, notwithstanding this law, to make *special direction for issuing an Execution,* before the first day of June, I think, a continuance under the first process, would be the proper mode, because the interference of the Executive suspends the Effect of the Law, which if left to operate would render the issuing of a new Fi Fa[30] after the first of June next, necessary."

The Board feel themselves bound to declare that the postponement of execution until the 1st Day of June next may put the Debt in danger. It is therefore advised that the Solicitor be directed immediately to take the Steps pointed out by the Attorney General as stated above for effectually securing to the Commonwealth the said debt. And it is farther advised that the Solicitor do, as soon as may be, report to the Governor all cases of Sheriffs or Collectors, or their securities upon whose property any execution has been levied.

All which matters so advised the Governor orders accordingly.

> James Wood
> Jos. Jones
> Carter Braxton
> Robt. Goode

Wednesday March 4th 1789

Present

The Governor

Mr. Wood	Mr. Jones
Mr. McClurg	Mr. Braxton
	Mr. Goode

The Governor laid before the board a Claim of the present Sheriff of Prince Edward amounting to fifty two pounds eleven shillings and ten pence for Commissions on Execution vs Thomas Flournoy late Sheriff of the said County and for expences of keeping Negroes. Whereupon it is advised that the said Claim be rejected; as a matter not coming properly before this board.

The Governor laid before the board a letter from Mr. Harry Heth desiring the Instructions of the executive as to the mode in which he shall settle the account of William Gilbert with the public Foundery. Whereupon it is advised that Mr. Heth be directed to settle the account of the said Gilbert agreeably to the Statement of the same upon the public books, and that in all cases of paper money he make the Scale of depreciation established by law his guide. If Mr. Gilbert should be dissatisfied with the account as it is stated on the Public books, Mr. Heth will receive any Vouchers which he may produce in support of his claim and report them specially to the board for their determination.

---

30. "Fi Fa" is short for *fieri facias,* which is a writ authorizing a sheriff to obtain satisfaction of a judgment in debt or damages from the goods and chattels of a defendant.

It is advised that Abram Davis[31] be continued on the pension List with his former allowance, twelve pounds per annum, from the first of January last.

All which matters so advised the Governor orders accordingly.

James Wood
Jos. Jones
Carter Braxton
Robt. Goode

Thursday March 5th 1789

Present

The Governor

Mr. Wood   Mr. Jones
Mr. McClurg   Mr. Braxton
Mr. Goode

On consideration of a petition from Thomas Hugard late Sheriff of Augusta, and the Solicitors statement of his case, It is advised that the one per cent damages and the interest from the first of May to the 21st of October 1786, on the amount of the Judgment obtained against the said Hugard for the revenue taxes of 1785, be remitted.

Col. Davies having represented that the counties are in some instances inconveniently arranged in the different Districts allotted to the persons appointed to collect Vouchers in support of the accounts of this State against the United States, It is advised that Col. Davies be authorized to make any changes in the said arrangement which he may think proper; and to assure the persons appointed to collect the said Vouchers that full compensation shall be made them in proportion to their trouble and expence.

On consideration of the petition of George Bridges praying for the remission of a fine of 400 lbs. of tobacco imposed on him by the Court of Henrico for nonattendance as a juryman; it is advised that the same be rejected.

The Governor laid before the board a letter from Col. Davies inclosing a protest of the Agents of this State for settling the accounts thereof against the United States, whereby it appears that it will be necessary in order to secure the interests of the Commonwealth that some person should be immediately sent on to Congress to represent the particular situation of the said accounts. Whereupon it is advised that Col. William Davies the Commissioner on the part of this State be authorized to proceed immediately to the Seat of the foederal Government and to take such steps as shall appear to him proper to effect

---

31. The name appears to be "Abin Davis" in the clerk's index.

this purpose; that, while he is employed in the execution of this business it be recommended to him to confer with the senators and representatives of this State in Congress, in all cases of difficulty which shall occur, and that he communicate from time to time to the Executive the progress he shall make; It is further advised that Col. Davies be allowed so much in addition to his present salary as will amount to four dollars by the day for his travelling to, staying at and returning from the seat of the foederal government. And that fifty pounds be granted him, out of the Contingent fund, upon account.

The Governor laid before the board a letter from Mr. Harry Heth inclosing the account of William Gilbert as it stands Stated upon the books of the public foundery and an account of sundry charges exhibited by the said Gilbert which do not appear upon the said books. Whereupon it is advised that Mr. Heth be directed to disallow the whole of the charges as exhibited by Mr. Gilbert, they not appearing to be supported by satisfactory vouchers; that he extend the item of the account for six months wages which at present stands blank at the rate of seven pounds ten shillings per month. But that before Mr. Heth finally close this Account, he inquire at the Auditors and treasury office, whether any Warrant issued or money was paid upon the Warrant from the war office charged to Mr. Gilbert.

It is advised, that Thomas Edgar be appointed Public Jailor for the District of Greenbriar and Botetourt, at Lewisburg; James Roberts for the same District, at Botetourt courthouse; Christopher Acklin, for the District of Montgomery, Washington and Russell, at Washington courthouse; James McGavock for the same District, at Montgomery courthouse; and [. . .]32 Roberts for the District including Northumberland courthouse.

It is advised that a register issue for the Schooner Betsey, satisfactory proof having been made in due form of law.

All which matters so advised, the Governor orders accordingly.

> James Wood
> Jos. Jones
> Carter Braxton
> Robt. Goode

Tuesday March 10th 1789

Present

The Governor

Mr. Wood	Mr. Jones
Mr. McClurg	Mr. Braxton
	Mr. Goode

32. Blank in the journal.

The Governor informed the board that on the 7th instant, he continued on the List of pensioners Joseph Watkins with twelve pounds per annum. approved.

On recommendations It is advised that a Commission issue for adding William Randolph, John Dunbar and John Gregory gentlemen to the Commission of the peace for Charles City, and that a Commission issue appointing Dudley Digges Gentleman Sheriff of James City County in the room of Samuel Griffin who hath been chosen a representative in Congress.

The Governor laid before the board an application for certain Warrants drawn in favor or Richard Winston, for sundries furnished in the Illinois Department, to be placed on the aggregate fund. Whereupon it is advised that the said application be rejected.

The Governor laid before the board an account of James M. McRea amounting to twenty three pounds one shilling for expences of the boat allowed him as Searcher at Alexandria, also an account of John Conner amounting to two pounds two shillings and seven pence as a balance due him from this State for the rent of his house occupied by the Commissioners for settling the Accounts between this State and the United States. Whereupon it is advised, That the said Accounts be referred to the Auditor for settlement and Warrants on the Contingent Fund for what shall appear to be due thereon (to be paid).

The Governor laid before the board a letter from Col. Davies inclosing some tobacco notes which were found among the public papers in his office, and which appear to have been received by Pierce or by James Warren, from York County, under the order of Governor Jefferson. Whereupon it is advised that the Clerk deliver the said notes to Mr. Harry Heth, in order that he may collect from the Inspectors the money for the said notes.

The board having received information that the Clerks office of the County of Westmoreland has been robbed of many material records and papers; It is advised that a Commission issue appointing Robert Carter, Richard Parker, John Turberville, Daniel McCarty, John Rose, Richard Buckner, Beckwith Butler, Corbin Washington, and Philip Lee gentlemen, or any five of them, Commissioners for the County of Westmoreland, to take Depositions respecting the destruction of the records and papers of the said County, pursuant to the act of assembly "for the relief of persons who have been or may be injured by the destruction of the records of County Courts."

The Governor laid before the board two recommendations of fit persons to be added to the commission of the peace for the County of Westmoreland, one dated June 1785, and the other March 1788. Whereupon it is advised that an additional Commission issue appointing George Turberville, William Stock Jett, Edward Sanford, Henry Washington, Christopher Collins and George Garner gentlemen Justices of the peace for the said County, pursuant to the first recommendation; and that the second be rejected, there appearing to be a sufficient number of Justices already commissioned for the said County.

On consideration of a letter from Martin Oster esquire of the 2d instant requesting that the Suspension of the Order to the Sheriff of Dinwiddie to aid in the execution of a Consular decree against John Cauvy may be taken off, It is advised that, as the said Cauvy has become a citizen of this Commonwealth, as appears by the Certificate of the Clerk of Henrico Court, he is no longer subject to the Consular power and cannot be arrested but under the Laws of this State.

On consideration of a Petition of Thomas Underwood praying that a number of Warrants in his possession, drawn on the Treasurer for supplies furnished in the Illinois Country, may be placed on the aggregate fund; It is advised that the same be rejected.

On consideration of a letter from Harry Heth, concerning the account of William Gilbert against the Westham Foundery, It is advised, that the said Gilbert be allowed credit for the hire of two negroes, on his producing a certificate from one of the managers of the Foundery, Specifying that they were hired on public account, and for what price and time; and that no credit be allowed him for the bed without further proof.

It is advised, that Cosby Foster, Joseph Sandidge and Thomas Davis be continued on the List of pensioners with their former allowances.

It is advised that Roger Mallory be appointed a Public Jailor for the District including Brunswick County.

The Governor informed the board that probably similar cases to that of the late Sheriff of Spotsylvania might occur in the recess of the Council, and he therefore now wished to take their opinion as to the mode to be pursued thereon. Whereupon it is advised that in all Cases where it shall appear by report of the Solicitor that property which had been taken in execution by any Sheriff or Coroner remains unsold for want of buyers, the same measures be taken as were directed in the Case of George Stubblefield late Sheriff of Spotsylvania.

All which matters so advised the Governor orders accordingly.

James Wood
James McClurg
Jos. Jones
Carter Braxton
Robt. Goode

Friday March 20th 1789

Present

The Governor

Mr. Wood   Mr. Jones
Mr. McClurg   Mr. Braxton
                    Mr. Goode

The Governor informed the Board that in the recess he granted a pardon to Negro Isaac who was condemned by the Town Court of Petersburg for burglary, and recommended as an object of mercy. That not being able to find out proper persons to be public Jailors on the Eastern shore and at new London, he put into the hands of the Judges going to those Districts, blank commissions to be filled up by them. That he directed to be paid out of the contingent fund to Matthew Anderson sixty one pounds ten shillings for expences incurred in overhauling damaged tobacco at Deaconsneck warehouse; to Samuel Eddins thirty six pounds thirteen shillings and four pence for the hire, clothing, feeding, and taxes of the negroes belonging to the boat allowed him as Searcher at York. That he directed a Warrant on the Aggregate fund in lieu of a warrant for forty pounds ten shillings issued the 11th of June 1783 "to Captain Benjamin Biggs, on account, agreeably to resolution of Assembly in lieu of a paper money warrant issued Feby. 12, 1781 taken in and reaudited according to law;" and Warrants on the Contingent fund to Doctor Turpin for one hundred pounds for the last years rent of the Council Chamber, and to the Rev. Benjamin Blagrave for fifteen pounds for a Quarters salary due him the 14th instant as Ordinary to the public Jail.

That on recommendations from the respective county courts he issued commissions appointing Thomas Lee senr. a Justice of the peace for the County of Prince William; Robert Poage Coroner and William Patton Escheator for the County of Pendleton; Mills Wills Inspector and Lemuel Lightfoot additional inspector at Smithfield and Fulghams warehouse in Isle of Wight; Mills Godwin inspector and Henry Godwin additional inspector at Milners warehouse in Nansemond. That on the usual proofs being made, he granted registers for the Schooner Shelela, Sloop Yankey, and Brig Daniel. That on the Solicitors report of the case of William Nall late Sheriff of Rockingham, relative to the revenue taxes for the year 1784, he considered the Debt as in danger, and therefore, in pursuance of the advice of the 10th instant, directed similar steps to be taken by the Solicitor, as were ordered in the case of George Stubblefield late Sheriff of Spotsylvania, and the property to be removed to Shenandoah Courthouse for sale. That he issued a commission appointing Peterson Goodwin a Colonel of the Militia of Dinwiddie County, he having produced a certificate from the Court of the said County, declaring as their unanimous opinion that he is innocent of the peculation with which he was charged by Doctor Greenway; and that he gave the following directions to the Solicitor, to wit, "Mr. Henry Anderson having produced to me a certificate from the Clerk of the County Court of Amelia declaring that the said Anderson did at a Court held for the said County in the month of February last enter into bond for three thousand five hundred pounds with sufficient Security for the payment of one moiety of the taxes for the year 1785 with which Millington Roach late a Deputy Sheriff to Christopher Hudson was chargeable. The Solicitor will therefore agreeably to a resolution of the General Assembly of the 17th of December 1788 consider the Executors and Estate of Christopher Hudson as exonerated from any Claim of the public for the said moiety of the said taxes; and will procure from the records of the Said County of Amelia an authenticated Copy of the Bond given by the said Anderson as aforesaid in order that he may be prepared if it shall be necessary to institute the proper proceedings thereon." Approved.

On recommendation, It is advised that a Commission issue appointing Luke Cannon an additional inspector at Quantico Warehouses, in Prince William County.

It is advised that William Andrews be continued on the List of pensioners with his former allowance, eighteen pounds per annum.

A Doubt being suggested whether the Naval Officers of this State have authority to enforce the payment of Duties after the new foederal Government goes into operation, It is advised that the Governor immediately direct the Naval Officers at the different Ports to insist on the payment of all Duties as heretofore until they shall receive Instructions from the Executive to the contrary.

On consideration of a letter from Col. Davies, It is advised that Captain Archibald Denham be appointed to Collect Vouchers etc. in Gloster District, in the room of Captains Buckner and Butler; and that ten pounds be advanced to Mr. Denham, upon account.

It is advised, that a Warrant issue on the contingent fund for six pounds, to Philip Southall for his trouble in copying the report of the Commissioners appointed to adjust the Claims for two expeditions against the Wabash and Shawanese indians (to be paid).

The Governor laid before the board a protested bill of exchange, drawn by Oliver Pollock, on Penet Dacoston freres and Company the 17th of June 1780. Whereupon it is advised that the Auditor be directed to compare the said bill with the report of the Commissioners appointed to examine the Claim of the said Pollock, and to report whether it be one of these bills, the amount of which is directed to be retained by a resolution of the General Assembly of the 7th of January 1786.

It appearing that Susannah Rowland[33] comes within the requisi-

---

33. "Susanna Rowland" in the clerk's index.

tions of the pension law; It is advised that She be put on the List of pensioners with an allowance of eight pounds per annum from the 1st of January 1786. It is also advised that Mary Rowland and Susannah Rawlings be continued on the List of pensioners, the former with ten pounds and the latter with twelve pounds per annum from January 1789.

All which matters so advised the Governor orders accordingly.

James Wood
James McClurg
Jos. Jones
Robt. Goode

Monday March 23d 1789

Present

The Governor

Mr. Wood	Mr. Jones
Mr. McClurg	Mr. Braxton

Mr. Heth

The Governor informed the board that on the 21st instant He issued an additional commission appointing Addison Lewis, Thomas Lewis, Peter Beverley Whiting, Armistead Smith, Robert Cary and Mordecai Cooke gentlemen Justices of the peace for the County of Gloucester, they having been recommended according to law; and that, on the usual proofs, he granted a register for the Brigantine Virginia Packet. (Approved.)

It is advised that the Treasurer be directed to borrow from any fund, pursuant to the 5th section of the Act "to amend the several laws for appropriating the public revenue" the sum of One thousand pounds to be applied to the payment of the Debts due to the Scouts and Rangers on the Western frontier, in the same manner as was directed by the Executive on the 2d of January last.

The Governor laid before the board an application for placing on the aggregate fund, a Warrant issued the 18th of July 1782 to David White for thirty six pounds 4/1. for cleaning and repairing arms as per agreement with the board of war. Whereupon it is advised that the said application be rejected.

The Governor laid before the board a Claim of William Armistead for the hire of three negroes viz, Jim, Jess and Sam. Whereupon it is advised that the Auditor be directed to settle the said Claim agreeably to Contract with Philip Moody, late Superintendant of Artificers; and to grant a Warrant on the Aggregate fund for the Sum due.

It is advised that the Accounts of Jacob Richards, Peter Cornelison, Thomas Herbert, and James Tanner, for their Services as Scouts in the county of Harrison, be referred to the Auditor for settlement in the usual way.

It appearing that there was a mistake made in the Commission issued for the County of Notaway in point of Seniority, and the same being returned; It is advised that a new Commission issue appointing Stephen Cocke, Peter Lamkin, Samuel Sherwin, William Cryer, Raleigh Carter, William Cross Cradock, Peter Randolph, William Greenhill, Freeman Eppes, Abner Osborne, and William Yates gentlemen Justices of the peace for the said County.

All which matters so advised, the Governor orders accordingly.

James Wood
James McClurg
Jos. Jones

Saturday March 28th 1789

Present

The Governor

Mr. Wood	Mr. Jones
Mr. McClurg	Mr. Heth
Mr. Goode	

The Governor informed the board that in the recess he directed to be paid out of the Contingent fund, to Jane West three pounds for nursing Catherine Cruls[34] child agreeably to contract; and that on recommendation, he issued an additional Commission appointing John Bracken (Clerk), Robert H. Water and Robert Greenhow, gentlemen, Justices of the peace for the County of James City. Approved.

It is advised that registers issue for the Ship Ulysses and the Sloop, Sally and Nancy; Satisfactory proofs having been made in due form of law.

On recommendation, It is advised that an additional Commission issue appointing James Callaway, John Callaway, William Meridith, Mathew Pate, William Harris and Michael Graham, gentlemen, Justices of the peace for the County of Bedford, the said James Callaway to be of the quorum.

The Governor laid before the board a letter from Col. Davies inclosing one from Mr. Dunscombe[35] stating some difficulties which he apprehended might occur in conducting the office for Settling continental accounts during Col. Davies's stay at New York, expressing a wish that it might be declared by some act of the Executive that the late change in that office did not arise from any malconduct on the part of

34. "C. Cralle" in the clerk's index.
35. "Dunscomb" in the clerk's index.

Mr. Dunscombe and desiring an increase of Salary. Whereupon it is advised that Col. Davies be informed that the Executive did not intend, when they assented to his going to New York, to take upon themselves responsibility for any part of the business of his office but that they expect he will give such full instructions for the prosecution of the business to his Assistant that no injury whatever may be sustained by the public in consequence of his absence. That they do not think it either necessary or proper to give any opinion on the propriety of Mr. Dunscombs conduct whilst the office was under his direction and that no good reason appears for making any addition to his Salary.

On consideration of a petition of William Lantrop praying for the remission of a fine of ten pounds imposed on him by the Court of Prince George for retailing liquors without license; It is advised that the same be rejected.

The Governor laid before the board sundry accounts of the Scouts for Madison County. Whereupon it is advised that the said Accounts be referred to the Auditor for settlement in the usual way.

On consideration of a letter from Col. Walter Crocket of Montgomery County, It is advised that two Scouts be allowed for the said county, with the usual pay.

All which matters so advised the Governor orders accordingly.

James Wood
James McClurg
Jos. Jones
Will Heth
Robt. Goode

Wednesday, April 1st 1789

Present

The Governor

Mr. Wood   Mr. Jones
Mr. McClurg   Mr. Heth
               Mr. Goode

The Governor laid before the board a letter from the Treasurer inclosing one from Mr. Matthew Anderson concerning the public tobacco at Deacons neck warehouses. Whereupon it is advised, That Mr. Heth, the Agent, be instructed to apply for the Notes and dispose of the said tobacco on the best terms he can, keeping a distinct account of the Sales.

On consideration of a letter from the Attorney General, and in pursuance of the District law, It is advised that Col. Meriwether be requested to contract for the conveying of Hugh Dowdall and Susanna Dowdall to the District of Dumfries; and Susanna Murphy to the

District of New London: And that the Governor give orders to the Keeper of the public Jail for the delivery of the said prisoners.

It is advised that the Treasurer be desired to borrow, pursuant to the 5th section of the act "to amend the Laws for appropriating the public revenue" the Sum of six hundred sixty six pounds thirteen shillings and four pence to answer a Draft in favor of William Hortshorne, Treasurer for the Potowmack Company, on Account of the Shares of this State in the said company.

The Governor laid before the board an application from Daniel Broadhead for putting on the aggregate fund, three warrants issued in favor of John Johnston, Christopher Kind and Frederick Rath for bounty money. Whereupon it is advised, that the same be rejected.

The Governor laid before the board an Account of the Solicitor for extra services performed in the last year. Whereupon it is advised that a Warrant issue on the Contingent fund for fifteen pounds as compensation to the Solicitor for his extra services. (To be paid)

The Governor laid before the board a letter from Mr. Edmund Randolph mentioning that out of the money, allotted for his expenditure on Mr. Dunscombs accounts, he retained ten guineas for the use of Mr. Charles Hay, who had been engaged by him in a particular service, with the approbation of the board, which money was still in his hands, as Mr. Hay had never informed him of what he had done in the business; and requesting instructions on the subject. Whereupon it is advised, that Mr. Randolph be desired to return the money to the Treasurer, Mr. Chas. Hay having informed the Governor that he had taken no step in the business as he found it would be impracticable for him to compleat it.

It appearing that there is no money now in the Treasury belonging to the funds appropriated to the payment of the Salaries of the Judges and other officers of Civil Government, It is advised that the Treasurer be directed to borrow from any other funds such a sum of money as will be sufficient to discharge the warrants issued for the last quarters salary to the said Judges and other officers of civil Government.

The Governor laid before the board a state of the Cash in the Treasury on the 31st Day of March. Whereupon it is advised that the Treasurer be informed that the Executive are of Opinion that there is a sufficient sum of money in hand to allow of two thousand pounds being applied as it is appropriated by law, but that he do not pay to a greater amount than the said two thousand pounds on account of any appropriation without first consulting the Executive.

All which matters so advised the Governor orders accordingly.

James Wood
James McClurg
Jos. Jones
Will Heth
Robt. Goode

Saturday April 4th 1789

Present

The Governor

Mr. Wood   Mr. Braxton
Mr. McClurg   Mr. Heth
Mr. Jones   Mr. Goode

The Governor informed the board that in the recess he directed to be paid out of the contingent fund, To Col. Wm. Davies seventy five pounds for his last quarters salary as Commissioner for settling the accounts of this State with the United States; To Robert Sayers six pounds for his trouble and expences in conveying Susanna Murphy to the District of New London, agreeably to contract: and That he directed two of the Clerks in Col. Davies's office to be dismissed; Col. Davies having certified that their services might be dispensed with for the present. Approved.

It is advised that Ann Shepherd be continued on the pension List with five pounds per annum from the first of January last.

On recommendation; It is advised that a Commission issue appointing Creed Taylor Coroner for the County of Cumberland.

The Governor laid before the board an account of Henderson, Fugusson and Gibson amounting to one pound six shillings for the freight of twenty boxes of arms down quantico Creek. Whereupon it is advised that the said account be referred to the Auditor for a warrant on the Contingent fund for the amount thereof. to be paid.

It is advised that Warrants issue on the contingent fund, To Col. Davies for ten pounds upon account, for the contingent expences of his office; To George Rice for fifteen pounds for his trouble and expences in furnishing Vouchers in support of the Claims of this State against the united States; To Joseph Leiplong for six pounds upon Account, for conveying prisoners to Dumfries agreeably to Contract: and To William Pierce for thirty pounds for his last years Salary as Keeper of the public buildings. (To be paid)

The Governor laid before the board the Accounts of John Darby, Robert and Emanuel Johnson for pay due them as artificers while in service as six months men. Whereupon it is advised that the said accounts be rejected.

The Governor laid before the board the Claim of Mr. John H. Norton making a balance in his favor of seven thousand eight hundred and ninety four pounds of tobacco as stated by the Auditor. Whereupon, It is advised that the Auditor be directed to settle the said tobacco at the rate of nineteen shillings per hundred, and grant a warrant on the Aggregate fund for the Sum due, allowing interest on 6889 lbs. of said tobacco from the 30th of September last.

The Governor laid before the board a protested bill of exchange drawn by Oliver Pollock, the 17th of June 1780, on Messrs. Penett Dacosta freres and Company, for twelve thousand two hundred dollars, which appears to be one of the bills for which a part of Mr. Pollocks claim was retained by order of the Executive, the 14th of January 1786, in pursuance of a resolution of the General Assembly of the 7th of January 1786. Whereupon it is advised that the Auditor be directed to issue a Warrant on the foreign fund, for the above sum of twelve thousand two hundred Dollars with eighteen per cent damages, and six percent interest from the 1st day of August 1782.

All which matters so advised, the Governor orders accordingly.

> James Wood
> James McClurg
> Jos. Jones
> Carter Braxton
> Will Heth
> Robt. Goode

Monday April 6th 1789

Present

The Governor

Mr. Wood	Mr. Braxton
Mr. McClurg	Mr. Heth
Mr. Jones	Mr. Goode

The Governor laid before the board an account of McCall and Cunli[ef][36] amounting to two pounds ten shillings for coal furnished for this office. Whereupon it is advised that a warrant issue on the contingent fund for that Sum. (To be paid)

It is advised that a register issue for the Brigantine Julia; satisfactory proof having been made in due form of law.

On consideration of Col. Meriwethers reports concerning the point of Fork; It is advised that Warrants issue to Captain Langham for seventy two pounds twelve shillings being the last quarters pay of the Guard; and one hundred and twenty one pounds six and two pence being the balance due the Superintendant and Artificers for the last quarter, (the money to be borrowed pursuant to law); That the Superintendant be instructed to engage the artificers for another year on the best terms he can: to pay for the necessary clothing of the guard out of the money arising from the sale of the public negroes: and to contract for inclosing the ars[e]nal and magazines at the Point of Fork with a Wall ten feet high to be built of plank and Locust posts properly fixed in the ground with braces.

---

36. "McColl and Cunlief" in the clerk's index.

It is advised that William Criddle be continued on the List of pensioners with fifteen pounds per annum from the first of January last: and that a new certificate be granted the said Criddle for his last years pension; it appear[ing] that the former certificate is lost.

The board took under consideration the cases of the malefactors having conditional pardons, Whereupon it is advised that pardons issue to Thomas Poe and Thomas Cole, the only two now at Work on the canal; and that the Attorney General be instructed to prosecute John Fowler, now in the public Jail, for having violated the conditions of his pardon. The Governor laid before the board a letter he had prepared in answer to one of the 22d of March from Mr. Oster vice consul of France, concerning the case of John Cauvy; which letter, being read, is approved and Ordered to be registered.

All which matters so advised, the Governor orders accordingly.

The Governor notified to the board his intention to be absent, which is ordered to be inserted on the Journal.

> James Wood
> James McClurg
> Jos. Jones
> Carter Braxton
> Robt. Goode

Monday April 13th 1789

Present

The Governor

Mr. Wood	Mr. Jones
Mr. McClurg	Mr. Braxton
	Mr. Goode

Mr. Wood informed the Board that in the recess and absence of the Governor, He, as Lieutenant Governor, issued an additional commission appointing Andrew Kincade, James Brown, Charles Smith junr., Thomas Fletcher, James Smith, George Mountjoy, and William Griffith gentlemen Justices of the peace for the County of Bourbon: Also an additional Commission appointing Jacob Kiser, Layton Yancy, Ezekiel Harrison, Mathias Lair, Archibald Hopkins Junr., John Ervin Senr., Reubin Harrison junr. and John Rice gentlemen Justices of the peace for the county of Rockingham agreeably to recommendations from the respective county courts. Approved.

It is advised that a warrant issue on the contingent fund for four pounds to Joseph Liplong[37] for the balance due him for his trouble and expences in conveying prisoners to Dumfries. (To be paid)

---

37. "Lieplong" in the clerk's index.

Pursuant to a resolution of the General Assembly of the 10th of November 1787. It is advised that James Cotman[38] be put on the pension List with an allowance of ten pounds per annum from the first of January 1788.

It is advised that Col. Meriwether be instructed to dispose of the public negroes, in possession of the Public Jailor, on the best terms he can for cash or tobacco, allowing three months credit.

The Governor informed the board that in consequence of the order for selling all the Negroes at the Point of Fork David the Waggoner was sold and bought by Captain Langham who is willing to restore him to the public, as a Waggoner is absolutely necessary at the post. Whereupon it is advised that the said David be retained as public property, and Major Langham exonerated from the purchase.

It is advised that a pardon issue for Negro Tom, the property of William Dunet, condemned to death by the Court of Caroline for larcency; he having been recommended as a proper object of mercy.

The Governor laid before the board an Account of Hunter Banks and Company with William Armistead as Agent for this State. Whereupon it is advised that the said Account be referred to the Solicitor for examination and report.

Application having been made for the following Warrants to be placed on the Aggregate fund to wit. A Warrant issued the 6th of November 1787 to David Piles for fourteen pounds one shilling and three pence as a Spy from the County of Monongalia; Also a warrant issued the tenth of January 1786, to Samuel Waples for nine pounds twelve Shillings for six months donation as Lieutenant in the Continental Line agreeable to Act of Assembly; It is advised that the same be rejected.

The Governor laid before the board an account of George Pickett[39] amounting to eleven hundred and seventy seven pounds of tobacco for broad axes furnished Philip Moody as Superintendant of artificers, as appears by the said Moodys certificate. Whereupon it is advised that the Auditor be directed to settle the said Account, rating the tobacco at fifteen shillings per hundred, and grant a warrant on the aggregate fund for the Sum due.

It is advised that a commission issue appointing Thomas Smith Sheriff of Isle of Wight.

All which matters so advised, the Governor orders accordingly.

James Wood
James McClurg
Jos. Jones
Carter Braxton
Robt. Goode

38. "Cotton" in the clerk's index.
39. "George Picket" in the clerk's index.

Saturday April 18th 1789

Present

The Governor

Mr. Wood   Mr. Jones
Mr. McClurg   Mr. Braxton
                  Mr. Goode

The Governor informed the board that in the recess, he directed John Poage as Surveyor of Augusta, and John Stovall as Surveyor of Henry County, to give bond in their respective County Courts in the penalty of two thousand pounds each, that he issued a register, on the usual proofs, for the Schooner Active, and that he directed to be paid out of the contingent fund, to Richard Adams seven pounds ten shillings, for a quarters rent of the Chancery office up to the 25th Ultimo. Approved.

The Governor laid before the board an account of John Roper amounting to nineteen pounds sixteen shillings and three pence for railing in the Jail; Whereupon it is advised that the same be referred to the Auditor for a Warrant on the contingent fund.

It is advised that a register issue for the Schooner Paragon satisfactory proofs having been made according to law. The Governor laid before the board sundry accounts for Jail expences etc., amounting to twenty two pounds six shillings and six pence as Certified by the court of Chancery and district Court of Richmond. Whereupon it is advised that the said accounts be referred to the auditor for warrants on the Contingent Fund. (To be paid)

It is advised that the Treasurer be directed to borrow, pursuant to the 4th section of the act to amend the appropriation laws two hundred pounds to satisfy a Warrant to that amount issued the 22d of December last in favor of Joseph Hornsby for the use of the Lunatic Hospital.

The Governor laid before the board a warrant to Wm. Coulter for two pounds two shillings for guarding Criminal the last term to and from court. Whereupon it is advised that the same be paid out of the contingent fund.

On recommendation, It is advised that an additional Commission issue appointing Abraham Claypool and John Elliott, gentlemen, Justices of the peace for the County of Randolph.

On consideration of the state of the sinking fund, It is advised That the Auditor be directed to issue a warrant in favour of the agent of the said fund for such sum of money or quantity of Tobacco as the Treasurer shall certify to him he has set apart for the use of the said Fund agreeably to the 2d section of the act to amend the several Laws for appropriating the public revenue.

The Governor laid before the board a letter from Samuel Hanway,

F. Warman and James Dougherty, charging Jesse Martin, Archibald Minzies, Charles Martin, David Scott and others with assaulting and seizing on the body of Thomas Laidley, a Justice of the peace for the County of Monongalia during the Session of the Court of the said County, and whilst the said Laidley was in the discharge of his duty as a Magistrate. Whereupon it is advised That the said Letter together with the affidavits in support of the facts charged as above be referred to the Attorney General, and that he be desired immediately to institute the proper prosecutions against the perpetrators of so flagrant a violation of the peace and dignity of the commonwealth.

It is advised that Mr. Wood, Mr. McClurg and Mr. Jones be appointed to examine the Treasurers accounts up to the end of the last quarter, pursuant to law.

On consideration of a Letter from Mr. John Wilson, It is advised That the Treasurer be desired to pay the proportion allotted for Captain James Westfalls Company of Rangers in the County of Randolph during the last year, notwithstanding the County Lieutenants Order does not accompany the Warrant.

All which matters so advised the Governor orders accordingly.

> James Wood
> James McClurg
> Carter Braxton
> Jos. Jones
> Robt. Goode

Thursday April 23d 1789

Present

The Governor

Mr. Wood	Mr. Jones
Mr. McClurg	Mr. Braxton
	Mr. Goode

The Governor informed the board that in the recess, he issued a Warrant on the Contingent Fund for one pounds four shillings to John Ammonet for expences in conveying a prisoner to the District of Petersburg for trial. Approved.

It is advised that a register issue for the Ship Powhatan, satisfactory proof having been made in due form of law.

It is advised that the auditor be directed to issue Warrants to William Peake for the arrearages of pension due him from the 15th November 1783, to the first of January 1786; it appearing that his pay as a Serjeant in Lees Legion ceased on the said 15th of November 1783.

On recommendation It is advised that a Commission issue appointing Samuel Crabb an additional inspector of tobacco at Yeocomoco and Kinsale warehouses in Westmoreland County.

The Governor laid before the board a letter from Thomas Smith refusing to accept and execute the office of Sheriff of Isle of Wight, to which he was lately appointed. Whereupon it is advised, that a commission issue appointing James Wills Sheriff of the said County; and that the Solicitor be instructed to move against the said Thomas Smith for his refusal to accept and execute the said office.

The Governor laid before the board an account of Clotworthy Stephenson for work done on the houses and Lot appropriated for the use of the Governor. Whereupon it is advised that Col. Meriwether be requested to have the several articles of work charged in the said Account valued by competent workmen, and report such valuation to this board.

Mr. John Beckley Clerk of the house of Delegates having absented himself from this State and there being good reason to believe that he has accepted of the Office of Clerk to the House of representatives for the United States, it becomes the Duty of the Executive to put the records of the General Assembly into the hands of some confidential person who will be responsible for their safe keeping. It is therefore advised that Mr. Charles Hay be requested immediately to take charge of the office and papers of the General Assembly.

The Governor laid before the board a letter from Mr. Mayo Carrington giving information of the Sale of sundry negroes belonging to the public, to satisfy the Debts of Mr. John Reveley, the manager of the Buckingham Furnace; and offering his service to procure the said negroes again. Whereupon it is advised that the Governor write to Mr. Carrington thanking him for the tender of his services, and authorizing him to demand the said Negroes on behalf of the Commonwealth: (see letter recorded in the letter book).[40]

All which matters so advised the Governor orders accordingly.

> James Wood
> James McClurg
> Jos. Jones
> Carter Braxton
> Robt. Goode

---

40. Beverley Randolph to Mayo Carrington, 24 Apr. 1789, Letter Book 1788–1792, Governor's Office.

Saturday April 25th 1789

Present

The Governor

Mr. Wood   Mr. Jones
Mr. McClurg   Mr. Braxton
                Mr. Goode

On consideration of the case of Lawrence Conner; It is advised that he be continued on the List of pensioners and that his allowance be increased to twelve pounds per annum from the first of January last.

The Governor laid before the board a letter from Mr. Daniel Herring late Sheriff of Isle of Wight complaining that a certain John Sinclair had rescued his property, which had been taken by execution; from the hands of the Deputy Sheriff. Whereupon it is advised that the said Letter be referred to the Attorney General in order that he may proceed against the said Sinclair as the Law directs.

It is advised that Mr. Jones, Mr. Braxton, and Mr. Heth be appointed a Committee to visit and examine the offices of the Auditor and Solicitor, and report the situation of the same.

On report from the Solicitor, Whereas it appears that a Judgment was obtained, in October 1783, against Sir John Peyton, late Sheriff of Gloster for £3232.7.8. for the revenue taxes of 1782, and that the property which was taken in execution to satisfy such judgment hath not been sold for want of buyers, as appears by a return to that effect. The board advise that the officer to whom any subsequent process may be directed (provided the said property cannot be sold agreeable to the Direction of such subsequent process) cause the same to be removed to the Court house of York County and there exposed to sale by as early a day as possible, allowing reasonable time to give notice of the day and place of sale, and that payment may be made for the said property in money or such Warrants or other Government Securities of this State, as were receiveable in the revenue taxes of 1782: And Whereas the Board have reason to believe that the postponement of execution against the said Sir John Peyton until the 1st of June next, under the Act "for granting relief to Sheriffs and Collectors of the public revenue in certain cases" might put the Debt in danger, They advise that the Solicitor be directed to proceed in the same manner in this case, as was ordered on the 3d of March last, in the case of George Stubblefield, late Sheriff of Spotsylvania.

It is further advised that similar measures to the above, be taken against the following persons who appear to be in a similar predicament to wit.

Stephen Ruddle, against whom as Sheriff of Hampshire, Judgment was obtained, in October 1783, for £618.12.6½ for the revenue taxes of 1782, the property to be removed to Hampshire Court house for sale on the same terms; the said Ruddle being now a resident of Hardy County which was taken from the county of Hampshire:

Robert Jones, against whom, as Sheriff of Sussex, Judgment was obtained, in April 1783 for £1888.10.6 for the revenue taxes of 1782, the property to be removed to the Town of Petersburg, in the County of Dinwiddie, for sale on the same terms:

Gross Scruggs, against whom as Sheriff of Bedford judgment was obtained, in December 1784, for £2062.0.6. for the revenue taxes of 1783, the property to be removed to Amherst Courthouse and there sold for money or such warrants or other Government Securities of this State as were receiveable in the revenue taxes of 1783:

William McClenahan, against whom as Sheriff of Botetourt, Judgment was obtained in December 1786, for £2299.19.9½ for the revenue taxes of 1783, the property to be removed to Staunton in Augusta, for sale on the same terms:

John Slaughter, against whom, as Sheriff of Culpeper, Judgment was obtained in October 1785, for £1212.8.0¾ and ninety five pounds of tobacco, for the revenue taxes of 1783, the property to be removed to Fredericksburg in Spotsylvania, for sale on the same terms:

Sir John Peyton, against whom, as Sheriff of Gloster Judgment was obtained, in June 1784, for £4218.9.10½ for the revenue taxes of 1783, the property to be removed to the Courthouse of York County, for sale on the same terms:

John Harris, against whom, as Sheriff of Powhatan, Judgment was obtained, in October 1784, for £1642.4.9 and 665 lbs. Tobacco for the revenue taxes of 1783, the property to be removed to Manchester in Chesterfield, for sale on the same terms:

John Thomas, against whom as Sheriff of Rockingham, Judgment was obtained, in October 1784 for £1636.12.1 for the revenue taxes of 1783, the property to be removed to Shenandoah Courthouse for sale on the same terms:

Robert Jones against whom as Sheriff of Sussex, judgment was obtained in October 1784, for £898.7.9 for the revenue taxes of 1783, the property to be removed to Petersburg in Dinwiddie, for sale on the same terms:

Henry Whiting, against whom as Sheriff of Berkeley, Judgment was obtained in December 1786 for £851.17.11 for the one per cent tax of 1784, the property to be removed to Frederick Courthouse and there sold for money or such Warrants or other government securities of this State as were receiveable for the said one per cent tax:

Abraham Shelton against whom as Sheriff of Pittsylvania, Judgment was obtained in December 1785, for £372.13.6 for the one per cent. tax of 1784, the property to be removed to Halifax Courthouse for sale on the same terms.

William Bowyer, against whom as Sheriff of Augusta, Judgment was obtained in December 1785 for £1992.1.4 for the revenue taxes of 1784, the property to be removed to Rockbridge Courthouse, and there sold for money or such Warrants or other government Securities of this State as were receiveable for the revenue taxes of 1784:

William Callaway against whom as Sheriff of Bedford, Judgment was obtained in December 1785 for £1932.18.2 for the revenue taxes of 1784, the property to be removed to Amherst Courthouse for sale on the same terms:

John Johns against whom as Sheriff of Buckingham Judgment was obtained in October 1785, for £967.11.2½ for the revenue taxes of 1784, the property to be removed to Prince Edward Courthouse for sale on the same terms:

James Barbour against whom as Sheriff of Culpeper, Judgment was obtained in June 1786 for £1786.14.8 for the revenue taxes of 1784, the property to be removed to Fredericksburg in Spotsylvania, for sale on the same terms:

Geddis Winston against whom as Sheriff of Hanover Judgment was obtained in December 1785, for £3477.4.2½ for the revenue taxes of 1784, the property to be removed to the City of Richmond for sale on the same terms:

Abraham Penn, against whom as Sheriff of Henry Judgment was obtained in December 1785 for £953.6.3½ for the revenue taxes of 1784, the property to be removed to Pittsylvania Courthouse, for sale on the same terms:

Abraham Shelton, against whom as Sheriff of Pittsylvania, Judgment was obtained in December 1785, for £1885.5.9 for the revenue taxes of 1784, the property to be removed to Halifax Courthouse, for sale on the same terms:

Richard Graham against whom as Sheriff of Prince William, Judgment was obtained in October 1785, for £1889.5.3½ for the revenue taxes of 1784, the property to be removed to Alexandria for sale on the same terms:

Alexander Macher against whom as Sheriff of Shenandoah, Judgment was obtained in December 1787, for £313.16.3 for the revenue taxes of 1784, the property to be removed to Frederick Courthouse for sale on the same terms:

David Mason against whom as Sheriff of Sussex Judgment was obtained in June 1786 for £644.10.7 for the revenue taxes of 1784, the property to be removed to Petersburg for sale on the same terms:

William Callaway against whom as Sheriff of Bedford, Judgment was obtained in October 1786 for £1768.11.5 for the revenue taxes of 1785, the property to be removed to Amherst Courthouse and there sold for money or such Warrants or other government securities of this State as were receiveable for the revenue taxes of 1785:

Patrick Lockhart against whom as Sheriff of Botetourt, Judgment was obtained in April 1787 for £1112.18.11 for the revenue taxes of

1785 the property to be removed to Montgomery Courthouse for sale on the same terms:

James Barbour against whom as Sheriff of Culpeper, Judgment was obtained in December 1786, for £544.4/10. for the revenue taxes of 1785, the property to be removed to Fredericksburg for sale on the same terms:

Abraham Penn against whom as Sheriff of Henry Judgment was obtained in October 1786 for £1207.0.0¾ for the revenue taxes of 1785, the property to be removed to Pittsylvania Courthouse for sale on the same terms:

Morgan Morgan against whom as Sheriff of Berkeley Judgment was obtained in December 1787 for £3839.18.4 for the revenue taxes of 1786, the property to be removed to Frederick Courthouse and there sold for money or such warrants or other Government securities of this State as were receiveable for the revenue taxes of 1786:

Henry Bell, against whom as Sheriff of Buckingham, Judgment was obtained in April 1788 for £573.6.4 for the revenue taxes of 1786, the property to be removed to Prince Edward Courthouse for sale on the same terms:

John Houston against whom as Sheriff of Rockbridge, Judgment was obtained in April 1788, for £1040.6.8 for the revenue taxes of 1786, the property to be removed to Staunton in Augusta for sale on the same terms:

Thomas Allen against whom as Sheriff of Shenandoah Judgment was obtained in April 1788 for £282.1.6 for the revenue taxes of 1786, the property to be removed to Frederick Courthouse for sale on the same terms:

William A. Washington against whom as Sheriff of Westmoreland, Judgment was obtained in December 1787 for £1950.18.8½ for the revenue taxes of 1786, the property to be removed to Richmond Courthouse for sale on the same terms: and

William Call against whom as Sheriff of Prince George Judgment was obtained in April 1788 for £1362.9.10 for the revenue taxes of 1786, the property to be removed to Petersburg for sale on the same terms.

It is further advised that similar measures so far as relates only to the issuing of Executions prior to the 1st of June next, be pursued against the following persons, to wit,

John Dixon against whom as Sheriff of Gloster, judgment was obtained in April 1786 for £495.8.4½ for the one per cent. tax of 1784:

Patrick Lockhart against whom as Sheriff of Botetourt, Judgment was obtained in June 1787 for £1014.7.11 for the revenue taxes of 1784:

John Dixon against whom as Sheriff of Gloster Judgment was obtained in April 1786, for £3749.10.1 for the revenue taxes of 1784:

Stephen Sampson against whom as Sheriff of Goochland Judgment was obtained in December 1787 for £145.12.4 for the revenue taxes of 1784:

Soloman Shepherd against whom as Sheriff of Nansemond, Judgment was obtained in April 1786 for £1454.4.10 for the revenue taxes of 1784:

Stephen Sampson against whom as Sheriff of Goochland Judgment was obtained in April 1788 for £382.19.4 for the revenue taxes of 1785:

Lawrence Baker against whom as Sheriff of Isle of Wight, Judgment was obtained in October 1786 for £1588.16.3½ for the revenue taxes of 1785: and

Lawrence Baker against whom as Sheriff of the said County Judgment was obtained in April 1788 for £3274.7.3 for the revenue taxes of 1786.

And it is also advised, That the Solicitor be instructed to take the opinion of the Attorney General concerning the claim made by William Duval and James Boswell to certain property which was taken in execution to satisfy a Judgment obtained in October 1785, against Thomas Johnson as Sheriff of Louisa, for £2752.0.4 for the revenue taxes of 1784; and whether proceedings ought not to be pursued against the Securities of the said Thomas Johnson for the balance due the Commonwealth.

All which matters so advised the Governor orders accordingly.

> James Wood
> James McClurg
> Jos. Jones
> Carter Braxton
> Robt. Goode

Thursday April 30th 1789

Present

The Governor

Mr. Wood	Mr. Braxton
Mr. McClurg	Mr. Goode

The Governor reported that he yesterday granted a register to the Sloop Ranger, satisfactory proofs having been made in due form of law. approved.

For reasons appearing to the board, It is advised that a pardon issue to William Crittendon one of the labouring criminals.

In pursuance of a resolution of the General Assembly of the 29th and 30th of December 1788, It is advised that the Auditor be directed to issue a duplicate Certificate in the name of Tarpley Machanis[41] for

---

41. "Tarpley Machinis" in the clerk's index.

sixty three pounds four shillings and two pence in lieu of the original which appears to have been lost; on affidavit being made by Henry Wade, who claims the said certificate, as to the destruction of it, and on his giving bond with security to indemnify the commonwealth.

On consideration of a letter to Mr. A. Dunscomb, from Mr. Charles Russell one of the persons employed to collect Vouchers in support of the claim of this State against the United States, It is advised that the several persons employed in that business be informed, that, on application, the Sum of ten pounds will be advanced to each of them, upon account, to defray expences.

All which matters so advised, the Governor orders accordingly.

The Governor notified to the board his intention to be absent which is ordered to be entered on the journal.

James Wood
James McClurg
Carter Braxton
Robt. Goode

Thursday May 7th 1789

Present

The President, who presides as Lieutenant Governor,
in the absence of the Governor.

Mr. McClurg   Mr. Braxton
Mr. Jones   Mr. Heth

Mr. Goode

The Lieutenant Governor laid before the board, a letter from the Governor informing that, upon finding from the Treasurers return, an increase of cash in the Treasury, he had advised the applying of two thousand pounds more towards the legal appropriations; and that in pursuance of the advice of the 30th of April he had directed ten pounds to be paid out of the Contingent fund to William Price, upon Account, as one of the Collectors of Vouchers. Approved.

The Lieutenant Governor informed the board, that in the recess of Council, the Governor inclosed to him before he left town two letters, dated the 25th ultimo, one from Col. John Evans and the other from Mr. Wm. McClerry, of Monongalia, giving information of hostilities committed by the Indians on the inhabitants of that County, etc.: Upon which Letters he took the advice of Mr. McClurg, Mr. Braxton and Mr. Goode, being the only members present, and gave orders to the Lieutenant of Monongalia to continue, until further orders, two of the Scouts ordered by him into service, and authorized him to call into service a Lieutenant and twenty five rangers for repelling any future attacks of the enemy, cautioning him not to continue them longer than real danger shall make it absolutely necessary; and transmitted to the President of the United States, copies of the aforesaid Letters together with the above orders:

That he referred to the Auditor for settlement in the usual way the account of Thomas Laidley who came express with the above dispatches:

That he also referred to the Auditor for Settlement in the usual way, the payrolls and account of disbursements of the public boats for the last quarter; and authorized Captain Taylor to draw on the Naval Officer of Eliza[beth] river District, for money to purchase the necessary subsistence of the Crews of the said boats:

That on recommendations, he issued a Commission appointing Henry Chowning additional inspector at Urbanna Warehouses in the room of James Dunlevy deceased, and an additional Commission appointing John Holman, William Turpin, Benjamin Allen Senr., Richard Booker, Stephen Cooke, Walter Warfield, Anderson Cocke, Marshall Booker, William Macon, William Cocke, Robert C. Harrison and Coddrington Carrington gentlemen Justices of the peace for the County of Cumberland: and

That he directed to be paid out of the contingent fund, fifty pounds to the Solicitor, upon account, to defray the expence of sending out notices etc. and ten pounds to Mr. Thos. Drew for his trouble in collecting Vouchers in support of the claim of this State against the United States. Approved.

On the application of the reverend Benjamin Blagrave in behalf of Absalom Allard, and Agnis Smith, two malefactors under sentence of death; It is advised, that they be reprieved until Friday the 22d instant.

The Lieutenant Governor laid before the board several petitions in behalf of Francis Suttle,[42] who is said to be under condemnation, by the Judgement of the district Court at New London, for horsestealing; Whereupon it is advised, that, as the report of the Court respecting the said Suttle has not yet come to hand, a reprieve be granted him until the first Friday in June next.

The Lieutenant Governor laid before the board the account of Samuel McDonald amounting to Ninety nine pounds and nine pence for supplies furnished the post at the Point of Fork the last quarter, as certified by Col. Meriwether: also the account of Elias Wells, amounting to nineteen pounds ten shillings, for plank furnished the said post agreeably to contract with Major Langham. Whereupon it is advised that the said accounts be referred to the Auditor for settlement and warrants for the sums due. (The money to be borrowed.) It is also advised that Col. Meriwether be instructed to renew the Contract with Mr. McDonald for supplying the post at the Point of Fork for another year.

---

42. "Little" in the clerk's index.

The Lieutenant Governor laid before the board the Account of Mr. Thomas Drew for his trouble and expences in collecting Vouchers in support of the claims of this State against the United States, amounting to £19.10.0: Whereupon it is advised that the said ac[count] be referred to the auditor for examination and settlement; and that he grant a warrant on the contingent fund for the balance due, after deducting the ten pounds allowed Mr. Drew the 4th instant: (to be paid).

All which matters so advised, the Lieutenant Governor orders accordingly.

> James McClurg
> Jos. Jones
> Carter Braxton
> Will Heth
> Robt. Goode

Friday May 8th 1789

Present

The Lieutenant Governor

Mr. McClurg   Mr. Braxton
Mr. Jones   Mr. Heth
                    Mr. Goode

On consideration of the petition of William English praying to be released from imprisonment; It is advised that the same be rejected.

The Lieutenant Governor laid before the board a letter from Major John Nelson inclosing a certificate from Mr. Chas. Hay that he had searched the office of the General Assembly and could not find the petition of the said Nelson and Deposition of Mr. Edward Archer which were referred to the Executive by the General Assembly on the 17th of December last. Whereupon the Board taking into consideration the aforesaid resolution, Advise, that the Auditor be directed to settle the Claim of Major Nelson for the pay and depreciation of pay due him, leaving the Account for monies advanced him for the purchase of horses open for future consideration, on Major Nelsons producing the deposition of Mr. Archer relative thereto.

It is advised that a Warrant issue on the contingent fund for ten pounds to Mayo Carrington, upon account, as one of the Collectors of Vouchers in support of the claims of this State against the United States.

On recommendation It is advised that a Commission issue appointing Henry Anderson Sheriff of Amelia, in the room of Stephen Coke who falls into the new County Notaway.

The Lieutenant Governor laid before the board the petition of

John Strother praying for the remmission of the damages on the amount of a Judgment obtained against the Sheriff of Culpeper for the taxes of 1782. Whereupon it is advised that the same be rejected.

Application having been made for the following Warrants to be put on the aggregate fund, to wit. A Warrant issued the 4th of June 1782 to Andrew Hamilton for twenty pounds in part for making cloaths for Col. George Gibsons regiment of State troops as per Settlement made by Wm. Armistead the clothier general: also a Warrant issued the 9th of April 1785 to Walter Scott for eight pounds six shillings and eight pence balance due for his services as superintendant of the Laboratory at Richmond in 1780. It is advised that the same be rejected.

Some difficulties having arisen from the mode prescribed by the Executive for the payment of the monies set apart for the Scouts and rangers, It is advised that the orders of the 2d of January and 23d of March last relating thereto, be changed so far as the signature of the County Lieutenant is made necessary to the payment of the Warrants; That the Auditor be directed to make an immediate return to the Treasurer of the amount of Warrants issued by him, since his last return, for services rendered by the Scouts and rangers in the year 1788, rations included, and like returns from time to time; and that, in future, he distinguish the Warrants which may be issued to the said Scouts and Rangers for their Services in the current year, rations included. It is further advised that the Treasurer be directed to pay in due proportion, as the Warrants for the said services of 1788 shall be presented, such sums as have been, or shall be directed, by this board to be so applied.

It is advised that Robert Andrews and James Southall Esqrs. be authorized and requested to rent out for one year on the best terms they can, the building on the public square in the city of Williamsburg, formerly used as the Secretary's office.

All which matters so advised, the Lieutenant Governor orders accordingly.

James McClurg
Jos. Jones
Carter Braxton
Will Heth
Robt. Goode

Thursday May 14th 1789

Present

The Governor

Mr. Wood　　　　　　　　Mr. Braxton
Mr. McClurg　　　　　　　Mr. Heth
Mr. Jones　　　　　　　　Mr. Goode

The Governor informed the board that since his return to Town, he issued registers to the Brigantine Greyhound and Ship Le Dominique; satisfactory proofs having been made in due form of law. Approved.

Mr. Wood informed the board that in the recess of Council, and absence of the Governor, he, with the concurrence of Mr. McClurg, Mr. Jones and Mr. Braxton, granted a pardon to Thomas Miller, who was condemned by the District Court at Winchester for horsestealing; he having been recommended as a proper object of mercy: that he directed John Martin, orphan of George Martin, to be continued on the pension list with an allowance of six pounds per annum from the 1st of January last; and that he granted a register for the Brigantine Cincinnatus, satisfactory proof having been produced in due form of law. Approved.

It is advised that Warrants issue on the Contingent fund, to John Harvie, for thirty pounds, for the last years rent of his office as Register: and, to Archibald Blair for twenty five pounds, for four months Salary as Keeper of the public Seal, ending the 4th instant.

On consideration of a letter from the Attorney General in behalf of Agnis Smith and Absolom Allard, under sentence of Death the former for murder and the latter for horsestealing; It is advised that they be pardoned.

It is advised that Frederick Fender, James Robertson and Dennis O'Farrell[43] be continued on the List of pensioners with eight pounds each per annum from the 1st of January last, that Henry Townsend[44] be continued with ten pounds, Martin Griffin with fifteen pounds and Leonard Cooper with fifty pounds per annum from the said 1st Day of January last, and that the pension of Joseph Sandidge be increased to fifteen pounds per annum from January 1789; it appearing to the satisfaction of the board that the allowance made him in March last is insufficient.

The Governor laid before the board an account of Messrs. Marsden Maxwell and Company making a balance in their favour of 18403½ lbs. of tobacco. Whereupon it is advised that the Auditor be directed to settle the said account at the rate of fifteen Shillings per hundred for the tobacco, with five per cent. interest from January

43. "Dennis OFarrell" in the clerk's index.
44. "Henry Townshend" in the clerk's index.

1781, and to grant a Warrant on the Aggregate fund for the sum due; taking bond of Nicholas B. Seabrook (the Agent of Marsdens administratrix) to indemnify the public against the Certificate given to Marsden by William Armistead ascertaining the debt, if hereafter produced, or if it shall appear to have been heretofore paid.

It is advised that a register issue for Schooner Dilligent Ann, Satisfactory proofs having been made in due form of Law.

It is advised that Mr. Harry Heth be instructed to report as soon as may be, a state of the balances which appear to be due from individuals to the public Foundery, specifying such as have been actually Settled.

It is advised that a letter be written to the Senators of this State in Congress, requesting them to make an offer of the public boats to the United States.

All which matters so advised, the Governor orders accordingly.

James Wood
James McClurg
Jos. Jones
Carter Braxton
Will Heth
Robt. Goode

Monday May 18th 1789

Present

The Governor

Mr. Wood	Mr. Braxton
Mr. McClurg	Mr. Heth
Mr. Jones	Mr. Goode

It is advised that a warrant issue on the Contingent Fund for thirty pounds to the Solicitor, upon account, to defray office expences, and of a temporary Clerk. (To be paid)

On consideration of the petition of John Bryan, It is advised that the fines of fifty pounds and of ten pounds imposed on him by the County Court of Henrico in March 1788 for retailing Liquors without License, be remitted.

The Governor laid before the board an account of Matthew Patton for horsemens accoutrements furnished Major John Stith for the Continental army. Whereupon it is advised that the same be rejected.

The Governor laid before the board an Account of William Morris as Superintendant of the Shipyard at Cumberland. Whereupon it is advised that the same be rejected for want of sufficient Vouchers.

All which matters so advised, the Governor orders accordingly.

James Wood
James McClurg
Jos. Jones
Carter Braxton
Will Heth
Robt. Goode

Saturday May 23d 1789

Present

The Governor

Mr. Wood   Mr. Braxton
Mr. McClurg   Mr. Heth
Mr. Jones   Mr. Goode

The Governor informed the board that in the recess, he with the concurrence of four members, issued a pardon to Francis Suttle who was condemned to Death by the District Court at new London. Approved.

The Governor laid before the board the account of Samuel Swan amounting to one pound nineteen shilling[s] for cleaning and mending a Bureau belonging to the public. Whereupon it is advised that the said Account be referred to the Auditor for a warrant on the Contingent fund. (To be paid).

It is advised that a Warrant issue on the Contingent fund for ten pounds to Capt. Thomas Parker, upon Account, as a Collector of Vouchers in support of the Claims of this State, against the United States. (To be paid)

It is advised that a pardon issue to Joseph Warden who stands condemned by the District Court of Suffolk; he appearing to be a proper object of mercy.

On consideration of the Solicitors report on the Claims of Hunter, Banks and Company. It is advised that the Claim of thirty five thousand five hundred and seventy four pounds of tobacco be rejected: that the Auditor be directed to settle the Claim of thirty nine thousand three hundred and fifty five pounds of Tobacco, at fifteen shillings per hundred, and grant a warrant on the aggregate fund for the Sum due.

On consideration of a petition from Stephen and Moses Austin setting forth that they are about establishing a manufactory of Shot, and praying a loan of a quantity of lead to enable them to begin the work; It is advised that Col. Meriwether be instructed to give an order in favor of Messrs. Stephen and Moses Austin, on the Keeper of the public Lead for twenty Tons, taking their bond with approved Security for the return of the said lead on demand.

Application having been made for putting on the aggregate fund, a Warrant issued the 17th of November 1788, to Richard Brasheur for one hundred and five pounds for seven months pay and rations as a Captain in the Illinois, It is advised that the said application be rejected.

The Governor laid before the board an Account of John Moore, Searcher at West Point, for his expences in prosecuting certain Vessels. Whereupon it is advised that the same be rejected.

On consideration of the Cases of the following persons who were fined each Sixty pounds by the Court of Henrico County in May 1788, for retailing Liquors without License, to wit, William Green, James Bisset, Joshua Morris, Nicholas Conway, James Roach, Elizabeth Alley, Benjamin Smoole, Robert Mims, Crouch and Rock, Richard Sharpe Junr. and William Lipscomb, It is advised that the whole of the fine on Nicholas Conway, and fifty pounds of each of the other fines, be remitted.

The Governor laid before the board the account of Robert Armistead amounting to eighteen pounds two shillings for fitting up a house for the use of the District Court of Petersburg etc. Whereupon it is advised that the same be rejected; the Executive conceiving themselves unauthorized to order payment of such accounts.

On consideration of a letter from the Attorney General in favor of Ephraim Willard[45] who stands charged with counterfieting and passing the public Securities of the United States, It is advised that the said Willard be pardoned.

The Governor laid before the board a letter without signature, which as he is informed by Mr. Renick, the bearer thereof, was written by George Clendinnen esqr., County Lieutenant of Greenbriar, informing that he had ordered out a party of Rangers, and had purchased 200 lbs. of gunpowder, etc.; and a letter which he had written in answer to Mr. Clendinnen; which answer being read is approved and ordered to be registered. [See Letter book][46]

On consideration of a petition of David Fergusson praying for the remission of a Fine of forty pounds imposed on him by the Court of Prince George County for keeping a retail Store without license; It is advised that the Same be rejected.

All which matters so advised, the Governor orders accordingly.

James Wood
James McClurg
Jos. Jones
Robt. Goode

---

45. "Wallard" in the clerk's index.
46. Beverley Randolph to George Clendenin, 23 May 1789, Letter Book 1788–1792, Governor's Office.

Monday May 25th 1789

Present

The Governor

Mr. Wood	Mr. Braxton
Mr. McClurg	Mr. Heth
Mr. Jones	Mr. Goode

The Governor laid before the board a Draft of the Directors of the James river company for six hundred fifty pounds on account of the Shares in the said company. Whereupon it is advised that the Treasurer be directed to borrow the money pursuant to the 5th section of the Act "to amend the several laws for appropriating the public revenue."

On consideration of the petition of George Bridges praying for the remission of a Fine imposed on him by the Court of Henrico for non attendance as a juryman, It is advised that the same be remitted.

On recommendation, It is advised that an additional commission issue appointing Benjamin Cook gentleman Justice of the peace for the County of Franklin.

It appearing that Thomas Powell Edmondson[47] comes within the requisitions of the pension law; It is advised that he be continued on the List of pensioners with an allowance of fifteen pounds per annum from January 1786.

On the further report of the Solicitor,

Whereas it appears that a Judgment was obtained in December 1784, against Gross Scruggs, late Sheriff of Bedford for £563.11.11 for the certificate tax of 1783; and that the property which was taken in execution to satisfy such judgment hath not been sold for want of buyers, as appears by a return to that effect.

The Board advise that the officer to whom any subsequent process may be directed (provided the said property cannot be sold agreeable to the direction of such subsequent process) cause the same to be removed to Amherst Courthouse and there exposed to sale by as early a day as possible, allowing reasonable time to give notice of the day and place of sale, and that payment may be made for the said property in money or such warants or other government Securities of this State as were receiveable in the Certificate taxes of 1783; And whereas the board have reason to believe that the postponement of execution against the said Gross Scruggs until the 1st day of June next under the Act "for granting relief to Sheriffs and Collectors of the public revenue in certain cases" might put the debt in danger, They advise that the Solicitor be directed to proceed in the same manner in this case as was ordered on the 3d of March last, in the case of George Stubblefield, late Sheriff of Spotsylvania.

47. "P. T. Edmondson" in the clerk's index.

It is further advised that similar measures to the above be taken against the following persons who appear to be in a similar predicament to wit.

William McClenachan against whom as Sheriff of Botetourt judgment was obtained in December 1786, for £1119.0.9 for the certificate tax of 1783, the property to be removed to Staunton for sale on the same terms:

Philemon Holcomb, against whom as Sheriff of Prince Edward judgment was obtained in April 1785, for £234.19.7 for the certificate tax of 1783, the property to be removed to Charlotte Courthouse for sale on the same terms:

Geddis Winston, against whom as Sheriff of Hanover judgment was obtained in December 1785, for £1047.4.2 for the certificate tax of 1784, the property to be removed to Richmond and there sold for money or such warrants or Government Securities of this State as were receiveable in payment for the certificate taxes of 1784:

Richard Graham, against whom as Sheriff of Prince William, judgment was obtained in October 1785, for £646.15.9 for the Certificate tax of 1784, the property to be removed to Alexandria for sale on the same terms:

David Mason, against whom as Sheriff of Sussex, judgment was obtained in December 1786 for £43.4.0 for the Certificate tax of 1784, the property to be removed to Petersburg for sale on the same terms:

William Callaway against whom as Sheriff of Bedford, judgment was obtained in December 1786 for £2366.5.3 for the Certificate tax of 1785; the property to be removed to Amherst Courthouse and there sold for money or such warrants or other government Securities of this State as were receiveable in payment for the certificate tax of 1785:

It is further advised that similar measures so far as relates only to the issuing of executions prior to the first of June next be pursued against the following persons viz:

Goodrich Willson, against whom as Sheriff of Isle of Wight, judgment was obtained in June 1785, for £415.—.2 for the one per Cent: tax of 1784:

John Dixon against whom as Sheriff of Gloster judgment was obtained in April 1786 for £1009.9.3¾ for the Certificate tax of 1784:

Solomon Shepherd against whom as Sheriff of Nansemond, judgment was obtained in December 1786, for £2480.4.2 for the Certificate tax of 1785: and

It is also advised that the Solicitor be instructed to take the opinion of the Attorney General as to the steps proper to be taken in the case of Thomas Flournoy against whom as Sheriff of Prince Edward Judgment was obtained in December 1787 for £2054.1.2¼ for the revenue tax of 1786.

All which matters so advised, the Governor orders accordingly.

James Wood
James McClurg
Jos. Jones
Robt. Goode

Saturday May 30th 1789

Present

The Governor

Mr. Wood   Mr. Braxton
Mr. McClurg   Mr. Goode

The Governor informed the board that during their recess he granted a pardon to Jim, a negro man slave condemned by the Court of Powhatan for a rape; the Court having certified that they had been convinced of the Error of their Judgment:

That, on the information of Mr. Wm. Hay that a quantity of Glass imported for the Capitol had been stop[p]ed by the Naval Officer for want of the Duties being paid, he directed the said Glass to be delivered to the Order of the Directors of the public buildings:

That he directed a dismission of the motion against Catesby Jones as Clerk of Northumberland for not rendering an account of one third of his fees; it being certified by Doctor Jones that the said Catesby was too unwell at the time to attend to any business:

That he directed to be paid out of the contingent Fund the account of Thomas Brend amounting to five pounds one shilling and six pence for blank books, etc. furnished for the Auditors office; and

That he issued a register for the Ship Sally on the usual proofs being produced. Approved.

It is advised that a pardon issue in favor of Negro Frank, condemned by the Court of Norfolk for felony; he having been recommended as a proper object of mercy.

The Deputy Sheriffs of Albemarle having been prevented from collecting the taxes on certain Lands in the said County by the removal of the high Sheriff to Georgia so that no sales of land could be legally made to discharge the taxes due thereon; for remedy of which inconvenience the General Assembly, did, at their last Session pass a law authorizing William Clarke "to sell and convey so much of the lands in the said County whereon sufficient Distress could not be made for that purpose, as would discharge the taxes respectively due for such lands in the years of 1786 and 1787["]: and it appearing to be unreasonable to demand the interest on so much of the balance due from the said Deputy Sheriffs as was occasioned by the removal of their principal, The board, therefore, advise that the Solicitor be directed to remit so much of the interest as shall appear to have accrued in consequence of the impediments which were thrown in the way of the collection as stated above.

It is advised that a register issue for the Ship Mary; Satisfactory proofs having been made in due form of law.

Upon good cause shewn, It is advised that the Execution against Louis Segoine,[48] for duties, be suspended until the 1st of July.

The Governor laid before the board a petition of sundry persons, praying that the interest on the Judgment obtained against John Hunter late Sheriff of Campbell for the taxes of 1784, may be remitted. Whereupon it is advised that the same be rejected.

The Governor laid before the board an account of John Webb amounting to twenty five pounds two shillings and six pence for signing 40,200 Bills issued under the resolve of congress of the 18th of March 1780. Whereupon it is advised that the said account be referred to the Auditor for settlement and a Warrant on the aggregate fund for the sum due, provided the same hath not been heretofore paid.

It is advised that Jett Roach and George Quick, who were condemned to death by the District Court at Dumfries, be reprieved until the first friday in July.

It is advised that the Account of C[lot]worthy Stephenson for Carpenters Work etc. done about the lots and houses occupied by the Governor, amounting to sixty four pounds eighteen shillings and seven pence, per valuation, be referred to the Auditor for a warrant on the contingent fund (to be paid).

On the recommendation of Henrico County Court, It is advised that the fine imposed in May 1788, on Benjamin Smoole on presentment of the grand jury, be remitted.

On consideration of a letter dated the 16th instant, from the President of the United States in answer to one of the 4th from the Lieutenant Governor, It is advised that copies of the Presidents letter be transmitted to all the frontier counties, with instructions, in case of future depredations, south of Ohio, by the Indians, to give information thereof as early as possible to the nearest post of the troops stationed on the Ohio: That all the Scouts and rangers, except those of Washington, Montgomery and Russell be immediately discharged: and That, in consideration of the great distance the above excepted Counties are from any continental post, the present system of defence within the same be continued, until the general government shall provide therefor, or the further orders of the Executive. It is further advised that the President of the United States be informed of the above advice.

---

48. "Seigoine" in the clerk's index.

All which matters so advised, the Governor orders accordingly.

James Wood
James McClurg
Carter Braxton
Robt. Goode

Thursday June 4th 1789

Present

The Governor

Mr. Wood   Mr. Braxton
Mr. McClurg   Mr. Heth
Mr. Jones   Mr. Goode

The Governor informed the board that he yesterday issued a commission appointing James Skidmore Escheator of Pendleton; he having been recommended by the Court. Approved.

It is advised that the Account of Thomas B. Lacy[49] as an Express from Harrison County be referred to the Auditor for settlement in the usual way.

The Governor laid before the board the claims of James McDowell and David Knox for their services as Clerks to the Commissioners appointed for settling the Militia Accounts for services rendered in Kentucky. Whereupon it is advised that the said Claims be rejected; the law having made no provision for such claims.

Mr. Henry Banks having produced some further Certificates in support of the Claims of Messrs. Hunter Banks and Company, It is advised that the same be referred to the Solicitor for examination and report.

The Governor laid before the board a letter from Col. Arthur Campbell inclosing one from Mr. John Anderson giving information of certain murders committed by the Indians on Clinch river. Whereupon it is advised that copies of the said Letters be transmitted to the President of the United States; and that Col. Campbell be informed of the proceedings of the 30th ultimo relative to the Western counties.

The Governor laid before the board an account of Turner Southall amounting to twenty four pounds for wood furnished for the use of the Auditors office to the 13th of March last as certified by Mr. Pendleton. Whereupon it is advised that the said Account be referred to the Auditor for settlement and a Warrant on the Contingent fund for the sum due: (to be paid).

It is advised that a Commission issue appointing John Goodrich,

---

49. "B. Thomas Lacy" in the clerk's index.

Sheriff of Isle of Wight, in the room of James Wells, who hath declared his inability to give security for the collection of the taxes.

The Governor laid before the board the report of Mr. Harry Heth concerning the foundery accounts. Whereupon it is advised that Mr. Heth be desired to fill up the blank charges which appear in the different accounts on the Foundery books at such prices as were current at the time of delivery of the articles to which no price is affixed in the said books.

It appearing that Captain John Stokes (late an officer in the continental army) has never received commutation of half pay; It is advised that the Auditor be directed to issue Warrants to the said Stokes for the arrearages of pension due him from the 1st of May 1783, the time of his pay ceasing, to the 1st of January 1787, the time the pension allowed him by the Executive commenced.

The time for which the present Council Chamber hath been rented, being about to expire with the present quarter; It is advised that Mr. McClurg, Mr. Jones and Mr. Braxton, be appointed a Committee, to examine the several apartments in the new Capitol, and report whether the Executive can be accommodated therein, until the Council Chamber and office are finished.

All which matters so advised, the Governor orders accordingly.

> James Wood
> James McClurg
> Jos. Jones
> Carter Braxton
> Will Heth
> Robt. Goode

Tuesday June 9th 1789

Present

The Governor

Mr. Wood	Mr. Braxton
Mr. McClurg	Mr. Heth
Mr. Jones	Mr. Goode

The Governor informed the board that during the recess, he issued a proclamation for apprehending Jett Roach and George Quick, two criminals under sentence of death, who made their escape from the District Jail of Dumfries; and offered a reward of fifty dollars each: that, on recommendation, he issued a commission appointing John Pollard Sheriff of King George; that he directed to be continued on the pension List with his former allowance John King: and that he issued a register for the Brig Kitty, on the usual proofs. Approved.

It is advised that a warrant issue for two thousand two hundred and eighty three pounds, ten shillings and eight pence half penny, to Captain Anthony Singleton, upon account, as Agent of the Sinking fund.

It is advised that Commissions issue appointing James Ross Notary Public for the District of Urbanna; and James Jones for the District of Hobshole.

It is advised that Mr. Harry Heth in settling the value of Mr. John Reveleys salary as Superintendant of the Westham Foundery reduce the paper money by the Scale at the different dates when the contracts were respectively made and that in all cases when Tobacco has been made the criterion he take as a rule for establishing the value of the said tobacco, the valuation made by the grand Jury at the last Session of the general court in each year and reduce the paper money by the scale of depreciation.

Mr. James Henry appeared and qualified as a Judge of the General court.

The Committee consisting of Mr. McClurg, Mr. Jones and Mr. Braxton, report that they have reason to believe, the board may be accom[m]odated in the public building by the time of the expiration of this quarters rent of the present Council Chamber. Whereupon It is advised that the Clerks take measures for moving the books and papers of the Executive to the new Capitol by next Saturday.

{ Letter to the Inspectors at Lynches warehouse in answer to theirs concerning duties on tobacco. (See letter book)[50]

All which matters so advised, the Governor orders accordingly.

> James Wood
> James McClurg
> Jos. Jones
> Carter Braxton
> Will Heth
> Robt. Goode

Saturday June 13th 1789

Present

The Governor

Mr. Wood	Mr. Braxton
Mr. McClurg	Mr. Heth
Mr. Jones	Mr. Goode

The Governor informed the board, that during their recess he had ordered payment of a Warrant formerly issued for the use of the Lunatic Hospital; that he had issued a Register for the Schooner

---

50. Beverley Randolph to William Martin and James Rucker, 10 June 1789, Letter Book 1788–1792, Governor's Office.

Fortune of sixty tons burthen, satisfactory proof having been made according to law; and that he had ordered a Warrant on the Contingent Fund in favour of Richard Yarbrough[51] for ten pounds on account for collecting vouchers to support the account of this State against the United States (to be paid:) of which several matters the board approve.

On recommendation it is advised, that the following Commissions issue, viz: An additional commission appointing William Fitzgerrald, Edmund Wills junior, William Watson, Samuel Pincham, John Doswell and Richard Bland, Gentlemen, Justices of the peace for the County of Nottoway; Commissions appointing Samuel Sherwin Gentleman, Coroner and Peter Lamkin Gentleman Sheriff for the said county; and an additional commission appointing Robert Carter and John Rose, Gentlemen, Justices of the peace for the county of Westmoreland.

On consideration of a letter from the Auditor, stating that the merchants of Alexandria have failed to renew their retail Licence agreeable to an act of Assembly passed October session 1786, and that Richard Conway, James Wren and John Moss Commissioners for the County of Fairfax have neglected to proceed against them for the recovery of the fine imposed by that Act, It is advised, that the Attorney General be directed to instruct his deputy for the said County to examine into the delinquencies aforesaid and institute such proceedings against the said merchants and Commissioners for neglecting their respective duties as the laws will Warrant.

It is advised, that the application of Joseph Parkason to have sundry Warrants, granted for expences incurred on account of an expedition meditated against Detroit, placed on the aggregate fund, be rejected.

The Governor laid before the board sundry accounts for the Wages of Scouts employed in the County of Fayette for the year 1788, whereupon it is advised, that the said accounts be referred to the Auditor for settlement in the usual way.

On consideration of Mr. John Reveley's account with the Westham Foundery as stated by Mr. Harry Heth, it is advised, that Mr. Heth be directed to restate the said Accounts and instead of applying the scale of depreciation to each particular Article of debit and credit, he strike the balance of paper money, and scale that agreeable to the act of assembly "directing the mode of adjusting and settling the payment of certain debts and contracts and for other purposes;" and that he adopt this mode in settling all other paper money accounts upon the books of the said Foundery.

It is advised, that the Treasurer be instructed to borrow from any fund two thousand pounds to be applied to the payment of the Warrants granted to the Scouts and Rangers employed in the year 1788.

---

51. "Richd. Yarborough" in the clerk's index.

All which matters so advised, the Governor orders accordingly.

James Wood
James McClurg
Jos. Jones
Carter Braxton
Will Heth
Robt. Goode

Monday June 15th 1789

Present

The Governor

Mr. Wood   Mr. Jones
Mr. McClurg   Mr. Braxton

On consideration of a Letter from the Treasurer of this date, It is advised, that Mr. Ambler be instructed to contract for securing the Windows of the Treasury office in the Capitol, in such manner, and with such person as he may think proper.

On recommendation, it is advised, that an additional Commission issue appointing William R. Fleming, Isaac W. Pleasants, Thomas W. Royster, John Geurrant junr., Howell Lewis and Thomas Miller Gentlemen justices of the Peace for the county of Goochland.

Pursuant to his appointment, John Tyler Esquire, appeared and took the Oath prescribed for a Judge of the General Court.

It is advised, that the directors of the public buildings be requested to report to the Executive when the rooms intended for the public offices will be ready for the reception of the different public officers.

All which matters so advised the Governor orders accordingly.

James Wood
James McClurg
Jos. Jones
Carter Braxton

Wednesday June 17th 1789

Present

The Governor

Mr. Wood   Mr. Braxton
Mr. McClurg   Mr. Heth
Mr. Jones   Mr. Goode

The Governor informed the Board that he had on the 16th instant pursuant to a recommendation issued a commission appointing Peter Saunders Gentleman Sheriff of Franklin; of which the board approve.

It is advised, that the following Warrants issue, to wit; A Warrant on the contingent fund to John Mayo for twenty five pounds being for the last quarters rent of the late council Chamber, and a Warrant on the same fund (to be paid) to Samuel Paine for One pound being the hire of Waggons to move the books and papers of the Executive to the Capitol: Also a Warrant in favour of the Commissioners of the Marine Hospital for the sum of five hundred pounds to be paid to Robert Borland the undertaker. And it is further advised, that a letter be written to the said Commissioners requiring a copy of the original contract between them and the said Undertaker, together with the present state of the Building. (See letter book.)[52]

On recommendation, it is advised that a Commission issue appointing Richard Evers Lee Gentleman, an Alderman for the Borough of Norfolk.

It is advised, that a Register issue for the sloop Endeavour, satisfactory proofs having been made according to law.

It appearing, that Smith Stephens[53] comes within the requisitions of the Pension law, it is advised, that he be put on the list of Pensioners with an allowance of twelve pounds per Annum to commence the first day of January 1786.

All which matters, so advised, the Governor orders accordingly.

James Wood
James McClurg
Jos. Jones
Carter Braxton
Will Heth
Robt. Goode

Friday June 19th 1789

Present

The Governor

Mr. Wood
Mr. McClurg
Mr. Jones
Mr. Braxton
Mr. Heth
Mr. Goode

On recommendations, It is advised that a Commission issue appointing James Miller Sheriff of Ohio County: Also a commission appointing William Robertson Sheriff of Prince George County; and an additional commission appointing Moses Johnson jun. and John Rosser Justices of the peace for the county of Greenesville.

The Governor laid before the board the account of William

52. Beverley Randolph to Dr. James Taylor, 18 June 1789, Letter Book 1788–1792, Governor's Office.
53. "Smith Stevens" in the clerk's index.

McKenley and Company for sixty four rations furnished the Scouts and rangers of Ohio for the year 1788 at 6d. per ration. Whereupon it is advised that the same be referred to the Auditor for settlement in the usual way.

On consideration of the petition of Hector McNeel praying for a suspension of the execution against him for certain duties; It is advised that the same be rejected.

For reasons appearing to the board; it is advised that the Solicitor be instructed to continue all motions against County Lieutenants until the next court.

On recommendation, It is advised that a commission issue appointing John Baller Sheriff of Botetourt in the room of Samuel Todd who hath refused to give security for the collection of the taxes.

Mr. William Hay having informed the board that the offices in the new Capitol are ready for the reception of the several executive boards; It is advised that the Governor notify the same to the said boards, and require them to move as soon as may be into their respective apartments.

All which matters so advised the Governor orders accordingly.

> James Wood
> James McClurg
> Jos. Jones
> Carter Braxton
> Will Heth
> Robt. Goode

Tuesday June 23d 1789

Present

The Governor

Mr. Wood	Mr. Braxton
Mr. McClurg	Mr. Heth
Mr. Jones	Mr. Goode

The Governor laid before the board a letter from the President of the United States inclosing a Copy of an Act of Congress intituled "an Act to regulate the time and manner of administering certain oaths." Whereupon it is advised that the said act be printed in the public paper for the information of all those whom it may concern, that two hundred copies thereof be struck, and that two of them be transmitted to each of the superior and county courts within this State.

On recommendation, It is advised that an additional commission issue appointing John Hipkins, Thomas Rootes, John Chiles, Laurence Battaile, Thomas Miller and William Harrison gentlemen Justices of the peace for the county of Caroline.

On consideration of the case of Negro Jim who stands condemned to be castrated, by the Judgment of Powhatan Oyer and Terminer Court, for an attempt to commit a rape, It is advised that the said Jim be pardoned.

All which matters so advised the Governor orders accordingly.

> James Wood
> James McClurg
> Jos. Jones
> Carter Braxton
> Will Heth
> Robt. Goode

Saturday June 27th 1789

Present

The Governor

Mr. Wood   Mr. Jones
Mr. McClurg   Mr. Braxton

The Governor informed the board that in the recess he directed to be paid out of the contingent fund, To John Carter, Clerk to the Auditor, fifteen pounds upon account to purchase stationary etc. for the use of that office; and To Jane West, three pounds, upon account, for nursing Catherine Crulles child. That on recommendation he issued an additional commission appointing Thomas Onsley, James Davis, William Montgomery junr. and William Patton gentlemen Justices of the peace for the County of Lincoln. Approved.

It is advised that a register issue for the Schooner Industry, Satisfactory proofs having been made in due form of law.

The Governor laid before the board an offer which had been made to the Agent of the Sinking Fund of twenty two shillings per hundredweight for the whole of the Tobacco now in his hands to be paid on or before the 1st Day of January next. Whereupon it is advised that the said Agent be instructed to accept the offer, on condition that the purchasee give his bond for the amount of the said tobacco and moreover lodge as a security for the payment thereof military Certificates to the amount of £2000. and good bonds to be approved by Captain Singleton to the amount of £3000 specie; The Certificates and bonds so deposited to be liable to public Sale in the City of Richmond on the expiration of the stipulated credit, if payment shall not be then made; The overplus of the Sales if any to be returned to the person making the deposit, the deficiency to be recovered upon the bond.

All which matters so advised the Governor orders accordingly.

> James Wood
> James McClurg
> Jos. Jones
> Carter Braxton

Tuesday June 30th 1789

Present

The Governor

Mr. Wood   Mr. Braxton
Mr. McClurg   Mr. Heth
Mr. Jones   Mr. Goode

The Governor informed the board that in the recess of Council, he issued a Warrant on the Contingent Fund for twenty two pounds ten shillings to Col. Charles Tompkins for removing Cannon to Taylors ferry and putting them under cover agreeably to contract. Approved.

The Governor laid before the board an account of Samuel Swann[54] amounting to ten pounds two shillings and six pence for mending presses etc. belonging to the Council office: Also an account of John Groves amounting to two pounds seventeen shillings and three pence for freight and expences of bringing the Marquis Fayettes bust from Maryland. Whereupon it is advised that the said accounts be referred to the Auditor for examination and warrants on the Contingent Fund for the sums due. To be paid.

Application having been made for placing on the aggregate fund a warrant issued the 23d. february 1785 for seven pounds four shillings payable to John Scarbrough in lieu of six months donation, It is advised that the same be rejected.

On recommendations, It is advised that commissions issue appointing William Harmanson Sheriff of Northampton County; and Tunstal Quarles Sheriff of Fluvanna County.

Col. Meriwether having resigned his office of third Clerk to this board and it appearing unnecessary that more than two Clerks be employed hereafter, It is advised that Mr. Coleman, the assistant Clerk, be directed in addition to the duties at present performed by him to discharge those heretofore assigned to Col. Meriwether, and that he be allowed as a compensation for his trouble therein the additional sum of One hundred pounds per annum.

It is advised that Mr. Wood, Mr. Jones and Mr. Goode be appointed a committee to examine the Treasurers Accounts up to this day, pursuant to law.

It appearing that there is no money now in the Treasury belonging to the funds appropriated to the payment of the salaries of the officers of Civil government, It is advised that the Treasurer be directed to borrow from any other funds such a sum of money as will be sufficient to discharge the Warrants issued for the salaries due the said officers this day.

---

54. "Swan" in the clerk's index.

All which matters so advised, the Governor orders accordingly.

James Wood
James McClurg
Will Heth
Robt. Goode

Monday July 6th 1789

Present

The Governor

Mr. Wood   Mr. Heth
Mr. McClurg   Mr. Goode

The Governor informed the board that during the recess, he issued registers for the Sloop Fanny and Agnes, and the Sloop Eagle; the usual proofs having been made; he examined and certified for payment the Account of Mr. Pendleton for his last quarters salary as Auditor of public accounts; he directed a warrant on the contingent fund for thirty four pounds nine shillings payable to the Solicitor upon account for sending out notices, etc.; and he directed the usual warrants to Major Langham for one hundred and twenty two pounds nine and three pence for balance of pay due the Superintendant and artificers, and seventy two pounds twelve shillings, being the amount of pay due the guard at the Point of Fork up to the 30th of June last. Approved.

The Governor laid before the board a State of the public tobaccoes now in the hands of the Agent and informed them that the said Agent had reported to him that he had visited some of the principal markets but could get no offer higher than fourteen shillings and six pence for the Northern, nineteen shillings for the Petersburg, and twenty shillings for the Richmond tobacco. Whereupon it is advised that the said Agent be instructed to receive in payment for two thirds of any Tobaccoes which he may hereafter dispose of, military or Loan Office Certificates at the rate of five shillings in the pound, that he may give a credit of four months for specie, that no credit for warrants on military or Loan Office Certificates be extended beyond the 20th of December next, but that the purchaser may at any time before the day of payment pay cash in lieu of Certificates at the rate of five shillings in the pound, And that he require a deposit in military Certificates at one fourth of their nominal value.

The Governor laid before the board a letter dated the 17th ultimo from Governor Hancock of Massachusetts, covering the proceedings of the supreme Judicial Court of that Commonwealth upon the examination of James Brown and William Davis charged with having committed Piracy in this State. Whereupon it is advised that Governor

Hancock be informed that Steps shall be immediately taken for the removal of the offenders to this State for trial.

On consideration of the petition of Joseph Selden praying for a suspension of the execution against him as Security for certain duties, It is advised that the same be rejected.

All which matters so advised, the Governor orders accordingly.

The Governor notified to the board his intention to be absent which is ordered to be entered on the Journal.

> James Wood
> James McClurg
> Will Heth
> Robt. Goode

Saturday July 11th 1789

Present

The President who presides as Lieutenant Governor
in the absence of the Governor

Mr. McClurg   Mr. Heth
Mr Braxton   Mr. Goode

The Lieutenant Governor informed the board that he yesterday issued a register for the Sloop Content, satisfactory proofs having been made in due form. Approved.

It is advised that a warrant issue on the Contingent Fund for fifteen pounds to the Reverend Benjamin Blagrave for the last quarters salary due him as ordinary to the public Jail But that such salary cease in future, as the law establishing District Courts hath made no provision for such an office.

The Lieutenant Governor informed the board that James Echkols had apprehended and brought to this City, Jonas Jordon, one of the criminals who escaped from labour. Whereupon it is advised, That the said Jonas Jordan be pardoned, That a warrant issue on the Contingent fund for ten pounds payable to the said Echkols as a reward for apprehending the said Jordan and that it be notified in the public gazette that no reward will be paid hereafter for apprehending any of the Criminals who received conditional pardons and have escaped from labour.

It is advised that a Commission issue appointing William Malory Sheriff of Isle of Wight in the room of John Goodrich who is unable to give security according to law.

All which matters so advised, the Lt. Governor orders accordingly.

> James McClurg
> Will Heth
> Robt. Goode

Tuesday July 14th 1789

Present

The Lieutenant Governor

Mr. McClurg   Mr. Heth
Mr. Braxton   Mr. Goode

The Lieutenant Governor laid before the board the accounts of William Rose amounting to three pounds seventeen shillings and sixpence for cleaning out the Courtroom during the last terms of the supreme Courts, as per Certificates from the said Courts. Whereupon it is advised that the same be referred to the Auditor for warrants on the Contingent fund.

Application having been made by Mr. Gernon for the duty on 70 tons which was overpaid in March 1787 on the tonnage of the Brig L'Amazon, to be refunded, It is advised that the same be rejected.

It is advised that Robert Todd who hath been commissioned as Surveyor of Fayette, be required to give bond in the penalty of one thousand pounds.

On recommendation, It is advised that an additional Commission issue appointing Edward Payne, William Ward, John Parker, Charles Morgan, Percival Butler, John Mason, William Boush, James McMillian, John Maxwell, John Hawkins, Thomas Young, Walter Carr and James McDowell gentlemen Justices of the peace for the County of Fayette.

It is advised that a register issue for the Sloop Phoenix, satisfactory proofs having been made in due form of law.

All which matters so advised, the Lieutenant Governor orders accordingly.

James McClurg
Will Heth
Robt. Goode

Tuesday July 28th 1789

Present

The Governor

Mr. Wood   Mr. Heth
Mr. McClurg   Mr. Goode

The Governor informed the board that in the recess he issued Commissions appointing John Clark Sheriff of Prince Edward County; Nathaniel Beavans Sheriff of Accomack County, and Roger Quarles Sheriff of Caroline County; they having been recommended according to law: that on recommendation from the Court of Brunswick County, he issued an Additional commission appointing John Stith, Edward Birchett, Thomas Jones, and Wright Tucker gentleman Justices of the peace for the said county: that he directed the Treasurer to borrow twenty five pounds to answer a Draft of the Directors, on account of the Shares of this State in the James river Company; there appearing to have been an omission of that much in their late Draft: that he remitted a fine of ten shillings imposed on Langston Ford by a court martial of Hanover for not attending muster; also a fine imposed on Richard Sharp jun. by the Court of Henrico for retailing liquors without license: that he referred the accounts and payrolls of Mercer Scouts and rangers for services rendered in 1788, to the Auditor for settlement in the usual way: that he wrote to Christopher Greenup County Lieutenant of Mercer in answer to his letter of the 8th Ultimo, and inclosed to him a copy of the dispatches of the 1st of June concerning Western defence: That, upon the receipt of the Act of Congress "for laying a Duty on goods, wares and merchandizes imported into the united States," He, in pursuance of the Act of the General Assembly concerning certain public Establishments, and with the concurrence of Mr. Wood, Mr. Heth and Mr. Goode, issued a proclamation requiring all Naval Officers, collectors of duties and Searchers to cease the exercise of the powers vested in them by virtue of their respective Offices from and after the 1st day of August next, required the said Naval Officers and Searchers to make up their Accounts as soon as possible and deliver up their books and official papers to the Solicitor or his order, directed the Inspectors at the different Warehouses to demand, after the said first of August, no other duties upon tobacco exported than that of six shillings per hogshead, reserved by law for inspection duties; and that he wrote to Captain Taylor desiring him to come immediately to Richmond with his payrolls and Accounts made up to the 1st of August in order to prepare for the discharge of the Officers and Crews of the public boats Liberty and Patriot. Approved.

The Governor laid before the board the payrolls and accounts of the public boats up to the 1st of August, Whereupon it is advised that the said payrolls and accounts be referred to the Auditor for settlement in the usual way.

The Board resumed the consideration of the "Act concerning certain Public establishments." Whereupon it is advised that Captain Richard Taylor be authorized to sell for the best price that can be obtained in military or Loan Office Certificates of this State the public boats Liberty and Patriot, the whale boat and the boat in possession of the Searcher at Norfolk together with their Guns rigging apparel and furniture, and that he allow a credit till the 31st Day of December next, taking bond and good security for the payment of the purchase money on that Day, and if sold for certificates the purchaser in case of Failure to pay all the Interest accruing on the amount of the Certificates contracted so to be paid; That Captain Taylor give passes to the two public negroes employed on board the boats, and that in consideration of their faithful services to the commonwealth since the commencement of the late War the Governor recommend them to the Legislature for an act of emancipation to pass in their favour. It is further advised that the Searchers at the ports of City point, York and Alexandria be desired to dispose of the boats employed by them in the execution of the duties of their offices for the highest price that can be obtained in ready money; and that they discharge the hands hired by them to row the said boats if free men and if slaves hired by the year that they dispose of the remainder of their time upon as good terms as possible.

It is advised that Captain Richard Taylor be replaced on the pension List with his former allowance to commence from the first of January last.

It is advised that Bazell Brown[55] be continued on the List of pensioners with twelve pounds per annum from the 1st of January 1786, and Matthew Amacks with nine pounds per annum from the first of January last.

It appearing that Sarah Booker comes within the requisitions of the pension law; It is advised that She be put on the List of pensioners with an allowance of eight pounds per annum from the first of January last.

The Governor laid before the board recommendations for an additional number of Justices for the County of Frederick. Whereupon, it is advised, that the same be rejected; there not being a Majority of Justices present when the said recommendations were made.

On recommendation, It is advised that a commission issue appointing Richard Stith Sheriff of Campbell County.

The Governor laid before the board an account of Dabney Minor amounting to forty two pounds twelve shillings and a penny for building a necessary for the use of the Executive boards. Whereupon it is advised that the said Account be referred to the Auditor for settlement and a warrant on the contingent fund for the sum due.

The Governor laid before the board his report of the State of the Magazine Arsenal etc. at the post of the point of Fork. Whereupon it is advised that the Superintendant be directed immediately to engage two Artificers in addition to those now in service who are to be constantly employed in the business of repairing and making stocks, That he enlist fifteen men for three months upon the same terms that the present guard are engaged, whose particular employment it shall be to clean and prepare as expeditiously as possible for the arsenal all the old arms, That he dispose of all the old musket, fusee and riffle barrels which after a careful examination shall appear to him not to be worth repair and that he report to the executive an estimate of the

---

55. "Bazel Brown" in the clerk's index.

expence of putting in compleat repair such as may in his opinion deserve it.

All which matters so advised the Governor orders accordingly.

James Wood
James McClurg
Carter Braxton
Will Heth
Robt. Goode

Tuesday August 4th 1789

Present

The Governor

Mr. Wood	Mr. Braxton
Mr. McClurg	Mr. Heth
	Mr. Goode

The Governor informed the board that in the recess, he issued Commissions appointing John Simmons Sheriff of Southampton County; Andrew Cowan Sheriff and James Gibson Coroner of Russell County: that he issued a Warrant on the Sinking fund in favor of Captain Singleton, the Agent, for four hundred and seventy eight pounds twelve shillings and six pence upon Account; and a Warrant on the contingent fund for twelve shillings to Christopher Tomkins[56] for finding and putting a Lock on the cannon-house. Approved.

The Governor laid before the board a Talk from the Warriors and Chiefs of the Cherokee nation of Indians delivered by Mr. Bennit Ballew accompanied by Nantoacka and Keewocannoh two Chiefs of the said nation. Whereupon it is advised that a letter be written to the President of the United States recommending to his attention the interest of the Cherokee nation, That the Sum of twenty pounds be advanced to Mr. Ballew for the purpose of defraying the expences of himself and his companions traveling from hence to New York:

That an answer be sent to the talk of the Indians expressive of the readiness of Virginia to assist their views and of their inclination to preserve perpetual peace and union with them.

That an address be particularly sent to the Draging Canoe informing him that the Governor has received by the hands of Nantooacka the pipe which he sent him as a token of his friendship to the Virginians which shall be forever preserved in the Council-house, and that he be requested to accept as a mark of the regard of Virginia a Silver medal:

It is farther advised that Captain Coleman be directed to purchase

---

56. "Christopher Tompkins" in the clerk's index.

four good white Shirts, two pair leggins, one to be of Scarlet, the other of blue cloth, a sufficiency of blue cloth for two breach-Clouts, and two black barcelona handkerchiefes to be presented to the two Chiefs who accompany Mr. Ballew.

The Governor laid before the board an account of Mrs. Cuff amounting to sixteen shillings and six pence for dieting and lodging the indians, Also an Account of William Geddy amounting to seventy pounds 4/4. for ironwork done about the Capitol. Whereupon it is advised, that the said Accounts be referred to the Auditor for settlement and Warrants on the Contingent fund. (To be paid)

On recommendation, It is advised that an additional Commission issue appointing Josiah Butt, James Wilson senr., Robert Butt, James Grimes, William Wilson junior and John Hudson gentlemen Justices of the peace for the County of Norfolk.

It appearing that John Cowan, Sheriff of Mercer County, hath refused to give bond and security for the collection of the taxes for the year 1787; It is advised, that a Commission issue appointing Hugh McGary in the room of the said Cowan; and that the Receiver for the District of Kentucky be instructed, to move against the said Cowan as the law directs for his refusal to give bond as aforesaid.

The Governor laid before the board the Claims of sundry Scouts for the County of Mercer. Whereupon it is advised, that the said Claims be rejected for want of the County Lieutenants certificate.

It is advised, that a Warrant issue on the Contingent Fund, to Archibald Denham,[57] for the further sum of seven pounds, upon account as a Collector of Vouchers in support of the Claims of this State against the United States: Also a Warrant, on the same fund, to Armistead Long for ten pounds upon account for the same purpose. (The said warrants to be paid.)

It is advised that a pardon issue to George Quick who was condemned to death by the District Court at Dumfries for horsestealing; he appearing to be a proper object of mercy.

The Governor laid before the board the payroll of Leonard Morris's Company of Montgomery Rangers, for services rendered in the year 1788. Whereupon it is advised that the said payroll be referred to the Auditor for settlement in the usual way.

Augustine Deneuville,[58] a subject of his most Christian Majesty, resident in this commonwealth for the purposes of commerce, having complained that he has been called upon in the County of New Kent to do Militia duty, The Board are of opinion, that the Subjects of all foreign powers in amity with the United States ought to be exempted from being of the Militia of this Commonwealth and from all calls for personal service for the protection or defence thereof; and the Governor is advised to notify the same whenever necessary to the

---

57. "Denholm" in the clerk's index.
58. "Deneuvill" in the clerk's index.

several militia officers, or to give a Certificate of exemption or discharge to any foreigner applying for such certificate.

All which matters so advised, the Governor orders accordingly.

> James Wood
> James McClurg
> Carter Braxton
> Will Heth
> Robt. Goode

Tuesday August 11th 1789

Present

The Governor

Mr. Wood   Mr. Braxton
Mr. McClurg   Mr. Heth
                Mr. Goode

The Governor informed the board that during the recess, he directed to be paid out of the Contingent fund: ten pounds to Col. Wm. Davies upon account to purchase stationary for the use of his office; ten pounds to Robert Porterfield, upon account, as a Collector of Vouchers in support of the Claims of this State against the united States; eight pounds one shilling and seven pence to Wright Southgate for goods furnished the Indians; and two pounds seventeen shillings and six pence to William Cocke for the board of Bennett Ballew and the two indian Chiefs who are on their way to Congress: that he issued a Commission appointing James Steel Sheriff of Augusta, he having been recommended according to law; And that he issued a register for the Ship Dauphin, satisfactory proofs having been produced: Approved.

It is advised that a warrant issue on the Contingent fund for three pounds to William and George Richardson for making a Silver medal for the Dragging Canoe. To be paid.

It is advised that the account of Samuel McDonald for supplies furnished the post at the Point of Fork up to the 1st instant agreeably to contract, amounting to ninety two pounds sixteen shillings and six pence half penny, be referred to the Auditor for settlement in the usual way.

On consideration of the Treasurers statement of monies in the Treasury, It is advised that so much be borrowed from the funds to which the said monies belong, as will discharge the Warrants issued up to this day to Scouts and rangers for services rendered in the year 1788.

It is advised that the Warrant issued the 31st of July 1783 for sixty three pounds fifteen shillings to Thomas Prosser for house rent for storing hemp and flour, as per order of Henrico Court, be put on the aggregate fund.

On recommendations, It is advised that Commissions issue appointing John Watkings and William Cave Coroners, and Robert Johnson Escheator, for the county of Woodford; and Andrew Hynes Sheriff for the county of Nelson: It is also advised that an additional Commission issue appointing John Handly, Will. Worthington, Robert Abell and Will. Harden, gentlemen, Justices of the peace for the said County of Nelson.

On consideration of a letter from Mr. Hillary Moseley[59] requesting a Suspension of an execution against him as security for certain duties, It is advised that the said request be rejected. Mr. Dabney Minor having requested that the Treasurer be directed to pay the warrant granted him on the contingent fund the 28th ultimo for building a necessary for the use of the Executive boards, and the Work having been revalued at the instance of this board and reduced to forty one pounds four shillings and seven pence; It is advised that a warrant issue on the contingent fund to Mr. Minor for the above sum in lieu of the one granted him before; and that the Treasurer be instructed to pay the same.

The Governor laid before the board a letter from Col. Davies desiring the Instructions of the executive as to the mode of conveying the books and papers of his office to new york and asking their authority to carry with him the Journals of the Council for 1781 and those of other boards. Whereupon it is advised that Col. Davies be requested to contract for the carriage of his books and papers by land upon as good terms as can be obtained, and that he be authorized to take with him the Journals of the Council for 1781 and such books belonging to any of the Executive boards as may be necessary to support the claim of this State against the United States, but that he suffer none of those books to be returned unless in the care of some very confidential person in the employment of the State.

All which matters so advised the Governor orders accordingly.

The Governor notified to the board his intention to be absent which is ordered to be entered on the Journal.

James Wood
James McClurg
Robert Goode

---

59. "Hillary Mosely" in the clerk's index.

Tuesday August 18th 1789

Present

The Governor

Mr. Wood   Mr. Jones
Mr. McClurg   Mr. Goode

The Governor informed the board that in the recess he issued a Warrant to Captain Anthony Singleton for One hundred and twenty five pounds one shilling and seven pence upon account as agent of the sinking fund; That he issued a commission appointing James Pendleton Sheriff of Culpeper, he having been recommended according to law. And That he directed Simeon Walton to give bond and Security as Surveyor of Nottoway in the penalty of two thousand pounds. approved.

Mr. Wood informed the board that in the recess of Council and absence of the Governor, he as Lieutenant Governor issued a register for the Schooner Liberty, satisfactory proofs having been made in due form. Approved.

Present Mr. Braxton.

The Governor laid before the board a letter from Col. Davies, Commissioner of Continental Accounts stating that it will be necessary for him to carry on with him one Clerk besides Mr. Dunscombe, that this Clerk in consequence of the greater expence of living at new york asks an addition to his salary, and as he will travel with the waggon which carries the books and papers, he will want a horse, and that it will also be necessary that he rent a room as an office. Whereupon it is advised, that such Clerk as Col. Davies shall carry on with him be allowed twenty pounds in addition to his present salary, that a horse and saddle not to exceed twenty five pounds be purchased for him to ride, which immediately upon his arrival at New York shall be sold for the best price that can be obtained and that Col. Davies be empowered to rent on public account a room proper for his office.

On recommendations, It is advised that Commissions issue appointing John Moore an additional Inspector at Pitts Landing, Guilford and Pungoteague Warehouses in accomack County, and John Bull Coroner of the said County.

It is advised that a warrant issue on the Contingent Fund to Archibald Denholm for the further Sum of five pounds, upon account, as a Collector of Vouchers in support of the Claims of this State against the United States. (To be paid)

It appearing that Priscilla Chowning comes within the requisitions of the pension law; It is advised that She be put on the List of pensioners with an allowance of six pounds per annum from the first of January 1789.

All which matters so advised the Governor orders accordingly.

James Wood
James McClurg
Carter Braxton
Robt. Goode
Jos. Jones

Thursday August 20th 1789

Present

The Governor

Mr. Wood   Mr. Braxton
Mr. Jones   Mr. Goode

The Governor laid before the Board a letter from Colonel Clendinen, Lieutenant of Green Briar County, stating several murders and Robberies, lately committed in his county, and informing the Executive, that he had, notwithstanding their order of the 23d of May, continued in Service, twenty six Rangers with the necessary number of Officers for a compleat company: Whereupon it is advised, that a copy of the Governor's circular letter, of the first of June last, to the different county Lieutenants, of the Western Frontier, be forwarded to Colonel Clendinen, and that he be directed to govern himself, by the instructions therein contained. It is further advised, that copies of the Letters of the 16th of May, and 15th of July, from the President of the United States, be also inclosed to him; And that he be informed, that the Executive cannot authorize the settlement of the Accounts, for the rations and service of more Rangers than were directed by them to be called into Service.

It is advised, that the following commissions issue, viz; appointing Thomas Lewis, Robert Clendinen, Francis Watkins, Charles McClung, Benjamin Strother, William Clendinen, David Robinson, George Alderson, Leonard Morris and James Vanbibber justices of the Peace; and appointing Thomas Lewis Sheriff for the county of Kanawha; and on recommendation appointing John Gay Sheriff for the county of Rockbridge.

It is advised, that the Auditor be directed to issue the following Warrants, viz; To Reuben Slaughter,[60] on Contingent Fund, as Express, from the county Lieutenant of Greenbriar; the usual Warrant to captain John Morton, late a district Commissioner, for his services from the 8th of September 1781, to the 14th of January 1782, and Twenty nine days extra service, at 7/6 per day, agreeably to a certificate of Mr. John Pierce; and to Mr. Andrew Dunscomb, for fifteen pounds, on the Contingent Fund, for the purpose of bearing his Expences to

60. "Reubin Slaughter" in the clerk's index.

New York, as a clerk to the Commissioner, for settling the Account of this State with the United States.

The Governor laid before the Board a letter from Mr. Mayo Carrington, informing him, that he had, agreeable to the former instructions of the Executive, taken into his possession, several negroes, the property of the public, heretofore employed at the Buckingham Furnace. Whereupon it is advised, that Mr. Carrington be desired, after giving sufficient notice, to offer them for sale at Cumberland Court house, on six months credit, for Specie, taking Bond with sufficient security, for the amount of the purchase money.

The Governor laid before the Board a Letter from Colonel William Davies, stating, that he had been informed, by Captain John Morton, late a Commissioner for the District of Prince Edward, that there was still due, and might be collected, from the District, at least £250. specie, provided he was now empowered to collect it. Whereupon it is advised, that Captain Morton be desired to collect any money which may be due on account of Specifics, etc. in the said District and make report thereof to this Board.

The Governor informed the board that in the recess he issued a commission appointing Anderson Scott Sheriff of King and Queen. approved.

All which matters so advised the Governor orders accordingly.

The Governor signified his intention to be absent for a few days, which is ordered to be entered in the Journal.

James Wood
Jos. Jones
Carter Braxton
Robt. Goode

Tuesday August 25th 1789

Present

The Governor

Mr. Wood	Mr. Braxton
Mr. McClurg	Mr. Goode

General Wood informed the Board, that in the recess thereof, and in the absence of the Governor, he had on the 24th Instant, as Lieutenant Governor, on recommendation, issued a commission appointing Henry Lee Surveyor for the county of Mason, directing him to give Bond, conditioned for the faithful discharge of the duties of his office, in the sum of two thousand pounds; and that he had ordered a Warrant on the Contingent Fund, for fifteen pounds to William Cocke, on account for transporting the Books and Papers for supporting the claim of this State against the United States, to the seat of the Foederal Government. (To be paid.) Of which several matters the Board approve.

The Governor laid before the Board a Letter from Colonel Davies, requesting an advance of money for himself and Clerks, in part of their salaries to defray their expences in going to New York. Whereupon it is advised, that Mr. Burnley be allowed ten pounds to defray his expences, in attending the Books and Papers to the seat of the Foederal Government, and that Twenty five pounds be advanced him on account of his salary: That Mr. Davies be advanced seventy five pounds, on account of his Salary, and Mr. Dunscomb fifty pounds on the same account. It is further advised, that Colonel Davies and his Clerks, be allowed to draw quarterly, on the Governor, for the amount of their salaries, and that they be assured, whatever sums may be respectively due them, shall be punctually paid.

On consideration of the Solicitor's Report upon the Claim of Mr. Henry Banks for Hunter Banks and Company, to him referred, It is advised, that the said Claim be rejected.

The Governor laid before the Board a statement of, and the Bonds taken for, the sales of the Public Boats Liberty and Patriot and the whale Boat, Searchers Boat etc. at Norfolk. Whereupon it is advised, that the said Bonds be lodged with the solicitor for collection as they may become due.

On Recommendation it is advised, that a Commission issue, appointing Abraham Bird, Sheriff for the county of Shenandoah.

The Governor laid before the Board an account of Captain Richard Taylor, for superintending the sales of the public boats Liberty and Patriot and the Whale Boat, Searchers boat etc. at Norfolk. Whereupon it is advised, that the said Account be referred to the Auditor for settlement; and that a warrant issue on the Contingent fund for the sum which may appear to be due. (To be paid.)

It is advised, that Warrants issue to John Roney and Michael Ford, for fifteen pounds one shilling each, being the Amount of Salary due them, to the 24th Instant, as Clerks to the Commissioner, for settling the account of this State with the United States; and to John Lyne, for Eleven Pounds, on the Contingent Fund, for the rent of the Auditor's and Solicitor's offices, from the first of April until the twenty second of June 1789. (To be paid.)

It is advised, that a Register issue for the sloop Eliza, satisfactory proof having been made in due form.

The Governor laid before the Board a Letter from Colonel William Heth, resigning his seat at this Board as a member of the Council of State. Whereupon it is advised, that the said Letter be transmitted to the General Assembly.

All which matters, so advised, the Governor orders accordingly.

> James Wood
> James McClurg
> Carter Braxton
> Robt. Goode

Tuesday September 1st 1789

Present

The Governor

Mr. Wood   Mr. Braxton
Mr. McClurg   Mr. Goode

The Governor informed the board that during the recess, he issued commissions appointing William Vaughan Sheriff and John Jones Coroner of the county of Brunswick and Michael Thomas Sheriff of Albemarle, that he referred to the Auditor for settlement in the usual way the claim of Thos. Piety for sixty one days services as a Scout in Nelson County; and directed Warrants to issue on the contingent fund to William Robenson[61] for four pounds for services rendered in Col. Davies's office, and to William Graves for twenty four pounds five shillings for the hire of hands and expences of the Searchers boat at Norfolk previous to the sale of the said boat: approved.

On recommendations, It is advised that commissions issue appointing Robert Harvie Sheriff of Botetourt, and John Lucas Sheriff of Greenesville.

The Governor laid before the board an Account of Doctor Foushee amounting to twenty three pounds twelve shillings for attendance on criminals in the public Jail previous to the establishment of the District Courts, and for three quarters services in examining pensioners. Whereupon it is advised that the said account be referred to the Auditor for settlement and a warrant on the Contingent fund for ths sum due. (To be paid.)

For reasons appearing to the board, It is advised, that the Fine of twenty pounds imposed at the last October General Court on William English for a misdemeanour be remitted, and that the said English be forthwith discharged from prison.

It is advised that the claim of Adam Miller as a scout of Nelson County from the 8th of March to the 9th of April 1789, be referred to the Auditor for settlement and a Warrant expressing for services rendered in the year 1789.

All which matters so advised, the Governor orders accordingly.

James Wood
James McClurg
Carter Braxton
Robt. Goode

---

61. "Robinson" in the clerk's index.

Tuesday September 8th 1789

Present

The Governor

Mr. Wood	Mr. Braxton
Mr. McClurg	Mr. Goode

The Governor informed the board that during the recess, he authorized Captain Singleton the Agent of the Sinking fund, to lend Mr. Richard Hartshorne One thousand pounds on the terms mentioned in the said Agents Letter of the 4th instant; that he wrote to Mr. George Reid and the Executors of Mr. Wm. G. Munford assuring them that Mr. John S. Langhornes[62] descriptive receipts of any Vouchers they may furnish him with in support of the claims of this State against the United States, shall answer every purpose that the originals would in the settlement of their accounts with the Auditors of public accounts; that he directed to be paid out of the Contingent fund ten pounds to Mr. Langhorne upon account as a Collector of vouchers, Seven pounds ten shillings to Mr. Richard Adams for a quarters rent of the Chancery Office, One pound ten shillings to Mr. Edward Voss for whitewashing the Governors house, that he referred to the auditor for settlement to be paid out of the Contingent Fund the Accounts of Clotsworthy Stephenson amounting to forty nine pounds sixteen and eight pence for work done to the Treasury Office and forty four pounds sixteen and six pence for work done to the Auditors office as certified by the Treasurer and Auditor and reported reasonable by Samuel Dobie; that he referred to the auditor for settlement in the usual way the claims of Evan Thompson, Hugh Gibbs and Daniel Ashby for services as Scouts for Mercer county in the year 1788 and that he issued Commissions appointing William Short Sheriff and William Todd Coroner of Pittsylvania; they having been recommended according to law. Approved.

It is advised that the application for placing on the aggregate fund, a warrant issued the first of February 1788 to Bland Ballard for two hundred and sixty five pounds nine shillings and eight pence for services as Quarter Master and Commissary of purchases in the Illinois Department, be rejected.

On recommendations, It is advised that commissions issue appointing David Gass Sheriff of Madison, and John Cornick Sheriff of Princess Anne County.

It is advised that Thomas Brown be continued on the List of pensioners with an allowance of twelve pounds per annum from January 1786; and that twenty shillings per annum be allowed Mary Hogan in addition to her former pension from January last.

---

62. "Wm. Langhorne" in the clerk's index.

The Governor laid before the board the Claims of Robt. H. Waller Clerk of York Court, and George Dunlevy Deputy Clerk of James City Court, amounting to twenty shillings each, for copies of Vouchers furnished Mr. Langhorne in support of the Claims of this state against the United States. Whereupon it is advised that the said Claims be paid out of the Contingent fund.

The Governor informed the board that Mr. Harry Heth, the Agent for selling the public tobacco, had been offered fourteen shillings specie per hundred for the lower Rappahannock and Potowmack tobaccoes, and wished to have the opinion of the board thereon. Whereupon it is advised, that the said Agent be authorized to accept the offer.

It is advised that a warrant issue on the Contingent fund to Archibald Blair for twenty five pounds for four months Salary as Keeper of the public Seal.

On application, It is advised that a commission issue appointing Joseph Cabell, the Elder, William Perkins, John Moseley, Thomas Landers, Robert Moseley, Josias Jones, Clough Shelton, Joseph Cabell the younger and Thomas Anderson, or any three of them, Gentlemen, to take Deposition, in the County of Buckingham touching the Destruction of the records of the said County, pursuant to the Act in that case made.

All which matters so advised the Governor orders accordingly.

The Governor notified to the board his intention to be absent which is ordered to be entered on the Journal.

> James Wood
> James McClurg
> Carter Braxton
> Robt. Goode

Saturday September 26th 1789

Present

The Governor

Mr. Wood	Mr. Braxton
Mr. McClurg	Mr. Goode

Mr. Wood informed the board that during the recess and in the absence of the Governor, He, as Lieutenant Governor, issued an additional Commission appointing Francis Muir, Bullar Claiborne, John Baird junr., Henry Spain, Elisha King and Winfield Mason gentlemen Justices of the peace for the County of Dinwiddie; they having been recommended according to law; Also commissions, on recommendations, appointing Robert Throckmorton Sheriff of Berkley, Cornelius Westfall Sheriff of Randolph, Peter Thweat and Henry Thweat Inspectors and George Pegram jr. additional Inspector at Robert Bollings warehouse in Dinwiddie County; That he directed to be paid out of the contingent Fund, To William Eskridge ten pounds upon account as a collector of Vouchers in support of the Claims of this State against the United States, to the Solicitor Fifty pounds on Account for sending out Executions etc. against delinquents; That he referred to the Auditor for settlement in the usual way the claim of Levy Morgan for services rendered as a Scout in Monongalia from the 25th April to the 1st of July 1789. Also the following Claims for rations furnished the rangers of Randolph County in 1788, to wit, James Westfall for 549 rations, John Hadden 366, John Johnson 183, and James Bodkin 183, and the Claims of John Jackson and Charles Parsons for sixty one days services each as Scouts for the said County in 1788. And that with the concurrence of such members as were in Town, he granted pardons to John Woodram and Hugh Shavers, two culprits condemned to death at the last District Court held in Richmond, they having been recommended as proper objects of mercy. Approved.

The Governor informed the board that after his return to Richmond he consulted with Mr. Wood, Mr. McClurg, and Mr. Goode, the only members present, concerning the quantity and quality of the public tobacco on hand, and, with their concurrence directed the agent immediately to advertize the said tobacco for sale at public auction in the City of Richmond on the 19th of October, one half the purchase money to be paid down, the other half on the 19th January 1790, taking the usual Deposits and security for payment; That with the concurrence of the same members, and on recommendations, he issued Commissions appointing Edmund Read Sheriff of Charlotte, and John Napier coroner of Fluvanna, continued on the pension List Martin Murphey with his usual allowance eighteen pounds per annum from January 1789, Appointed David Mead Randolph Notary Public for the District of Bermuda hundred and city point, Directed to be paid out of the contingent Fund ten pounds twelve shillings and six pence to Mr. Charles Hay for the purchase of parchment for the use of the General Assembly, Referred to the Auditor for settlement the account of James M. McRea, late Searcher at Alexandria, amounting to twenty pounds eleven shillings and five pence, Directed the Treasurer to borrow money for the payment of all warrants which have been issued prior to the 24th instant to Scouts and Rangers for services rendered in the year 1788, And that he directed the Solicitor to return to Mr. Lindsay, late naval officer, the Bonds which Mr. Bedinger his Deputy lodged with him through mistake, Mr. Lindsay conceiving that he was intitled to the collection of the said bonds, But the Solicitor had some objections to the delivering the bonds to Mr. Lindsay, and requested that the matter might be reconsidered. Approved except as to the order concerning the bonds.

The board took under consideration the Solicitors objections to returning certain bonds to Mr. Lindsay and the first Sect. of the Act of

Assembly intituled "An Act concerning certain public establishments." Whereupon the board are of opinion that the Naval Officers are not authorized, after the first of August last to retain in their possession or to collect the bonds taken at their offices under the laws of this state. But as it is a point of law, the Governor is advised to take the Opinion of the Attorney General, and act conformably thereto.

The Governor laid before the board the Claims of the following persons certified by the last District Court held in Richmond to wit, William Rose for £38.11.0 for maintenance of criminals from 4th April to 31st August last, Joseph Harrell and Archd. Rose for £1.4.0 for guarding criminals, William Rose £1.0.0 for taking Irons off criminals, William Carter for £2.12.9. for medicine furnished Criminals, and John Roper for £10.0 for wood furnished for the use of the public Jail. Whereupon, It is advised that the said Claims be referred to the Auditor for settlement and Warrants on the Contingent fund.

It is advised that a warrant issue to General Daniel Morgan on the aggregate Fund, for the sum of Sixty three pounds ten shillings and a penny voted him by the general assembly the 21st and 23d November 1782; It appearing from the Auditors Certificate that no warrant has heretofore issued for the same.

It is advised that a warrant issue on the Contingent Fund for five pounds sixteen shillings and eight pence to Richard Adams per rent of the Chancery Office up to the 4th instant (to be paid). That the claim of Thomas Machens late Master Builder at the public Shipyard be referred to the Auditor for settlement and a warrant on the aggregate Fund for the sum due: and That the claim of Alexander McRoberts and David Lambert amounting to one pound sixteen shillings for laying off the additional prison bounds as Directed by the last District Court held in Richmond be referred to the Auditor for settlement and a warrant on the Contingent fund for the Sum due.

On recommendation, it is advised that Commissions issue appointing James Withers and William Wallace Inspectors and Nathaniel Fox additional Inspector at Dixons Warehouse in Stafford County.

All which matters so advised, the Governor orders accordingly.

James Wood
James McClurg
Carter Braxton
Robt. Goode

Thursday October 15th 1789

Present

The Governor

| Mr. Wood | Mr. Jones |
| Mr. McClurg | Mr. Braxton |

Mr. Goode

The Governor informed the board that in the recess he directed to be paid out of the Contingent fund, sixty five pounds to Augustine Davis for parchment furnished the Land office, and five pounds twelve shillings and two pence for postage of public Letters to the 6th instant; to William Cocke eight pounds sixteen shillings and eight pence balance due him for carrying the books and papers of Col. Davies office to New York; to Jane West, three pounds, for three months pay as Nurse to Catherine Crulls child; and to the Solicitor fifty pounds upon account: That he referred to the Auditor for settlement in the usual way the Accounts of Major Langham amounting to one hundred and twenty nine pounds five and eleven pence, the pay of the Superintendant and Artificers at the point of Fork for the last quarter, and eighty nine pounds twelve shillings the pay of the Guards for the same time, and directed a Warrant to Maj. Langham for seventy pounds upon account to lay in forage for the post: That on recommendations he issued commissions appointing William Farrow and Howson Hooe Junr. Inspectors and Matthew Harrison Senr. additional inspector at Dumfries warehouses; William Hewit Sheriff of Stafford; John Moseley Sheriff and Henry Bell coroner of Buckingham; and an additional commission appointing Cary Selden, Joseph Meridith, Robert Brough, George Wray junr., Charles Jennings, Michael King and William Ap Thomas Parsons justices of the peace for Elizabeth City County; That he examined and certified for payment the auditors account per his last quarters salary; That he directed the Solicitor to allow credit on the executions against John Johns as Sheriff of Buckingham for the revenue and certificate taxes of the Buckingham Furnace; That he granted exemptions from militia duty to [. . .][63] Defargue and Charles Olone subjects of his most Christian Majesty; And that with the concurrence of Mr. Jones, Mr. Braxton and Mr. Goode, he directed to be continued on the pension List Peter Parchment and Mary Ogle with twelve pounds per annum each from January 1786, and granted a warrant to Samuel McDonald for one hundred pounds upon account as Contractor for supplying the Post at the Point of Fork with provisions. Approved.

On consideration of the case of Martin Pearce, It is advised that the sum of six pounds six shillings established by the Judgment of

---

63. Blank in the journal.

Cumberland County court as the treble tax of the said Pearce *for not rendering an account of his riding chair with his List of taxable property to the Commissioners*, be remitted.

The Governor laid before the board the account of Samuel Swann[64] for work done about the house occupied by the Governor, and for repairing a press belonging to the Council office, amounting to eight pounds three shillings and six pence. Also the account of Aug. Davis amounting to six pounds sixteen shillings for printing work done by order of the executive. Whereupon it is advised that the said Accounts be referred to the Auditor for settlement and warrants on the Contingent fund for the sums due (to be paid).

It is advised that a warrant issue on the Contingent Fund to Mr. Charles Russell for twenty pounds as full compensation for his trouble and expences in furnishing vouchers in support of the Claims of this State against the United States. (to be paid) It is also advised that the warrant issued the 20 September 1782, to Ulrick Marks for one hundred and sixty seven pounds for a horse and accoutrements lost in charging the enemy in the year 1781, per resolution of Assembly, be put on the aggregate fund.[65]

On recommendations It is advised that commissions issue appointing Thomas Maccubbin Sheriff of Hampshire; Thomas Bronaugh Sheriff of Fauquier, and Edmund King Coroner of Halifax County, and that an additional commission issue appointing Edmund Drumgoold, Richard Fletcher, Joseph Mason, Sack Pennington, Daniel Huff and Theophilus Harrison gentlemen Justices of the peace for the County of Brunswick.

On consideration of the Claim of John Crow for the maintenance of nine Indian prisoners and for barrack hire, It is advised that the same be rejected.

It is advised that the claim of Robert Poage for 96 Days service as a Scout of Mercer County in 1788, be referred to the Auditor for settlement in the usual way, provided the same has not been already settled.

The Governor laid before the board a recommendation of twelve persons to be added to the commission of the peace for Halifax County. Whereupon it is advised that the same be rejected; there appearing to be a sufficient number already in commission.

On consideration of a letter from Mr. Griffin Stith concerning the Lands of the Gingaskin Indians on the Eastern shore; It is advised that the said letter be laid before the general assembly; and that Mr. Stith be requested to pursue all legal measures to prevent encroachments on the Lands of the said Indians, the expences of which shall be defrayed by the public.

---

64. "Swan" in the clerk's index.
65. Beside this paragraph is the marginal note: "N.B. General Wood issued a warrant for this money to Mr. Russell Deceased 5th. 89. (See Dec. 9)."

The Governor laid before the board a letter from the Secretary of the Treasury, of the 26th of September, inclosing resolutions of the house of representatives of the 21st of same month directing him to apply to the Supreme executives of the several States for Statements of their public Debts etc. Whereupon it is advised that the Governor be requested to furnish the Secretary with the amount of such loan office certificates and other public Securities of the United States as may be in the Treasury of this State, and to inform him that the Statement he requires cannot be compleatly furnished until the Legislature shall provide funds in lieu of the impost in discharge of the interest of the public debts.

On consideration of a letter from the Secretary at War of the 6th instant informing that the Governor of the Western Territory hath instructions to call forth the militia of the nearest counties for the protection of the frontier Inhabitants from the hostile incursions of the Indians, limiting the number to a thousand men to be called from Virginia etc. It is advised that the Governor of the Western Territory be furnished with the best state of the militia of the western counties in order to facilitate the calling forth the said militia.

All which matters so advised, the Governor orders accordingly.

> James Wood
> James McClurg
> Jos. Jones
> Carter Braxton
> Robt. Goode

Saturday October 17th 1789

Present

The Governor

Mr. Wood	Mr. Jones
Mr. McClurg	Mr. Braxton
	Mr. Goode

The board conceiving that a longer credit would be the means of the public tobacco's selling to greater advantage, Advise that the Agent be directed to allow credit 'til the 20th of December for one half of the sales, and for the other half until the 20th of February.

The Governor laid before the board the claims of Jacob Richards, Peter Cornelius, Job Hughes, Richard Hall, John Brown and John Radliff as Scouts of Harrison County for services rendered in 1789. Whereupon it is advised that the said Claims be referred to the auditor for settlement in the usual way.

On recommendation, It is advised that a commission issue appointing John Powers Sheriff of Harrison County.

It is advised that the Warrant issued the 27th January 1783, to Walter King Cole for fifty pounds, in part of Walter Kings estate escheated and sold agreeable to law, be put on the aggregate fund.

Piomingo or mountain leader a Chief of the Chickasaw nation of Indians being on his way to new york to lay before the President some matters of dispute between the South Carolinians and his nation and to request a supply of ammunition to defend themselves against their enemies, It is advised that it be recommended to him to return to his nation from hence, that he be furnished with 500 lbs. of good powder together with the old fixed ammunition and Keg of damaged powder at the point of Fork and 1500 lbs. lead, and that the expences of himself and other indians, while in Richmond, be paid by the public.

It is advised that the Clerk provide for the use of the Council Chamber a floor Cloth and Table Cloth.

All which matters so advised, the Governor orders accordingly.

> James Wood
> James McClurg
> Jos. Jones
> Carter Braxton
> Robt. Goode

Monday October 19th 1789

Present

The Governor

Mr. Wood	Mr. Jones
Mr. McClurg	Mr. Braxton
	Mr. Goode

The Governor laid before the board a letter he had prepared stating sundry matters for the consideration of the General Assembly, which Letter was read approved and ordered to be registered.

It is advised that the account of Mr. Augustine Seaton[66] amounting to nine pounds seven shillings and eleven pence half penny for dieting the Chickasaw indians, be referred to the Auditor for settlement and a warrant on the Contingent fund for the sum due. To be paid.

On recommendation, It is advised that a commission issue appointing Isaac Younghusband Gentleman Sheriff of Henrico County.

All which matters so advised the Governor orders accordingly.

> James Wood
> James McClurg
> Jos. Jones
> Carter Braxton
> Robt. Goode

66. "Austin Seaton" in the clerk's index.

Tuesday October 20th 1789

Present

The Governor

Mr. Wood   Mr. Jones
Mr. McClurg   Mr. Braxton
            Mr. Goode

On recommendation, it is advised that a commission issue appointing William Fleet gentleman Coroner of King and Queen County.

A letter was written to the General Assembly inclosing to them a remonstrance of sundry Inhabitants of the District of Kentucky, who were also Members of the Convention for the District, against the discharge of the Scouts and rangers, together with an account of the Depredations committed in the District of Kentucky by the Indians since the 1st Day of May 1789.

The Governor laid before the board a payroll of Ensign Millers company of Rangers for Nelson County employed in 1789, and the Claims of Saml. McGrady, Daniel Rhodes and Michael Rely as Scouts for the said county, for services rendered in 1788: Also the claims of James Stuart and Lewis Field as Scouts for Jefferson County, for services rendered in 1789; And the Claims of John Lime and William Bruce as Scouts for Bourbon county for services rendered in 1789. Whereupon it is advised that the same be referred to the Auditor for settlement in the usual way.

On recommendations It is advised that Commissions issue appointing John Horsley and William Bibb Inspectors, and William Warwick additional Inspector at Swan Creek warehouse in Amherst County, and Alven Mountjoy Sheriff of Bourbon County.

All which matters so advised, the Governor orders accordingly.

James Wood
James McClurg
Jos. Jones
Carter Braxton

Wednesday October 21st 1789

Present

The Governor

Mr. Wood   Mr. Jones
Mr. McClurg   Mr. Braxton
            Mr. Goode

The Governor laid before the board the Claim of James Mitchell as a scout for Ohio County, for services rendered in 1789; and the Claim of Asa Searcy as a Scout for Madison County for services rendered in

1788: Whereupon it is advised, that the said Claims be referred to the auditor for settlement in the usual way.

On consideration of a letter from the County Lieutenant of Ohio, It is advised that the account of Robert McClure and Company be referred to the Auditor for examination, so far as relates to the balance of forty nine pounds seven shillings for supplies furnished the Ohio rangers agreeably to contract, and if the said balance be just, that he grant the usual warrant therefor.

On consideration of a letter from the County Lieutenant of Bourbon expressing doubts whether he has authority to act under the Invasion and Insurrection laws of this State, as Congress have passed no act concerning the militia; It is the Opinion of this board that all Laws concerning the militia are in force until Congress shall pass laws on the subject.

It is advised that the Treasurer be instructed to borrow money according to law to pay off all warrants issued to Scouts and rangers for services rendered in 1788 up to this day.

On recommendation It is advised that a commission issue appointing James Coleman Sheriff of Loudon County.

All which matters so advised, the Governor orders accordingly.

> James Wood
> James McClurg
> Jos. Jones
> Carter Braxton
> Robt. Goode

Thursday October 22d 1789

Present

The Governor

Mr. Wood	Mr. Jones
Mr. McClurg	Mr. Braxton
Mr. Goode	

It is advised that the Payroll of Lieutenant Dudley Evans's company of Monongalia Rangers for services from the 1st of June 1789 to the last of the same month, and the Claims of Thomas Pindell and John Davis for 630 rations furnished the said rangers, be referred to the Auditor for settlement.in the usual way.

It is advised that John McKenny be continued on the pension list with his former allowance of fifteen pounds per annum, from January last.

On recommendations It is advised that commissions issue appointing Eli Cleveland Sheriff of Fayette County; and William Tunstal Sheriff of Henry county: and that an additional commission issue appointing Walter Beall, Michael Campbell and Thomas Monton Gentlemen Justices of the peace for Nelson County.

To prevent impositions in the settlement of the Claims of Scouts and rangers It is advised that Captain Coleman be directed to call on the auditor for a state of all payrolls and accounts of Scouts and rangers already settled for services rendered in the present year, that he examine whether the same are conformable to the instructions of the executive authorising the employment of Scouts and rangers, and report to this board; And that, previous to any order being given for settlement of such claims hereafter, He first examine the same and report whether the number of men and quantity of rations are agreeable to the Instructions of the Executive.

All which matters so advised, the Governor orders accordingly.

> James Wood
> James McClurg
> Jos. Jones
> Carter Braxton
> Robt. Goode

Monday October 26th 1789

Present

The Governor

Mr. Wood	Mr. Jones
Mr. McClurg	Mr. Braxton

Mr. Goode

The Governor informed the board that in the recess, he directed to be paid out of the Contingent Fund, to Captain Thomas Parker, the further Sum of twenty five pounds twelve shillings 4 3/4 upon account as a Collector of vouchers; it appearing that he had already expended fifteen pounds twelve shillings and 4 3/4 in the business; and to Mr. William Price the further Sum of twenty pounds upon account, as a collector of Vouchers: And that on recommendations he issued commissions appointing George Williamson Sheriff of Powhatan: Samuel Ritchie Sheriff of Russell County in the room of [. . .][67] Cowan who is a member of the Assembly; and Randal Fouqua, Inspector of tobacco at Boyds warehouses in Prince George, and administered the oath of office to the said Randal. Approved.

On recommendations, It is advised that a commission issue appointing Samuel Goode Sheriff of Mecklenburg; and an additional Commission appointing John Montgomery a Justice of the peace for the County of Lincoln.

On consideration of a memorial of divers inhabitants of the district of Kentucky praying that a sufficient number of Militia may be ordered

---

67. Blank in the journal.

out for the protection of the great bone Lick; It is advised that the same be rejected; the executive having no authority on the subject.

The Governor laid before the board an account of Cohen and Isaacs amounting to twenty seven pounds ten shillings for rent of the General Court Office from the 20th of October 1788 to the 20th of September 1789, as certified by the Clerk of the said Court: also an Account amounting to forty one pounds one shilling and five pence half penny for sundry expences of the public Treasury since the 24th of November last as certified by the Treasurer. Whereupon it is advised that the said accounts be referred to the Auditor for examination and Warrants on the contingent fund for the sums due (to be paid).

It is advised that the Treasurer be desired to borrow money for the payment of all Warrants issued up to this day for the expences of Scouts and rangers for services rendered in 1788.

All which matters so advised, the Governor orders accordingly.

> James Wood
> James McClurg
> Jos. Jones
> Carter Braxton
> Robt. Goode

Tuesday October 27th 1789

Present

The Governor

Mr. Wood   Mr. Jones
Mr. McClurg   Mr. Braxton
                    Mr. Goode

It is advised that a warrant issue on the Contingent fund to Messrs. Boyd and Ker for three pounds twelve shillings for eight yards of Cloth for the table of the Council chamber. (To be paid)

The Governor laid before the board the account of Jacob Westfall[68] amounting to five pounds nine shillings for conveying the proportion of arms and ammunition allotted for the county of Randolph from Job Weltons in hardy county to the said county of Randolph. Whereupon it is advised that the said account be referred to the Auditor for settlement and a warrant on the contingent fund for the sum due. (To be paid)

It is advised that the claim of John Ballard for services as Deputy Commissioner of provisions under John Brown and John Pierce from 1st of August 1781 to the 14th of January 1782, be referred to the

---

68. "Jacob Westfal" in the clerk's index.

Auditor for settlement in the usual way, provided the said Ballard has fully settled his account, and has not been paid before.

On consideration of the petition of Nathan Ryan praying for duplicates of two Warrants for twenty four pounds each for pensions of James Powell Edmondson, which he had lost, It is advised that the same be rejected, the Executive having no authority to grant duplicate warrants.

It is advised that the pension of James Davenport be encreased to twelve pounds per annum from January last.

The Governor laid before the board a resolution of the General Assembly of the 23d and 26th of October 1789, desiring the executive to furnish Piomingo a chief of the Chickasaw nation of Indians with such quantity of gun powder not exceeding two thousand weight and lead proportioned thereto, and to furnish such of the said nation of Indians as are in this City with such articles as may be proper for them; and also to make a suitable compensation to the two white men who accompany the said Indians. Whereupon it is advised, that orders be given to the Superintendant of the post at the point of Fork to deliver to the said Chief 2000 lbs. of the best powder, and to Mr. McGavack to deliver to him 6000 lbs. of the public lead in his possession, in lieu of the powder and lead ordered the 17th instant; that the Superintendant employ the necessary number of waggons to convey the said powder and lead to the mouth of Redstone creek by as early a day as possible; that he furnish each of the three white men who attend the Indians with such a gun as they may choose out of the repaired muskets or fusils; that General Wood be requested to take measures that each of the Indians be furnished with a good rifle on their way to redstone. It is further advised that the sum of nine pounds be given to Piomingo, six pounds to the other principal chief and three pounds to each of the other indians to be laid out by Mr. Coleman in such articles as they shall respectively choose, And that the sum of twenty pounds be given to Mr. Fry the Interpreter, fifteen pounds to Mr. King and six pounds to the other white man who attends the said chiefs, as a compensation for their services. It is likewise advised that the contractor at the Point of Fork be desired to furnish the Indians and white men with what rations they may want for their journey.

On consideration of a letter from Col. Wm. Davies, of the 16th instant, It is advised that a letter be written to Mr. Yarbrough to know whether he means to proceed in the business of collecting vouchers in support of the Claims of this State against the United States; and, if not, that he be desired to deliver his Instructions to Major Peter Williams, with a letter from the Governor requesting him to undertake the business: It is also advised that Col. Davies be written to for further information relative to the mileage claimed by the Easte[r]n militia.

All which matters so advised the Governor orders accordingly.

James Wood
James McClurg
Jos. Jones
Carter Braxton
Robt. Goode

Wednesday October 28th 1789

Present

The Governor

Mr. Wood   Mr. Jones
Mr. McClurg   Mr. Braxton

The Governor laid before the board an account of Bazzell Fry and Robert King amounting to thirty pounds nine shillings for cash advanced to, and sundry expences of the Indians. Whereupon it is advised that the said account be referred to the Auditor for settlement and a warrant on the Contingent fund for so much thereof as shall appear to be due from satisfactory vouchers. To be paid.

It is advised that William Moore be continued on the pension list with an additional allowance of three pounds per annum from January 1789.

All which matters so advised the Governor orders accordingly.

James Wood
James McClurg
Jos. Jones
Carter Braxton

Thursday October 29th 1789

Present

The Governor

Mr. Wood   Mr. Jones
Mr. McClurg   Mr. Goode

It is advised that a letter be written to Mr. Thomas Brown at Redstone, requesting him to take measures for facilitating the passage of the Chickasaw Indians and their baggage down the river; and assuring him that the public will defray all expences not exceeding twenty pounds.

It appearing that Messrs. Fry and King have neglected to take the proper vouchers for the monies advanced by them on account of the Indians; It is advised that the Auditor be desired to accept such other evidence as shall be satisfactory to him in support of their Claim; but, if no such evidence can be adduced, that he then grant a warrant for twenty pounds in lieu of all expences incurred by the Claimants.

In pursuance of a resolution of the general Assembly of the 26th and 28th instant, It is advised that the Auditor be directed to examine and settle the account of William Morris as Superintendant of the public Shipyard at Cumberland, according to the scale of depreciation, and grant a Warrant on the aggregate fund for what shall appear due; he having produced to the board sufficient proof of the propriety of his claim.

In pursuance of an Act of the general Assembly 'to regulate the inspection of flour and bread' It is advised that a Commission issue appointing Samuel Wiseagar an Inspector of flour and bread at Manchester, the Court of Chesterfield County having failed to nominate and appoint according to law.

On recommendation It is advised that an additional commission issue appointing John Archer, Joshua Chaffin, John Finney, Francis Anderson jun., Efford Bentley, William Samuel Peachey and David Meade gentlemen Justices of the peace for Amelia County.

All which matters so advised the Governor orders accordingly.

Mr. Cyrus Griffin appeared and produced a certificate from Turner Southall (a Justice of the peace for Henrico County) of his having qualified as a member of this board.

> James Wood
> James McClurg
> Jos. Jones
> Robt. Goode

Saturday October 31st 1789

Present

The Governor

| Mr. Wood | Mr. Jones |
| Mr. McClurg | Mr. Goode |

Mr. Griffin

It is advised that the account of William Cocke for dieting the Chickasaw Indians be referred to the Auditor for Settlement and a warrant on the Contingent fund for the Sum due. (To be paid)

On consideration of a petition of sundry Inhabitants of the counties of Prince William, Stafford, Fauquier and Culpeper in favour of John Chancillor late inspector of tobacco at Dumfries, It is advised that the same be laid before the General Assembly.

For reasons appearing to the board, It is advised that a pardon issue to John Fowler alias John Anderson who was attainted of felony in December 1785, and pardoned the January following on condition of his performing bodily labour for five years.

On recommendation, It is advised that a commission issue appointing James Ball Sheriff of Lancaster.

All which matters so advised, the Governor orders accordingly.

James Wood
James McClurg
Joseph Jones
Robt. Goode

Monday November 2d 1789

Present

The Governor

| Mr. Wood | Mr. Braxton |
| Mr. Jones | Mr. Goode |

On consideration of a letter from the Secretary at War, of the 19th ultimo, It is advised that the Auditor be instructed to make out an exact List, agreeably to the form forwarded by the Secretary, of all the military Invalids to whom pensions have been granted and paid by the State of Virginia in pursuance of the resolves of the late Congress of the United States: and a Return of the Officers' Widows or orphans who have received from this State the seven years half pay stipulated by the resolve of Congress of the 24th of August 1780, stating the rank and time of the officers death, the amount of the annual pension paid to the Widows or orphans, and the years for which it has been paid. It is further advised that Capt. Coleman furnish the Auditor with the places of residence of the Invalid pensioners as far as can be ascertained from his office.

It is advised that Warrants issue on the Contingent fund to William McCraw for twenty pounds as a compensation for his services in furnishing vouchers in support of the Claims of this State against the United States; to William Clayton for one pound one shilling for sundries furnished the Chickasaw Indians on their way to Richmond; and to Archibald Blair, Clerk of the Council, for twelve pounds, upon Account, to purchase Stationary for the use of this office. to be paid.

The Governor laid before the board an account of William Cook amounting to two pounds two shillings for 21 days pay as a seaman on board the public boats, he having been left out of the payrolls as certified by Lieutenant Barron. Whereupon it is advised that the said account be referred to the Auditor for settlement in the usual way, provided the said Cook hath not been included in the payrolls.

It is advised that Robert Williams be continued on the pension List with his former allowance fifteen pounds per annum from January last.

On consideration of the cases of Thomas Anderson, Benjamin

Burton Hope and Zack Pullar It is advised that the Fines imposed on them by the Courts martial of Louisa County be remitted.

The Governor laid before the board a report of the committee of Council appointed to examine into the State of the Solicitors office. Whereupon it is advised that a copy of the said report be transmitted to the general Assembly, And that the Solicitor do in no case admit the credits for drawbacks endorsed upon the back of the Duty bonds by the naval officers, but where the 60th section of the Act to amend the several Acts of Assembly concerning naval officers and the collection of Duties has been fully complied with, unless the Attorney General shall declare it to be his opinion that such endorsations are sufficient to entitle the Claimants to such credits. It is further advised that the Solicitor do (agreeably to the act concerning certain public establishments) immediately cause all the books and papers belonging to the different naval officers, Collectors and Searchers to be brought to his office and there duly preserved.

It appearing that the buildings appointed for holding the Court of the County of Fauquier are in so ruinous a condition as to be unfit for the purpose to which they were appropriated, It is advised that a proclamation issue directing that the Courts for the said County be hereafter holden in the house of Thomas Maddux in the said County until the said buildings shall be rebuilt.

All which matters so advised, the Governor orders accordingly.

James Wood
Jos. Jones
Carter Braxton
Robt. Goode

Saturday November 7th 1789

Present

The Governor

Mr. Wood   Mr. Braxton
Mr. Jones   Mr. Goode

The Governor informed the Board that in the recess he directed to be paid out of the contingent fund, to Captain Langham eighty pounds upon account to defray expences of transporting powder and lead to redstone for the Chickasaw Indians: and to Mayo Carrington twenty pounds upon account as a Collector of Vouchers: that he issued commissions appointing Richard Bagby Inspector in the room of George Stephens deceased and Thomas Bagby additional Inspector at Mantipike and Fraziers warehouses in King and Queen and King William: and that, on consideration of the complaint of Mr. Robert Tare who thought himself intitled to a remission of Interest on his bonds in the Solicitors office, and the Solicitors state of the case; he gave it as his opinion to the Solicitor that Mr. Tare ought to pay Interest. Approved.

On recommendation It is advised that a Commission issue appointing James Ross Sheriff of Middlesex.

It is advised that the account of Samuel McDonald for supplies furnished the post at the point of Fork up to the 31st ultimo, making a balance in his favour of sixteen pounds and a penny as certified by Captain Coleman, be referred to the Auditor for the usual Warrant.

It is advised that a commission issue appointing Thomas Butler Sheriff of King William in the room of William D. Claiborne who declines acting another year.

On consideration of the Claim of Ann Gist adm[inistra]t[rix] of Thomas Gist for the arrears of pension due said Thomas, at forty pounds per annum, It is advised that the same be rejected, for want of proof of the Death of the pensioner and the vouchers required by law.

The Governor laid before the board an account of James Little for express hire and services rendered in the militia. Whereupon it is advised that the auditor be directed to settle the said account so far as relates to express hire and grant a Warrant on the Contingent fund for the sum due. (to be paid)

The Governor laid before the board a Certificate of Baker Ewings having served 16 days as a Commissioner settling the Claims for Militia services in two expeditions carried on from the Kentucky District against the neighbouring Indians, and having rode 150 miles. Whereupon it is advised that the Auditor settle the said Claim in the usual way allowing ten shillings per diem and 4d. per mile.

It is advised that the Account of Mr. Charles Lynch with the papers accompanying it, be referred to the Auditor for examination and special report.

On consideration of a letter from Col. William Davies of the 24th ultimo. It is advised that Captain Coleman be directed to procure from the Clerk of the house of Delegates a state of the distances from the several counties to the Seat of Government; and, from the Auditor, an Account of the Donations which have been given by this State to the Officers and Soldiers of Virginia on continental Establishment, which the Governor is requested to forward to Col. Davies.

It is also advised that a Warrant issue on the Contingent Fund, in favor of Col. Davies, for fifteen pounds upon account for the contingent expences of his office; and that Messrs. Stot and Donaldson of Petersburg be written to on the subject of supplying Col. Davies, and receiving his salary as it shall become due.

All which matters so advised, the Governor orders accordingly.

James Wood
Carter Braxton
Robt. Goode

Tuesday November 10th 1789

Present

The Governor

Mr. Wood   Mr. Braxton
Mr. McClurg   Mr. Goode

The Governor informed the board that in the recess, having received a letter from Major Langham informing that Piomingo was desirous of changing his route by the way of Holston instead of redstone; he wrote to the Major desiring him to forward the Powder and Lead by the way most agreeable to the Indian Chief, and to purchase the rifles for him, taking care to destroy the order to Mr. Kean for procuring them and the letter to Mr. Brown at redstone desiring him to facilitate the passage of the Indians down the Ohio, and that he issued a warrant on the Contingent Fund to Major Langham for twenty two pounds ten shillings upon account to pay a Mr. Quarles for certain work done at the point of Fork agreeably to contract. Approved.

For reasons appearing to the board It is advised that the Solicitor be directed to dismiss all prosecutions against County Lieutenants for not making returns of their militias and Fines in the last year.

It is advised, that a Warrant issue on the Contingent Fund to John S. Langhorne[69] for twenty pounds upon account as a Collector of Vouchers; and that the Account of Dabney Minor amounting to twelve pounds for repairing book cases for the General court and Court of Appeals Office be referred to the Auditor for settlement and a warrant on the contingent fund for the sum due. To be paid.

On recommendation, It is advised that an additional commission issue appointing Francis Kertley a Justice of the peace for the county of Rockingham.

All which matters so advised the Governor orders accordingly.

James Wood
James McClurg
Carter Braxton
Robt. Goode

Thursday November 12th 1789

Present

The Governor

Mr. Wood   Mr. Jones
Mr. McClurg   Mr. Braxton
              Mr. Goode

69. "Wm. Langhorne" in the clerk's index.

The Governor informed the board that in the recess, he granted a reprieve to negro Robin who was condemned to death by the judgment of Brunswick Court, until the second friday in December; to give time for a full state of his case to be laid before the Executive. Approved.

On consideration of a letter from the Secretary of the Treasury, It is advised that the Auditor be directed to make out as soon as possible a statement of all Debts due from this commonwealth, pursuant to the resolve of the house of representatives of the United States, bearing date the 21st of September 1789.

It is advised that Catherine Helphinstones pension of twenty pounds per annum be continued to her for life from June last, pursuant to a resolve of the General Assembly of the 28th and 29th of November 1788.

It is advised that a warrant issue on the contingent fund to Jno. Otey for one pound ten shillings and six pence for necessaries furnished the Chickasaw Indians on their way to Richmond.

It is advised that Job Weltons bond be delivered up; he having satisfactorily complied with his Contract for the transportation of Arms and Ammunition to the Counties of Monongalia, Harrison and Randolph.

All which matters so advised, the Governor orders accordingly.

James Wood
James McClurg
Jos. Jones
Carter Braxton

Saturday November 14th 1789

Present

The Governor

Mr. Wood   Mr. Jones
Mr. McClurg   Mr. Braxton
                  Mr. Goode

The Governor informed the board that in the recess, he granted a warrant on the Contingent fund to Mr. John Carter, Clerk to the Auditor for twenty pounds upon account to purchase Stationary for that office. Approved.

The Governor laid before the board a state of the prizes taken by the brig Liberty during the late war as taken from the late agents books. Whereupon it is advised that the Solicitor be Instructed to take measures for the recovery of the balances due.

It is also advised that a letter be written to Mr. Raleigh Colston to know whether he ever forwarded to Mr. Parsons of Guadalupe, the Governors dispatches of the 31st of May 1786 concerning the prizes of the brig Muskeeto; and another to Mr. Richard Harrison, late agent at Martinique, requesting a state of the said prizes.

Mr. Wilkinson and Mr. Selden having waited on the Executive, in pursuance of an order of Henrico Court, to represent certain difficulties attending the county Jail and District Jail being united; the Sheriff of said County having demanded a Jail to be assigned him, It is advised that Mr. Goode be appointed to confer with Mr. Wilkerson and Mr. Selden on measures proper to be taken for reconciling the said difficulties and report to this board.

All which matters so advised the Governor orders accordingly.

> James Wood
> James McClurg
> Jos. Jones
> Carter Braxton
> Robt. Goode

Tuesday November 17th 1789

Present

Mr. Wood who presides as Lieutenant Governor,
the Governor being unable from sickness to perform his duty.

| Mr. McClurg | Mr. Braxton |
| Mr. Jones | Mr. Goode |

The Lieutenant Governor informed the board that in the recess he issued a Warrant to Stott and Donaldson for forty nine pounds seventeen shillings on account of Col. William Davies. Approved.

James Higginbotham having been appointed Surveyor of Amherst County; It is advised that he be required to give bond in the penalty of two thousand pounds.

It is advised that a commission issue appointing John Anderson Sheriff of Greenbriar in the room of William Renick who refuses to act another year.

On recommendation, It is advised that an additional commission issue appointing David Allen, William McCraw, Daniel Willson, Thomas Watkins, Samuel Pointer, Gregory Bagham, John Wimbish, John Stone, Thomas Thweat, William Hall, William Owen Senr., Richard Jones (Fork) and William Thompson gentlemen Justices of the peace in Halifax County.

All which matters so advised, the Lt. Governor orders Accordingly.

> James McClurg
> Jos. Jones
> Carter Braxton
> Robt. Goode

Friday November 20th 1789

Present

The Lieutenant Governor

Mr. McClurg   Mr. Braxton
Mr. Jones   Mr. Goode

The Lieutenant Governor informed the board that in the recess, he directed that Reubin Slaughter, Surveyor of Kanawha, should give bond in the county Court in the penalty of two thousand pounds before he entered on the duties of his office. Approved.

On recommendations It is advised, that additional Commissions issue appointing Samuel Brown, Isaac Estill and William Hains gentlemen Justices of the peace for the county of Greenbriar; Littleton Upshur, John Tompkins, Custis Kendall and Isaac Smith gentlemen Justices of the peace for the County of Northampton; and that a Commission issue appointing Elijah Hunt Sheriff of Halifax.

James Mercer esqr. appeared and qualified as a Judge of the Court of appeals by taking the oath of fidelity, the oath of office, and the oath to support the Constitution of the United States, a Certificate whereof was delivered to him.

The Lieutenant Governor laid before the board an account of Mayo Carrington for his trouble and expences as a collector of Vouchers, including Clerks fees on 200 copies of orders of courts. Whereupon it is advised that the Auditor be directed to settle the said Account allowing Mr. Carrington at the rate of a Dollar per day for 143 days riding on the business, exclusive of expences, and grant a Warrant on the contingent fund for the sum due, taking care to deduct what has been advanced to Mr. Carrington. To be paid.

The Lieutenant Governor laid before the board an account of William Graves, late Searcher at Norfolk, for office rent and Stationary. Whereupon it is advised that the said account be rejected, the law having made no provision for such claims.

All which matters so advised, the Lieutenant Governor orders accordingly.

James McClurg
Carter Braxton
Robt. Goode

Saturday November 28th 1789

Present

The Governor

Mr. Wood   Mr. Braxton
Mr. McClurg   Mr. Goode

Mr. Wood informed the board that in the recess, he, as Lieutenant Governor, issued an additional Commission appointing, William Russell, Abraham Archer and William Waller gentlemen Justices of the peace for the County of York; they having been recommended according to law. Approved.

On consideration of a letter from Matthew Anderson esquire a member of the Senate informing that a negro Man Slave the property of Mr. John Lawson was found guilty by the court of Gloster County and sentenced to suffer death on the fourth day of next month for robbery, but that the Clerk of the court had informed him that the precise proof adduced against him was that the Negro did in the day time enter into a dwelling house (the door of which was open) stole out sundry cloaths and was making off when a young woman who had been out getting wood, and was returning to the house, observed and followed him a little way calling to him and begging that he would return the Cloaths which he refused. The board advise that a reprieve be granted to the said negro until the third friday in next month in order that the record of the court and a full state of the case may be had.

It is advised that a warrant issue on the Contingent Fund for twenty pounds to Mr. Samuel Paine for the passage of two piratical prisoners from Boston. (To be paid.)

All which matters so advised, the Governor orders accordingly.

James Wood
James McClurg
Carter Braxton
Robt. Goode

Wednesday December 2d 1789

Present

Mr. Wood, who presides as Lieutenant Governor,
the Governor being unable from sickness to perform his duty.

Mr. McClurg   Mr. Braxton
                    Mr. Goode

Mr. Charles Carter having been appointed a privy councillor, he produced a Certificate of his having qualified before Turner Southall a Justice of the peace for the County of Henrico, and took his seat at the board.

It is advised that the letter prepared by the Governor, to the Governor of North Carolina, in pursuance of the resolves of the General Assembly of the 19th and 24th ultimo, concerning the boundary line between north Carolina and this State, be approved and forwarded by express.

It is advised that a warrant issue on the Contingent fund for eight pounds to Joseph Leiplong[70] upon account as an Express. to be paid.

On consideration of a petition of Hugh Patton complaining of Mr. Harry Heth's having failed to comply with a contract for the sale of a certain quantity of public Tobacco, It is advised that in all disputes between the Agent and Individuals there should be no interference of the Executive, but that all such differences should be settled either by arbitration, or suit at law.

Application having been made for placing on the aggregate fund two warrants, the one issued the 12 of December 1783, to William Parks for £1.15.0 for two blankets and a bridle furnished the montgomery Militia ordered to the aid of the Southern States, and the other on the 18th of November 1783 to Jacob Vermeter for £62.10.0 for salt furnished the Troops stationed in the Western department, It is advised that the same be rejected.

It is advised that Mary Boush's application to be put on the pension List, be rejected; the time limited for the admission of persons on the pension list, according to the spirit of the resolution of assembly of the 1st and 4th of December 1788, having expired.

All which matters so advised the Lieutenant Governor orders accordingly.

> Jas. McClurg
> Carter Braxton
> Robt. Goode
> Chs. Carter

Thursday December 3d 1789

Present

The Lieutenant Governor

Mr. McClurg   Mr. Goode
Mr. Braxton   Mr. Carter

The Board took under consideration the report of Captain Coleman concerning the Claims of Scouts and rangers, Whereupon it is advised,

That the payrolls of Captain James Gibson's company of rangers of Russell County for services rendered in April and August 1788; the Claims of Archibald Prater, Roland Gray, Joseph Johnson, Willobe Lewis, Robert Boucher, William Howard, Alexander McFarling for services rendered as Scouts in the same year; the Claims of Samuel Oxen, John Damron, Austin Boush, David Lewis for services rendered as Scouts in 1789; the several Claims for rations furnished the rangers of the said County: Also the payroll of Captain John Finnies Company of Rangers of Fayette County for services rendered in 1788; the payroll of a Detachment of rangers under the command of Ensign William

---

70. "Lieplong" in the clerk's index.

Young, for services in the same year; the payroll of a Detachment of rangers under the command of Lieutenant Col. Johnson, for services rendered in the same year; the payroll of Captain William Steels company of rangers for services in the same year; the payroll of a detachment of rangers under the command of Lieutenant Field for services rendered in the same year; the payroll of a detachment of rangers under the command of Ensign Samuel McIlvain for services rendered in the same year; the Claims of Wm. P. Sportman, Achiles Eubanks and Philip Boush for services as Scouts in the same year; the Claims of David Stacker and Nicholas Tomlinson for services rendered as Scouts in 1789; the several Claims for rations furnished the rangers of the said County; Also the payroll of a part of Captain Chas. Kavanaughs company of rangers of Madison County for services rendered in 1788: Also the Claim of William Elms for services rendered as a Scout in Jefferson County for 1788: Also the Claim of John Wilson, for services rendered as a Scout for Nelson County in 1788: Also the Claims of Robert McGary and John Arnol for services as Scouts in Mercer County for 1788; the Claims of Stephen Arnold and John Arnold for services as Scouts in the same county in 1789; Also the Claims of James Cockran, Abram Highly, and Ury Bains for services as Scouts in Monongalia County in 1789: Also the Claims of Chas. Gallif, George Painter, James Hamilton, George Neal, Ebenezer McKenny, and Demsey Ward for services as Scouts in Lincoln County in 1788; and the Claim of Charles Ruunell and Samuel Lowe for services as Scouts in the said County in 1788, be referred to the Auditor for settlement in the usual way; taking care in every instance that the number of officers and quantity of rations be proportioned to the number of men in service.

That the several payrolls of the militia of Madison County for services rendered in 1789; Also the Claim of Benja. Dunn for services as a Guard in Mercer County in 1789; and the several payrolls and Claims for services rendered and rations furnished in Lincoln County in 1789, be rejected; the said services having been ordered without authority from the Executive.

That the Claim of Michael Montgomery for services as a Scout in Harrison County in 1789, be rejected as a supernumerary:

That the Claim of David Robinson for 28 Days services as a Scout in Greenbriar in the room of Jno. Young, and the Claims of William Butler and John Bell for services as Scouts in Lincoln County in 1788, be rejected for want of satisfactory certificates; and

That the Claim of William Steel for the ferriages of the Fayette rangers be rejected.

For reasons appearing to the board, It is advised that negro Robbin who stands reprieved until friday next, be further reprieved until the first Friday in January next.

The Lieutenant Governor laid before the board an account of

Hart and Stephenson amounting to seventeen pounds fourteen shillings and eleven pence for four new presses furnished the registers office and for repairs to old ones, as certified by the register. Whereupon It is advised that the said Account be referred to the Auditor for settlement and a Warrant on the contingent fund for the sum due.

All which matters so advised, the Lieutenant Governor orders accordingly.

James McClurg
Carter Braxton
Robt. Goode

Wednesday December 9th 1789

Present

The Governor

| Mr. Wood | Mr. Braxton |
| Mr. McClurg | Mr. Goode |

The Governor produced credentials of his reelection and qualification, which are filed.

The Governor informed the board that in the recess he issued a Commission appointing Thomas Marshall jur. Surveyor of Woodford County, and directed him to give bond in the penalty of three thousand pounds, that he wrote to the Secretary of the Treasury on the subject of the public Debts of this State and to Col. Davies in answer to his favor concerning vouchers for the support of the Claims of this State against the united States (which letters he read to the board); and that he referred to the auditor for settlement the Accounts of Thomas Jefferson esquire for the disbursements of the monies advanced on account of the purchase of Arms in Europe, the Statue of General Washington, and the bust of the Marquis de la Fayette. Approved.

Mr. Wood informed the board that in the recess, he, as Lieutenant Governor issued a pardon to George, a negro Slave, belonging to Alexander G. Strachan, of the Town of Petersburg, condemned to Death by the Judgement of the Court of the said Town of Petersburg for felony; the said George having been recommended by the Court as a proper object of mercy: that he issued a warrant, pursuant to the advice of the 15th of October last, to Mr. Charles Russell for twenty pounds; and that he directed to be paid out of the Contingent fund five pounds five shillings to John Conner for the rent of his house for an office for the Chancery up to the 4th instant as Certified by the Clerk of said office; and that he issued Commissions appointing John Roy an inspector at Roys Warehouses in Caroline in the room of John Catlett deceased and Peyton Stern additional Inspector in the room of the said John Roy. Approved.

Joseph Jones esquire appeared and took the oath of office as a Judge of the General court, and the Oath to support the Constitution of the United States, a Certificate whereof was delivered to him.

On order of the Directors of the lunatic hospital, It is advised that a Warrant issue on the Contingent fund for two hundred pounds to Joseph Hornsby, treasurer of the said Hospital, upon account, for the present support thereof. to be paid.

On recommendation It is advised that a Commission issue appointing William Maclin Sheriff of Greenesville County in the room of John Lucas deceased.

It is advised that a Warrant issue on the contingent fund for fifteen pounds to David Bates and John Richardson for apprehending and delivering George Quick to the Jailor of Dumfries District agreeably to proclamation. Also a Warrant on the same fund to James Cowper for two pounds one and sixpence for necessaries furnished the Chickasaw Indians on their way to Richmond. (to be paid)

For reasons appearing to the board It is advised that negro James who stands reprieved until next friday week, be further reprieved until the first Friday in January next.

It appearing that Catherine Crulle has recovered from her insanity and is desirous of having her child again, It is advised that her Child be returned to the said Catherine.

All which matters so advised the Governor orders accordingly.

> James Wood
> James McClurg
> Carter Braxton
> Robt. Goode

Saturday December 12th 1789

Present

The Governor

Mr. Wood	Mr. Braxton
Mr. McClurg	Mr. Goode
	Mr. Carter

The Governor informed the board that he yesterday directed a Warrant to issue on the contingent fund in favor of Jane West for three pounds the balance of a years pay for nursing Catherine Crulles Child. Approved.

On recommendations It is advised that commissions issue appointing Joseph Jones Sheriff of Dinwiddie, and Alexander Robertson Sheriff of Mercer County in the room of Hugh McGarry whose indisposition prevents his executing the duties thereof.

It is advised that a warrant issue on the contingent fund for fifteen pounds to Samuel Wood as the reward for apprehending Jett Roach.

The Auditor having requested the Instruction of the Executive whether the Day books of his office ought to be forwarded to Col. Davies, as the same have not been Journalized, It is advised that the said Day books ought not to be parted with until they are journalized.

On report of Captain Coleman It is advised that the Claims of John Miller and Vachel Dickeson for services as Scouts in Ohio County in 1789, be referred to the Auditor for settlement in the usual way.

The Governor laid before the board two Second Bills drawn by William Shannon on the Treasurer of Virginia, to wit, one dated the 13th September 1779 for two hundred and fifty Dollars in favour of Andrew Ray, and the other the 20th September 1779 for thirteen hundred and one Dollars in favour of Nicholas Peaurault, also an account of said Nicholas for seven hundred and fifty dollars. Whereupon it is advised that the same be rejected.

On recommendation It is advised that an additional Commission issue appointing Albert Russell, John Gunnel and Charles Bennett gentlemen Justices of the peace for the County of Loudoun.

Pursuant to an Act of the General Assembly for the purchase and manumitting Negro Caesar, It is advised that Miles King esquire be appointed to contract with Mary Tarrant for the purchase of the said negro Caesar.

On consideration of a letter from the County Lieutenant of Amherst inclosing the declaration of the field officers and captains of the Militia of the said county relative to their power of holding Courts martial etc. under the Militia laws of this State, It is advised that a copy of the opinion of the Executive of the 21st of October concerning the Militia Laws of this State, be inclosed to the County Lieutenant of Amherst.

All which matters so advised, the Governor orders accordingly

>James Wood
>James McClurg
>Carter Braxton
>Robt. Goode
>Chs. Carter

Tuesday December 15th 1789

Present

The Governor

Mr. Wood   Mr. Braxton
Mr. McClurg   Mr. Goode
                  Mr. Carter

The Auditor having suggested that he has some doubts whether the Executive meant that the scale of depreciation should be applied to the Account of William Morris monthly as stated by him, or to reduce the nominal balance at the close of the transactions agreeably to the customary rule of the office; It is advised that he be informed that the Executive could never mean to make any distinction between the Creditors of the State; but that the same rule Should be pursued in all similar cases.

On recommendation It is advised that Commissions issue appointing William Strother, and John Morton Inspectors and John Moss additional Inspector at Scotts warehouses in Woodford county.

The Board resumed the consideration of the case of Negro Robin under sentence of death by the Judgment of Brunswick County court for robbing Bottom Steagal [of] a gun and wounding him with a knife, Whereupon it is advised that a pardon be granted to the said Robin; he appearing to be a proper object of mercy.

On report from Captain Coleman It is advised that the Claim of William Drinnin for services as a Scout in Jefferson County in 1789, be referred to the auditor for settlement in the usual way.

The Governor laid before the board an account of Hart and Stephenson amounting to six pounds twelve and ten pence for bookcases etc. made for the Auditors office, as certified by the auditor, Whereupon it is advised that the said account be referred to the auditor for settlement and a warrant on the Contingent fund for the sum due.

On consideration of the case of Cornelius Conway, It is advised that the Fine of fifty pounds imposed on him by the Court of Berkley County for an assault, be remitted.

In pursuance of the resolves of the general assembly of the 10th and 14th instant, It is advised that the Governor write to the general Assembly of Maryland inclosing a copy of the Act for the Cession of ten miles square or any lesser quantity of territory within this State to the United States in Congress Assembled for the permanent seat of the general government; and to propose to the said Assembly to unite with this State in advancing a sum of money to Congress for erecting public buildings, on the terms proposed by the above recited resolves; And also to write to the Directors of the Potowmack Company requesting them to furnish, as soon as possible, the Information directed by the Assembly to be procured of the present State of the navigation of the river potowmack etc. in order to its being forwarded to Congress, at the commencement of its next Session: And that there may be no delay in the business; it is further advised, that the letter to the Directors be forwarded open to Col. Fitzgerald with a request that he procure a meeting of the Directors for considering the subject, as soon as possible.

All which matters so advised, the Governor orders accordingly.

> James Wood
> James McClurg
> Carter Braxton
> Chs. Carter

Thursday December 17th 1789

Present

The Governor

Mr. Wood   Mr. Braxton
Mr. McClurg   Mr. Goode
                   Mr. Carter

It is advised that a copy of the Act of the general assembly authorizing the governor to convey certain lands to the United States for the purpose of building a lighthouse be forwarded to the President of the United States.

The board took under consideration a resolution of the general assembly of the 11th and 14th instant requesting the Executive to appoint some proper person to examine the situation and condition of the materials formerly provided by the state for the purpose of erecting a Lighthouse etc. Whereupon they are of opinion that it would be best for one of their body to proceed to Cape Henry before the first of January next with full power (after having examined the situation and condition of the materials aforesaid) to contract with some person or persons to secure the same on the best terms he can. And it is advised that General Wood be appointed to do this business, whose pay as a member of this board shall be the same as if present, and that his reasonable expences be paid by the public.

It is advised that a warrant issue on the Contingent fund for three pounds to Joseph Clarke upon account as an express with dispatches to the Governor of Maryland.

It is advised that a commission issue appointing Archelaus Hughes, George Hairston, John Dillard, John Wells, William Carter, George Waller, James Lyon, Abraham Penn and David Lenear, or any three of them, gentlemen, Commissioners pursuant to an act of the general assembly for supplying the loss of the entry books and field notes of the Surveyor for Henry County.

It is advised that a commission issue appointing Martin McFarran Sheriff of Botetourt County in the room of Robert Harvey, who, being a member of the Assembly, declines the appointment.

It is advised that the account of Martin Hawkins for riding express to Mr. F. Eppes in Chesterfield with dispatches from the President to Mr. Jefferson, be referred to the Auditor for settlement in the usual way.

On consideration of a letter from Col. Davies of the 3d instant, It is advised that such of the Day books of the Auditors office as are necessary for the support of the claims of this State against the United States, be forwarded to Col. Davies, notwithstanding they are not journalized; it appearing from the information of the Auditor that they have been posted, and will probably not be wanted 'til they are returned: that captain Coleman make out copies of the Instructions inclosed by Col. Davies to the several collectors of vouchers; and that he procure from the Clerk of the Assembly a state of the mileage from the several counties to Williamsburg, to be forwarded to Col. Davies.

It is advised that a commission issue appointing John Byrd, James Southall and Benja. C. Waller gentlemen to supply the vacanc[i]es in the Court of Directors for the public Hospital in the City of Williamsburg, occasioned by the Death of Thomas Nelson and resignations of John Dixon and Henry Tazewell.

The Governor laid before the board sundry Depositions taken in New Kent County concerning lost records, pursuant to a Commission bearing date the 21st of June 1788, together with the said commission. Whereupon it is advised that the said Depositions be transmitted to the General assembly.

Mr. James Belcher having petitioned that a warrant issued to him the 28th November 1783 for ninety one pounds 13/. for 305 ½ bushels of salt furnished for the use of the Continental army may be placed on some productive fund; It is advised that the same be rejected; the Executive having no power to apply any funds to that purpose.

On consideration of the petition of the men of Captain Thomas Whites company of Hanover Militia, It is advised that the Fines imposed on them by a Court martial held for the said County, on the 25th of November 1788, be remitted so far as relates to their nonattendance at the general Muster in the said month of November 1788.

All which matters so advised, the Governor orders accordingly.

> James Wood
> James McClurg
> Carter Braxton
> Robt. Goode
> Chs. Carter

Saturday December 19th 1789

Present

The Governor

Mr. Wood	Mr. Braxton
Mr. McClurg	Mr. Goode
	Mr. Carter

The Governor informed the board that in the recess, he directed the Auditor to settle the Account of Captain Roane amounting to fourteen pounds fourteen shillings and eleven pence for the hire of negroes and their expences while employed by him as Searcher at City point, after deducting the Sale of the boat which was allowed him for the purposes of his office. Approved.

It is advised that the Auditor be directed to issue a warrant on the Aggregate Fund to David Coupland for three hundred and thirty pounds pursuant to the Act of the general assembly concerning the escheated property of James Coupland decreased.

On report of Captain Coleman, It is advised that the Claims of Macum McClullum and John Connel for services rendered as Scouts in Nelson County for 1788, of William Foster for services as a Scout in Same County in May, June and July 1789, of Edward Robertson for sixty three Days services in the same County and year, be referred to the Auditor for settlement in the usual way; and that the Claim of Serjeant Samuel Mairs company of eight men of Montgomery Rangers for services in 1789, be rejected, the services having been ordered with authority from the executive.

On recommendation It is advised that a commission issue appointing Miles King Sheriff of Elizabeth City County.

In pursuance of a resolve of the general Assembly of the 12th and 14th instant It is advised that Aug. Davis be employed to print 2000 copies of the Acts of Congress, 500 copies of the Journal of the House of representatives of the United States, and 200 Copies of the Journal of the Senate of the United States, on the following terms: viz. the Laws at the rate of £12.10 per Sheet, the Journals of the house of representatives at £2.15 per Sheet and the Journal of the Senate at £2. per Sheet, the whole to be printed according to the sample produced with an addition of five or six lines more on a page and to be completed in time to go out with the Laws of the State.

The Governor laid before the board a letter he had prepared to the Courts of the Counties in which the District Jails are, in pursuance of a resolve of the General assembly of the 15th and 16th instant, which being read and approved is ordered to be registered.

All which matters so advised the Governor orders accordingly.

> James Wood
> James McClurg
> Carter Braxton
> Robt. Goode
> Chas. Carter

Monday December 21st 1789

Present

The Governor

Mr. Wood	Mr. Braxton
Mr. McClurg	Mr. Goode
	Mr. Carter

The Governor informed the Board that in the recess he issued a

Warrant on the Contingent fund for twenty pounds payable to Major Robert Porterfield upon account, as a Collector of Vouchers in support of the Claims of this State against the United States. Approved.

The Governor laid before the board an account of Joseph Leiplong for riding express to North Carolina with public despatches. Whereupon it is advised that the said account be referred to the Auditor for settlement in the usual way, allowing ten shillings per day for the time he was detained by the General Assembly of North Carolina.

Mr. John Dawson having been elected a member of the privy council, he produced a certificate of his qualification before John Pendleton gentleman a Justice of the peace for the County of Henrico, and took his seat at the board.

It is advised that the Auditor be instructed to prepare in conformity to the act of the General Assembly intituled "an act concerning invalid pensioners," a List to be forwarded to the several County Courts of such pensioners as are provided for by Congress and a separate List of such as are to be paid by the State. The List of Continental pensioners to be headed thus "*a List of pensioners provided for by Congress for the payment of which no Orders of Court are to be granted*" In those cases where full pay is allowed any officer by special Act of Assembly, the Auditor will insert one half in the Continental List, and the other half in the State List.

Mr. John H. Briggs having been elected a member of the privy Council, he produced a Certificate of his qualification before John Pendleton gentleman a Justice of the peace for the county of Henrico, and took his seat at the board.

It is advised that Mr. Wood, Mr. McClurg and Mr. Braxton be appointed a Committee to visit and examine the offices of the Treasurer, Auditor and Solicitor pursuant to the Act of the general Assembly empowering the Executive to superintend and arrange the Offices of the Treasurer, Auditor and Solicitor.

On consideration of a petition of Thomas Underwood praying that a number of Warrants in his possession, issued for flour etc. furnished the Garrison at Fort Nelson as per Certificates from the Commissioners appointed for settling Western Claims, may be put on the aggregate fund; It is unanimously advised that the same be rejected.

Pursuant to a resolve of the General Assembly of the 14th and 19th instant, It is advised that the Auditor be instructed to adjust and settle the Accounts of the Directors of the public buildings for all the several appropriations heretofore made, in their hands, and of the Disbursements thereof.

It is advised that Captain Langham be desired to employ Thomas Harris, late an armourer in the service of this State, at the point of Fork and allow him such wages as he may think his services deserve.

It is advised that the account of McColl and Cunlieff[71] for 400 bushels of coal furnished for the Council Chamber be referred to the Auditor for settlement and a warrant on the Contingent fund for the sum due. to be paid.

All which matters so advised, the Governor orders accordingly.

James Wood
James McClurg
Carter Braxton
Robt. Goode
Jno. H. Briggs
Chs. Carter
J. Dawson

Tuesday December 22d 1789

Present

The Governor

Mr. Wood   Mr. Goode
Mr. McClurg   Mr. Briggs
Mr. Braxton   Mr. Carter
Mr. Dawson

The Governor laid before the board a resolution of the general assembly of the 18 and 19 instant respecting the Sinking fund. Whereupon it is advised, That the Agent for the Sinking fund be instructed to apply the money in the fund, in his discretion, to the actual purchase of the public securities of this commonwealth, or of the United States bearing an interest of six per centum, and to no other purpose whatsoever, That the Treasurer, agreeably to the 7th Section of the Act 'providing a sinking fund for the gradual redemption of the public debt,' cause to be registered in a book to be kept for that purpose all such public Securities as shall be delivered to him by the Agent or which shall be brought into the Treasury in payment of taxes; and that he annually deliver to the Auditor of public Accounts a copy of such register with a Certificate that he has received such public securities, Upon which register so certified the auditor shall issue Warrants to the agent for the sinking fund for the interest so due.

On reconsidering the account of Joseph Leiplong for express hire. It is advised that the Auditor be directed to allow him at the rate of 15/. per day, deducting 5/. per day for the five days he was detained by the Assembly of North Carolina.

---

71. "McColl and Cunlief" in the clerk's index.

The Governor laid before the board a bill of exchange for three thousand three hundred thirty three and a third dollars drawn by James F. Moore[72] in favor of George Wilson for flour etc. furnished the Troops stationed in the Illinois department, presented to him for payment. Whereupon it is advised that the same be rejected.

On consideration of a letter from George Clendinnin Lieutenant of Greenbriar, and the report of Captain Coleman, It is advised that the payroll of Captain William Clendinnins Company of Greenbriar rangers for 1789. Also the Claims of William Morris, William Boggs and John Morris for rations furnished the said rangers, also the claims of Charles McClung, John Young, Leonard Cooper and Charles Alsbury as Scouts for the same year and the Claim of John Stuart for 200 lbs. gunpowder furnished for the use of the rangers, be referred to the Auditor for settlement in the usual way.

It is advised that the act of the general assembly, "concerning the erection of the District of Kentucky into an independent State" be transmitted to the Representatives of this commonwealth in Congress pursuant to the direction of the said act.

On recommendations It is advised that an additional Commission issue appointing Abner Prior, Joseph Woods and William Morres gentlemen Justices of the peace for the County of Kanawha; and that commissions issue appointing William Boggs and Wm. Droddy Coroners for the said County.

In pursuance of a resolution of the general Assembly of the 19th instant, It is advised that the petitions of the serveral persons named in the said resolution together with the several resolutions thereupon be transmitted, in a letter from the Governor, representing it as the earnest wish of the general Assembly, that the Claims of the said petitioners be inquired into, and paid, if they be found just and right, to the Secretary at War; and that, in case he should not be the proper officer of the foederal Government for taking cognizance of such cases, he be requested to forward the said petitions and resolutions to the proper officer.

All which matters so advised, the Governor orders accordingly.

> James Wood
> James McClurg
> Carter Braxton
> Robt. Goode
> Jno. H. Briggs
> Chs. Carter
> J. Dawson

---

72. "Francis More" in the clerk's index.

Wednesday December 23d 1789

Present

The Governor

Mr. Wood	Mr. Goode
Mr. McClurg	Mr. Briggs
Mr. Braxton	Mr. Dawson

On consideration of a petition from the Directors of the Potowmack Company; It is advised that the Treasurer be directed to borrow from any funds money sufficient to pay five pounds for each public share in the said company: It is also advised that the treasurer borrow a sufficient sum to pay the present quarters salary of the Officers of Civil Government.

The Governor laid before the board the Solicitors Account for expences in forwarding executions and notices previous to the last court, Whereupon it is advised that the same be referred to the Auditor for settlement and a warrant on the Contingent fund for the sum due. (To be paid).

All which matters so advised, the Governor orders accordingly.

James Wood
James McClurg
Carter Braxton
Robt. Goode
Jno. H. Briggs
J. Dawson

Thursday December 24th 1789

Present

The Governor

Mr. Wood	Mr. Goode
Mr. McClurg	Mr. Briggs
Mr. Braxton	Mr. Dawson

It is advised that a warrant issue on the Contingent Fund for twenty pounds to Captain Archibald Denholm upon account as a Collector of Vouchers. To be paid.

On recommendation, It is advised that an additional Commission issue appointing James Martin, Edward Macarty, Isaac Parsons, Virgil Mecrakin, Solomon Jones and Jonathan Purcell gentlemen Justices of the peace for the County of Hampshire.

For reasons appearing to the board It is advised that Negro James who stands condemned to Death by the Judgment of Gloster county court, be further reprieved until Friday the 15th of January next.

On consideration of the opinion of the Attorney General, to whom the question was submitted, whether the Executive had the power of borrowing for the purpose of paying the warrants issued to Scouts and rangers for services in 1788, It is advised that the provision by loan be not extended to such warrants.

All which matters so advised, the Governor orders accordingly.

> James Wood
> James McClurg
> Carter Braxton
> Robt. Goode

Wednesday January 6th 1790

Present

The Governor

| Mr. McClurg | Mr. Goode |
| Mr. Braxton | Mr. Carter |

The Governor informed the Board, that during the recess, he had on the 28th Ultimo, issued a Commission appointing Thomas Cheney Gentleman, Sheriff of the county of Harrison, recommended in the room of John Powers Gentleman who is certified unable to procure security: that on the 31st, he had ordered a Warrant on the Contingent Fund, to Joseph Clarke for riding Express to Annapolis, with dispatches for the Governor of Maryland, for so much as may appear to be due: that on the first Instant, he had directed the Auditor to give an order to the Treasurer to receive of Jacob Rinker County Lieutenant of Shenandoah, the sum of twenty pounds one Shilling and six pence half penny, being the balance of his account of fines received for Militia Delinquencies for the years 1783 and 1784, in his county: And that he had examined and certified for payment, the Salary of the Auditor for the last quarter, Of which several matters the Board approve.

It is advised, that the Auditor be directed to issue a Warrant on the contingent fund, to Armistead Long, for twenty Pounds on account as a Collector of Vouchers to support the Account of this state against the United States, (to be paid); Also a Warrant to the Auditor on said fund, for Seventeen pounds twelve shillings on Account to purchase Stationary for the use of his Office; the Usual Warrants to Elias Langham for the balance of pay due the superintendant and Artificers at the Point of Fork, for a quarters Wages due the 31st of December 1789, being One hundred and twenty two pounds eighteen shillings and eight Pence; for the Amount of pay due the Guards at said Post for the same time being One hundred and seven pounds twelve Shillings; and for the sum of seventy one Pounds eight shillings and five Pence, being a balance due the said Elias Langham for monies advanced by him to defray the Expences incurred by the transportation of the Powder and Lead given to the Chickasaw Indians, and for other contingent Expences.

The Governor laid before the Board, a Letter from Elias Langham, on consideration of which, it is advised, that Mr. Samuel McDonald, Contractor to furnish the Post at the Point of Fork with Provision, be discontinued, and that Mr. Langham take the necessary steps to furnish the Post with supplies, until a New Contract can be made, which he is authorized to do, subject to the Approbation of the Executive, previously advertising, that he will receive Proposals for such Contract: It is also advised, that Mr. Langham have leave of Absence from the Post at the Point of Fork, from the 15th of April until the 15th of July next, he furnishing a person properly qualified to execute the business of the Post at his expence, and for whose conduct he will be responsible:

And it is further Advised, that Mr. Langham reinlist the Guards for said Post, whose time of service will shortly expire, for the same time as heretofore and upon the best terms he can.

On consideration of a Letter from the Secretary of the Department of War for the United States, inclosing an Order on Mr. Thomas Holt, for the delivery of two thousand pounds of Gun powder, and a proportionable quantity of Lead, as furnished the Chickasaw Indians by this state, It is advised, that Mr. Langham repair to New London, and request of the said Thomas Holt, permission to examine the powder in his care and report the quality thereof to this Board.

In pursuance of an Act of Assembly, for paying a sum of Money to John Cox, It is advised, that the Auditor be informed, that the Penalty of the Bond to be given by the said John Cox, agreeable to the said Act, ought, in the opinion of the Executive, to be five hundred Pounds.

On consideration of a Letter from the Directors of the James River Company, It is advised, that the Treasurer be directed to borrow from any Funds, money sufficient to pay five pounds for each public Share in said Company.

The Governor laid before the Board a Letter from Mr. William Hay, one of the Directors of the Public Buildings. Whereupon it is advised, that in pursuance of the Act of Assembly for appropriating a further sum of money for building the Capitol, the Treasurer be directed to borrow from any funds, the sum of nine hundred pounds for the purposes of the said Act.

On consideration of a Letter from Colonel Davies, of the 24th Ultimo, it is advised, that a Letter be written to General Edward Stevens, inclosing the form of an affidavit tending to support the charge of this state against the United States of Mil[e]age for the Militia; also a letter of the same nature to Colonel David Mason; And a letter to Mr. Grisset Davis requesting him to furnish an authentic statement of the supplies and services of every kind, which were obtained by George Elliot for the purposes of the War, and which were not paid for by the Continent: It is also Advised, that a letter be written to Mr. Richard Yarborough, and sent by Express, covering copies of Letters to him of the 28th of October and 18th of December last on the subject of Collecting Vouchers to support the Account of this State against the United States, and requesting him to forward by the Express any Vouchers, which he may have collected on this subject:

And it is further advised, that Mr. Samuel Coleman be directed to make out and Authenticate a Statement of all Cordage and other property furnished by Mr. Charles Thomas, as Agent of this state, to all public Vessels or others for the purposes of the War.

The Governor laid before the Board, a Letter from the Solicitor, inclosing a copy of an advertisement of the Sale of the public Boats Liberty and Patriot etc. and a copy of a bond from Moses Myers and James Douglass[73] to the Governor, and stating that payment of said Bond had been tendered by Mr. James Heron in Military Certificates, on which the Interest had been drawn to the first Instant, and requesting Instructions of the Executive whether he shall receive payment of the said Bond in Military Certificates without the Interest which became due thereon for the last year, Whereupon it is advised, that the solicitor be directed to submit the Question to the Attorney General, whose opinion thereupon he will make the rule of his conduct.

All which matters so advised the Governor Orders Accordingly.

> James McClurg
> Carter Braxton
> Robt. Goode
> Chs. Carter

Monday January 11th 1790

Present

The Governor

Mr. McClurg   Mr. Goode
Mr. Braxton   Mr. Carter

The Governor informed the Board, that in the Recess he had directed the Auditor to issue a Warrant on the Contingent Fund to Clotworthy Stephenson for the sum of two pounds nine Shillings and ten pence for Work done in the solicitors office as certified by the solicitor. Also a Warrant on the same fund to Joseph Liplong[74] for One

---

73. "Myres" and "Douglas" in the clerk's index.
74. "Leiplong" in the clerk's index.

pound four shillings on Account for going Express to Richard Yarbrough. to be paid: That he issued Commissions appointing William Rowlett Inspector and John Rowlett additional Inspector at John Bollings warehouses; that on Recommendation he had issued a Commission appointing John Holloway surveyor for the county of Mecklenburg directing him to give bond for the faithful execution of his office in the Penalty of £1000; That he had received a letter from Mr. Harry Heth Agent for selling the public Tobacco, stating that an offer had been made him for 150 to 200 Hogsheads of upper Rappanhannock and Potowmack Tobacco, viz: Seventeen shillings specie per Hundred or Nineteen shillings half Cash and half Warrants payable in four months and requesting his Advice, upon which he gave it as his opinion that Mr. Heth should accept the offer of nineteen shillings half Cash and half Warrants but should endeavour to have the credit so far as it concerned cash limited to the first of April, and of which several matters the Board approve.

On Consideration of sundry letters and papers respecting the conviction of James a negro man slave the property of John Lawson of Robbery by the County Court of Gloucester on the 2d day of November 1789, who is now under sentence of death for the same, it is advised, that the said negro man slave be pardoned, he appearing to be proper object of mercy.

It is advised that the Auditor be directed to issue a Warrant on the Contingent Fund to John Hague and Company for the rent of the old Treasury Office from 1st of April to 22d of June 1789 being eight pounds five shillings as certified by the Treasurer, to be paid: also a Warrant to Clotworthy Stephenson on the Contingent fund for eighteen shillings being for the removal of the Bust of the Marquis De la Fayette from the Old Council Chamber to the present office of the Executive.

All which matters so advised the Governor orders accordingly.

James McClurg
Carter Braxton
Robert Goode
Chs. Carter

Wednesday January 13th 1790

Present

Mr. Wood who presides as Lieutenant Governor, the Governor being unable from sickness to perform his duty.

Mr. McClurg	Mr. Goode
Mr. Braxton	Mr. Carter

The Lieutenant Governor laid before the board his report concerning the situation of the materials formerly collected at Cape Henry for the purpose of erecting a Lighthouse. Whereupon it is advised, that the said Materials be offered to the general Government in their present state, and That copies of the proceedings of the Legislature concerning the same, and of the consequent proceedings of the Executive be transmitted to the Governor of the State of Maryland.

It is advised that the Account of Joseph Leiplong making a balance in his favor of two pounds three and seven pence for express hire, be referred to the Auditor for settlement in the usual way.

All which matters so advised, the Lieut. Governor orders accordingly.

James McClurg
Carter Braxton
Robert Goode
Chs. Carter

Monday January 18th 1790

Present

The Lieutenant Governor

Mr. McClurg   Mr. Briggs
Mr. Braxton   Mr. Carter
Mr. Goode   Mr. Dawson

Mr. Thomas Madison having been elected a member of the Privy Council, he produced a certificate of his qualification before John Harvie, gentleman, a Justice of the peace for the County of Henrico, and took his seat at the board.

For reasons appearing to the board, It is advised that Negro Phil, now under sentence of death, by the Judgment of New Kent County court, be reprieved until the third Friday in February: Which the Lieutenant Governor orders accordingly.

James McClurg
Carter Braxton
Jno. H. Briggs
Thos. Madison
Chs. Carter
J. Dawson

Thursday January 21st 1790

Present

The Lieutenant Governor

Mr. Braxton	Mr. Madison
Mr. Goode	Mr. Carter
Mr. Briggs	Mr. Dawson

The Lieutenant Governor informed the board that in the recess he sent on, to New York, the Vouchers lodged in this office for Col. Davies, by Joseph Leiplong and granted him a warrant on the Contingent fund for eighteen pounds upon account to defray his expences; that he issued a Warrant in favor of Andrew Dunscombe[75] for one hundred sixty six and sixty ninetieths Dollars on Account of wages due him; Also a Warrant in favor of Thomas McClaskey for eight pounds two shillings for bricks furnished for a Well on the lot occupied by the Governor: and that on recommendations he issued an additional Commission appointing Benjamin Goodrich, John Goodwyn, John Fisher and William Sykes Gentlemen Justices of the peace for the County of Greenesville and a Commission appointing Lockett Mitchell Coroner for the said County. Approved.

The Lieutenant Governor laid before the board a Draft of Col. William Davies in favor of Messrs. Stott and Donaldson for five hundred and fifty two dollars on account of wages due him. Whereupon it is advised that the same be paid out of the Contingent fund.

On consideration of a letter from the Solicitor concerning the prizes of the Brigg Liberty; It is advised that the several persons from whom balances appear to be due, be written to requiring them to make immediate settlements thereof.

The board took under consideration the eighth section of the act of the general assembly to amend the act concerning pensioners. Whereupon it is advised that a circular letter be written to the several county courts requiring a reexamination of the pensioners in their respective Counties payable by this State, and a special report of their respective situations specifying age, disability, number and ages of children, and indigency of circumstances, previous to their being continued on the pension List for the year 1790.

On consideration of the proceedings of the Court of New Kent and a state of the evidence against negro Phill, the property of William Tyree, adjudged to Death by the said Court for felony; It is advised that a pardon be granted to the said Phil there appearing to be an error in the judgment against him.

The Board being informed that Catherine Crulle had gone off and left her child in the hands of Jane West its former nurse, It is

---

75. "Dunscomb" in the clerk's index.

advised that the said Jane West be allowed at the rate of twelve pounds per annum for nursing and cloathing the said child.

All which matters so advised, the Lieutenant Governor orders accordingly.

> Carter Braxton
> Robt. Goode
> Jno. H. Briggs
> Thos. Madison
> Chs. Carter
> J. Dawson

Monday January 25th 1790

Present

The Governor

Mr. Wood	Mr. Briggs
Mr. Braxton	Mr. Madison
Mr. Goode	Mr. Carter

Mr. Dawson

The Governor informed the board that he had in the recess administered the oath of office to William Rowlett as an Inspector of tobacco at John Bollings warehouse in Chesterfield, and granted a warrant on the Contingent fund for six pounds three and two pence to William Usher for digging and bricking a well on the lott occupied by the Governor. Approved.

The Governor laid before the board a Draft of Reuben Burnley for one hundred and six $\frac{19}{90}$ dollars on account of Wages due him up to the 1st instant of Clerk to Col. Davies. Whereupon it is advised that the same be referred to the auditor for settlement in the usual way.

The Board took under consideration what allowance ought to be made Mr. Harry Heth as Agent for selling the public tobacco. Whereupon it is advised that he be allowed, for the last year, at the rate of three quarters per cent. on thirty one thousand four hundred and ninety eight pounds two shillings and a penny, and thirty nine pounds 9/2. actually expended by him in the execution of his office.

It being suggested that some of the inferior officers of the Treasury Auditor and Solicitor's offices are concerned in speculating in the public Securities, The Board, conceiving such practices to be highly improper, advise, that a letter be written to the heads of the above offices directing them to take measures to prevent their Clerks being concerned in such practices in future.

Present Mr. McClurg.

It is advised that the Account of Mr. William Price for his Services in collecting Vouchers, be referred to the Auditor for settlement, allowing him a Dollar per day for 152 Days riding, exclusive of expences, and a warrant on the contingent fund for the sum due (to be paid).

All which matters so advised, the Governor orders accordingly.

James Wood
James McClurg
Carter Braxton
Robt. Goode
Jno. H. Briggs
Thos. Madison
J. Dawson
Chs. Carter

Thursday January 28th 1790

Present

The Governor

Mr. Wood	Mr. Briggs
Mr. McClurg	Mr. Madison
Mr. Braxton	Mr. Carter
Mr. Goode	Mr. Dawson

The Governor informed the board that in the recess he referred to the auditor for settlement in the usual way, the account of Thomas Parker as a Collector of Vouchers, allowing him a Dollar per day for one hundred Days riding exclusive of expences. Approved.

It is advised that a Commission issue appointing John Hill Sheriff of King William County in the room of Thomas Butler who hath not been able to give bond according to law.

On consideration of the account of Mr. John Morton as a District Commissioner, It is advised that the Auditor be directed to allow him a credit for one hundred pounds in full compensation for his services, leaving the unvouched articles of the said account open until Mr. Morton can procure the Vouchers, which he assures the board shall be speedily done. It is also advised that Mr. Morton be authorized to receive any public securities of this State or the United States bearing an Interest of six per cent, at not more than 8/ in the pound, for the Debts due from the individuals in his District.

It is advised that a warrant issue on the contingent fund for twenty five pounds to Archd. Blair for four months salary as Keeper of the public seal ending the 4th instant.

It is advised that the account of John L. Langhorne[76] as a collector of Vouchers be referred to the Auditor for settlement in the usual way

---

76. "Wm. Langhorne" in the clerk's index.

allowing him a Dollar per day for one hundred and six days employed in riding and writing.

It is advised that a commission issue appointing Lyddall Wilkerson Sheriff of New Kent County in the room of Wm. H. Macon who refuses to serve a second year.

All which matters so advised, the Governor orders accordingly.

> James Wood
> James McClurg
> Carter Braxton
> Robt. Goode
> Jno. H. Briggs
> Chs. Carter
> J. Dawson
> Thos. Madison

Monday February 1st 1790

Present

The Governor

Mr. Wood	Mr. Braxton
Mr. McClurg	Mr. Dawson

The Governor informed the board that in the recess, he issued a Commission appointing Daniel Hankins Sheriff of Pittsylvania, in the room of William Short who is unable to give Security: also a commission appointing George Guy Sheriff of Caroline County in the room of Roger Quarles deceased. Approved.

On recommendation, It is advised that an additional Commission issue appointing John Starke, Elisha Meredith, John Thompson jr., James Doswell, John Bullock, Thomas Macon and Meriwether Jones gentlemen Justices of the peace for the county of Hanover.

On consideration of the proceedings of a court of Oyer of Lancaster County, and a state of the evidence against negro James, the property of Joseph Shearman, condemned to death by the said court for felony; It is advised that a pardon issue in favor of the said James, he appearing to be a proper object of mercy.

It is advised that a commission issue appointing Cason Moore Sheriff of Princess Anne county in the room of John Cornick who is unable to give security.

All which matters so advised, the Governor orders accordingly.

> James Wood
> James McClurg
> Carter Braxton
> J. Dawson

Friday February 5th 1790

Present

The Governor

Mr. Wood	Mr. Goode
Mr. McClurg	Mr. Briggs
Mr. Braxton	Mr. Carter

Mr. Dawson

The Governor informed the board that in the recess he directed to be paid out of the Contingent fund three pounds to Jane West in advance for nursing Catherine Crulls child, that he referred the account of Samuel McDonald, amounting to sixty nine pounds six and five pence for supplies furnished the post at the Point of Fork from the 1st of November to the 31st December last, and the Account of Elias Langham amounting to twenty eight pounds 18/8 for supplies furnished the said post for the month of January, to the Auditor for settlement in the usual way. Approved.

It is advised that a Warrant issue on the Contingent fund for eleven pounds eighteen shillings and three pence to General Wood for the expences of his trip to Cape Henry on public service. To be paid.

It is advised that the account of Charles Lynch as manager of the Lead mines, be referred to the Auditor for settlement according to the Vouchers produced, and a Warrant for the sum due, provided that Mr. Lynch is not a Debtor to the Commonwealth on the books of the Auditor in his own office or that of the Solicitor.

On consideration of a letter from Alexander Macauley[77] to the Treasurer requesting a further credit 'til the 1st of April next for four hundred and fifty pounds due the 20th instant to Mr. Heth for the purchase of public tobacco, It is advised that Mr. Macaulay be allowed the indulgence he asks, provided the Deposits remain in Mr. Heths hands subject to be sold without notice should the public be in absolute want of money at any time between the 20th instant and the first of April next.

It is advised that a Commission issue appointing Thomas Coleman Sheriff of King and Queen County in the room of Anderson Scott who hath failed to give bond.

On consideration of a letter from the Solicitor, dated the 4th instant; It is advised that he be directed to pay into the Treasury all Military Certificates and interest Warrants received by him for the sale of the public boats, to be applied to the purposes of the Sinking Fund.

The Governor laid before the board a second bill of exchange, for 1490 Dollars, drawn by Jas. Frs. Moore D. C. P. Illinois Department the

---

77. "McCauley" in the clerk's index.

17 July 1780, presented to him for payment. Whereupon It is advised that the same be rejected.

All which matters so advised, the Governor orders accordingly.

> James Wood
> James McClurg
> Carter Braxton
> Robt. Goode
> Jno. H. Briggs
> Chs. Carter
> J. Dawson

Monday February 8th 1790

Present

The Governor

Mr. Wood	Mr. Goode
Mr. McClurg	Mr. Briggs
Mr. Braxton	Mr. Carter

Mr. Dawson

The Governor informed the board that in the recess he issued a Commission appointing Joseph Parkinson a principal Inspector of tobacco at Littlepages warehouses in the room of Richard Graves deceased. Approved.

On consideration of a letter from the Auditor It is advised that he be authorized to engage a temporary Clerk in the room of Mr. Southall whose ill state of health requires a recess from business for a while, which said temporary Clerk shall be paid out of the contingent fund during the necessary absence of Mr. Southall.

It is advised that the account of Joseph Clark[78] amounting to three pounds fifteen shillings for express hire in carrying dispatches from the President of the United States to Mr. Jefferson, be referred to the Auditor for settlement in the usual way.

It is advised that the Treasurer be directed to pay a warrant lately issued to Archd. Blair for twenty five pounds for four months Salary as Keeper of the public seal.

All which matters so advised, the Governor orders accordingly.

> James Wood
> James McClurg
> Carter Braxton
> Robt. Goode
> Chs. Carter
> J. Dawson

---

78. "Clarke" in the clerk's index.

Friday February 12th 1790

Present

The Governor

Mr. Wood	Mr. Goode
Mr. McClurg	Mr. Carter
Mr. Braxton	Mr. Dawson

It is advised that a Commission issue, to take effect from and after the first Day of May next, appointing Walter Crocket, James McGavock, Andrew Boyd, William Davies, James Newell, Robert Sayers, William Ward, William Love, *John* Stephens,[79] John Adams, David McGavock, Flower Swift and William Thompson gentlemen justices of the peace for the County of Wythe, the first eight of whom to form a quorum; And that a commission issue (to take effect the same time) appointing James Newell Sheriff of the said County.

It is advised that a warrant issue to Henry Mann for one pound eight shillings for framing a map of the Potowmack river etc. to be paid out of the contingent fund.

The Governor laid before the board an Account of William Rose amounting to three pounds four shillings for maintenance of John Fowler in the public Jail from the 1st of October to the 3d of November 1789. Whereupon it is advised that the said account be referred to the auditor for settlement and a warrant on the Contingent fund for the sum due. (to be paid)

On recommendation, It is advised that commissions issue appointing Roe Cowper and John Hunter Coroners and Benja. Bryan Escheator for the County of Elizabeth City.

The Governor laid before the board the Account of Joseph Leiplong who was employed to go to new york with certain books and vouchers for Col. Davies, in support of the Claims of this State against the United States. Whereupon it is advised, that the Auditor be directed to settle the said account so far as relates to stage hire only, according to the Vouchers produced; and to grant a Warrant on the Contingent fund for the sum due together with thirty four Dollars as a compensation for his services; taking care to deduct the eighteen pounds granted to Mr. Leiplong upon acount. (To be paid)

The Governor laid before the board a letter from Mr. William Tatham accompanied with a copy of the Map of Potowmack river which he was requested to take for the use of the Executive, and for which he refuses any pecuniary compensation. Whereupon it is advised that the Governor return the thanks of this board to Mr. Tatham for the trouble he has been at; and inform him that he may

---

79. The word "Jehu" is written in the margin beside the name "*John* Stephens" in the text.

have free access to any public papers which will aid him in the execution of the Work he proposes to engage in.

All which matters so advised, the Governor orders accordingly.

James Wood
James McClurg
Carter Braxton
Robt. Goode
J. Dawson
Chs. Carter

Wednesday February 17th 1790

Present

The Governor

Mr. Wood	Mr. Goode
Mr. McClurg	Mr. Carter
Mr. Braxton	Mr. Dawson

The Governor informed the board that in the recess he directed to be paid out of the Contingent fund to Clotworthy Stephenson twelve pounds four shillings and six pence for making book presses etc. for the Chancery office. Approved.

On report from Captain Coleman It is advised that the Claim of Charles Parpoint for thirty two Days Services as a Scout in Nelson County from the 8th of March 1789, be referred to the Auditor for settlement in the usual way.

It is advised that the Auditor be directed to settle in the usual way the Account of Armistead Long as a Collector of Vouchers allowing him a Dollar per day for 261 Days employed in riding.

On consideration of a letter from Col. Thomas Newton of this date, It is advised that he be desired to retain the Continental final settlement for four thousand Dollars, lodged in his hands as security for the payment of an execution served by him, when Sheriff, on Captain Thomas Brown for a Debt due the Commonwealth, until the Executors of the said Brown shall pay up *all* balances due from him to the Commonwealth; and that, should any suit be commenced against the said Newton for recovery of the final settlement aforesaid, *all* Damages and costs, if he be cast, shall be paid by the public.

Present Mr. Carter.

Upon application made and for good cause shewn, It is advised that fourteen per cent damages on the amount of the judgment obtained against Thomas Newton as Sheriff of Norfolk County for the certificate tax of 1786 be remitted, on his producing to the Governor a certificate of his having paid the balance of principal and interest, with one per cent Damages on said judgment.

On report from the Solicitor, It is advised that he be directed to take measures according to law for the removal of the property on which a Fi. Fa. hath been levied, to satisfy a judgment obtained against William McClanahan, as Sheriff of Botetourt for the revenue tax of 1782, to Bedford courthouse, there to be sold by as early a Day as possible, giving reasonable Notice of the time and place of sale; and that payment may be made for the said property in money or such Warrants or other government Securities of this state as were receiveable in the revenue tax of 1782.

That similar measures be taking for the removal and sale of such of the following property as may be of a movable nature, to wit:

Property taken to satisfy a judgment against Vivion Brooking, as Sheriff of Amelia, for the revenue tax of 1782, to be removed to Powhatan courthouse and sold on the same terms.

Property taken to satisfy a judgment against John Calaway, as Sheriff of Campbell, for the revenue tax of 1785, to be removed to Bedford courthouse and sold for money or such warrants or other Government securities of this state as were receivable in the revenue tax of 1785.

Property taken to satisfy a judgment against Abraham Shelton, as Sheriff of Pittsylvania for the revenue tax of 1785, to be removed to Halifax courthouse and sold on the terms next above.

Property taken to satisfy a judgment against John Johns as Sheriff of Buckingham for the certificate tax of 1785, to be removed to Cumberland Courthouse and sold for money or such Warrants or other government Securities of this State as were receivable in the certificate tax of 1785.

Property taken to satisfy a judgment against John Callaway as Sheriff of Campbell for the Certificate tax of 1785, to be removed to Bedford Courthouse and sold on the same terms.

Property taken to satisfy a judgment against Stephen Sampson, as Sheriff of Goochland for the certificate tax of 1785 to be removed to the City of Richmond and sold on the same terms.

Property taken to satisfy a judgment against Abram. Shelton as Sheriff of Pittsylvania for the certificate tax of 1785, to be removed to Halifax Courthouse and sold on the same terms.

Property taken to satisfy a Judgment against William Moore as Sheriff of Orange for the certificate tax of 1785 to be removed to Culpeper Courthouse and sold on the same terms.

Property taken to satisfy a judgment against William Washington as Sheriff of Westmoreland for the certificate tax of 1785, to be removed to King George courthouse and sold on same terms.

Property taken to satisfy a judgment against John Rogers as Sheriff of Southampton for the certificate tax of 1785, to be removed to Greenesville Courthouse and sold on the same terms.

Property taken to satisfy a judgment against Thomas Hugard as

Sheriff of Augusta for the revenue tax of 1786 to be removed to Rockbridge Courthouse and sold for money or such warrants or other government Securities of this State as were receivable in the revenue tax of 1786.

Property taken to satisfy a judgment against William Leftwich as Sheriff of Bedford for the revenue tax of 1786, to be removed to Campbell Courthouse and Sold on the same terms.

Property taken to satisfy a judgment against John Callaway, as Sheriff of Campbell, for the revenue tax of 1786, to be removed to Bedford Courthouse and sold on same terms.

Property taken to satisfy a judgment against Martin Pickett as Sheriff of Fauquier for the revenue tax of 1786, to be removed to Prince William Courthouse and sold on same terms.

Property taken to satisfy a judgment against Robert Woods as Sheriff of Franklin for the revenue tax of 1786 to be removed to Henry Courthouse and sold on the same terms.

Property taken to satisfy a judgment against Stephen Sampson as Sheriff of Goochland for the revenue tax of 1786, to be removed to the City of Richmond and sold on same terms.

Property taken to satisfy a judgment against John Lacy as Sheriff of New Kent for the revenue tax of 1786 to be removed to the City of Richmond and sold on same terms.

Property taken to satisfy a judgment against William Moore as Sheriff of Orange for the revenue tax of 1786, to be removed to Culpeper Courthouse and sold on same terms.

Property taken to satisfy a judgment against William Todd as Sheriff of Pittsylvania for the revenue tax of 1786, to be removed to Halifax Courthouse and sold on same terms.

Property taken to satisfy a judgment against George Rives as Sheriff of Sussex for the revenue tax of 1786, to be removed to Petersburg and sold on the same terms.

Property taken to satisfy a judgment against John Rogers as Sheriff of Southampton for the revenue tax of 1786, to be removed to Greenesville Courthouse and sold on same terms.

Property taken to satisfy a judgment against William Leftwick as Sheriff of Bedford for the certificate tax of 1786, to be removed to Campbell courthouse and sold for money or such warrants or other government Securities of this State as were receivable for the Certificate of 1786.

Property taken to satisfy a judgment against Morgan Morgan as Sheriff of Berkeley for the Certificate tax of 1786, to be removed to Winchester in Frederick and sold on same terms.

Property taken to satisfy a judgment against John Callaway as Sheriff of Campbell for the certificate tax of 1786 to be removed to Bedford Courthouse and sold on same terms.

Property taken to satisfy a judgment against Maurice Langhorne as Sheriff of Cumberland for the Certificate tax of 1786, to be removed to Powhatan Courthouse and sold on same terms.

Property taken to satisfy a judgment against Martin Pickett as Sheriff of Fauquier for the Certificate tax of 1786, to be removed to Prince William Courthouse and sold on same terms.

Property taken to satisfy a judgment against Robert Woods as Sheriff of Franklin for the certificate tax of 1786, to be removed to Henry Courthouse and sold on the same terms.

Property taken to satisfy a judgment against John Rogers as Sheriff of Southampton for the Certificate tax of 1786, to be removed to Greenesville Courthouse and sold on same terms.

Property taken to satisfy a judgment against George Rives as Sheriff of Sussex for the Certificate tax of 1786, to be removed to Petersburg and sold on same terms.

Property taken to satisfy a judgment against Joseph Fox as Sheriff of Westmoreland for the Certificate tax of 1786, to be removed to King George Courthouse and sold on the same terms.

All which matters so advised, the Governor orders accordingly.

> James Wood
> James McClurg
> Carter Braxton
> Robt. Goode
> Chs. Carter
> J. Dawson

Monday February 22d 1790

Present

The Governor

Mr. Wood	Mr. Goode
Mr. McClurg	Mr. Carter
Mr. Braxton	Mr. Dawson

The Board proceeded to the choice of a President in conformity to the Constitution or Form of Government and Mr. Wood being proposed was unanimously elected.

It is advised that a commission issue appointing William Henderson gentleman Sheriff of Campbell, in the room of Richard Stith who hath failed to give security according to law.

The Governor laid before the board a certificate of the Solicitor Stating that a bond dated the 5th of September 1787 given by Philip le Bayley and Bernard Maynier for £537.15.11 ½ the amount of Duties on the cargo of the Brig Dispatch part of which sum is for 11752 gallons of brandy of which quantity 11606 gallons appear to have been exported so that there remains 146 gallons still subject to Duty but the owner suggests that the said 146 gallons are exempted from Duty under the act of 1787 chapter 29. Whereupon it is advised that the Solicitor be directed to give credit for the amount of the Duty on the 146 Gallons of brandy on a bond of Mr. Quesnels[80] for duties now in his hands and that he inform Mr. Quesnel of this act of the Executive.

Mr. Tatham having offered to the board a scheme for obtaining Information relative to a Map and succinct history of the Southern part of the United States; They have no difficulty in expressing their wish that he may succeed in the application he makes to respectable characters in the several counties of this State for their aid in forwarding this work.

It is advised that Mr. Tatham be requested to mark off the Counties in Kentucky and the western parts of this state, on the Map transmitted by the Secretary of War for that purpose; and that the Governor make Mr. Tatham a reasonable allowance for so doing, to be charged to the United States.

All which matters so advised, the Governor orders accordingly.

> James Wood
> James McClurg
> Carter Braxton
> Robt. Goode
> J. Dawson
> Chs. Carter

Monday March 8th 1790

Present

The Governor

Mr. Wood	Mr. Braxton
Mr. McClurg	Mr. Goode
	Mr. Dawson

Mr. Wood informed the board that during the recess and indisposition of the Governor, he, as Lieutenant Governor, issued an additional Commission appointing David Bell, Josias Jones, Peter Guirrant, William Allen, Charles Moseley, Edmund Glover and George Ducguid gentlemen Justices of the peace for Buckingham County, they having been recommended according to law, that he issued a commission appointing Thomas Roane Sheriff for the County of King and Queen in the room of Thomas Coleman who refuses to qualify as a Justice of the peace by taking the Oath to the United States: Also Commissions appointing George Pegram jun. an Inspector of

---

80. "Queshel" in the clerk's index.

Tobacco at Robert Bollings warehouse in the room of Peter Thweat deceased and Robert Williams additional Inspector in the room of said Pegram: And that he directed to be paid out of the Contingent fund twenty five pounds to the Solicitor upon account for office expences. Approved.

The Governor laid before the board an account of Dabney Minor amounting to eleven pounds and seven pence half penny for carpenters work done on the public tenement occupied by the Governor. Whereupon it is advised that the said account be referred to the Auditor for settlement and a warrant on the Contingent fund for the sum due. (To be paid)

On the order of the Directors of the Lunatic Hospital, It is advised that a warrant issue to Joseph Hornsby Treasurer of the said Hospital, for two hundred pounds upon account. (To be paid)

It is advised that a commission issue appointing Robert Greenhow and Champeon Travis, gentlemen, to supply the vacancies in the Court of Directors for the public Hospital in the City of Williamsburg occasioned by the resignations of John Blair and James Innes esquires.

It is advised that the Auditor be directed to settle the account of William Price for his services in collecting Vouchers for Col. Davies, allowing him a Dollar per day for nine Days riding, and two Dollars per Day for two Days employed in examining and copying Capt. Peytons Accounts.   to be paid out of the Contingent fund.

The Governor laid before the board a letter from Mr. Harry Innes resigning the office of Attorney general for Kentucky District. Whereupon it is advised, that a temporary Commission issue appointing George Nicholas esqr. to that office.

It is advised that the pension of Mary Anne Jolly, who has no child to maintain, be reduced to seven pounds per annum from the 1st of January last.

It is advised that a warrant issue to William Pierce for thirty pounds for the last years Salary as Keeper of the public buildings (to be paid out of the Contingent fund).

Martin Oster esquire Vice Consul of France having certified to the Executive in due form of law, that he had taken cognizance of a certain controversy arising between the Sieur Alexis François Joseph Dauchy, represented by his brother the Sieur Pierre Franço[is] Dauchy, complainant, and the Sieurs Adrian Wiscart and Augustine de Neuville Defendants and, had, on the 10th of September 1788, determined the same by condemning the Defendants to render good and sufficient accounts of their management of the Cargoe of the Ship St. Allegonde, belonging to the complainant and to pay him the balance, and the whole costs of suit etc., with in five months from the Day on which notice of this Sentence shall be given to the Sieur Peter Robert de Neuville their representative, under penalty of being constrained thereto, and imprisoned, And the said Martin Oster having requested aid for executing the said determination, It is advised that an order issue to the Sheriff of Hanover, in the usual form, for executing the said Determination.

On consideration of a letter from Col. Arthur Campbell of the 20th Ultimo informing that the ammunition lately granted to the Chickasaw Indians is at present deposited in a very unsafe place, and requesting permission of the Executive to order a guard for its protection, It is advised that Mr. Campbell be informed that the executive do not think themselves authorized, under the present circumstances, to order a guard, but they recommend to the good citizens, in its neighbourhood, to embody themselves as Volunteers for the protection of the property of our allies on the approach of an enemy. It is also advised that Mr. Campbells letter be transmitted to the President of the United States: And that the account of James Davis, the Express who brought the said letter, be referred to the Auditor for settlement; allowing him six dollars for the time he has been detained in Richmond. to be paid out of the Contingent fund.

The Governor submitted to the consideration of the board a letter of the 18 of January, from Governor St. Clair informing that incursions have been made by parties from this State into the territory of the United States with a design of committing depredations on the Tribes of Indians in amity with the United States, and requesting the interposition of the Executive to prevent such unjustifiable conduct. Whereupon it is advised that a circular letter be written to the Lieutenants of the Western Counties enjoining them to exert all their authority to prevent such injurious practices in future; and that Governor St. Clair be informed of these measures.

All which matters so advised, the Governor orders accordingly.

> James Wood
> James McClurg
> Carter Braxton
> Robt. Goode
> J. Dawson

Friday March 12th 1790

Present

The Governor

Mr. Wood	Mr. Goode
Mr. McClurg	Mr. Briggs
Mr. Braxton	Mr. Dawson

It is advised that the Agent for selling the public Tobacco be directed to render to the Executive as soon as he conveniently can an account of his Agency stating the quantity of tobacco received by him, the price at which it was received into the Treasury, the price at which it has been actually sold, the quantity now on hand and the sums not yet collected from the different purchasers.

It is advised that a commission issue appointing Samuel Todd Sheriff of Botetourt County in the room of Martin Mcfarren who refuses to accept the said office: and that the Solicitor be instructed to move against the said Mcfarran for his refusal to accept and execute the said office.

It is advised that a Duplicate Certificate be granted to John Smith placing him on the pension List with twelve pounds per annum from January 1786, he having produced satisfactory proofs of the loss of his original Certificate, and of his receiving no part of his said pension.

Mr. Briggs, Mr. Carter and Mr. Dawson are appointed a Committee for the examination of the Treasury books.

It is advised that the account of John Conner amounting to five pounds five shillings for house rent as an office to the High Court of Chancery up to the 4th instant, be referred to the auditor for settlement and a warrant on the contingent fund for the sum due. (To be paid)

All which matters so advised, the Governor orders accordingly.

James Wood
James McClurg
Carter Braxton
Robt. Goode
Jno. H. Briggs
J. Dawson

Monday March 15th 1790

Present

The Governor

Mr. Wood   Mr. Goode
Mr. McClurg   Mr. Briggs
Mr. Braxton   Mr. Carter
Mr. Dawson

The Governor informed the board that in the recess, he directed Judith Miller to be put on the pension List with an allowance of ten pounds per annum from the 1st of January 1786; it having been certified that She is in indigent circumstances, and has three children. Approved.

It is advised that a duplicate certificate be granted to Albeon Gordon as a pensioner with eighteen pounds per annum; it appearing that his original certificate is lost.

For reasons appearing to the board, It is advised that the Instruction of the 12th to the Solicitor for proceeding against Martin Mcfarran for refusing the Office of Sheriff, be rescinded.

The Commissioner for selling Gosport Lands having reported that he has a number of Certificates, received on Account of the Sales of said lands, and sundry bonds that are still due, It is advised that the said Certificates be returned to the Treasurer for the purposes of the Sinking fund, and the bonds to the solicitor that he may take measures for the collection of the same: And it is further Advised that the Treasurer be instructed to grant Deeds to the purchasers of Lots, on payment being made for them.

The Governor laid before the board the accounts of Major Porterfield, and Mr. Johnson his assistant in collecing Vouchers in support of the Claims of this State against the United States. Whereupon it is advised that Major Porterfield be allowed thirty two pounds twelve shillings and eight pence in addition to the thirty pounds advanced him, and Mr. Johnson eighty pounds, in full compensation for their services and expences. To be paid out of the Contingent fund.

All which matters so advised, the Governor orders accordingly.

James Wood
James McClurg
Carter Braxton
Robt. Goode
Jno. H. Briggs
Chs. Carter
J. Dawson

Thursday March 18th 1790

Present

The Governor

Mr. Wood	Mr. Goode
Mr. McClurg	Mr. Briggs
Mr. Braxton	Mr. Carter

Mr. Dawson

The Governor informed the board that he had received confirmation of the death of Col. Wm. Grayson, which occasions a vacancy in the Senate of the United States. Whereupon the board agree to make a temporary appointment of a Senator in the room of the said Grayson on Thursday next.

It appearing to the board that Robert Andrews late Sheriff of James City stands charged with a sum of money which was collected by his predecessor in office, It is advised that the Solicitor be directed to give a credit to the said Robert Andrews for such Sums as he shall produce authentic Vouchers proving the payment to have been to his predecessor, and that he move for judgment (agreeably to the 12th Section of the Act for the more speedy recovery of Debts due to the Commonwealth) against the Sheriff who proceeded to collect such money without having given bond according to law.

All which matters so advised, the Governor orders accordingly.

> James Wood
> James McClurg
> Carter Braxton
> Robt. Goode
> Jno. H. Briggs
> Chs. Carter
> J. Dawson

Thursday March 25th 1790

Present

The Governor

Mr. Wood	Mr. Goode
Mr. McClurg	Mr. Briggs
Mr. Braxton	Mr. Carter

Mr. Dawson

The Governor informed the board that in the recess he issued a Commission appointing David Clarke a Collector of the taxes due in Pittsylvania for the year 1787, in the room of John Buckley who hath failed to give Security: that he granted a pardon to negro Joe condemned to death by the Judgment of Nottaway County, for attempting the murder of his master by administering poison; the said Joe having been recommended by the court as a proper object of mercy; and that he issued a Warrant on the contingent fund in favor of Colonel Davies for fifteen pounds on account of the expences of his office. Approved.

By virtue of the constitution of the United States of America, It is advised, that George Mason esquire be appointed to act as a Senator for this Commonwealth, in the room of Wm. Grayson deceased, until the next meeting of the Legislature; and that a Commission be made out in due form and transmitted to Mr. Mason by express.

It is advised that Elizabeth Shipwash who is 45 years old and have three children, be continued on the List of pensioners with an allowance of ten pounds per annum from the 1st of January 1786.

It is advised that a warrant issue on the Contingent Fund for twenty pounds payable to Major Pryor as compensation for his services in furnishing Vouchers in support of the Claims of this State against the United States. (to be paid)

It is advised that a Commission issue appointing John Fenton

Public Jailor for the District of Williamsburg in the room of John Crump deceased.

On recommendations, It is advised that an additional Commission issue appointing Thomas Barbee a Justice of the peace for the county of Mercer: and that a commission issue appointing William Overton Callis Escheator for the county of Louisa.

On consideration of a letter from the Solicitor stating that his health is so far impaired as to render a recess from business indispensably necessary; It is advised that he be permitted to retire from public business for a while, and that Mr. Shepherd be authorized to act during his necessary absence.

It is advised that a warrant issue on the Contingent fund for four pounds to Joseph Leiplong upon account, to defray his expences in going express to Mr. Mason. (To be paid)

The Governor laid before the board a letter from the Auditor stating that the Collectors of the revenue conceived themselves at liberty to discharge the arrearages of taxes in facilities or tobacco without the returns required by the laws which regulated the different collections, that he doubted whether this construction of the 11th section of the Act of the last Session of Assembly for enforcing the collection and payment of the Debts due to the Commonwealth and for other purposes could be supported, had refused to admit such payments although the law had not prescribed any mode by which he could distinguish the particular periods at which the collections were made, that in consequence thereof the arrearages of taxes will come in slowly and the public be thereby greatly injured and requesting the direction of the Executive as to the manner in which he shall proceed in future. Whereupon it is advised that the Auditor be directed to admit all payments in such facilities or Tobacco as are receiveable by law.

All which matters so advised, the Governor orders accordingly.

> James Wood
> James McClurg
> Carter Braxton
> Robt. Goode
> Jno. H. Briggs
> Chs. Carter
> J. Dawson

Monday March 29th 1790

Present

The Governor

Mr. Wood	Mr. Goode
Mr. McClurg	Mr. Briggs
Mr. Braxton	Mr. Carter
Mr. Dawson	

The Governor informed the board that in the recess he issued Commissions appointing Francis Duvall inspector at Poropotank warehouse in the room of Richard Taliaferro deceased, and John Jones an additional Inspector at the said warehouse in the room of the said Duvall: Also a commission appointing John Davenport Coroner for the County of Berkeley, he having been recommended by the Court. Approved.

It is advised that a commission issue appointing Thomas Walke Sheriff of Princess anne county in the room of Cason More who is unable to give security.

The Governor laid before the Board an account of Archibald Denholm for his trouble and expences in collecting Vouchers. Whereupon it is advised that the Auditor be directed to settle the said Account allowing Mr. Denholm 4/. per Day from the 14th of April 1789 to the 26th november following for his trouble, exclusive of expences; and to grant a warrant on the contingent fund for the sum due. (To be paid.)

On recommendation, It is advised that an additional commission issue appointing John Dangerfield, George William Smith, Richard Banks jun., Richard Gatewood, Robert Beverley junr., James Garnett, Sthreshley Rennolds, Thomas Corbin and Paul Micow jun. Justices of the peace for the county of Essex.

On consideration of a letter from Alexander Donald, It is advised that he be allowed until the first of May next to make payment for the tobaccoes purchased by him of the public Agent provided the Deposits remain in Mr. Heths hands subject to be sold without notice should the public be in *absolute* want of money at any time before the said first Day of May.

It is advised that 1000 Copies of the Act of Congress "providing for the enumeration of the inhabitants of the United States" be printed and distributed in the several Counties.

Upon application made and for good cause shewn It is advised that the Damages on the amount of the Judgments obtained against James Upshaw as Sheriff of Caroline for the Certificate taxes of 1785 and 1786 be remitted.

It is advised that Mary Rowling, Sarah Stacy, Susanna Rawlings, alias Rowland, and Eve Clark[81] be continued on the pension List for the year 1789, with their former allowances.

On report from the Solicitor, It is advised that he be directed to take measures according to law for the removal of the property which has been taken to satisfy the judgments obtained against John Lawrence as Sheriff of Hanover for the revenue taxes of 1785 and 1786 and certificate tax of 1786, to the City of Richmond; there to be sold by as early a day as possible, giving reasonable notice of the time and place of sale; and that payment may be made for the said property in money

---

81. "Clarke" in the clerk's index.

or such Warrants or other government securities of this State as were receiveable in the revenue and certificate taxes for the respective years afore said. That similar measures be taken for the removal and sale of such of the following property as may be of a moveable nature to wit:

Property taken to satisfy the judgments obtained against James Ewell as Sheriff of Prince William for the revenue taxes of 1785 and 1786 and certificate taxes of 1786, to be removed to Alexandria and sold on the same terms.

Property taken to satisfy a judgment obtained against Newman Brockenbrough as Sheriff of Essex for the Certificate tax of 1785, to be removed to Caroline Courthouse and sold for money or such warrants or other government securities of this State as were receiveable in the Certificate tax of 1785, and

Property taken to satisfy a judgment obtained against Lawrence Baker as Sheriff of Isle of Wight for the Certificate tax of 1785, to be removed to Suffolk in Nansemond and sold on the same terms.

All which matters so advised, the Governor orders accordingly.

> James Wood
> James McClurg
> Charles Braxton
> Robt. Goode
> Jno. H. Briggs
> Chs. Carter
> J. Dawson—but he dissents

from the determination of the board in the case of Mr. Donald, because he thinks the power of granting such indulgences *clearly* taken from the Executive by a Resolution of the last assembly, and the practice injurious to the sinking Fund.

Wednesday March 31st 1790

Present

The Governor

Mr. Wood	Mr. Goode
Mr. McClurg	Mr. Briggs
Mr. Braxton	Mr. Carter

Mr. Dawson

The Governor informed the Board that he yesterday issued a commission appointing James Taylor junr. Surveyor of Caroline, and directed him to give bond in the penalty of two thousand pounds. approved.

George Mason esquire having refused to Act as a Senator of the United States, It is advised that a commission be made out in due form appointing John Walker esquire in the room of Mr. Mason.

It is advised that the Account of McColl and Cunliffe amounting to seven pounds five and ten pence for coal furnished for the use of the Auditor's office, also the account of Joseph Leiplong for express hire in going to Mr. Mason, be referred to the Auditor for settlement and warrants on the Contingent fund for the sums due (to be paid).

On recommendations It is advised that an additional Commission issue appointing Thomas Posey, John Herndon, Edward Herndon jr., Lewis Holladay, Stockley Towles, Francis Thornton junr., and Charles Carter junr., justices of the peace for the County of Spotsylvania, also a commission appointing Hezekiah Ellis an additional Inspector at Roystons warehouses in said county; and a Commission appointing Peter Eppes Coroner of Prince George County in the room of William Eppes who hath resigned.

The Governor laid before the board the account of the Solicitor for his trouble in collecting the Sales of the public boats. Whereupon it is advised that the Auditor be directed to settle the said account allowing Mr. Wood one per centum on his collections as full compensation (to be paid).

It is advised that the Treasurer be directed to borrow from any funds, money sufficient to pay the present quarters salary due to the officers of civil Government; taking care to replace the same as soon as possible.

All which matters so advised, the Governor orders accordingly.

James Wood
James McClurg
Carter Braxton
Robt. Goode
Jno. H. Briggs
Chs. Carter
J. Dawson

Tuesday April 13th 1790

Present

The Governor

Mr. Wood   Mr. Goode
Mr. Braxton   Mr. Briggs

The Governor informed the board that in the recess he issued an additional commission appointing Richard Gains Junr., Thomas Bedford, Quin Morton, James Pattillo, Gideon Spencer, and Hillery Moseley gentlemen Justices of the peace for the County of Charlotte; they having been recommended for that purpose; that on recommendations he issued Commissions appointing Benjamin Edmondson Sheriff for Charles City County; Donald Campbell an Alderman for the borough of Norfolk; and William E. Broadnax Coroner for the County of Brunswick, that he examined and certified for payment the Auditors account for his last quarters salary, that he directed to be paid out of the Contingent fund Col. Daviess draft for forty pounds in part of his quarters salary due the 1st instant, five pounds to Col. Cameron for his services in copying certain Vouchers for Col. Davies, also eight pounds to Mr. Veriker, who is engaged in the like business, upon account; also three pounds to Jane West in advance for nursing Catherine Crulls child; also thirty five pounds to the Solicitor upon account for sending out executions etc. And thirty pounds to Edmund Randolph esquire upon Account to enable the compilers of the laws to employ a transcribing Clerk: And that he referred to the Auditor for settlement in the usual way the accounts of Captain Langham amounting to One hundred and thirty six pounds nineteen shillings for pay due the Superintendant and Artificers at the Point of Fork up to the first instant and seventy two pounds twelve shillings due the guard up to the same time, as certified by Capt. Coleman: Approved.

On recommendations It is advised that Commissions issue appointing Richard Ogleby Coroner for the County of Amelia; Richard Evers Lee Recorder for the Borough of Norfolk, and John Skidmore Sheriff for the County of Pendleton.

It is advised that the following Accounts for Jail expences as certified by the District Court held in the City of Richmond be referred to the Auditor for settlement and Warrants on the Contingent fund for the Sums due viz.

Doctor Wm. Carters Account for medicine etc.	£8.	14.	9½
John Ropers Ditto for fuel	19.	10.	0
Wm. Claibornes Ditto for a load of straw	0.	9.	0
Z. Tatte and Jos. Harwell for guarding the prisoners from Goal to the Capitol for trial	1.	4.	0
William Rose for provisions	12.	4.	0

This last account to be paid.

On consideration of the accounts of Elisha Price and J. B. Clausel for expences in cleaning out the Court room, and the Accounts of Joseph McCaughey and Southall and Trower for repairs done to the District Jail in this City; It is advised that the same be rejected; The board conceiving it to be the Duty of Mr. Pierce who receives an annual Salary as Keeper of the public buildings, to have the court rooms cleaned out occasionally; and of the county court to keep the Jail in repair.

On application from the Directors of the public buildings, It is advised that the Auditor be directed to grant them a Warrant for two hundred and sixty pounds upon account to be applied to the purpose of building a pediment roof on the Capitol the money to be borrowed pursuant to law.

All which matters so advised, the Governor orders accordingly.

James Wood
Carter Braxton
Robt. Goode
Jno. H. Briggs
Chs. Carter

Saturday May 1st 1790

Present

The Governor

Mr. Wood   Mr. Goode
Mr. McClurg   Mr. Briggs
Mr. Braxton   Mr. Carter
Mr. Dawson

The Governor informed the board that in the recess he directed to be paid out of the contingent fund two hundred pounds being the balance of the order of the Directors of the Lunatic Hospital to Joseph Hornsby upon account for the purposes of the said Hospital, and fourteen pounds to John Groves in payment for the floor cloth furnished for the Council chamber, that he referred to the Auditor for settlement in the usual way the account of Thomas Nicolson for printing advertizements etc. per order of the Treasurer; also the account of Thos. Brend for record books and stationary furnished for the use of the Registers office as per his certificate; also an account for stationary furnished for the use of the Treasury office; also the account of Colonel William Davies for the balance of his last quarters Salary as commissioner for settling the Accounts of this State with the United States; Also the Accounts of Andrew Dunscombe[82] and Reubin Burnley for their last quarters salary as Clerks to Col. Davies; that on recommendations he issued additional Commissions appointing John Beel and James Caruthers gentlemen justices of the peace for the County of Rockbridge; John Lovell (son of Lancaster), Erasmus Haynes, Peter Evans, Thomas Wishart, junr., William Walke, James Blamire and James Dawley gentlemen Justices of the peace for the County of Princess Anne; George Rutledge, James Barnett, Samuel Eason, Andrew Lewis, Rowland Madison, James Woods, John Kent, Thomas Goodson and William Goodson gentlemen Justices of the peace (and of the quorum) for the county of Montgomery, that on recommendations he issued commissions appointing Henry Hill and Robert Coleman Coroners for the county of Culpeper, Nathl. Chapman Hunter an additional inspector at Dumfries warehouses in the

---

82. "Dunscomb" in the clerk's index.

room of Matthew Anderson who hath resigned, that he issued a commission appointing William Love Sheriff of Wythe County in the room of James Newell who is about to remove out of the said county, the he directed to be paid to Captain Langham Sixty seven pounds fourteen shillings and four pence upon account to purchase clothing for the use of the Post at the Point of Fork agreeably to estimate; And that with the concurrence of Mr. Wood, Mr. McClurg and Mr. Goode he directed the Treasurer to borrow a sufficient sum of money to pay fifty shillings on each public share in the James river company. Approved.

In pursuance of an act of the General Assembly "for selling certain escheated Lands in the County of Norfolk" It is advised that the Escheator for the said county be instructed to sell as soon as may be, on twelve months credit for Cash, giving due notice of the time and place of sale, a tract of land in the County of Norfolk, late the property of John Bowness but now vested in the commonwealth by escheat; taking bond and good security for the amount of such sale, which bond he will transmit to this board without delay.

Upon applications made and for good cause shewn, It is advised, that the Damages on the amount of the following Judgments be remitted, viz. a Judgment against Joseph Moore as Sheriff of Rockbridge for the revenue taxes of 1787, Judgments against John Houston as Sheriff of the said County for the revenue and certificate taxes of 1786; a judgment against Henry Skipwith as Sheriff of Cumberland for the revenue taxes of 1787, a judgment against Goodrich Willson as Sheriff of Isle of Wight for the revenue taxes of 1784, a judgment against Richard Crump as Sheriff of Powhatan for the revenue taxes of 1786, judgments against John Blackwell as Sheriff of Fauquier for the revenue taxes of 1784 and 1785, Judgments against Martin Pickett as Sheriff of Fauquier for the certificate taxes of 1786 and revenue taxes of 1787, and a judgment against Newman Brockenbrough as Sheriff of Essex for the Certificate tax of 1785.

The Governor laid before the board a Contract of Tunstal Quarles for furnishing the Post at the point of Fork with provisions, Whereupon it is advised that the same be approved.

It is advised that Spencer Martin alias David Patterson who stands attainted of horsestealing by the judgment of Petersburg District Court, and James Johnston attainted of burglary by the Judgment of the District Court held at Richmond in April last, be pardoned; they appearing to be proper objects of mercy.

It is advised that the Auditor be directed to issue a warrant in favor of the commissioners of the Marine Hospital for four hundred pounds upon account for the purposes of the said hospital agreeably to the act of Assembly in that case made.

It is advised that the account of the Solicitor amounting to sixty two pounds eight and eleven pence for office expences, be referred to the auditor for settlement and a warrant on the contingent fund for the sum due (to be paid).

On consideration of a letter from Col. Anthony Thornton Lieut. of Caroline, concerning the militia fines of the said County; It is advised that he be directed to proceed to collect the said fines according to the directions of the tenth Section of the Act "to amend and reduce into one Act the several laws for regulating and disciplining the Militia and guarding against invasions and insurrections."

All which matters so advised, the Governor orders accordingly.

James Wood
James McClurg
Carter Braxton
Robt. Goode
Jno. H. Briggs
Chs. Carter
J. Dawson

Monday May 3d 1790

Present

The Governor

Mr. Wood   Mr. Goode
Mr. McClurg   Mr. Briggs
Mr. Braxton   Mr. Carter
             Mr. Dawson

On consideration of the case of Solomon Shepherd late Sheriff of Nansemond, It is advised that the Solicitor be directed in settling the interest on the judgment obtained against the said Shepherd for the revenue taxes of 1784, to calculate the same from the 25th of June 1785; it appearing that the bond for collection was not executed until the March Court in 1785.

On recommendation It is advised that a commission issue appointing William Cook Escheator for the County of Louisa in the room of William Overton Callis who hath resigned.

Upon application made and for good cause shewn It is advised that the Damages on the amount of the judgment against Matthew Simn as Sheriff of Halifax for the revenue taxes of 1787, be remitted; it appearing that the balance due was lodged in the treasury the first instant, though not finally settled until today.

It is advised that the auditor be directed to issue the usual warrant to Captain Langham for eighty five pounds sixteen shillings and four pence for supplies furnished the post at the Point of Fork from the 1st of February to the thirtieth of April last as certified by Capt. Coleman.

Upon application made and for good cause shewn, It is advised that the damages on the amount of the judgment against Maurice Langhorne as Sheriff of Cumberland for the revenue taxes of 1786 be remitted; it appearing that the balance was paid into the treasury the 1st instant.

A memorial from the honorable James Mercer respecting the situation of Sr. John Peytons Estate in consequence of certain resolutions of the last Assembly suspending any further proceedings on the Judgments obtained by the said Sr. John against the Estates of John Fox and Peter B. Whiting until the 1st of October next, being laid before the board, they are of opinion that no injury could have been intended to Sr. J. Peyton by the Legislature, and therefore, although they have no power to suspend the Executions, they recommend to the Solicitor to direct the Sheriff of Gloster to postpone all Sales of Sr. J. Peytons estate on account of the Executions against him as high Sheriff of the County until the 1st October next.

All which matters so advised the Governor orders accordingly.

> James Wood
> James McClurg
> Carter Braxton
> Robt. Goode
> Jno. H. Briggs
> J. Dawson
> Chs. Carter

Friday [i.e., Tuesday] May 11th 1790

Present

The Governor

Mr. Wood
Mr. McClurg
Mr. Braxton

Mr. Goode
Mr. Briggs
Mr. Dawson

The Governor informed the board that in the recess he issued commissions appointing Richard Davis and William Hackney inspectors and John Sutton additional inspector at Kemps warehouses in Middlesex county; John Glenn Sheriff of Lunenburg, Daniel Hankens Collector of the revenue tax of 1789 in Pittsylvania, and James Johnson, Vincent Shelton, Crispin Shelton, jr., William Wilkinson, William Clark, Gilbert Hunt, William Durrett, George Adams and Samuel Calland gentlemen Justices of the peace for the said County of Pittsylvania, the said appointments being agreeable to recommendations, that with the concurrence of Mr. Wood, Mr. Goode and Mr. Dawson he directed to be paid out of the Contingent fund twenty five pounds to A. Blair for four months salary as Keeper of the public seal ending the 4th instant and nine pounds to Major Peter Williams for his

services in collecting Vouchers in support of the Claims of this State
against the United States; that he appointed Mr. Peter Woodlief[83] in
the room of Major Williams to compleat the collection of the said
Vouchers in his district: and that he issued a Commission appointing
John Holman, Coroner for the County of Cumberland. Approved.

On consideration of the case of John Ross, It is advised that his
pension be reduced to six pounds per annum from January last.

The Governor laid before the board a letter from Mr. Madison,
one of the representatives of this State in Congress, informing that
some persons are taking advantage of the officers and soldiers of the
Virginia and North Carolina lines of the late army in whose favor an
appropriation was made at the last Session of Congress; and recommending that some measures should be taken to prevent such unjust
speculations. Whereupon it is advised, that, to accommodate those who
may be prevented from attending in person at the Seat of Government,
Captain Anthony Singleton be appointed Agent with authority to
receive, from all such original Claimants who may think proper to
confide their Interest to him, powers of Attorney duely authenticated,
and to secure to their use the benefit of the said appropriation; and that
the Clerk publish in the Gazettes the substance of this determination.

On recommendations, It is advised that Commissions issue appointing Lewis Parham and William G. Baptist Coroners for Mecklenburg County; and that an additional Commission issue appointing
Granville Smith, Christopher Manlove, William McKinzie, Thomas
Burfoot, Thomas Railey, Matthew Cheatham and Thomas A. Taylor
gentlemen Justices of the peace for the county of Chesterfield.

On consideration of the memorial from Philip Pendleton, Moses
Hunter, and David Hunter concerning the Claim of Denny Fairfax to
certain lands in the Northern neck, It is advised that a copy of the said
Memorial be referred to the Attorney General with Directions to
inquire how far the right or dignity of this Commonwealth may be
concerned in the dispute between the Memorialists and Denny Fairfax
stated in the said Memorial; And that he take all proper Steps to secure
the Interests of the Commonwealth if they shall appear to him to be at
all engaged therein.

The Governor laid before the board the Account of Wm. J.
Vereker[84] for his services in examining the books and papers of
Richard Claiborne; late Deputy Quarter master, and of his assistants,
and selecting therefrom sundry Accounts returns and Vouchers to be
exhibited by this Commonwealth as Claims against the United States.
Whereupon it is advised that Mr. Vereker be paid out of the Contingent fund twenty eight pounds in addition to the eight pounds
received, as full compensation for his said services.

83. "Peter Woodleif" in the clerk's index.
84. "Veriker" in the clerk's index.

It is advised that a Warrant issue on the Contingent fund in favor of Doctor Foushee for ten pounds being the balance of pay due him to the 1st of January last for examining and reporting the wounds of invalid pensioners; and that the annual allowance to the Doctor for such services be discontinued from the said first of January.

On consideration of a letter from Col. Thomas Newton, and the report of Capt. Coleman concerning certain cannon, It is advised that Col. Newton be desired not to suffer the cannon claimed by Col. Finnie as continental property to be removed until the right of the United States be fully shewn to the Executive, and their order obtained for the removal of the same, that he be requested to examine and report the present situation of the cannon dispersed about in his part of the Country, the grounds on which the Claim of the state to them is founded, and an estimate of the probable expences of collecting and securing the said Cannon; and that Captain Coleman be directed to take measures for removing and securing the cannon found in the woods near this City.

All which matters so advised, the Governor orders accordingly.

James Wood
James McClurg
Carter Braxton
Robt. Goode
Jno. H. Briggs
J. Dawson

Wednesday May 12th 1790

Present

The Governor

Mr. Wood	Mr. Goode
Mr. McClurg	Mr. Briggs
Mr. Braxton	Mr. Dawson

On application made, It is advised that the property taken to satisfy the judgment obtained against Stephen Sampson as Sheriff of Goochland for the revenue taxes of 1786, be removed for sale to the Point of Fork in Fluvanna, instead of the City of Richmond.

The Governor laid before the Council the report of the committee appointed to visit and examine the offices of the Treasurer, Auditor and Solicitor, Whereupon it is advised that the same lie for examination.

It is advised that Mr. Goode, Mr. Briggs and Mr. Madison be appointed a Committee, for the present quarter, to visit and examine the above offices.

All which matters so advised, the Governor orders accordingly.

James Wood
James McClurg
Carter Braxton
Robt. Goode
Jno. H. Briggs
J. Dawson

Saturday May 15th 1790

Present

The Governor

Mr. Wood	Mr. Goode
Mr. McClurg	Mr. Briggs
Mr. Braxton	Mr. Dawson

The Governor informed the board that in the recess he issued a commission appointing Leonard George Surveyor for Middlesex County and required him to give bond in a thousand pounds penalty; and that he referred to the Auditor for settlement in the usual way, the Account of Capt. Eskridge allowing him a Dollar per day for 130 Days services in collecting Vouchers. Approved.

The Governor laid before the board a protested bill of exchange drawn by Oliver Pollock the 26th of May 1780, on Messrs. Penett Da Costa freres and Company for three thousand two hundred and seventy eight Dollars, which appears to be one of the bills for which a part of Mr. Pollocks claim was retained by order of the Executive the 14th of January 1786 in pursuance of a resolution of the General Assembly of the 7th of same month. Whereupon it is advised that the Auditor be directed to issue a Warrant on the foreign fund for the above sum of 3278 Dollars, with eighteen per cent damages and six per cent interest from the first of August one thousand seven hundred and eighty two.

On recommendation, It is advised that an additional Commission issue appointing William Murray and Pleasant Roberts gentlemen justices of the peace for the County of Amelia.

The Governor laid before the board the Contract of the Directors of the public buildings with Samuel Dobie to put a flat roof on the capitol, together with the said Dobies account in consequence thereof. Whereupon it is advised, in pursuance of the resolve of the General Assembly authorising the Executive to compromise with the said Dobie, that he be allowed one hundred pounds as full compensation on account of said contract.

On consideration of the case of Matthew Cox, It is advised that the fine of ten shillings imposed on him by a Court of enquiry for Cumberland County for not attending Muster in November 1787, be remitted.

All which matters so advised the Governor orders accordingly.

James Wood
James McClurg
Carter Braxton
Robt. Goode
Jno. H. Briggs
J. Dawson

Tuesday May 18th 1790

Present

The Governor

Mr. Wood	Mr. Goode
Mr. McClurg	Mr. Briggs
Mr. Braxton	Mr. Dawson

Alexander Herring having been appointed Surveyor of Rockingham County; It is advised that he be required to give bond in one thousand pounds penalty.

On recommendations It is advised that an additional Commission issue appointing Benjamin Temple, John White, Robert Pollard, Thomas Nelson, William F. Gaines, Edward Pye Chamberlaine, John Roane Junr., and William Gregory gentlemen justices of the peace for the county of King William; and that a Commission issue appointing John Botte Sheriff of Chesterfield County.

It being uncertain when Mr. Madison will return, It is advised that Mr. Dawson be appointed in his room, one of the Committee to visit and examine the public offices.

All which matters so advised, the Governor orders accordingly.

James Wood
James McClurg
Robt. Goode
Carter Braxton
Jno. H. Briggs
J. Dawson

Friday May 21st 1790

Present

The Governor

Mr. Wood   Mr. Goode
Mr. McClurg   Mr. Briggs
                    Mr. Dawson

The Governor informed the board that upon application made and for good cause shewn, during the recess, he directed the remission of damages on the amount of a judgment obtained against Joseph Winn as Sheriff of Lunenburg for the revenue taxes of 1787, it appearing that the balance was paid up prior to the first instant. Approved.

The board resumed the consideration of the report of the Committee appointed to visit and examine the Public Offices, and, having prepared some Instructions thereon, advise that the further consideration of the said report be postponed.

All which matters so advised the Governor orders accordingly.

James Wood
James McClurg
Robt. Goode
Jno. H. Briggs
J. Dawson

Tuesday May 25th 1790

Present

The Governor

Mr. Wood   Mr. Goode
Mr. McClurg   Mr. Briggs
Mr. Braxton   Mr. Carter
                    Mr. Dawson

The Governor laid before the board an Account of Aug. Davis amounting to four hundred and four pounds seventeen shillings and six pence for printing a number of copies of the Laws and Journals of the first Session of Congress, Whereupon It is advised that the said account be referred to the Auditor for settlement and a Warrant on the Contingent fund for the sum due (to be paid).

The Governor laid before the board a letter from the County Lieutenant of Goochland inclosing the proceedings of a Court martial held for his County on the sixth Day of April last which proceedings are as follows, viz. "At a court martial held at the Courthouse, on Tuesday the 6th of April 1790, present John Guerrant jr. Col., Ro. H. Saunders

Lt. Col., Howell Lewis Capt. of Cavalry, Gideon Hatcher, David Mullin, John Brett, Archelaus Perkins, Samuel Pryor, William Sampson, Stephen Ellis and Heath J. Miller gentlemen Captains, This Court taking into consideration the authority vested in them by the Federal constitution, are of opinion "that they have no constitutional power to impose fines upon the delinquencies which have occurred since the last Court Martial. Ordered that all fines assessed for delinquences since the adoption of the new constitution be remitted, Howell Lewis Captain of Cavalry, dissenting from the above determination.

Signed

John Guerrant jr. Col.

a copy Teste Tho. F. Bates Clk."

Whereupon it is advised that so much of the said proceedings as relate to the remission of Fines assessed upon militia Delinquents Subsequent to the adoption of the new foederal constitution be declared to be illegal and that the County Lieutenant be directed to proceed according to law in the collection of any fines which have been assessed within his county notwithstanding the order of the abovementioned court martial.

All which matters so advised the Governor orders accordingly.[85]

James Wood

James McClurg

Carter Braxton

Robt. Goode

Jno. H. Briggs

Chs. Carter

J. Dawson

Saturday May 29th 1790

Present

The Governor

Mr. Wood	Mr. Goode
Mr. McClurg	Mr. Briggs
Mr. Braxton	Mr. Carter

Mr. Dawson

The Governor informed the board, that during the Recess he had referred to the Auditor for settlement, an account of Captain Samuel Eddins as Searcher at the Port of York for the hire of Negroes as Oarsmen from the 5th of March to the 1st of August 1789 and had ordered a Warrant on the Contingent fund for the sum due (to be paid) which was approved.

<hr>

85. *See* page 346 for the additional journal entry dated 25 May 1790.

On recommendation it is advised, that a Commission issue appointing Charles Russell, Coroner for the county of Prince George in the room of Peter Eppes, who declines accepting that office.

It is advised, that Sarah Wilkinson,[86] Susanna Rowland, Susanna Rawlings, Mary Rowland,[87] Sarah Stacey[88] and Eve Clark be continued on the list of Pensioners, Wilkinson and Stacy with an allowance of six pounds each, Susanna Rowland and Eve Clark[89] with Eight pounds each, and Susanna Rawlings and Mary Rowland with ten pounds each yearly, commencing the first day of January 1790.

The Governor laid before the Board the petition of John Halcombe in behalf of Thomas Flournoy late High Sheriff of Prince Edward County setting forth, that he has been prevented from obtaining a considerable credit against an Execution levied upon the Estate of the said Flournoy in consequence of the Commissioners of the Tax having failed to attend according to notice given on the day appointed for selling certain lands for the Taxes due upon them, Whereupon it is advised that although the Executive have no power to suspend Executions, it be, from the peculiar hardship of the case, recommended to the Solicitor to direct the Sheriff to postpone the sale of the said Flournoy's property until the 20th day of August, that he may receive the benefit which he is entitled to from the sale of the said land; provided the same can be done without relieving the property from the operation of the Execution at present levied on it.

All which matters so advised the Governor orders accordingly.

> James Wood
> Carter Braxton
> Robt. Goode
> Jno. H. Briggs
> J. Dawson
> J. M. McClurg—dissents

from the Opinion on Holcombe's petition; because the Executive are restrained by law from suspending executions for arrearages of taxes due before November 1788; and the Sollicitor, from the general controul of this board over his Office, will probably construe their advice, into an order. Otherwise, he must suppose from this recommendation of the board, that the power of suspending executions against Sheriffs resides in himself, by virtue of his office, which would be an opinion dangerous and improper to be countenanced by the Executive.

---

86. "Sarah Wilkerson" in the clerk's index.
87. "Mary Rowling" in the clerk's index.
88. "Sarah Stacy" in the clerk's index.
89. "Clarke" in the clerk's index.

Monday May 31st 1790

Present

The Governor

Mr. Wood	Mr. Goode
Mr. McClurg	Mr. Carter
Mr. Braxton	Mr. Dawson

It is advised that James Ridley,[90] who stands attainted of Horse-stealing by the Judgment of Winchester District Court the 15th of April last, be pardoned, he appearing to be a proper object of mercy.

The Governor laid before the Board an offer of Captain Samuel Eddins, to purchase the disabled brass cannon at Hanover Court House; Whereupon it is advised, that Mr. Samuel Coleman be empowered to make sale of the said Cannon, subject to the Approbation of this Board.

All which matters so advised the Governor orders accordingly.

James Wood
James McClurg
Carter Braxton
Robt. Goode
Chs. Carter
J. Dawson

Saturday June 5th 1790

Present

The Governor

Mr. Wood	Mr. Goode
Mr. McClurg	Mr. Briggs
Mr. Braxton	Mr. Dawson

The Governor informed the Board, that during the Recess he had pursuant to Recommendation issued a Commission appointing William Plume Gentleman an Alderman for the Borough of Norfolk in the room of Benjamin Pollard Gentleman resigned: and that he had issued a Duplicate of a Pension Certificate to Judah Levi, satisfactory proof having been made to him of the original being lost: which was approved.

The Governor laid before the Board, a letter from the Honourable James Madison covering the copy of a Letter from the secretary of the Treasury addressed to the Collectors and surveyors of the state of Virginia on the subject of the Tobacco Inspection law directing them to forward to such persons as the Executive of the state may point out, lists

90. "Riddley" in the clerk's index.

or manifests of all Tobaccos shipped from their respective ports as has heretofore been the practice: Whereupon it is advised, that a circular letter be written to the said collectors and Surveyors requesting them to forward returns of the aforesaid lists or manifests quarterly to the auditor of public accounts.

It being certified to the Governor that there are two Vacancies in the Court of Directors of the Hospital for the cure of persons of unsound minds occasioned by the Death of Dudley Digges and the resignation of Edmund Randolph Gentlemen: It is advised, that a Commission issue appointing William Pasteur and Robert Hall Waller Gentlemen to fill the said Vacancies, they being nominated by the said Court.

The Governor laid before the Board, the opinion of the Attorney General upon the Question stated to him relative to the demand made by Mr. Carter Page Executor to Archibald Cary Esquire deceased, for the Governor's receipt upon the delivery of two Certificates of the Treasurer for monies paid by his testator into the public Treasury on account of Mr. John Lidderdale and messrs. Capel and Osgood Hanbury British Subjects: Whereupon it is advised that the Governor grant to Mr. Page his receipt for the said Certificates according to the Act of the General Assembly for sequestering British property, enabling those indebted to British Subjects to pay off such debts and directing the proceedings in suits where such subjects are parties.

The Governor laid before the Board a Draft of the Directors of the James River Company for fifty shillings on Account of each public share in the said Company; Whereupon it is advised, that the Treasurer be directed to borrow the money pursuant to the 5th section of the act to amend the several laws for appropriating the public revenue.

It is advised, that an account of the Solicitor for Expences attending notices to sheriffs and others on public account, be referred to the auditor for settlement and a Warrant on the Contingent fund for the sum due. (To be paid.)

All which matters so advised, the Governor orders accordingly.

> James Wood
> James McClurg
> Carter Braxton
> Robert Goode
> Jno. H. Briggs
> J. Dawson

Wednesday June 9th 1790

Present

The Governor

Mr. Wood	Mr. Goode
Mr. McClurg	Mr. Briggs
Mr. Braxton	Mr. Dawson

The Governor informed the Board, that during the recess he had referred to the Auditor for settlement and the usual Warrants for the sums due, the claims of Matthew Harman, Solomon Shutton and Daniel Harman for services rendered as Scouts in the county of Montgomery for the year 1789, they being reported just; which was approved.

For good cause shewn it is advised, that the damages on a Judgment against the Sheriff of Fluvanna for balance of the Revenue tax of 1787, be remitted.

It is advised, that Priscilla Chowning and Jane Burn be continued on the list of Pensioners the former with six pounds and the latter with eight pounds annually commencing the first day of January 1790.

On recommendations it is advised, that an additional Commission issue appointing Joseph Martin, James Anthony, William Banks and Charles Forster Gentlemen Justices of the Peace for the County of Henry; and that a Commission issue appointing James McCraw Gentleman Coroner for the county of Halifax in the room of Edmond King Gentleman, who refuses to give bond and security according to law.

All which matters so advised, the Governor orders accordingly.

James Wood
James McClurg
Carter Braxton
Robt. Goode
Jno. H. Briggs
J. Dawson

Friday June 11th 1790

Present

Mr. Wood as Lieutenant Governor the Governor being sick

Mr. McClurg	Mr. Goode
Mr. Braxton	Mr. Briggs
Mr. Dawson	

The Governor by a note to the Lieutenant Governor reported, that during the recess, he had, upon a certificate of Doctor William Carter and the emaciated appearance of John Ross, who was continued on the list of Pensioners with an allowance of six pounds on the fifteen of May last, increased his allowance to twelve pounds per annum commencing the first day of January 1790; and that he had issued a Commission appointing William Lee Gentleman Sheriff of James City in the room of Dudley Digges Gentleman deceased. Approved.

On Recommendations, it is advised, that an additional Commission issue appointing John Page, George Murray, Rawleigh Colston, Matthew Wright, Cornelius Baldwin and John Gatewood Gentlemen Justices of the peace for the county of Frederick; and that a Commission issue appointing Moore Brokenbrough sheriff for the county of Richmond.

An account of John Conner for a quarter's rent of the office for the High Court of Chancery amounting to five pounds five shillings being presented to the Board, it is advised, that the same be referred to the Auditor for a Warrant on the Contingent Fund. (To be paid.)

All which matters, so advised, the Lieutenant Governor orders accordingly.

> James McClurg
> Carter Braxton
> Robt. Goode
> Jno. H. Briggs
> J. Dawson

Tuesday June 15th 1790

Present

The Lieutenant Governor, the Governor being sick

Mr. McClurg   Mr. Goode
Mr. Braxton   Mr. Briggs
            Mr. Dawson

The Lieutenant Governor informed the Board, that in the Recess he had ordered a warrant on the Contingent Fund to Stott and Donaldson pursuant to a Draft of Colonel William Davies for twenty pounds on account for contingent Expences of his office to be paid; and that on Recommendation he had issued a Commission appointing John Simmons Sheriff of the county of southampton. Approved.

The Lieutenant Governor laid before the Board a Letter from the Speaker of the House of Representatives of the United States notifying the Death of Theodorick Bland esquire, a Representative of this State in Congress, whereupon it is advised, that Writs of Election issue, pursuant to the Constitution of the United States, to the Sheriffs of the Counties of Brunswick, Sussex, Greensville, Prince George, Dinwiddie, Mecklenburg, Lunenburg, Amelia, Nottoway, Cumber-

land and Powhatan, composing the District in which the said Theodorick Bland Esquire was elected, to fill the Vacancy; and that the
said Writs be forwarded by Express.

It is advised that the following usual Warrants issue in favour of
the Directors of the Public Buildings, to wit; One for Two hundred
pounds (to be paid), And another for two hundred and fifty pounds.

All which matters so advised, the Lieutenant Governor orders
accordingly.

James McClurg
Carter Braxton
Robt. Goode
Jno. H. Briggs
J. Dawson

Tuesday June 22d 1790

Present

The Governor

Mr. Wood	Mr. Goode
Mr. McClurg	Mr. Briggs
Mr. Braxton	Mr. Carter

Mr. Dawson

Mr. Wood as Lieutenant Governor reported, that in the recess of
the Board and during the Indisposition of the Governor, he had issued
Duplicates of Certificates to Nathaniel Wilkins and James Askew to
enable them to receive their Pensions of Mr. Heth the Agent of the
United States for payment thereof; it appearing that no improper use
could be made of the said Duplicates; that he had issued a Commission
appointing Robert Adams Gentleman Surveyor of the County of
Wythe, he having been examined and certified able according to law,
directing him to give Bond and security in the Penalty of two thousand
pounds, conditioned for the faithful discharge of the duties of his
office as the law directs; that he had referred to the Auditor for
settlement and the usual Warrant for the sum due, the claim of David
Piles for services as a Scout for the county of Monongalia from the 25th
of April until the 8th of June 1789, the same having been reported just
pursuant to an order of this board; and that he had ordered a Warrant
to issue in favour of Joseph Liplong[91] on the Contingent Fund for Nine
pounds on account for going Express with Writs of Election to fill the
vacancy occasioned by the Death of Colonel Bland. Of which several
matters the Board approve.

The Governor laid before the Board a Letter from the Secretary

---

91. "Leiplong" in the clerk's index.

for the Department of War of the United States relative to the Defence of the Western frontier of this Commonwealth. Whereupon it is advised, that a Letter be written to the county Lieutenant of Washington directing him, that, in case any serious attack be made upon the frontier of his County by the Indians, he immediately communicate the same to the Executive, that they may give such relief to the Inhabitants, as the President of the United States has authorized.

It is advised, that the usual Warrant issue in favour of the Directors of the Public Buildings for One hundred pounds.

The Governor laid before the Board the Petition of Job McKay praying the remission of a fine imposed on him by the county court of Frederick. Whereupon it is advised, that the said Petition be rejected.

For good cause shewn, it is advised, that the damages on a Judgment against the sheriff of Shenandoah for a Balance of the Revenue Tax of 1787 be remitted.

On Recommendation it is advised, that Commissions issue appointing Anthony Foster and John R. Gather Inspectors and James Brown Additional Inspector of Tobacco at Stewarts Creek Warehouse in the County of Nelson.

All which matters so advised the Governor orders accordingly.

The Governor notified to the Board his intention of being absent for some time.

> James Wood
> James McClurg
> Carter Braxton
> Robt. Goode
> Jno. H. Briggs
> Chs. Carter
> J. Dawson

Friday June 25th 1790

Present

The Lieutenant Governor

Mr. McClurg	Mr. Goode
Mr. Braxton	Mr. Briggs
	Mr. Carter

The Lieutenant Governor reported, that in the recess, he had upon recommendations issued Commissions appointing Job Welton Sheriff for the County of Hardy and William Holman sheriff for the county of Goochland; and that upon a Certificate of the Clerk of Princess Anne stating that Bond and Security had not been given for the Collection of the Revenue tax by the sheriff of the said County for the years 1788 and 1789, he had issued a Commission appointing

Thomas Walke Gentleman Collector of the Revenue Tax in the said County for the Years aforesaid. Of which several matters the Board approve.

The Lieutenant Governor laid before the Board a letter from the Honourable Spencer Roane Esquire stating that there is no Jailor for the Court of the District of Botetourt and Greenbriar: Whereupon it is advised, that Abraham Savine be appointed Jailor for the said District in the room of [. . .][92] Edgar, who hath refused to accept of the said office.

On Recommendations, it is advised, that an Additional Commission issue appointing William Dudley and William Digges Junr. Gentleman Justices of the Peace for the County of Warwick and a Commission appointing Thomas Lucas Coroner for the said County.

The Lieutenant Governor laid before the Board a Letter from Benjamin Johnson Esquire Lieutenant Colonel Commandant of the Militia of Orange stating the Vacancies in the said militia and the refusal of the County Court to recommend in order to their being filled: Whereupon it is advised, that Commissions issue to fill the said Vacancies.

All which matters so advised the Lieutenant Governor orders accordingly.

> James McClurg
> Carter Braxton
> Robt. Goode
> Jno. H. Briggs
> Chs. Carter

Saturday June 26th 1790

Present

The Lieutenant Governor

Mr. McClurg	Mr. Briggs
Mr. Braxton	Mr. Carter
Mr. Dawson	

The Lieutenant Governor laid before the Board, a Petition from a large number of the Inhabitants of the county of Pittsylvania together with a letter from John Willson Esquire, Setting forth that they labour under great Hardship and inconvenience from the payment of the Revenue Tax of the Year 1787, at this time arising from the former sheriffs having failed to give security for the collection of the said Tax, Praying that the collection may be postponed until the first of January next: Whereupon it is advised, that the said Petition be rejected, the

---

92. Blank in the journal.

Board being of Opinion, that they have no power to suspend the Operation of the law.

It is advised, that a Duplicate Pension Certificate be issued to John King to enable him to draw his Pension of the United States the original Certificate being left in the court of the County where he resides.

Mr. Wood, Mr. McClurg and Mr. Goode are appointed a Committee for the examination of the Treasury Books.

All which matters so advised the Lieutenant Governor orders accordingly.

> James McClurg
> Carter Braxton
> Jno. H. Briggs
> Chs. Carter
> J. Dawson

Tuesday June 29th 1790

Present

The Lieutenant Governor

Mr. McClurg	Mr. Briggs
Mr. Braxton	Mr. Carter
Mr. Goode	Mr. Dawson

On recommendation, It is advised that an additional Commission issue appointing John Hook, David Barton, Daniel Brown and John Muse gentlemen Justices of the peace for the county of Franklin.

On report from Captain Coleman, It is advised that the claim of Edward Pindell for his services as a scout in monongalia from the 28th of April to the 30th of June 1789, be rejected, the number of Scouts allowed that county having been already paid.

It appearing from the confession of James Arthur on his examination before the court of Dinwiddie County, that a certain Benja. Woodward hath been principally concerned in counterfeiting and passing certain Certificates and public Securities of this State: and there is reason to believe that the said Benjamin Woodward now absconds from justice. The Board advise that a proclamation issue offering a reward of one hundred and fifty Dollars for apprehending the said Woodward: and it is further advised that a copy of Arthurs confession be sent to the Governor of North Carolina.

It is advised that the Treasurer be directed to borrow from any funds money sufficient to pay the present quarters salary due to the Officers of civil government; taking care to replace the same as soon as possible.

All which matters so advised, the Lieutenant Governor orders accordingly.

> James McClurg
> Carter Braxton
> Robt. Goode
> Jno. H. Briggs
> J. Dawson

Wednesday June 30th 1790

Present

The Lieutenant Governor

Mr. McClurg	Mr. Carter
Mr. Briggs	Mr. Dawson

On consideration of a letter from Mr. Harry Heth; It is advised that a Warrant issue on the Contingent fund for the further sum of twelve pounds to Mr. Heth, upon account, as Agent for settling the Westham foundery accounts (to be paid) and The Lieutenant Governor orders accordingly.

> James McClurg
> Jno. H. Briggs
> J. Dawson
> Chs. Carter

Tuesday July 6th 1790

Present

The Governor

Mr. Wood	Mr. Goode
Mr. McClurg	Mr. Briggs
Mr. Braxton	Mr. Dawson

Mr. Wood informed the board that in the recess and absence of the Governor He as Lieutenant Governor examined and certified for payment the account of the Auditor for his last quarters salary; and that on the report of Captain Coleman, he referred to the auditor for settlement in the usual way the accounts of Captain Langham for the last quarters pay due the Superintendant, Artificers and Guards at the point of fork. Approved.

The Governor laid before the board a letter from Col. Davies stating that he will be able to discharge the Duties of his office with the assistance of one Clerk only, that Mr. Burnley is in his judgment to be preferred to Mr. Dunscombe, but he does not think himself authorized to discharge Mr. Dunscombe as he held his appointment under the immediate authority of the executive. Whereupon, It is advised that Col. Davies be empowered to discharge such of his Clerks as he may think proper, he being considered as responsible for the faithful executive of the business entrusted to him.

On consideration of a letter from the solicitors Clerk, with its inclosures; It is advised that he be directed to deliver up all bonds for duties which were entered into after the laws of the State concerning duties on imports ceased, agreeably to the decision of the General Court; And that the Auditor be directed to credit all such bonds accordingly, they having been illegally taken.

The Governor laid before the board the resolves of Congress of the 7th of June 1790 concerning the provision made for the officers, noncomissioned officers and privates of the lines of Virginia and North Carolina who are entitled to receive arrears of pay due for services in the years 1782, and 1783. Whereupon, It is advised that the advertizement of the Executive of the 11th of May be republished in the gazettes with so much of the said resolves as specifies the kind of power necessary for authorizing *others* than original Claimants to receive the said arrears, and that 200 copies of the same be printed and distributed in the respective counties for the better information of those concerned.

In order to give some mark of public respect to Col. Alexander McGillivray and the Chiefs and warriors of the Creek nation of Indians, It is advised that an entertainment be prepared for them at the Theatre in this City and that the Judges of the Court of Appeals, the gentlemen of the bar and heads of the Executive Departments be invited to it.

All which matters so advised, the Governor orders accordingly.

> James Wood
> James McClurg
> Carter Braxton
> Robt. Goode
> Jno. H. Briggs

Tuesday July 13th 1790

Present

The Governor

Mr. Wood	Mr. Braxton
Mr. McClurg	Mr. Goode
Mr. Briggs	

The Governor informed the board that in the recess he directed to be paid out of the Contingent fund, Ten pounds to Mr. Robert Anderson upon Account, to provide for entertaining Col. McGillivray and the Indian Chiefs; and Ten pounds to Mr. Peter Woodlief[93] upon Account as a Collector of Vouchers: And that he granted a pardon to Negro Abram condemned to Death by the Court of New Kent for felony and burglary, he having been recommended by the Court as an object of mercy. Approved.

On consideration of the case of Negro Jesse belonging to Mary B. Webb, under condemnation by the Court of New Kent County for felony and burglary; It is advised that he be pardoned.

The Governor laid before the board the payroll of Captain McMahans company of Ohio rangers for services in 1789, also the Claim of Willm. Boggs for his services as a Scout in the said county in the year 1788, and the Claims of Walter Buchanan, John Buskirk, Samuel Bready and Lewis Whitsel for services rendered in the said County in 1789: Whereupon it is Advised that the said payroll and Claims be referred to the Auditor for settlement in the usual way, they having been examined by Captain Coleman.

On report from Captain Coleman It is advised that the Claims of George Cox and Peter Cox for services in Ohio County as Scouts in 1789, be rejected; the said services having been ordered without authority.

The Governor laid before the board the Account of Mr. Anderson amounting to twenty eight pounds eighteen shillings and four pence for the expences of the entertainment provided for Col. McGillivray and the Indian Chiefs. Whereupon it is advised that a Warrant issue on the Contingent fund for eighteen pounds eighteen shillings and four pence being the balance of the said account deducting the ten pounds advanced. (To be paid)

On recommendation, It is advised that a Commission issue appointing John Boggs Sheriff of Ohio County.

On consideration of the cases of Lucy McDaniel, Mary Ogle and John Marshall It is advised that the said McDaniel be continued on the pension List with an allowance of six pounds per annum from January last, that the pension of the said Ogle be reduced to eight pounds per annum from the same time; and that the pension of the said Marshall be augmented to twelve pounds per annum from the same period.

Thomas Harris who was employed at the Point of Fork as an armourer having complained of ill treatment and dismission by Captain Langham, and charged him with misconduct in his office of Superintendant at the post, It is advised that copies of the said complaint and charges be transmitted to Captain Langham; and that enquiry be made thereon.

---

93. "Peter Woodleif" in the clerk's index.

All which matters so advised, the Governor orders accordingly.

James Wood
James McClurg
Carter Braxton
Robt. Goode
Jno. H. Briggs

Tuesday July 20th 1790

Present

The Governor

Mr. Wood   Mr. Braxton
Mr. McClurg   Mr. Goode
                 Mr. Briggs

The Governor informed the board that in the recess, on recommendations, he issued Commissions appointing Lawrance Smith Sheriff of Sussex, and John Billups and Peter Lamkin jr. Coroners of Lunenburg, that he directed a continuance of William Shaw on the pension List with his former allowance, that having received Dispatches from Russell County giving information of several murders committed by the indians, and stating that there was reason to apprehend an invasion by a large party, he answered the said Dispatches (which answer he read to the board) and forwarded the same to the Secretary at War, and that he referred the account of Ambrose Fletcher, who came express with the said Dispatches from Bedford court house, to the Auditor for settlement in the usual way. Approved.

On recommendations, It is advised that an additional commission issue appointing Thomas Pettus, Edward R. Yates, William Delony, John S. Field, George Tarry, James Harwell, and Henry Speed gentlemen Justices of the peace for the county of Mecklenburg; and that a commission issue appointing William Phillips Sheriff of Louisa.

On consideration of the case of Florence Mahony[94] it is advised that his pension be augmented to fifteen pounds per annum from January last.

All which matters so advised, the Governor orders accordingly.

James Wood
James McClurg
Carter Braxton
Robt. Goode
Jno. H. Briggs

---

94. "Florence Mahoney" in the clerk's index.

Tuesday July 27th 1790

Present

The Governor

Mr. Wood   Mr. Braxton
Mr. McClurg   Mr. Goode
                  Mr. Briggs

The Governor informed the Board that in the recess he issued Commissions appointing John Dunbar Coroner for Charles City and Samuel Clayton Sheriff of Culpeper, they having been recommended according to law, that he granted a reprieve to Negro Jack under sentence of death by the judgment of Spotsylvania County Court for burglary, in order to obtain the proceedings of the court, it having been represented that the condemnation was illegal; and that he granted a warrant on the contingent fund to Jane West for three pounds in advance for nursing and maintaining Catherine Crulls child. Approved.

On consideration of the case of Negro Dick the property of James Jones, under sentence of Death by the Judgment of Gloster County Court for felony and burglary; It is advised that the said Dick be pardoned, he appearing to be a proper object of mercy.

On recommendations, It is advised that an additional Commission issue appointing Grant Allin a justice of the peace for mercer County; also an additional Commission appointing Francis Ruffin, Edmund Harrison and William Call junr. Justices of the peace for the County of Prince George; and a Commission appointing Samuel Rust Sheriff of Westmoreland.

On consideration of the petition of Lieutenant John Bullock of the Hanover militia praying for the remission of a fine of three pounds imposed on him by the court martial for not attending the general muster in October 1787, Also the petition of James Fretwell of the Cumberland militia praying for a remission of the Fines imposed on him for not attending the general musters in October 1787 and in April and October 1788, It is advised that the said fines be remitted.

On consideration of a contract entered into in the year 1787, between Philip Bush, Agent for Mathias Bush, and Joseph Holmes, John Smith and Isaac Zane, for the rent of a certain tract of Land in Frederick County for the purpose of furnishing barracks, fuel, etc. for the Troops and prisoners of the United States; It is advised that the petitioner be referred to the General Government for payment of said Contract, as it appears to have been made for continental purposes.

The Governor laid before the board a recommendation of Parke

Goodall, John Syme, and Elisha White, as fit persons one of whom to be commissioned as Sheriff of Hanover County, together with the respective pretensions of those gentlemen to the office. Whereupon it is advised that a Commission issue to Mr. Syme it appearing that he has been longer in Commission as a Justice without having the Sheriffs office than either of the others.

All which matters so advised, the Governor orders accordingly.

James Wood
James McClurg
Carter Braxton
Robt. Goode
Jno. H. Briggs

Tuesday August 3d 1790

Present

The Governor

Mr. Wood   Mr. Braxton
Mr. McClurg   Mr. Goode
                Mr. Briggs

The Governor informed the board that in the recess, on the report of Capt. Coleman, he referred to the Auditor for settlement in the usual way the payroll of Captain Ballard Smiths company of Jefferson rangers for services rendered in 1789, also the Claim of Mark Thomas for services as a Scout in the said County in 1789, and the Claim of Samuel Hulton for like services in Mercer County in 1788, and that he directed the usual Warrant to issue for the last quarters Salary due Reubin Burnley one of Col. Davies's Clerks. Approved.

It is advised that the Auditor be directed to issue the usual Warrant for the last quarters salary due Andrew Dunscomb as one of Col. Davies's Clerks.

On application from St. George Tucker, It is advised that a receipt be granted for a loan Office Certificate (no. 24) dated the 4th of May 1780, for thirty six thousand six hundred and sixty six and two thirds Dollars paid into the said office by the Executors of the Estate of John Randolph of Cumberland County, to be applied to his credit in account with Capel and Osgood Hanbury, british subjects.

On consideration of the petition of Mary White praying for the remission of the fines imposed by the court martial of Henrico on her son Robert, who is under age, for not attending the general musters, It is advised that the said fines be remitted.

On recommendation, It is advised that a commission issue appointing John Cole Sheriff of Nansemond County.

All which matters so advised the Governor orders accordingly.

James Wood
James McClurg
Carter Braxton
Robt. Goode
Jno. H. Briggs

Friday August 6th 1790

Present

The Governor

Mr. Wood   Mr. Goode
Mr. Braxton   Mr. Briggs

For reasons appearing to the board, It is advised that the Agent of the Sinking fund be instructed to suspend entering into any engagements for public papers of any kind until further order; and The Governor orders accordingly.

James Wood
Carter Braxton
Robt. Goode
Jno. H. Briggs

Tuesday August 10th 1790

Present

The Governor

Mr. Wood   Mr. Goode
Mr. McClurg   Mr. Briggs

On report from the Solicitor It is advised that he be directed to take the usual steps for the removal and sale of such of the following property as may be of a moveable nature viz.

Property taken to satisfy the judgment obtained against Garland Anderson as Sheriff of Hanover for the revenue tax of 1782, to be removed to the City of Richmond.

Property taken to satisfy the judgments obtained against Stephen Sampson as Sheriff of Goochland, for the revenue taxes of 1784 and 1785, to be removed to the Point of Fork.

Property taken to satisfy a judgment obtained against Abram Penn; as Sheriff of Henry County for the revenue tax of 1784, to be removed to Pittsylvania Court house.

Property taken to satisfy the judgments obtained against William

Nall as Sheriff of Rockingham for the revenue and one per Cent taxes of 1784, to be removed to Orange Courthouse:

Property taken to satisfy the judgments obtained against John Pollard as Sheriff of Stafford for the revenue taxes of 1784 and 1785 and certificate tax of 1784 to be removed to Fredericksburg.

Property taken to satisfy the judgments obtained against Lawrence Baker as Sheriff of Isle of Wight, for the revenue taxes of 1785, to be removed to suffolk.

Property taken to satisfy the judgments obtained against Otway Byrd as Sheriff of Charles City for the revenue taxes of 1786 and 1787, to be removed to the City of Richmond.

Property taken to satisfy the judgments obtained against Simon Triplett, as Sheriff of Loudoun for the revenue and Certificate taxes of 1786, to be removed to Alexandria.

Property taken to satisfy the judgment obtained against John Bernard as Sheriff of Buckingham for the revenue tax of 1787, to be removed to Amherst Courthouse.

Property taken to satisfy the judgment obtained against James Upshaw as Sheriff of Caroline for the revenue tax of 1787, to be removed to Fredericksburg.

Property taken to satisfy the judgment obtained against Hugh Innes as Sheriff of Franklin for the revenue tax of 1787, to be removed to Henry Courthouse.

Property taken to satisfy the judgment obtained against William Roystor as Sheriff of Goochland for the revenue taxe of 1787, to be removed to the Point of Fork.

Property taken to satisfy the judgment obtained against Armistead Russel as Sheriff of new Kent for the revenue tax of 1787, to be removed to the City of Richmond.

Property taken to satisfy the judgment obtained against John McMillian as Sheriff of Prince William for the revenue tax of 1787, to be removed to Alexandria.

Property taken to satisfy a judgment obtained against Thomas Mountjoy as Sheriff of Stafford for the revenue tax of 1787, to be removed to Fredericksburg, And It is further advised that the Solicitor be directed to take the Opinion of the Attorney General in all cases where the Fi-Fa's levied upon lands have been returned "not sold for want of time."

The Governor laid before the board an Account of Tunstal Quarles amounting to eighty four pounds 4/10½ for balance due for rations furnished the Post at the Point of Fork up to the 31st of July last agreeably to contract, as certified by Capt. Coleman. Whereupon it is advised that the same be referred to the Auditor for settlement in the usual way.

On consideration of the case of Reubin Sneed, It is advised that the Fines imposed on him by the Courts martial of New Kent County for not attending the General muster in November 1787, a petty muster in March 1789 and a regimental muster in April 1789, be remitted.

On recommendations It is advised that an additional Commission issue appointing John Davis and John Thurman Justices of the peace for the County of Nelson: Also Commissions appointing Henry Lawson Sheriff and James Tapscott Coroner of Lancaster.

On consideration of a letter from the Secretary at War, dated the 28th of July, authorizing the Governor to order into Service under certain regulations, one Lieutenant, one Ensign, two Serjeants, two Corporals and twenty six privates of Russel Militia, if in his Opinion the peculiar extent of the said county and its situation render it necessary, It is advised, that the Governor give orders accordingly, it appearing that such a force is requisite for the protection of the said County.

All which matters so advised the Governor orders accordingly.

The Governor notified his intention to be absent on a visit to the Point of Fork, which is ordered to be entered on the journal.[95]

James Wood
James McClurg
Robt. Goode
Jno. H. Briggs

Tuesday August 17th 1790

Present

Mr. Wood who presides as Lieutenant Governor, the Governor being absent.

| Mr. McClurg | Mr. Goode |
| Mr. Braxton | Mr. Carter |

The Lieutenant Governor informed the board that in the recess, he issued a Commission appointing Gabriel Penn Sheriff of Amherst, he having been recommended according to law, And that he granted a further reprieve to negro John alias Jack until the first Friday in October next. Approved.

The Lieutenant Governor laid before the board a letter from Arthur St. Clair esquire Governor of the Western Territory, dated the 15th July 1790, stating that all prospect of peace with the Indians of the Ouabash and Miami, is at a greater distance than was expected, that an expedition is meditated against those Tribes, and requesting that an additional Number of the militia, situate on the Western Frontier should be held in readiness to cooperate with the regular Troops, under the command of General Harmer. Whereupon it is advised, That Instructions be immediately given to the Senior County Lieutenant of the District of Kentucky to cause five hundred of the Militia of

---

95. *See* page 350 for the additional journal entry dated 10 Aug. 1790.

the District with the proper proportion of Officers (in addition to the 575 heretofore directed to be embodied) to be held in constant readiness, and subject to the Orders of the said Governor of the Western Territory, the said 500 men to be duly proportioned to the respective counties according to the strength of their militia.

It is advised that the order of the sixth instant, directing the Agent of the Sinking Fund to suspend entering into any engagements for public papers or securities, be rescinded.

On consideration of the case of Negro John Alias Jack condemned to death by a Court of Oyer for Spotsylvania, for burglary and felony It is advised that the said John alias Jack be pardoned.

On recommendation, It is advised that Commissions issue appointing William Oldham and Richard Roult inspectors and Jeduthur Haynie additional Inspector at Coan Warehouses in the County of Northumberland.

It appearing from information on oath, that the House of Alexander Horsburgh, in the town of Petersburg, was, on the night of the 4th instant, feloniously set on fire in different places by some evil disposed person or persons, which endangered the public warehouses, therefore, It is advised, that a reward of two hundred Dollars be offered for apprehending the Incendiary or Incendiaries provided any one of them be prosecuted to conviction.

It is advised that Leannah Overstreet,[96] who has five children, and Hanah Thatcher who has two children be continued on the List of pensioners with an allowance of eight pounds each per annum.

All which matters so advised, the Lieutenant Governor order accordingly.

> James McClurg
> Carter Braxton
> Robt. Goode
> Chs. Carter

Tuesday August 24th 1790

Present

The Governor

Mr. Wood	Mr. Braxton
Mr. McClurg	Mr. Goode
	Mr. Briggs

Mr. Wood informed the board that in the recess he as Lieut Governor issued a warrant for one hundred pounds payable to Col Barbour on account of Col. Davies as Commissioner for settling the Account of this State with the United States as per said Davies's Draft Approved.

---

96. "Leanah Overstreet" in the clerk's index.

On recommendation, It is advised that a Commission issue appointing William Warring Sheriff of Essex.

The Governor laid before the board an application of Capt. Denholm for further compensation as a Collector of Vouchers, Whereupon it is advised that the same be rejected, he having been paid at the same rates allowed the other collectors.

On application of the Directors of the public buildings, It is advised that the Auditor be directed to issue a Warrant in favor of the said Directors for Sixty pounds in part of the sum appropriated by the last Assembly for building the Capitol. (To be borrowed)

It is advised that the Account of William Geddy amounting to fifty four pounds thirteen shillings for grates and other black Smiths work done for the Capitol, be referred to the Auditor for settlement according to the customary rates allowed for such work, to be paid out of the Contingent fund.

The Governor laid before the board the petition of Anthony Murphey, Smith Shepherd jur., William Shepherd jun., Paul Keeling, Matthew Pallat, John Pallat, William Pallat, Thomas Thompson, William Nottingham, William Deel Woodhouse and William Bishop; praying for the remission of the fines imposed on them, by the District Court held at Suffolk the 13th of May last, upon an Indictment for an Assault and false imprisonment. Whereupon, It is advised that the said petition be rejected.

All which matters so advised, the Governor orders accordingly.

> James Wood
> James McClurg
> Carter Braxton
> Robt. Goode
> Jno. H. Briggs

Tuesday September 7th 1790

Present

The Governor

Mr. Wood	Mr. Braxton
Mr. McClurg	Mr. Goode

The Governor informed the board that in the recess he directed to be paid out of the contingent fund, Thirty pounds to the Solicitor upon account to defray the expences of sending out executions against delinquents, one pound and ten pence to McColl and Cunlief for twenty five bushels of coal furnished the Auditor, and twenty eight pounds ten shillings to Mr. Richard Mayze for the expences of keeping seven horses belonging to Col. McGilivary, which last sum he should apply to the Secretary at War to have reimbursed as it was a Continental charge; that, on recommendations, he issued Commissions appointing

James Kee Sheriff of Surry and Richard Allen Sheriff of Cumberland; And that he granted a reprieve to Negro Joe, under sentence of death by the Judgment of Fauquier County Court, until the first Friday in October next; in order to give time for obtaining the proceedings of the Court and information concerning the said Joe. Approved.

The Governor laid before the board an account of Dabney Minor amounting to sixty nine pounds seventeen shillings and five pence for work done about the Governors Lott, etc. Whereupon it is advised that the same be referred to the auditor for settlement and a Warrant on the Contingent fund for the Sum due. (To be paid)

On recommendations, It is advised that Commissions issue appointing Thomas Parker, Isaac Basey, Cyrus Pinckard, Spencer Ball, Joseph Ball, Hopkins Harding, and Pressley Thornton gentlemen Justices of the peace for the County of Northumberland; Thomas Kennedy, John Goggins, James French, Samuel Estill, John Kincaid, James Anderson, Green Clay, and John Adams Gentlemen Justices of the peace for the County of Madison; John Bush, gentleman, an Alderman for the Borough of Norfolk; James Steel Sheriff for the County of Augusta, and Richard Young Sheriff for the County of Woodford.

It is advised that a warrant issue on the Contingent fund for twenty five pounds to Archd. Blair for four months Salary as Keeper of the Public Seal. to be paid.

All which matters so advised, the Governor orders accordingly.

The Governor notified to the board his intention to be absent which is ordered to be entered on the journal.

> James Wood
> James McClurg
> Carter Braxton
> Robt. Goode

Tuesday September 21st 1790

Present

Mr. James Wood who presides as Lieutenant
Governor, the Governor being absent.

Mr. McClurg   Mr. Goode
Mr. Braxton   Mr. Carter

The Lieutenant Governor informed the board, that, in the recess, and absence of the Governor, he, on recommendations, issued Commissions appointing Enock Osburn, Manitree Jones, Alexander Buchanan, James Maxwell, Nathaniel Frisbee, William Calfree, James Campbell, Joseph Patterson, Jesse Evans, Robert Adams, James Finley and Andrew Steel, Justices of the peace, and William Davis Coroner for the County of Wythe;

Mathew Wills Sheriff for the County of Warwick;

John Willoughby Sheriff and Thomas Bressie Escheator for the County of Norfolk;

Daniel Tompkins Collector of the Taxes due from the County of Henry for the year 1786;

Alexander Brown, Sheriff of Prince William;

Peyton Stern and Thomas Alcock inspectors, and William Buckner Senr. additional Inspector, at Roys Warehouses, in Caroline:

That he directed to be paid out of the Contingent fund, to Jane West, three pounds, in advance for nursing Catherine Crulls child, to John Conner, five pounds five shillings, for three months rent of his House as an office for the High Court of Chancery, ending the 4th instant:

That he directed the usual warrant to issue for twenty five pounds to Andrew Dunscomb upon account as Clerk to Col. Davies;

That he directed to be borrowed the sum of ten pounds for payment of so much adjudged by the District Court to be due to John Tyler esquire as a Judge; being the difference bewteen the time of his appointment and qualifications: that he granted a pardon to Negro Joe, Condemned to Death by Westmoreland County Court for felony; he having been recommended as a proper object of mercy.

That he granted a further reprieve, until the first friday in November next, to Negro Joe, condemned by Fauquier County Court for felony,

That, on the request of the President, through the Secretary at War, he directed the County Lieutenants of the Kentucky District to embody such proportions of their respective militias as may be called for by Govr. St. Clair and requested Cols. Benjamin Logan and Isaac Shelby to accompany the militia, even as volunteers, on the intended expedition against the Western Indians; and

That he directed to be settled in the usual way, the Account of Joseph Evans who came Express from Wythe County for military Commissions, as the Militia of said County could not be embodied without in case of an attack by the Indians, the same having never been arranged for want of recommendations. Approved.

On recommendation It is advised that a commission issue appointing William Hutcheson Sheriff of Greenbriar.

On consideration of the case of negro Joe the property of John Green jun., condemned to Death by the Court of Fauquier for felony; It is advised that he be pardoned.

On consideration of the petition of Edward Voss praying for the remission of a Fine of five pounds imposed on him by the District Court of King and Queen for leaving the Court as a Juror without permission; It is advised that the said fine be remitted.

It is advised that a Commission issue appointing John James Maund Notary Public for the District of Westmoreland, Richmond, Northumberland and Lancaster Counties.

The Lieutenant Governor laid before the board the account of E. B. Lacy (Clerk to the Treasurer) for expences in going to Petersburg with the charge of certain books and certificates which were thought necessary on the Trial of Torence Thynes, for passing counterfiet Securities; Whereupon it is advised that the said account be referred to the Auditor for settlement and a warrant on the Contingent fund for the sum due. To be paid.

It is advised that the Treasurer be directed to borrow from any funds, money sufficient to pay the present quarters salary due to the Officers of civil government; taking care to replace the same as soon as possible.

All which matters so advised, the Lieutenant Governor orders accordingly.

> James McClurg
> Carter Braxton
> Robt. Goode
> Chs. Carter

Tuesday October 12th 1790

Present

The Governor

Mr. Wood	Mr. Braxton
Mr. McClurg	Mr. Goode
	Mr. Dawson

The Governor informed the board that in the recess, he issued on recommendations, Commissions appointing Willliam Richardson and Charles Hundley inspectors and Hampton Wade additional Inspector at Meriwethers warehouses in hanover;

John Bush additional inspector at Swan Creek Warehouse in Amherst;

Charles Allen Surveyor of Prince William, and John Brown Surveyor of King and Queen, and directed each of them to give bond in the penalty of one thousand pounds;

That he issued an additional Commission appointing Andrew Waggoner, Alexander White junr., John Kerney and John Briscoe justices of the peace for the County of Berkeley;

That he directed to be paid out of the Contingent fund thirty pounds to the Solicitor upon account, to defray expences in sending out notices to delinquent Inspectors etc., twenty five pounds to Col. Davies, on Account, for the contingent expences of his Office, and

Seventy five pounds in part for salary due him, Fifteen pounds to Archd. Blair upon Account to procure stationary etc. for the use of this Office,

That on the report of Captain Coleman, he directed the usual warrants to issue in favor of Capt. Langham for one hundred thirty eight pounds nineteen shillings and sixpence due for the last Quarters salary of the Superintendant and Artificers at the Point of Fork, Seventy two pounds twelve shillings for pay of the Guard for the same time, and seventy pounds upon account to lay in forage for the Post,

That he referred the Account of Aug. Davis amounting to fourteen pounds two shillings and a penny for postage of public letters and the Gazettes for one year, to the Auditor for settlement and a Warrant on the Contingent Fund for the sum due. (To be paid)

That he granted a reprieve to Charles Burke, attainted of horse-stealing, until Friday the 22d instant on his Sollicitation for such indulgence,

That, on application of the Directors of the Public buildings, he directed Warrants to issue in their favor for the sums of sixty five pounds and nine pounds in part of the sum appropriated for building the Capitol, and directed the same to be borrowed, and

That he examined and certified for payment the Account of the Auditor for his last Quarters Salary. Approved.

Mr. Wood informed the board that in the recess and absence of the Governor, he as Lieutenant Governor directed to be paid a second Draft of Col. Davies in favor of the Rev. Benjamin Blagrave for sixty three pounds sixteen shillings, on account of Salary due to Col. Davies on the 31st of June last, and

That he issued a Commission appointing John Stewart Surveyor of Westmoreland, and required him to give bond in penalty of one thousand pounds. Approved.

The Governor reminded the board of the necessity of appointing a Door Keeper in the room of John Connor deceased. Whereupon it is advised, That the Salary be reduced to fifty pounds per annum; and that Mrs. Conner be allowed at that rate for the present quarter, provided She attends to cleaning out the Council chamber and office and procure some trusty lad of good character to do the other duties of Door Keeper.

The board resumed the consideration of the report of a committee appointed the 21st Day of December 1789, under the Act empowering the Executive to superintend and arrange the Offices of Treasurer, Auditor and Solicitor; together with the remarks of those Officers, on the opinions of the board, formed on the said report and sent to them previous to their becoming an Act of the Executive, with a request that they would state any objections, and suggest any alterations, or additions, which in their opinion would tend to make them more useful to the public, or more practicable in the offices. Whereupon it is advised, That the Opinions of the board, formed on the report of their Committee, be now affirmed and entered on the additional Journal as the Act of the Executive; and that copies thereof be transmitted to the General Assembly, the Treasurer, Auditor, and Solicitor.[97]

On consideration of the case of Doctor James Midlecott[98] under sentence of Death by the Judgment of the District Court held in Winchester the 11th September, for murder; It is advised that he be reprieved until Friday the 26th of November next.

It is advised that a commission issue appointing Park Goodall Sheriff of Hanover vice John Symm who hath failed to give bond according to law.

On consideration of the case of Charles Burke alias Burkes under Sentence of Death by the Judgment of the District Court held at Richmond the 10th of September, for horsestealing; It is advised that he be pardoned.

The Governor laid before the board a letter from Mr. Charles Simms informing that many Citizens of this State are like to be deprived of their property in Lands which have fallen within the limits of Pennsylvania by the establishment of the boundary between the two States, for want of authentic copies of the land laws of this State; and a letter from Mr. Edmund Randolph on the same subject. Whereupon it is advised that Mr. Edmd. Randolph be appointed an Agent to state to the board of property in Pennsylvania, the Laws of Virginia concerning Grants for lands, and to support the rights of those who claim under them, and that the President of the State of Pennsylvania be informed thereof.

It is advised that the account of Dabney Minor amounting to nine pounds one shilling and six pence for work done for the better Security of the Treasury, as certified by the Treasurer, be referred to the Auditor for settlement and a warrant on the Contingent fund for the sum due. (To be paid).

The Governor laid before the board the Petition of Thomas Anderson praying for the remission of a Fine of fifty pounds imposed on him by the Court of Mecklenburg County for assaulting and beating John Winkler; together with other papers in support of the allegations set forth in the said petition. Whereupon it is advised that the said fine be remitted.

On consideration of the report of Captain Coleman on the payroll of Captain Ballard Smiths Company of Cavalry for services rendered in Jefferson County for the year 1788, It is advised that the said Payroll as claiming the pay of Cavalry be rejected; but that the Auditor settle the same in the usual way as for Rangers taking care to proportion the Officers to the number of rangers in service.

---

97. *See* additional journal, pages 346-349.
98. "Medlicot" in the clerk's index.

All which matters so advised, the Governor orders accordingly.

> James Wood
> James McClurg
> Carter Braxton
> Robt. Goode
> J. Dawson

Friday October 15th 1790

Present

The Governor

Mr. Wood	Mr. Goode
Mr. McClurg	Mr. Briggs
Mr. Braxton	Mr. Carter

Mr. Dawson

The Governor informed the board that he had issued a Commission appointing John Grinnan Surveyor of Culpeper, and required him to give bond in penalty of £2000. Approved.

On recommendations It is advised that an additional Commission issue appointing Rhoderick Starling, William Lyne and Lyne Shackelford gentlemen Justices of the peace for the County of King and Queen; also commissions appointing, Henry Anderson Sheriff of Amelia; and Alexander Montgomery, Sheriff of Washington.

The Governor laid before the board an Account of Captain Langhan[99] amounting to Sixteen pounds sixteen shillings and eight pence being the balance due for transporting amunition to the Chickasaw Indians from Holston, as settled by arbitration. Whereupon it is advised that the same be paid out of the Contingent Fund.

On consideration of the Claim of William Claiborne amounting to nine hundred and twenty five pounds 3/11. as balance due him for the purchase of horses for the continental army during the late war; It is advised that the same be rejected for want of Funds.

All which matters so advised the Governor Orders accordingly.

> James Wood
> James McClurg
> Robt. Goode
> Jno. H. Briggs
> Chs. Carter
> J. Dawson

[99]. "Langham" in the clerk's index.

Monday October 18th 1790

Present

The Governor

Mr. Wood	Mr. Goode
Mr. McClurg	Mr. Briggs
Mr. Braxton	Mr. Carter

Mr. Dawson

On recommendations, It is advised that an additional Commission issue appointing James Samuels gentleman a Justice of the peace for the County of Nelson: Also Commissions appointing Ralph Cotton and David Glenn Inspectors and David Caldwell additional inspector at Parkers warehouses in the said County: Also a commission appointing James Lewis Sheriff of Spotsylvania County.

The Governor laid before the board an Account of Andrew Dunscomb for his pay and expences as a Clerk to the Commissioner for settling the Continental account, together with a letter from Mr. Edmund Randolph certifying that Mr. Dunscomb was under the necessity of engaging a house by the year at New York. Whereupon it is advised that the Auditor be directed to settle the said account allowing Mr. Dunscomb pay up to the time he left the office, thirty pounds for his expences in going to and returning from new York, and seven pounds ten shillings for loss sustained by house rent. (To be paid.)

It is advised that a commission issue appointing George Hairston Collector of the taxes due for the year 1786 in Henry, vice Daniel Tompkins who hath failed to give bond.

On consideration of a letter from the Solicitor inclosing an anonimous letter received by him pointing out a mode for securing the arrearages due from George Stubblefield late Sheriff of Spotsylvania, It is advised that the Solicitor be directed to send out executions against the property of the said Stubblefield said to be in Frederick, without dismissing the suit against his securities.

All which matters so advised the Governor orders accordingly.

James Wood
James McClurg
Carter Braxton
Robt. Goode
Jno. H. Briggs
Chs. Carter
J. Dawson

Tuesday October 19th 1790

Present

The Governor

Mr. Wood   Mr. Goode
Mr. McClurg   Mr. Briggs
Mr. Braxton   Mr. Carter
               Mr. Dawson

On recommendations It is advised that Commissions issue appointing Chiles Terrell and Jacob Oglesby inspectors and Harwood Bacon additional inspector at Hendersons warehouses in Albemarle, Charles Rogers and Joseph Carter inspectors and James Carter additional inspector at Davis's and Lowrys warehouses in Lancaster, James Martin Inspector at Cresaps warehouse, in Hampshire, in the room of James Tarpley who hath resigned, Lawson Hathaway additional inspector at Dymers and Indian Creek warehouses, Thomas Crowcher and Richard J. Rapier Inspectors and James Laythen additional Inspector at Bealls warehouse in Nelson.

Upon the appeal of Captain McColly of the Harrison militia arrested at the instance of Col. George Jackson, and tried by a General Court martial whereof Colonel Benjamin Wilson was President, charged with having subjected himself to liquor and demeaned himself unbecoming an Officer. The said Court martial were of opinion the said Captain McColly should be censured and that he should be suspended from his command as a Captain for one year. The board having considered the Evidence and facts, disapprove the sentence and proceedings and order that the said John McColly resume the command of his company in the militia of the County of Harrison.

It is advised that the Fines imposed by New Kent Court martial on Augustine Denneuville[100] for not attending a petty Muster the 18th of April 1789 and a regimental muster the 29th of the same month, be remitted; It appearing that he was at the time a Subject of his most christian Majesty.

All which matters so advised the Governor orders accordingly.

James Wood
James McClurg
Carter Braxton
Robt. Goode
Jno. H. Briggs
Chs. Carter
J. Dawson

---

100. "Deneuvill" in the clerk's index.

Thursday October 21st 1790

Present

The Governor

Mr. Wood	Mr. Goode
Mr. McClurg	Mr. Briggs
Mr. Braxton	Mr. Carter

Mr. Dawson

On recommendations, It is advised that additional Commissions issue appointing William Croghan, John Thruston, Philip Buckner, Martin Daniel, John Harrison, Robert Leman, Thomas I. Gwinn and Samuel Kirby, Justices of the peace for the county of Jefferson; Thomas Montgomery, James French and John Goggin Justices of the peace for the County of Madison; Also that Commissions issue appointing George Wilson Sheriff of Jefferson; Nicholas Hamner and Clifton Garland Inspectors and Jacob Morris additional Inspector at Nicholas's warehouses in Albemarle.

It is advised that a warrant in favor of John Carter, Clerk to the Auditor, for fifteen pounds upon account to purchase Coal and Stationary for the use of the Auditors office, be paid out of the Contingent fund.

On application of the Directors of the public buildings, It is advised that the auditor be directed to issue a warrant to them for one hundred and two pounds eleven pence half penny in part of the sum appropriated for building the Capitol. (Money to be borrowed).

It is advised that the Treasurer be directed to borrow pursuant to law, a sum sufficient to answer a Draft of the James river Company for Five pounds on each public Share in said Company.

On consideration of the petition of Daniel Miller praying for the remission of the Fine of six pounds imposed on him by the Court of Frederick County for a breach of the peace, It is advised that the said Fine be remitted.

It is advised that a Duplicate pension Certificate be granted to Thomas Hightower, it appearing that the original is lost.

On recommendation, It is advised that Commissions issue appointing Richard Sanford inspector and Philip Webster additional inspector at Alexandria warehouses in Fairfax.

All which matters so advised, the Governor orders accordingly.

James Wood
James McClurg
Carter Braxton
Robt. Goode
Jno. H. Briggs
Chs. Carter
J. Dawson

Friday October 22d 1790

Present

The Governor

Mr. Wood	Mr. Goode
Mr. McClurg	Mr. Briggs
Mr. Braxton	Mr. Carter

Mr. Dawson

It is advised that the Auditor be directed to grant the usual Warrant to Reubin Burnley for thirty pounds being for his last quarters salary as Clerk to Col. Davies.

On recommendations, It is advised that commissions issue appointing Samuel Judkins inspector and Thomas Bage additional inspector at Grays Creek warehouse in Surry; John Butler inspector and Stephen Ashby additional inspector at Harrods landing warehouse in Mercer County; and Alvin Mountjoy, Sheriff at Bourbon.

On the report of Captain Coleman It is advised that the payroll of a company of Russell rangers, under the command of John Carter, for services rendered in 1789, be referred to the Auditor for settlement in the usual way; allowing for the proper number of rations.

The Governor laid before the board a letter from George Thomson of Fluvanna, charging Tunstal Quarles at present Sheriff of the said County with such conduct as if proven satisfactory will render it improper to continue him a second year in the Office of Sheriff. Whereupon it is advised that copies of the charges be furnished the said Quarles and that the 18 Day of November next be appointed for hearing such evidence as may be adduced by either party on this subject; and that the parties be informed that written Testimony will be received so that each shall give to the other reasonable notice of the time and place at which they propose to take depositions.

It is advised that a warrant issue on the Contingent fund, for two hundred and fifty pounds, payable to John Brown, Clerk of the General Court, as full compensation for his services in preparing the causes for the District Courts, in pursuance of the District law, and for those rendered by him in the execution of the Act for amending the District law.

All which matters so advised, the Governor orders accordingly.

James Wood
James McClurg
Robt. Goode
Jno. H. Briggs
Chs. Carter
J. Dawson

Monday October 25th 1790

Present

The Governor

Mr. Wood	Mr. Briggs
Mr. McClurg	Mr. Carter
Mr. Goode	Mr. Dawson

On recommendations, It is advised that Commissions issue appointing Thomas Brookes and Joel Berry Inspectors and Daniel Teagar additional Inspector at Limestone Warehouses in Mason County; Edmund Lyne, Sheriff and Miles W. Conway, Coroner, for the said County, and Charles Tomkies Sheriff of Gloster County.

The Governor laid before the Board an account of Tunstal Quarles amounting to eighty three pounds 18/7½ for provisions furnished the post at the point of Fork to the 31st instant as certified by Capt. Coleman. Whereupon it is advised that the same be referred to the Auditor for settlement in the usual way.

All which matters so advised, the Governor orders accordingly.

> James Wood
> James McClurg
> Carter Braxton
> Robt. Goode
> Jno. H. Briggs
> Chs. Carter
> J. Dawson

Thursday October 28th 1790

Present

The Governor

Mr. Wood	Mr. Goode
Mr. McClurg	Mr. Briggs
Mr. Braxton	Mr. Madison

Mr. Carter

The Governor informed the board that he had issued a commission for continuing Samuel Goode Sheriff of Mecklenburg a second year he having desired the same. Approved.

On recommendations It is advised that Commissions issue appointing William Hogan Inspector and John Chiles additional inspector at Hickmans warehouses in Mercer County, and Alexander Robertson Sheriff of the said County.

The Governor laid before the board a petition signed by most of the respectable inhabitants of Fredericksburg, imploring a pardon for

Joshua alias Vitch Night, condemned to Death by the District Court for horsestealing; Whereupon it is advised that he be pardoned.

On consideration of the case of Daniel Herring late sheriff of Isle of Wight, The board recommend to the Solicitor to direct the Sheriff of said County, to postpone all Sales of the said Daniel Herrings estate, on account of the Executions against him for the taxes of 1788; to give him time to obtain redress; it appearing that he refused to collect for that year, and a commission issued appointing a successor.

Present Mr. Dawson.

The Governor laid before the board an account of the Treasurer amounting to thirty four pounds sixteen shillings and £7d½ for Stationary, fuel, postage of letters etc. Whereupon it is advised that the Auditor issue a Warrant on the Contingent Fund for the Sum due. (To be paid)

On recommendations It is advised that Commissions issue appointing Philip Taliaferro Sheriff of King and Queen vice Thomas Roan who refuses to act a second year; John Watkins Sheriff of Surry County Vice James Kee, who declines serving, being a member of the assembly; Isaac Shelby Sheriff of Lincoln County; John Haymond, Benjamin Coplin, Robert Lowther, William Martin, George Arnold, Joseph Davison, and John Radcliff, Justices of the peace for the county of Harrison; Henry Doring, Thomas Pindell, Dudley Evans and James Scott Justices of the peace for the County of Monongalia, and Thomas Laidley Sheriff of the said County.

On consideration of the Claims of Richard Hall, Adam Fletcher, Edward Tanner, and Peter Cornelius for services rendered in Harrison County, as Scouts in 1789; also the claim of Watson Clark amounting to 17/11 d. for provisions furnished a party of the militia of the said County, also the Claims of John Elliott, William Wamsby, Charles Parsons and John Jackson for Services as Scouts in Randolph County for the year 1789, It is advised that the same be refferred to the Auditor for settlement in the usual way, notwithstanding two of the Scouts in Harrison and all four in Randolph are unauthorized by the general regulations; it appearing by a letter from the Delegates of those Counties that the said Scouts were absolutely necessary.

On report from Captain Coleman It is advised that the account of James McAfee for rations furnished a company of Mercer Rangers in 1788, be referred to the Auditor for settlement in the usual way, disallowing the charges for rations furnished Scouts as also the claim for Waggons, packhorses etc. It is also advised that the Auditor be directed to settle in the usual way, the payrolls of Lincoln Rangers for services from the 23d of June to the 23d of October 1788, also the Claim of William Butler for services as a Scout in the said County from the 22d of April to the 16th of July 1788; and the Claims for 1980 rations furnished the said rangers.

The Governor laid before the board a letter from Mr. Tazewell and Mr. Tucker expressing a wish that two prisoners, Brown and Davis, convicted of robbery before the District Court held at Williamsburg, might be reprived until some further satisfaction can be obtained as to their identity as there was only one Witness against them, the woman robbed, who possibly might be mistaken, having seen the prisoners only once (and that on the morning of the same Day) *before* the robbery, which possibility was encreased by the earnest and steady assertion of the prisoners that they never were in Virginia until they were brought hither from Massachusetts in consequence of some pirati[cal] act they had been charged to have committed within our cape. Whereupon it is advised, that they be repriewed until Friday the 26 of next month; and that a Copy of Daviss confession, before two Justices of the State of Massachusetts, be transmitted to Doctor Barraud who is requested to interrogate the prisoners in such manner as will most likely draw from them the Truth, as to their being the very persons; and report the result of his enquiries to the board as soon as possible.

All which matters so advised, the Governor orders accordingly.

> James Wood
> James McClurg
> Carter Braxton
> Robt. Goode
> Jno. H. Briggs
> Thos. Madison
> Chs. Carter
> J. Dawson

Saturday October 30th 1790

Present

The Governor

Mr. Wood	Mr. Briggs
Mr. McClurg	Mr. Madison
Mr. Braxton	Mr. Carter
Mr. Goode	Mr. Dawson

On report from Captain Coleman It is advised that the payroll of a company of Russell Rangers under the command of Captain James Gibson, including two Scouts, William Dorton and Moses Dorton, also the Claims of Samuel Porter and John Alley, as Scouts in the said County for the year 1789, be referred to the Auditor for settlement in the usual way.

It is advised that the Treasurer be directed to borrow a sufficient sum to answer a Draft of the Patowmack Company for ten pounds sterling on each public Share in said Company.

All which matters so advised, the Governor orders accordingly.

> James Wood
> James McClurg
> Carter Braxton
> Robt. Goode
> Jno. H. Briggs
> Thos. Madison
> Chs. Carter
> J. Dawson

Tuesday November 2d 1790

Present

The Governor

Mr. Wood	Mr. Briggs
Mr. McClurg	Mr. Madison
Mr. Braxton	Mr. Carter
Mr. Goode	Mr. Dawson

On recommendations, It is advised that Commissions issue appointing, Andrew Shanklin, Sheriff of Rockingham; John Cralle, Sheriff, of Northumberland; and David Gass, Sheriff of Madison.

It appearing that the Resolution of the General Assembly of the 12th June 1781 for presenting Captain John Jouitt,[101] with an elegant Sword and pair of Pistols, has not been compleatly carried into execution, It is advised that General Wood be requested to provide an elegant Sword and present the same to Capt. Jouitt in pursuance of the said resolve of the Assembly.

All which matters so advised, the Governor orders accordingly.

> James Wood
> James McClurg
> Carter Braxton
> Robt. Goode
> Jno. H. Briggs
> Thos. Madison
> Chs. Carter
> J. Dawson

---

101. "Jouit" in the clerk's index.

Friday November 5th 1790

Present

The Governor

Mr. Wood	Mr. Briggs
Mr. McClurg	Mr. Madison
Mr. Braxton	Mr. Carter
Mr. Goode	Mr. Dawson

The Clerk of Bourbon County having certified that he had applied to the Commissioners of the Land-tax *for the books of the said tax, which books he had never received,* It is advised that the Solicitor be directed to proceed to recover the fine imposed on the said Commissioners for neglect, and to furnish the Clerk of the said County with an attested copy of the land tax from the last Statement on the equalizers books.

On recommendations It is advised that commissions issue appointing William Kinchelor and Richard Simmons: inspectors and Withers King additional inspector at Waltons warehouses in Nelson County.

All which matters so advised, the Governor orders accordingly.

James Wood
James McClurg
Carter Braxton
Robt. Goode
Jno. H. Briggs
Thos. Madison
Chs. Carter
J. Dawson

Tuesday November 9th 1790

Present

The Governor

Mr. Wood	Mr. Briggs
Mr. McClurg	Mr. Madison
Mr. Braxton	Mr. Carter
Mr. Goode	Mr. Dawson

It is advised that the proceedings of the executive be laid before the General Assembly pursuant to the Constitution of the Commonwealth and the late requisition of the Assembly.

On recommendation It is advised that commissions issue appointing Hudson Martin, Reubin Thornton, Samuel Higginbotham, William Warwick and John Thompson Gentlemen Justices of the peace for the County of Amherst; Charles Little Sheriff of Fairfax: and Peter Saunders, Sheriff of Franklin.

The Governor laid before the board the Claims of Col. William Finnie, referred to the Executive by the General Assembly, for additional compensation for his services as Quarter Master general for this State, for a sum of money advanced by him on public Account and for a further compensation for his trouble in procuring vouchers to support the account of this State against the United States. Upon consideration where of, It is advised that no farther compensation should be allowed for his servises in the Quarter masters Department he not having produced sufficient Documents to support his demand, that his Claim for money advanced cannot be admitted it not having been referred to this board by the assembly and that his Claim for supplying Vouchers to the continental account be rejected, the sum formerly allowed being deemed adequate to his trouble in that business.

The Governor laid before the board the terms of Mr. Augustin Davis for printing one thousand Copies of the Laws of the second Session of the Congress of the united States, pursuant to the Directions of the General Assembly, viz 1000 Copies of the said Laws to be printed on good paper, with a type two sizes smaller than those with which the laws of the first Session were printed, at ten pounds per Sheet. Whereupon it is advised that the said terms be accepted.

It is advised that the Claims of George Cox and Peter Cox for services as Scouts in Ohio County from the 14th of May to the 18th of July 1789, be referred to the Auditor for settlement in the usual way, the members of Assembly from that county having certified that their Services were absolutely necessary.

It is advised that the account of the Solicitor for expences in forwarding executions and notices for the November Court 1790, and office expences, making a balance of twenty four pounds one shilling and three pence be referred to the Auditor for settlement and a warrant on the Contingent fund for the sum due (to be paid).

The Governor laid before the board the account of James Campbell for express hire from Wythe County. Whereupon it is advised that the said account be referred to the Auditor for settlement in the usual way.

For reasons appearing to the board, it is advised that the Fine imposed by New Kent Court Martial held the 30th November 1787, on Major John Hockaday, for not attending the said Court martial, be remitted.

On consideration of a memorial of the officers of the militia and others inhabiting that part of Montgomery County which was lately part of Botetourt, concerning rank; It is advised that the same be rejected; the appointments of Militia officers having been made on the recommendations of the Court.

It is advised that the Governor open a correspondence with the President of the United States on the subject of establishing a woollen

Manufactory within this Commonwealth, agreeably to a resolution of the general assembly; and that he write to the Governor of Maryland relative to the disposal of the Light-house materials.

All which matters so advised, the Governor orders accordingly.

James Wood
James McClurg
Carter Braxton
Robt. Goode
Jno. H. Briggs
Chs. Carter
J. Dawson

Thursday November 11th 1790

Present

The Governor

Mr. Wood	Mr. Briggs
Mr. McClurg	Mr. Madison
Mr. Braxton	Mr. Carter
Mr. Goode	Mr. Dawson

On recommendations It is advised that Commissions issue appointing Robert Gaines an additional Inspector at Mantapike and Fraziers warehouses; William Cryer Sheriff of Nottoway; James G. Dowdale Sheriff of Frederick; and William Gooseley Sheriff of York.

On the application of the Directors of the public buildings It is advised that the Auditor be directed to issue a Warrant to them for eight hundred pound[s] in part of the sum appropriated for building the Capitol (money to be borrowed.)

For reasons appearing to the board It is advised that the fine of ten shillings imposed on Josiah Atkinson by a Court martial held for Hanover the 6th of October 1789 for not attending General Muster, be remitted; Also that the Fines amounting to forty shillings imposed on James Durham by the Courts Martial of Hanover for nonattendance, be remitted; it appearing that he is an invalid pensioner.

It is advised that the Account of Edward Pegram amounting to seven pounds for expences in bringing to Richmond Ben. Woodwards counterfeiting Implements agreeably to the Governors order, be referred to the Auditor for a Warrant on the Contingent fund for the sum due; It is also advised that the said Implements be lodged in the Treasurey Office; and that John Young and Tinsley Young be allowed ten Dollars each for discovering the said implements.

The board resumed the consideration of the Cases of Brown and Davis under sentence of Death, by the Judgment of the District Court held at Williamsburg, for robbery; when a letter from Doctor Barraud was read. Whereupon it is advised, that the said Brown and Davis be pardoned.

All which matters so advised, the Governor orders accordingly.

James Wood
James McClurg
Carter Braxton
Robt. Goode
Jno. H. Briggs
Chs. Carter
J. Dawson

Monday November 15th 1790

Present

The Governor

Mr. Wood	Mr. Briggs
Mr. Braxton	Mr. Carter
Mr. Goode	Mr. Dawson

On consideration of the petition of William Taylor praying for a remmission of a Fine of eleven pounds 15/8d. imposed on him by the Town Court of Petersburg for retailing Liquors without License, It is advised that the same be remitted.

It is advised that a letter be written to the Governor of North Carolina relative to the establishment of the boundary line between the two states, pursuant to the resolution of the General Assembly of the 21st of October last; And that General Martin be requested to present the same to the Executive of North Carolina, for which service his reasonable expences shall be paid by the public.

The Governor laid before the board a letter he had written to the President of the United States on the subject of establishing a Woollen Manufactory in this Commonwealth, which is approved and ordered to be registered (see letter book).[102]

Present Mr. McClurg.

The Governor informed the board that a quantity of crop Tobacco lay at Crows warehouse on James river which could not be sold. Whereupon it is advised that Mr. T. Madison be requested to have the same reexamined and such part of it as is merchantable transported by water to Richmond, and to sell the remainder for the public benefit. It is also advised that the notes for 4541 lb. nett transfer Tobacco be delivered to Mr. Madison and that he receive from the Inspectors the money for which it was sold and forward it to Mr. Harry Heth by the first safe opportunity.

102. Beverley Randolph to George Washington, 15 Nov. 1790, Letter Book 1788–1792, Governor's Office.

All which matters so advised, the Governor orders accordingly.

> James Wood
> James McClurg
> Carter Braxton
> Robt. Goode
> Jno. H. Briggs
> Chs. Carter
> J. Dawson

Thursday November 18th 1790

Present

The Governor

Mr. Wood	Mr. Goode
Mr. McClurg	Mr. Briggs
Mr. Braxton	Mr. Carter

Mr. Dawson

The Governor informed the board that he had issued a Commission, on recommendation, appointing Thomas Howle additional Inspector at Littlepages warehouses. Approved.

On recommendation It is advised that a Commission issue appointing Johnny Scott Sheriff of Orange County.

On consideration of a letter from Captain Langham It is advised that he be authorized to contract, on the best terms he can, for a false roof to be built over the Magazine and covered with shingles for the better security against leaks.

The board proceeded to consider the complaint exhibited by George Thompson against Tunstal Quarles and sundry Depositions as well in support of the Complaint as against the same having been read, It is advised that the further consideration thereof be postponed until tomorrow.

All which matters so advised the Governor orders accordingly.

> James Wood
> James McClurg
> Carter Braxton
> Robt. Goode
> Jno. H. Briggs
> Chs. Carter
> J. Dawson

Friday November 19th 1790

Present

The Governor

Mr. Wood	Mr. Goode
Mr. McClurg	Mr. Briggs
Mr. Braxton	Mr. Carter

Mr. Dawson

The board proceeded farther to consider the charges brought by George Thompson against Tunstal Quarles, whereupon, at the request of George Thompson, it is advised that further time be allowed to take Depositions as to the Charge of bribery and that the 30th Day of November be appointed to hear such Depositions as may be then produced by either party respecting that charge only.

In consequence of information received from the Attorney General "that Lewis A. Pauley demands of the Auditor warrants on the foreign fund agreeable to the decree of the High Court of Chancery at the last term notwithstanding it had been agreed by himself and the attorney for Mr. Pauley that an appeal should go which agreement prevented him from having the appeal entered in due form, and that he had no Doubt but upon application to the Chancelor the appeal would still be directed to be entered." It is advised that the Auditor be directed to suspend issuing Warrants to Lewis A. Pauley for the present; and that the Attorney General be desired to state to the board tomorrow fully the circumstances respecting the appeal directed in the case of Lewis A. Pauley.

On recommendation It is advised that a Commission issue appointing Francis Hall additional Inspector at Deacons neck warehouse.

All which matters so advised, the Governor orders accordingly.

James Wood
James McClurg
Carter Braxton
Robt. Goode
Jno. H. Briggs
Chs. Carter
J. Dawson

Saturday November 20th 1790

Present

The Governor

Mr. Wood	Mr. Goode
Mr. McClurg	Mr. Briggs
Mr. Braxton	Mr. Carter

Mr. Dawson

It is advised that a Commission issue appointing Worlich Westwood Sheriff of Elizabeth City County in the room of Miles King who declines acting a second year.

It is advised that a warrant issue on the Contingent Fund to Peter Woodlief[103] for twenty pounds upon account as a Collector of Vouchers. (To be paid)

On consideration of the application for the remission of a fine of seven pounds 10/. imposed by the Court of Hanover on Pitman Kidd for an assault on John Batkins, It is advised that the said application be rejected.

On consideration of a letter from the Attorney General and the resolution of the General Assembly referring the Claim of Lewis A. Pauley to the High Court of Chancery or General Court; It is advised that the order entered into yesterday directing the Auditor to postpone issuing warrants to the said Pauley be rescinded.

All which matters so advised, the Governor orders accordingly.

James Wood
James McClurg
Carter Braxton
Robt. Goode
Jno. H. Briggs
Chs. Carter
J. Dawson

Monday November 22d 1790

Present

The Governor

Mr. Wood	Mr. Goode
Mr. McClurg	Mr. Briggs
Mr. Braxton	Mr. Carter

Mr. Dawson

The board proceeded further to consider the charges brought against Tunstal Quarles by George Thompson when a letter was read from the said George Thompson stating that he had been induced by principles of public Duty to take the part he had done but that on investigating the subject he found that the charge exhibited against Quarles as Coroner had not been fully represented to him in as much as he conceived the said Coroner had never acted under a second execution against William Henry so that the money paid to Quarles by Napier which he had considered as a bribe for delaying to levy the first execution might be the legal fee on the second and requesting that the said charge may be withdrawn. Whereupon on mature consideration

---

103. "Peter Woodleif" in the clerk's index.

of the proofs adduced in support of the several charges and the said letter from Mr. Thompson, it is the opinion of the board that Mr. Quarles stands fully acquitted of the charges brought against him, and that a commission issue appointing him sheriff for the County of Fluvanna for the ensuing year.

On recommendation, It is advised that an additional Commission issue appointing James Neal Gentleman a Justice of the peace for the County of Harrison.

All which matters so advised, the Governor orders accordingly.

James Wood
James McClurg
Carter Braxton
Robt. Goode
Jno H. Briggs
Chs. Carter
J. Dawson

Thursday November 25th 1790

Present

The Governor

Mr. Wood	Mr. Goode
Mr. McClurg	Mr. Briggs
Mr. Braxton	Mr. Carter
	Mr. Dawson

On recommendations It is advised that Commissions issue appointing Christian Snidow and Jonathan Isom Justices of the peace; Abraham Trigg Escheator and Daniel Trigg Coroner of Montgomery County, and John McColly Sheriff of Harrison County.

On consideration of the petition of John Baptist alias Peter Piatt, It is advised that a fine of five pounds imposed on him by the Town Court of Petersburg for keeping open Shop and trafficking with Slaves on the sabbath Day, Also the fine of eleven pounds 15/8½ imposed on him by the said Court for retailing Liquors without License, be remitted.

For reasons appearing to the board, It is advised that the Fine of eleven pounds 15/8 imposed by the Town Court of Petersburg against William Cunningham[104] for retailing Spiritous Liquors without License, be remitted.

It is advised that Florence Blairs pension be reduced to eight pounds per annum from the 1st of January last.

The Governor laid before the board a resolution of the General Assembly referring the Accounts of William Shannon to the Executive for settlement. Whereupon it is advised that the said Claim be referred

---

104. "Cuningham" in the clerk's index.

to Captain Coleman who will examine the same, as well as the transactions of Mr. Shannons Deputies and report specially thereon to this board.

On consideration of the report of Captain Coleman relative to the Accounts of Mr. Charles Thomas late manager of the public rope walk and tannery, It is advised the said report together with the books and papers of the said Thomas be referred to the Auditor who will examine the same and state on the public books the balances which appear, and report thereon to the executive.

The Governor laid before the board a resolution of the general assembly referring to the Executive for settlement the Claim of William Claiborne. Whereupon it is advised that the Account of Mr. Claiborne be referred to the Auditor of public Accounts, that he be directed to compare the same with the public books, apply the scale of depreciation thereto in the customary manner and that he report specially to the board stating the balance which may appear to him to be due in specie.

The Governor laid before the board a letter from Doctor James Taylor President of the Commissioners of the Marine Hospital requesting that a warrant might be directed to William Newsom for his services as Clerk to the said Commissioners. Whereupon it is advised that the requisition be not complied with, the money in the fund being appropriated solely to the carrying on the building. It is also advised that the said letter together with the Treasurers state of the Marine hospital fund be laid before the General Assembly.

The Governor laid before the board a letter signed Thomas Carter and David Ward, representing the exposed situation of the County of Russell and the insufficiency of the measures taken by the General Government for its defence. Whereupon it is advised that the said Letter be transmitted to the President of the United States.

On consideration of a letter from Colonel Thomas Newton, It is advised that he be directed to deliver to Colonel Finnie all the Cannon which he supposes to belong to the United States; and that he be requested to have the twenty 4 and 6 pounders, six Cohuns or Caronades and one 12 pounder belonging to this State collected together and secured under cover.

All which matters so advised, the Governor orders accordingly.

> James Wood
> James McClurg
> Carter Braxton
> Robt. Goode
> Jno. H. Briggs
> Chs. Carter
> J. Dawson

Saturday November 27th 1790

Present

The Governor

Mr. Wood   Mr. Goode
Mr. McClurg   Mr. Briggs
Mr. Braxton   Mr. Carter
          Mr. Dawson

The Governor informed the board that he yesterday directed to be paid out of the Contingent Fund, thirty pounds, to Gen. Martin, upon account, to defray his expences in going to North Carolina on public business. Approved.

On consideration of a letter from Robert Bolling and Peterson Goodwin in behalf of John and Tinsley Young; It is advised that the further sum of seven pounds each be allowed to the said John and Tinsley Young as a reward for having discovered the implements of Ben Woodward; It is also advised that a further reward of two hundred and fifty Dollars be offered for apprehending the said Woodward.

It being represented that there is a quantity of tobacco waiting at Rockeyridge Warehouses for inspection which cannot be done, one of the principal and the additional Inspector for said Warehouses being unable to attend from sickness, It is advised that the case be laid before the General Assembly, the Executive not having power to remedy the inconvenience.

All which matters so advised, the Governor orders accordingly.

James Wood
James McClurg
Carter Braxton
Robt. Goode
Jno. H. Briggs
Chs. Carter
J. Dawson

Tuesday November 30th 1790

Present

The Governor

Mr. Wood   Mr. Goode
Mr. McClurg   Mr. Briggs
Mr. Braxton   Mr. Carter
          Mr. Dawson

It is advised that a commission issue appointing William Adams additional Inspector of tobacco at Grays Creek warehouses in the room of Thomas Bage who hath resigned.

The Governor laid before the board a resolution of the General Assembly requesting the executive to employ one or more Printers to print 200 Copies of the Journal of the second Session of Congress and the various treaties of the United States to be annexed to the acts of the Second Session of Congress. Whereupon it is advised that Mr. Davis be employed to print the above mentioned Treaties in the english language to be annexed to the said Acts on the same Terms that he has engaged to print the Acts; and that Mr. Blair be requested to apply to the other printers in this City to know by what time and for what price they can print the Journal, the time proposed by Mr. Davis for finishing the whole work being too long to be agreed to.

It is advised that the Claim of Stephen Smith, as an Express from Greenbriar, with Dispatches, from the County Lieutenant, to the Governor, be referred to the auditor for settlement in the usual way and a warrant on the contingent fund for the same due. (To be paid)

It is advised that Comfort Blonton be continued on the pension List with eight pounds per annum from January last.

On consideration of a memorial of John F. Mercer stating that he had defrayed several charges for the equipment of a Volunteer Corps of Cavalry raised at the request of the Marquis Fayette, and commanded by him, and that he was obliged to purchase a horse that cost him forty five Guineas which was killed in the service; The Board are of opinion that the memoralist ought to apply to the general government for reimbursement.

The Governor laid before the board an Account of Mr. Jas. McGavock for storage and delivery of the public lead under his care. Whereupon it is advised that a Warrant issue to Mr. McGavock on the Contingent Fund, for thirty pounds in full of all Accounts for storage and delivery of public lead and for his services in keeping the same; and that he be exonerated for the loss of 300 lbs. of lead stated in the same Account.

All which matters so advised, the Governor orders accordingly.

James Wood
James McClurg
Robt. Goode
Jno. H. Briggs
Chs. Carter
J. Dawson

Thursday December 2d 1790

Present

The Governor

Mr. Wood   Mr. Carter
Mr. McClurg   Mr. Dawson

On recommendation It is advised that a commission issue appointing Humphrey Marshall Surveyor of Woodford vice Thomas Marshall who hath resigned; and that he be required to give bond in penalty of two thousand pounds.

The Governor laid before the board an account of costs on an appeal from the Sentence of the court of admiralty in a suit, William Gatewood as Searcher, against Robert Fairclaugh amounting to 2145 lbs. tobacco at 12/6, and five pounds; Whereupon it is advised that, as the Commonwealth was interested one moiety in said Suit, the Auditor be directed to issue a warrant on the Contingent Fund in favor of the Clerk of appeals for one half of the said Costs (to be paid.)

All which matters so advised, the Governor orders accordingly.

James Wood
James McClurg
Chs. Carter
J. Dawson

Friday December 3d 1790

Present

The Governor

Mr. Wood   Mr. Briggs
Mr. McClurg   Mr. Carter
Mr. Goode   Mr. Dawson

The Governor produced credentials of his reelection to the office of Governor or chief Magistrate, and of his qualification before John Pendleton, a justice of the peace for the County of Henrico, which are ordered to be filed.

On recommendation It is advised that a Commission issue appointing Henry Buford Sheriff of Bedford.

It is advised that Captain Denholm be desired to continue collecting Vouchers in support of the Claims of this State against the United States until the first of March next; And that ten pounds be advanced him out of the Contingent fund upon account for that purpose.

The board took under consideration the State of the public tobacco now in the hands of the Agent. Whereupon it is advised that the agent be directed to advertize all the tobacco in his hands in the

Gazette stating the particular warehouses at which it lies and the quantity at each.

Present Mr. Braxton.

On consideration of the Depositions taken before Robert T. Hooe and John Moss gentlemen two of the Justices for the County of Fairfax touching the Conduct of the Inspectors at Alexandria warehouses It is advised that Charles Jomes, Richard Sanford and Philip Webster be removed from their offices of Inspectors, for breach of duty, And that Commissions issue appointing Jacob Cox and George Minor inspectors and Thomas Grafford additional inspector at the said Warehouses.

On recommendation It is advised that an additional Commission issue appointing Jacob Palsley, William Wilson, Matthew Whitman, Abraham Kittle, Zenah Osborn and William Parsons Gentlemen Justices of the peace for the County of Randolph.

The Governor laid before the board a resolution of the general Assembly referring to the Executive the petition of Walter Hopkins praying to be paid for his services in South Carolina as an Agent to purchase Goods. Whereupon the board are of Opinion that the letters and papers produced by the said Hopkins in support of his claim are not sufficient to charge this State with any allowance for his services it appearing that he entered into contract with and received his Instruction from William Finnie Deputy Quarter Master General for the Continent, and that this State had no other agency in the business farther than that the Executive were consulted by Col. Finnie on the occasion and approved the measure. It is therefore advised that the Claim be rejected, But that if Mr. Hopkins shall at any time hereafter produce such Vouchers as may render the State chargeable, The board will reconsider the case.

All which matters so advised, the Governor orders accordingly.

James Wood
James McClurg
Carter Braxton
Robt. Goode
Jno. H. Briggs
Chs. Carter
J. Dawson

Tuesday December 7th 1790

Present

The Governor

Mr. Wood	Mr. Goode
Mr. McClurg	Mr. Briggs
Mr. Braxton	Mr. Carter
Mr. Dawson	

The Governor informed the board that he had issued a Commission appointing Richard Beal Sheriff of Richmond County vice Moore Brokenborough deceased. Approved.

On consideration of a memorial from the Delegates of the Counties of Ohio, Monongalia, Harrison, Randolph, Kanawha, Greenbriar, Montgomery and Russell representing their Defenceless situation, It is advised that a Copy thereof be laid before the General Assembly and that another copy be forwarded to the President of the United States.

Mr. John Hopkins, Commissioner of Loans for the United States having requested that he might be furnished from the public offices of this State with the necessary Checks to prevent impositions in the funding of the Debts of this State; It is advised that he be referred to the Auditor for such Checks as he may be able to furnish.

The Governor laid before the board the report of Captain Coleman, on certain Claims presented for services rendered by Individuals, for the subsistence of a Lieutenant, for rations, and for physic and attendance furnished a troop of Cavalry raised for the defence of Jefferson County in the year 1788. Whereupon it is advised that the said Claims so far as they respect the rations and services rendered be referred to the Auditor for settlement in the usual way: that in the settlement thereof the Auditor be directed to allow the individuals for their services as Rangers and not as Cavalry, And that the Claims for physic and attendance and for the subsistence of a Lieutenant, be rejected.

The Governor laid before the board a letter from the Auditor requesting that some gentleman acquainted with the French language may be appointed to explain to him certain bills in the hands of Mr. Lewis A. Pauley directed to be paid by the High Court of Chancery to whom the same were referred by the General Assembly. Whereupon Mr. McClurg is requested to explain the said bills to the Auditor.

It is advised that a Commission issue appointing Thomas Jones Surveyor of Bourbon, and that he be required to give bond in the penalty of two thousand pounds.

It is advised that John McKenney[105] be continued on the pension List with his former allowance.

The board took into consideration the state of the office of the Commissioner for the Continental Accounts. Whereupon They are of opinion that as the business of the Commissioner is likely to be of longer continuance than was expected at the time of his appointment it is proper that his Salary should be reduced to a standing annual sum. It is therefore advised that from and after the first Day of January next he be allowed at the rate of four hundred pounds per annum and that when the business shall be compleated, the Executive will make him such

---

105. "Jno. McKenny" in the clerk's index.

further compensation as his services in their Opinion shall entitle him to.

It is advised that a Committee of the Council be appointed to examine the books of the Agent for selling the public tobacco and report particularly to this board the state of them: and that Mr. McClurg, Mr. Briggs and Mr. Dawson be appointed accordingly.

All which matters so advised, the Governor orders accordingly.

James Wood
Carter Braxton
Robt. Goode
Jno. H. Briggs
Chs. Carter
J. Dawson

Thursday December 9th 1790

Present

The Governor

Mr. Wood	Mr. Goode
Mr. McClurg	Mr. Briggs
Mr. Braxton	Mr. Carter

Mr. Dawson

The Governor laid before the board an account of Henry Lepner for ferriages of troops, and baggage during the War. Whereupon it is advised that the said Account, be rejected; the Executive having no authority to order the settlement of such accounts.

The Governor laid before the board a letter from Thomas Lawson and Dennis Dawley inclosing a petition of sundry Inhabitants of the County of Princes[s] Anne in favor of several persons who were fined by the District Court at Suffolk, On consideration whereof, the Board see no good cause for altering their Opinion entered the 24th of August last for rejecting the application for the remission of the said fines.

On consideration of the petition of Thomas Roane praying for the remission of a fine of fifty pounds imposed on him by the District Court of King and Queen for an assault, It is advised that the same be rejected.

The Board resumed the consideration of the account of Mr. William Claiborne. Whereupon it is advised that the said Account be again referred to the Auditor together with the remarks made upon his former report and other papers adduced by Mr. Claiborne in support of his claim and that he be requested after examining the same to report specially thereon and to inform the board what are in his opinion the measures most likely to acquire the vouchers necessary to a fair and just settlement of the account.

On recommendation, It is advised that an additional commission issue appointing Lemuel Bailey, John Southall, John Watkins, junior, James Allen Bradley, Thomas I'Anson and Benjamin Edwards Browne gentlemen Justices of the peace for the County of Surry.

It is advised that a commission issue appointing Edmund Booker senr. Sheriff of Amelia in the room of Henry Anderson who hath failed to give bond according to law.

It is advised that Augustine Davis be employed to print 200 Copies of the Journals of the 2d Session of Congress on the same type and paper used for printing the Laws, at the rate of four pounds per Sheet, he engaging to Compleat the same within forty days from the 25th instant.

It appearing by a Certificate from Colonel Posey that John Eagar was wounded on the 19th September 1777 at the battle of still Water, It is advised that the Governor certify as much on the said Eagars pension Certificate, the Commissioner of Loans refusing to pay the said pensioner without.

The Governor laid before the board Mr. Colemans report upon the Claims of Mr. William Shannon. Whereupon it is advised that the said report with Mr. Shannons accounts and Vouchers be referred to the auditor, that he be requested to compare the same with all entries on the public books which relate to the subject and state accounts shewing the just balance due to Mr. Shannon in paper money including as well the bills of exchange drawn in that species of money which have been heretofore protested and since taken up by him, as those which were drawn for the purpose of procuring supplies for the use of his department and are yet unpaid: And that he also state an account shewing the balance due in specie including his pay, and report the whole to the board with such observations as may serve to elucidate the business.

All which matters so advised, the Governor orders accordingly.

James Wood
James McClurg
Carter Braxton
Robt. Goode
Jno. H. Briggs
Chs. Carter
J. Dawson

Saturday December 11th 1790

Present

The Governor

Mr. Wood   Mr. Goode
Mr. McClurg   Mr. Briggs
Mr. Braxton   Mr. Carter
                 Mr. Dawson

It is advised that Commissions issue appointing Samuel Crabb an Inspector at Yeocomoco and Kinsale warehouses vice Jeremiah Rust deceased and Fleet Cox additional inspector at said warehouses vice the said Crabb.

The Governor laid before the board a letter from the Auditor assigning reasons why it is impossible for him immediately to enter into the examination of Mr. Shannons accounts as directed on thursday last. Whereupon it is advised that Mr. Coleman prepare and state to the board the Accounts in the manner required to be done by the Auditor and that Mr. McClurg and Mr. Dawson be a committeee to superintend the execution of the business.

All which matters so advised, the Governor orders accordingly.

James Wood
James McClurg
Carter Braxton
Robt. Goode
Jno. H. Briggs
J. Dawson
Chs. Carter

Tuesday December 14th 1790

Present

The Governor

Mr. Wood   Mr. Goode
Mr. McClurg   Mr. Briggs
Mr. Braxton   Mr. Dawson

On recommendation It is advised that a commission issue appointing James Southall Coroner of Charles City County.

The Governor laid before the board sundry protested bills of exchange, drawn by O. Pollock on Penet Dacosta freres and Company, Whereupon it is advised that the Auditor be directed to compare the said bills with the report of the Commissioners appointed to examine the Claim of the said Pollock, and report whether they be part of those bills, the amount of which is directed to be retained by a resolution of the General Assembly of the 7th of January 1786.

On the order of the Directors of the Lunatic hospital, It is advised that a warrant issue on the Contingent Fund, to Joseph Hornsby, for two hundred pounds upon account, for the support of the said Hospital (to be paid.)

On the application of the Directors of the public buildings It is advised that the Auditor be directed to grant them a Warrant for nine hundred pounds upon account, in part of the sum appropriated for building the Capitol (money to be borrowed).

On the Draft of Col. Davies in favor of Stott and Donaldson, It is advised that the auditor issue the usual Warrant to Col. Davies for three hundred and two Dollars on account of his Salary as Commissioner for settling the continental account. (To be paid)

For reasons appearing to the board It is advised that the Fine of four hundred pounds of tobacco imposed on John Goodrum by the District Court held at Brunswick, for nonattendance as a Grand Juror, be remitted.

The Governor laid before the board a letter from the Solicitors Clerk Stating that two Judgments had been rendered at the last general Court on bonds taken for duties by the naval officer of South Patowmack contrary to law, as adjudged in a similar case; and that the parties liable by the said Judgments had applied to him for such acquittances as will secure them against executions, the Clerk of the General Court refusing to give up their bonds; which acquittances he did not think proper to give without the Direction of the Executive. Whereupon the board are of Opinion that they have no power to interfere with such cases.

All which matters so advised the Governor orders accordingly.

> James Wood
> James McClurg
> Carter Braxton
> Robt. Goode
> Jno. H. Briggs
> J. Dawson

Thursday December 16th 1790

Present

The Governor

Mr. Wood	Mr. Goode
Mr. McClurg	Mr. Briggs
Mr. Braxton	Mr. Dawson

The Governor informed the board that he yesterday issued a Warrant on the Contingent Fund to Archibald Robertson for two pounds nineteen shillings and three pence for Coal furnished for the Council Chamber. Approved.

The Governor laid before the board an Account of Harry Heth for his pay and expences as Agent for selling the public tobacco. Whereupon it is advised that the same be referred to the Auditor for settlement, allowing Mr. Heth three Quarters per Cent: on the amount of the Sales of the said tobacco, and the reasonable expences of his agency.

On recommendation It is advised that an additional Commissi[on] issue appointing William Johnston, William Morrow, Henry Hunter, John Hutchison, William McKay and Elijah Richards gentlemen Justices of the peace for Greenbriar County.

It is advised that John McKenny be furnished with a Duplicate of his pension certificate for the year 1788, the original being lost.

On consideration of a letter from the Solicitor of this date, It is advised that he be instructed not to move against the Serjeant of Norfolk for retaining sundry Executions against Public Debtors for Duties, until the first of May next, if the Commonwealth can be benefitted thereby.

On report from Captain Coleman It is advised that the Claims of Jacob Hubbs, William Elme, Vincent Robins, John Sherley, Henry Smith, Wm. Dennin, Aron Vancleave, Thomas Neal, Mark Thomas and Peter Smith for Services rendered as Scouts in Jefferson County for the year 1788, and the Claim of Preserved Wilcox for services in the said County as a Scout for the year 1789, be referred to the Auditor for settlement in the usual way: And that the Claim of Henry Smith for twelve pounds and the Claim of Mathias Hester be rejected, for want of form the times of service not being specified.

All which matters so advised, the Governor orders accordingly.

> James Wood
> James McClurg
> Carter Braxton
> Robt. Goode
> Jno. H. Briggs
> J. Dawson

Saturday December 18th 1790

Present

The Governor

Mr. Wood	Mr. Goode
Mr. McClurg	Mr. Briggs
Mr. Braxton	Mr. Dawson

The Governor laid before the board an account of sundry expences attending the Agency of Mr. Heth in selling public tobacco, with a certificate from the Treasurer who was appointed with the Auditor by the Assembly to settle Mr. Heths Accounts, Specifying that they had compared the Items of the said Account with his books and found them to correspond; and requesting the executive to say whether the charges are approved. Whereupon the Board approve the Items in the said account of expences, except the charge of £4.4.0 for making a return of his proceedings at the instance of the legislature, and the Two pounds charged for an extra horse.

The Governor orders accordingly.

> James Wood
> James McClurg
> Carter Braxton
> Robt. Goode
> Jno. H. Briggs
> J. Dawson

Monday December 20th 1790

Present

The Governor

Mr. Wood	Mr. Goode
Mr. McClurg	Mr. Briggs
Mr. Braxton	Mr. Dawson

On Recommendation, it is advised, that a Commission issue appointing Joseph Jones Sheriff of Dinwiddie.

The Board resumed the consideration of Mr. Shannons accounts whereupon they are of opinion that the sum of two thousand and twenty six pounds, six shillings and one penny farthing appears to be due to the said Shannon and his Deputies as per account filed in the council office; It also appears that he drew One hundred and ten Bills on General Clarke amounting to One hundred and sixteen thousand nine hundred and sixty livres, five sols and six Deniers,[106] of which sundry appear to have been taken up by Clarke to the amount of ninety five thousand six hundred and forty nine Livres, and eight by Oliver Pollock amounting to fifteen thousand two hundred and forty six livres, That he drew sixty nine Bills on the Treasurer amounting to three hundred and eighty eight thousand six hundred and eighty nine Livres, That he also drew seventy Bills in paper money in the currency of this state amounting to four hundred and thirty three thousand two hundred and thirty seven pounds, of which twenty eight appear to have been settled by the Auditor and Warrants issued for the same to the amount of two hundred and one thousand five hundred and seventy seven pounds, seventeen shillings, and five by Shannon himself amounting to thirty three thousand one hundred and forty seven

---

106. A livre was a French monetary unit equal to twenty sols; a sol was a French coin equal to twelve deniers. A denier was a small silver coin used in France and western Europe from the eighth to the nineteenth centuries.

pounds, It further appears, that he drew Nine Bills on the Treasurer amounting to Nine hundred and fourteen pounds three shillings and three pence specie and gave four certificates to artificers amounting to thirty three pounds Six shillings: And that there are accounts of Articles Supplied to Support all the Bills drawn, but that those accounts which are produced in support of the specie Bills appear to be extravagant.

All which matters so advised the Governor orders accordingly.

James Wood
Jas. McClurg
Carter Braxton
Robt. Goode
Jno. H. Briggs
J. Dawson

Wednesday December 22d 1790

Present

The Governor

Mr. Wood	Mr. Goode
Mr. McClurg	Mr. Briggs
Mr. Braxton	Mr. Dawson

It is advised, that Elizabeth Cunningham[107] be continued on the list of Pensioners with an allowance of twelve pounds per Annum, commencing the first day of January last.

It appearing, that the longer confinement of John Rose, at present in custody in the public Jail, committed by the Sheriff of Henrico, on an Execution from the General Court in behalf of the Commonwealth, for nonpayment of certain duties, the 4th of October last, will be attended with no benefit to the public, It is advised, therefore in pursuance of a Resolution of the General Assembly of the 6th of January 1787, that the said John Rose be set at liberty without the usual proceedings in Court; and that the solicitor be directed to take proper steps for the recovery of the said Duties of the principal for whom Rose was security.

On Recommendation, it is advised, that an Additional Commission issue, appointing Corbin Washington, Philip Lee, Willoughby Newton, Alexander Parker, Walker Muse, and Archibald Campbell Gentlemen, Justices of the Peace for the County of Westmoreland.

On consideration of the act passed at the present session of the General Assembly directing Duplicates of Certificates and Warrants to be issued to certain Persons, it is advised, that a letter be written to the Speaker of the House of Delegates, stating, that in the case of John Henderson one of the persons who claims duplicates of certain Warrants under this Act, it appears that one of the Original Warrants

---

107. "Cuningham" in the clerk's index.

said to have been lost, has been actually paid at the Treasury and it is suggested, that others will be found also to have been paid upon a more accurate scrutiny. And that the Executive wish to know whether it is the sense of the Legislature, that Duplicates shall issue notwithstanding the Originals may have been paid at the Treasury.

All which matters, so advised, the Governor orders accordingly.

> James Wood
> Jas. McClurg
> Carter Braxton
> Robt. Goode
> Jno. H. Briggs
> J. Dawson

Thursday December 23d 1790

Present

The Governor

Mr. Wood	Mr. Goode
Mr. McClurg	Mr. Briggs
Mr. Braxton	Mr. Dawson

It is advised that the Auditor be directed to issue a Warrant to Robert Borland pursuant to the request of the Commissioners of the Marine Hospital for one hundred and fifty pounds upon account for the purposes of the said Hospital agreeably to the Act of Assembly in that case made; also a Warrant to William Newsum[108] as Clerk to the said Commissioners for twenty five pounds.

On recommendation it is advised, that an additional Commission issue appointing Andrew Donnally Gentleman a Justice of the Peace for the County of Kanawha.

The Governor laid before the Board a Judgment of a Court held for the County of Goochland against Solomon Williams, with an order of the said Court, dated December 1790. Whereupon it is advised, that the said Judgment and order be referred to the solicitor General and that he be directed to take the necessary steps to adjust the business according to right.

All which matters so advised the Governor orders accordingly.

> James Wood
> Jas. McClurg
> Carter Braxton
> Robt. Goode
> Jno. H. Briggs
> J. Dawson

---

108. "Wm. Newsom" in the clerk's index.

Friday December 24th 1790

Present

The Governor

Mr. Wood   Mr. Braxton
Mr. McClurg   Mr. Goode
                Mr. Briggs

Pursuant to the Act for dividing the County of Gloucester and of the Act concerning Wrecks, it is advised that Commissions issue appointing Thomas Smith Sheriff of the County of Matthews and Armistead Smith and Houlder Hudgen Gentlemen Commissioners of Wrecks for the said County. And it is further advised that a Commission issue appointing Thomas Smith, Thomas Smith Junior, Thomas Tabb, Machen Boswell, Armistead Smith, James Booker, Robert Cary, Richard Billups, Richd. Gregory, Mordicai Gregory, George Armistead and Ezekiel Lain Gentlemen Justices of the Peace for the County of Mathews.

All which matters so advised the Governor orders accordingly.

James Wood
Jas. McClurg
Carter Braxton
Robt. Goode
Jno. H. Briggs

Saturday December 25th 1790

Present

The Governor

Mr. Wood   Mr. Braxton
Mr. McClurg   Mr. Goode
                Mr. Briggs

On consideration of a Letter from Colonel Davies, It is advised, that the Treasury Receipt Books from the year 1775, to the 4th of January 1781, be forwarded to Colonel Davies for the purpose of supporting the account of this State against the United States.

And the Governor Orders Accordingly.

James Wood
James McClurg
Carter Braxton
Robt. Goode
Jno. H. Briggs

Monday December 27th 1790

Present

The Governor

Mr. Wood   Mr. Braxton
Mr. McClurg   Mr. Goode
            Mr. Briggs

In pursuance of the Act for forming a new county out of the counties of Augusta, Botetourt and Greenbriar, It is advised, that a Commission issue appointing Sampson Mathews Gentleman sheriff of the county of Bath, And it is further advised that a Commission issue appointing Sampson Mathews, Samuel Vance, John Wilson, Charles Cameron, John Baller, Alexander Crawford, John Deane, James Poage, William Poage, John Dickenson, John Kinkaid, George Poage, Jacob Warwick, John White, John Peebles, John Lewis, Samuel Shrewsberry and John Oliver Gentlemen Justices of the Peace for the said county of Bath.

All which Several matters so advised the Governor orders accordingly.

James Wood
James McClurg
Carter Braxton
Robt. Goode
Jno. H. Briggs

Tuesday December 28th 1790

Present

The Governor

Mr. Wood   Mr. Braxton
Mr. McClurg   Mr. Goode
            Mr. Briggs

The Governor laid before the board a resolution of the General Assembly providing for the defence of the Western Frontiers of this Commonwealth; but there not being time to go through the same, it is advised that the further consideration thereof be postponed until tomorrow, which the Governor orders accordingly.

James Wood
James McClurg
Carter Braxton
Robt. Goode
Jno. H. Briggs

Wednesday December 29th 1790

Present

The Governor

Mr. Wood   Mr. Braxton
Mr. McClurg   Mr. Goode
                Mr. Briggs

The board resumed the consideration of the Resolution of the General Assembly, authorizing the Executive to direct such temporary defensive operations in the frontier counties of this state as will secure the Citizens from the hostile Invasions of the Indian Enemy. Whereupon the board are of opinion, that the best system of defence which can be established under the present circumstances will be to order into service in the different Western counties a small number of men proportioned to the degree in which they are respectively exposed.

That the officers commanding these parties be instructed constantly to range the frontiers most open to invasion and either to alarm the Inhabitants upon the approach of a large body of the enemy or repel the incursions of predatory parties.

It is therefore advised that a Lieutenant, two Serjeants and forty rank and file be allowed to the County of Harrison; An Ensign, two serjeants and thirty rank and file to Monongalia; a Lieutenant, a Ensign, three serjeants and fifty rank and file to Ohio; a Lieutenant an Ensign, three serjeants and fifty rank and file to Kanawha; a Ensign, two serjeants and twenty rank and file to Randolph; an Ensign three serjeants and thirty two rank and file to Wythe; and a Lieutenant an Ensign and three serjeants and fifty Rank and file to Russel. The rangers to be ready for service by the first day of March next, to be stationed at such places as in the opinion of the commanding officer of each county respectively shall be most convenient to enable them be ranging the frontiers to given effectual protection.

That the Commanding officers of the several counties be directed to procure by Voluntary engagements the compliment of men allowed for the defence of their counties respectively; but should they be unable to obtain the required number by this means that they detach them with the necessary officers by detail and rotation of duty agreeable to the Act to amend and reduce into one Act the several laws for regulating and disciplining the Militia and guarding against invasions and insurrections.

That for the defence of Kentucky, it is advised, that a Brigadier General be appointed to command the whole militia of the District who shall be allowed the pay and Rations of a Lieutenant Colonel when in actual service.

That the said Brigadier General do immediately endeavour to procure by voluntary engagements two hundred and twenty six men to range the most exposed parts of the frontiers of the district to be s stationed as will in his judgment afford the best protection to the Inhabitants; but should he be unable to obtain the required number by voluntary engagements, that he direct the commanding officer of the respective counties composing the District to detach their just proportion with the necessary officers by detail and rotation of duty agreeable to the Militia law, the whole to be ready for service by the first day of March next.

That in the execution of this business he be not considered as in actual service nor have authority to appoint the Staff and other officers allowed by law, but shall be reimbursed all such reasonable expences as he may necessarily incur.

That the said Rangers be furnished with rations in such manner as the Brigadier General of Kentucky and the officers commanding the several counties without that District shall think proper—six pence to be allowed for each ration, a subaltern to be allowed two and the non commissioned and privates one ration each. The pay and rations of both officers and privates to be the same as is allowed by law to the continental troops.

That the following evidence of the service of the rangers be required,

1st. A return of the names, rank and time of service of each of the said Rangers.

2d. A Pay abstract or account for the number of said Rangers agreeable to the aforesaid return; these papers to be verified by the oath of the officers commanding the several Detachments and by the signature of the Brigadier General in Kentucky, or by that of the commanding officers of the several counties without that District.

3d. An abstract of the rations agreeably to the aforesaid return, to be signed by the officer receiving them and countersigned by the Brigadier General in Kentucky or by the Commanding officers of the several Counties without that district.

And it is further advised that Charles Scott be appointed Brigadier General of Kentucky.

On Recommendation, it is advised that a Commission issue appointing Henry Lee Gentleman sheriff of Mason in the room of Edmund Lyne Gentleman about to remove out of the county.

All which matters so advised the Governor orders accordingly.

> James McClurg
> Carter Braxton
> Robt. Goode
> Jno. H. Briggs

James Wood—I dissent from the opinion of the Board, in their advise respecting the pay of the militia, meant to be called into service, under the Resolutions of the General Assembly of the 20th day of this Instant;

for the following reasons 1st Because I consider it to be manifestly inconsistent to order any part of the militia into actual service, *under a law of the state,* and to assume the power of reducing the daily pay allotted to them by the same law. And 2dly Because it has a direct Tendency to defeat the Intentions of the Legislature in affording security and protection to an extensive and exposed frontier.

Thursday December 30th 1790

Present

The Governor

Mr. Wood	Mr. Braxton
Mr. McClurg	Mr. Goode

Mr. Briggs

It is advised that a letter be written to the public Printer informing him that unless he can give assurance that the laws will be printed upon good paper within thirty days from the first day of January next, the Board will be under the necessity of appointing other Printers to assist him agreeable to the Resolution of the Assembly of the 28th of December 1786.

It is advised that the Treasurer be directed to borrow from any funds, money sufficient to pay the present quarters salary due to the officers of civil government; taking care to replace the same as soon as possible.

All which matters so advised the Governor orders accordingly.

> James Wood
> James McClurg
> Carter Braxton
> Robt. Goode
> Jno. H. Briggs

Saturday January 1st 1791

Present

The Governor

Mr. Wood	Mr. Braxton
Mr. McClurg	Mr. Goode

Mr. Briggs

On consideration of a Letter from Colonel George Clendinen[109] complaining of the late provision made for the Western defence, It is advised, that the Governor inform him that the Board see no good cause for altering their Regulations on that Subject.

---

109. "Clendinnen" in the clerk's index.

Pursuant to an Act of the last Session of Assembly it is advised, that Mary Boush be put on the list of Pensioners with an allowance of half the pay of a Captain of the Navy of this State Yearly commencing the first day of January 1791.

In pursuance of a Resolution of the General Assembly of the 24th of December last, It is advised, that the Directors of the public Buildings be instructed to put in the balances due to the Commonwealth from the Estate of Archibald Cary deceased, with the Master Commissioner of the chancery, in order that the same may be levied upon the assets of the said Estate. It is also advised, that the Attorney General be directed to take such Steps for the recovery of a sum of money due to the Directors of the Public Buildings for the purchase of public Lots, as the law directs.

It being suggested that the constant attendance of the Solicitor at his office for the proper discharge of the duties thereof, is necessary, It is advised that the Governor inform him, that it is expected, he will attend accordingly.

It is advised, that Mr. McClurg, Mr. Braxton and Mr. Briggs be appointed a Committee to visit and examine the offices of the Treasurer, Auditor and Solicitor, pursuant to the Act of the General Assembly empowering the Executive to Superintend and arrange the said offices.

All which matters so advised the Governor orders accordingly.

James Wood
James McClurg
Carter Braxton
Robt. Goode
Jno. H. Briggs

Tuesday January 4th 1791

Present

The Governor

Mr. Wood   Mr. Braxton
Mr. McClurg   Mr. Goode
            Mr. Briggs

It is advised that a Warrant issue on the Contingent Fund to Jane West for six pounds in advance for nursing Catherine Crulls child. (to be paid)

The Auditors account for his Quarters salary, being examined the same is certified for payment.

On report from Captain Coleman It is advised that the Auditor be directed to issue the ususal Warrants to Major Langham for one hundred and six pounds fourteen shillings and eight pence ½ being the balance due the Superintendant and Artificers at the point of Fork up to the first instant: and for seventy two pounds twelve shillings being the amount of the payroll for the Guards at the Post to the same time.

The Governor laid before the board a letter from Major Langham Superintendant at the Point of Fork informing that he had taken the Liberty to have an addition made to the public mill at the post so as to grind meal which was done at small expence and without interfering with the original intention of the said mill, and he conceives the toll will supply the post with forage: and submitting to the board the propriety of entering into new contracts for supplying the post with rations. Whereupon it is advised that Major Langham take upon himself the expence of the alteration in the mill and that he have the profits arising therefrom until he shall be fully reimbursed; taking care that the grinding for toll shall on no occasion interfere in the business for which the mill was originally intended; And that he be directed to contract for supplying the post on the best terms he can.

On application from the Directors of the public buildings It is advised that the Auditor grant them a Warrant for three hundred and fifty three pounds nineteen shillings and a penny being the balance of a sum of money voted by the general assembly in 1789 for building the Capitol (to be paid).

The Governor laid before the board Mr. Amblers resignation of the Office of a Director of the public buildings, and the same is accepted.

The Governor laid before the board two bills drawn by William Shannon on the Treasurer of Virginia, One in favor of William Spangler for seven pounds ten shillings, and the other to James Querthom for five pounds fifteen shillings, which appear to be part of the specie bills allowed in the settlement of Mr. Shannons claim; Whereupon it is advised that the Auditor be directed to grant Certificates for the said bills pursuant to the Act of the general assembly "Granting a sum of money to William Shannon and others."

It is advised that a warrant issue on the Contingent Fund to Archd. Blair for Twenty five pounds for four months Salary as Keeper of the public Seal up to this Day. to be paid. It is also advised that the Treasurer be directed to pay a warrant granted by the Auditor, pursuant to an act of the general assembly, to William Courtney, for twelve pounds out of the Contingent Fund, for his present relief as a pensioner.

On consideration of the Letters from Col. George Clendinnen of the 1st and 4th instant, It is advised that he be informed, as the opinion of this board, that no partial alterations can be made with propriety in the general Orders given for the Defence of the Western frontiers.

All which matters so advised, the Governor orders accordingly.

James Wood
James McClurg
Carter Braxton
Robt. Goode
Jno. H. Briggs

Friday January 7th 1791

Present

The Governor

Mr. Wood	Mr. Goode
Mr. McClurg	Mr. Briggs
Mr. Braxton	Mr. Carter
	Mr. Dawson

It is advised that a commission issue appointing Samuel Vance Coroner for the County of Bath, to take effect from and after the first of May next.

The board took into consideration the situation of the Post at the Point of Fork, Whereupon it is advised that the Superintendant lay before the board by the 1st of April next a particular Statement of the number of arms that have been repaired in the last year, that he also prepare Estimates of the number of Arms that can be put into order quarterly by the artificers at present employed, that he use every exertion to have the bayonets which have been forged at the Post ground and prepared for service; and that he report to the board whether in his opinion the Guard will be sufficient without the aid of the Artificers to keep in order the arms that are already in repair.

The board resumed the consideration of the System established the 29th ulto. for the defence of the Western Counties, so far as relates to the pay and rations of the officers and privates to be employed; Whereupon it is advised that no alteration be made therein at present.

All which matters so advised, the Governor orders accordingly.

James Wood
James McClurg
Carter Braxton
Robt. Goode
Jno. H. Briggs
Chs. Carter
J. Dawson—When the General Assembly, on the 20th of the last month, passed the resolution authorizing the executive to direct temporary defensive operations in

the frontier counties of this state, their intention must have been to afford *effectual* relief to the defenseless citizens inhabiting those counties and to *secure* them against the hostile invasions of the Indian enemy. The system adopted, will, I am persuaded, defeat the laudable intentions of the legislature and endanger the lives of many of our valuable citizens. And when any part of the militia are called into actual service *under a Law of the state,* I humbly apprehend that they ought to receive the same pay and rations allotted to them by that Law.

For these reasons I dissent from the opinion of the board of this day, advising that no alterations be made in the system established on the 29th ultimo.

Tuesday January 18th 1791

Present

The Governor

Mr. Wood	Mr. Goode
Mr. McClurg	Mr. Dawson

The Governor informed the board that in the recess he directed the usual warrant for a Quarters salary due the first instant to Reubin Burnley as Clerk to the Commissioner for settling the Continental account and That he directed the Treasurer to pay to the Directors of James river Company thirty shillings on each of the public Shares in said company. Approved.

Pursuant to a resolution of the General Assembly of the 28th of December 1790, It is advised that William Foushee, Daniel L. Hylton and Alexander Montgomery esquires be appointed Directors of the public buildings in the room of Archibald Cary deceased, Edmund Randolph who hath removed out of the state, and Jaquelin Ambler who hath resigned.

All which matters so advised, the Governor orders accordingly.

James Wood
James McClurg
Robt. Goode
J. Dawson

Monday January 24th 1791

Present

The Governor

Mr. Wood	Mr. Goode
Mr. McClurg	Mr. Briggs
Mr. Braxton	Mr. Carter
Mr. Dawson	

The Governor laid before the Board a letter from Colonel Davies stating that he conceives the reduction of his Salary is injurious to him in as much as it is contrary to the terms upon which he engaged in the service; that the business is in its nature complicated and laborious, but that in consequence of the length of time which will be expended in the completion of the Work he is willing to receive five hundred pounds per annum for the present to be paid hereafter the arrears which may be due on the terms of the original contract and such farther compensation as the Executive think his services merit. Whereupon it is advised that in consideration of the particular circumstances stated by Col. Davies he be allowed at the rate of four hundred and fifty pounds per annum from the first Day of the present month whilst he shall continue in the service of the public But his claim to arrears, cannot be admitted, the executive conceiving that they have at all times a right to judge of the adequacy of the allowance made him.

It is advised that a warrant issue on the Contingent Fund to Aug. Davis for four pounds six shillings and four pence for the postage of public letters to the 1st instant. (To be paid.)

On application of the Directors of the public buildings, It is advised that the Auditor be directed to grant them a warrant for five hundred pounds in part of the sum voted by the last assembly for building the Capitol (to be paid).

On consideration of an opinion of Mr. John Taylor relative to the situation of Mr. John Pope as security for John Linton one of the Inspectors at Dumfries; It is advised that a copy of the said opinion, together with copies of the List of the Sales of the said Lintons estate under an execution of the Commonwealths, and of the previous notice of the said Sale, be referred to the Attorney General who will take the proper steps for securing the interest of the Commonwealth.

Mr. John Morton late District Commissioner having represented that the two suits brought by him in behalf of the public against Samuel H. Saunders and Col. Harris remain yet untried; the Defendants having found means to have them continued; and recommending that the same should be left to reference, Mr. Saunders being willing to do so. It is advised that Mr. Morton be instructed to consent to a reference provided that the award of the referrees be made the Judgment of the Court.

All which matters so advised, the Governor orders accordingly.

James Wood
James McClurg
Carter Braxton
Robt. Goode
Jno. H. Briggs
Chs. Carter
J. Dawson

Wednesday January 26th 1791

Present

The Governor

Mr. Wood   Mr. Goode
Mr. McClurg   Mr. Briggs
Mr. Braxton   Mr. Carter
                    Mr. Dawson

It is advised that a Warrant issue on the Contingent Fund for two hundred pounds to Mr. Joseph Hornsby for the use of the Lunatic Hospital, being the balance of the Directors order of the 10th of December last. (To be paid).
The Governor orders accordingly.

James Wood
James McClurg
Carter Braxton
Robt. Goode
Jno. H. Briggs
Chs. Carter
J. Dawson

Friday January 28th 1791

Present

The Governor

Mr. Wood   Mr. Goode
Mr. McClurg   Mr. Briggs
Mr. Braxton   Mr. Carter
                    Mr. Dawson

It is advised that the Treasurer be directed to pay the amount of a warrant drawn on the Contingent fund for fifteen pounds in favor of John Carter upon account, to purchase coal, books, etc., for the use of the Auditors office.

The Goveror laid before the board three protested bills of exchange drawn by Oliver Pollock on Messrs. Penett DaCosta freres and Company, one for three thousand Dollars, dated the 22d of June 1780, one for thirteen thousand Dollars dated the 28th of June 1780, and one for two thousand one hundred and fifty five Dollars dated the 13th of July 1780, which appear to be some of those bills for which a part of Mr. Pollocks Claim was retained bye order of the executive the 14th of January 1786, pursuant to a resolution of the General Assembly of the 7th of January 1786. Whereupon it is advised that the auditor be directed to issue Warrants on the foreign fund for the amount of the above three bills with 18 per cent Damages and six per cent interest from the 1st of August 1782. It is further advised that the balance of Mr. Pollocks claim cannot be paid unless he produce the original bills under proper protests.

It is advised that Priscilla Chowning be continued on the List of pensioners with an allowance of six pounds for the present year.

Cut silver coin no longer circulating but at the rate of six shillings and eight pence per ounce, It is advised that the Agent for selling the public tobacco, be instructed to receive no such money but at the above mentioned rate in payment of any balance now due to him on account of the public.

All which matters so advised the Governor orders accordingly.

> James Wood
> James McClurg
> Carter Braxton
> Robt. Goode
> Jno. H. Briggs
> Chs. Carter
> J. Dawson

Saturday January 29th 1791

Present

The Governor

Mr. Braxton Mr. Briggs
Mr. Goode Mr. Carter
Mr. Dawson

Upon application made It is advised that the Damages on the amount of a Judgment obtained against John George, as Sheriff of Middlesex, for the revenue tax of 1788, be remitted; he having produced a statement of his account with a receipt for the principal sum due on such judgment, together with the legal interest due thereon, and costs.

The Governor orders accordingly.

> Carter Braxton
> Robt. Goode
> Jno. H. Briggs
> Chs. Carter
> J. Dawson

Friday February 4th 1791

Present

Mr. Wood, as Lieutenant Governor, the Governor being sick.

Mr. McClurg   Mr. Goode
Mr. Braxton   Mr. Briggs
                  Mr. Carter

It is advised that a Commission issue appointing Samuel Neale Sheriff of Norfolk County in the room of John Willoughby who hath failed to give bond according to law; And that the Solicitor be directed to proceed against the said Willoughby for such failure, as the law directs.

Present Mr. Dawson.

It is advised that Captain Richard Taylor be continued on the List of pensioners with his former allowance from January 1790.

All which matters so advised, the Lieutenant Governor orders accordingly.

James McClurg
Robt. Goode
Jno. H. Briggs
J. Dawson

Tuesday February 8th 1791

Present

The Governor

Mr. Wood   Mr. Briggs
Mr. McClurg   Mr. Carter
Mr. Goode   Mr. Dawson

The Governor informed the board that in the recess he issued a Commission appointing Thomas Baytop additional Inspector at Deacons-neck warehouse in Gloster County. Approved.

The Governor laid before the board Col. Davies's Drafts in favour of Stott and Donaldson for one hundred and sixty five pounds twelve shillings in full for his salary to the first of January last, and for fifteen pounds for the contingent expences of his office. Also an account of Ross and Currie for one hundred and ninety eight bushels of Coal furnished for the use of the Executive amounting to eight pounds five shillings. Whereupon it is advised that the said Drafts and account be referred to the Auditor for Warrants for the Sums due. (To be paid.)

The Governor laid before the board a petition of William Alexander, attorney for the Creditors of Simon Nathan praying for the payment of a protested bill of exchange for fifteen thousand Livres drawn in favour of the said Nathan by the board of Trade the 21st of

March 1780. Whereupon it is advised that the same be referred to the Auditor to examine whether the said bill is mentioned in any of Mr. Nathans accounts with the state, heretofore settled, and make report.

It appearing that the State hath by a Decree of the High Court of Chancery confirmed by the court of appeals, a title to a tract of Land lying in the County of Prince William formerly the property of Robert Bristoe but confiscated in the year 1779 to the use of the Commonwealth, It is advised that Thomas Lee, Jr. esquire be authorized and empowered to recover all Rents which have or may become due after the confiscation aforesaid; He first giving bond with sufficient Security in the penalty of a thousand pounds to the Governor and his Successors for the payment into the public treasury of all Sums of money which may come into his hands in consequence of the Authority now given him.

All which matters so advised, the Governor orders accordingly.

James Wood
James McClurg
Robt. Goode
Jno. H. Briggs
J. Dawson

Saturday February 12th 1791

Present

The Governor

Mr. Wood   Mr. Goode
Mr. McClurg   Mr. Briggs
Mr. Braxton   Mr. Dawson

It is advised that a commission issue appointing Lydal Wilkerson Sheriff of New Kent, he having desired to be continued another year.

On consideration of a letter from the Treasurer, It is advised that he be informed, the Executive will have no difficulty in directing three hundred pounds to be advanced now towards the purchase of Shares in the James river Company in behalf of the commonwealth, and the remainder to complete such purchases, as the state of the Treasury will admit, hereafter.

On recommendation, It is advised that an additional Commission issue appointing Thomas Pleasants, Thomas Jones, William Mayo, John Mayo, Thomas Bowler Adams, Peter Skipwith Randolph, John Ellis (son of John) and William Price, gentlemen Justices of the peace for the County of Henrico.

The Governor informed the board that in the recess he referred to the Auditor to settle in the usual way, the account of Peter Woodlief[110]

---

110. "Peter Woodleif" in the clerk's index.

for 216 Days service in collecting Vouchers in support of the Claims of Virginia against the United States. Approved.

All which matters so advised, the Governor orders accordingly.

> James Wood
> James McClurg
> Carter Braxton
> Robt. Goode
> Jno. H. Briggs
> J. Dawson

Wednesday February 16th 1791

Present

The Governor

Mr. Wood	Mr. Goode
Mr. McClurg	Mr. Briggs
Mr. Braxton	Mr. Dawson

Mr. Wood, Mr. Briggs and Mr. Dawson are appointed a Committee to examine the Treasurers books according to law.

It appearing to the board that the Acts of the last Session of the General Assembly are printed upon paper of different sizes and quality, It is advised that a Committee of the Council be appointed to examine such of the laws as have not been forwarded to the different Counties and report to the Executive. It is farther advised that the said Committee call upon the public printer to shew that he has printed the number of copies directed and to examine the proportion which he allows the respective Counties. Mr. Wood and Mr. Goode are appointed a Committee for the above purpose.

All which matters so advised the Governor orders accordingly.

> James Wood
> James McClurg
> Carter Braxton
> Robt. Goode
> Jno. H. Briggs
> J. Dawson

Friday February 18th 1791

Present

The Governor

Mr. Wood	Mr. Goode
Mr. McClurg	Mr. Briggs
Mr. Braxton	Mr. Dawson

The Governor informed the board that in the recess, he issued ommissions appointing William Miller inspector of tobacco at Rockey ·idge Warehouse vice Stephen Pankey, deceased, and John Teabue, jr. idditional inspector vice said Miller. Approved.

It is advised that Robert White be continued on the List of 'ensioners from January 1790, with his former allowance.

The board resumed the consideration of the Claim of William ·laiborne, and he having requested to be allowed Counsel; It is advised hat the further consideration of the said Claim be postponed until ·riday next, when Counsel will be heard on behalf of the Claimant.

All which matters so advised, the Governor orders accordingly.

> James Wood
> James McClurg
> Carter Braxton
> Robt. Goode
> Jno. H. Briggs
> J. Dawson

Wednesday February 23rd 1791

Present

The Governor

Mr. Wood	Mr. Goode
Mr. McClurg	Mr. Briggs
Mr. Braxton	Mr. Dawson

The Governor informed the board that in the recess, he granted a pardon to negro James, belonging to William Adie, condemned by the Court of Prince William for burglary; he having been recommended as a proper object of mercy; and that he issued a Commission appointing Burdit Ashton, Coroner for the County of King George. Approved.

The Governor laid before the board official returns of the balances due from several Inspectors of tobacco by which it appears that many of them have retained in their hands those balances for several years, and that others have failed to make report agreeable to law of the Quantity of Tobacco shipped annually from the warehouses under their inspection. Whereupon it is advised that an Inquiry be immediately set on foot against the following Delinquents agreeable to the 28th section of the Tobacco law viz:

Pegram and Goodwin, at Petersburg, for failing to pay in the surplus of £598.16.3 from October 1785 to October 1786.

Dedman and Cosby, at York, for balance of 3/ duty from April to August 1786 .... £ 13. 6. 3.

Andrews and Jarrett at Low Point for balance
of tax on tobacco exported to October 83 .... £ 28.16. 4.

Vaughn and Blick at Cedar point for surplus
from September 1784 to September 1785 .... £107.16. 9.

Miskett and Garland at Beckwiths for Tobacco
sold that lay over two years .... £ 46.12. 9.

Lewis and Kirby at College Landing for 3/ Duty
on Tobacco to May 1786 .... £ 23. 8. 0

Lowry and Rogers at Davis and Lowrys for
balance of 3/. duty to October 1786 .... £ 19. 9. 0

Dunn and Minston at Bowlers for balance of
tax on Tobacco exported
to October 83   £ 16.12.10

     for balance ware-
     house rents ....   <u>15. 2.10</u>   £ 31.15. 8.

White and Stowers at Cabin Point for Surplus
October 1785 to October
1786 .... £ 29.16. 8

     for 4/ Duty-Do. 80.10. 9
     for 3/ Duty-Do. ....   <u>60. 8. 0</u>   £170.15. 5.

Bailey and Stone at Colchester for Surplus from
from October 1785 to Oc-
tober 1786 .... £197.10. 9

     for 4/. Duty-Do.   275. 6. 3
     for 3/. Duty-Do.   <u>206.10. 0</u>   £679. 7. 0.

Sullivan and Webb at Hobbs-hole for balance of
3/. Duty from October 1785 to October 1786 ..... £ 23. 7.10½

Debnam and Nutall at Deaconsneck, for tax on
Tobacco from October
1783 to October 84 ..... £ 10.16. 0

     For Do...Do ....   27. 0. 0.
     for balance of 4/.
     Duty from October
     1785 to October
     1786   <u>0. 0. 6</u>   £ 37. 16. 6

Dishman and Alexander at Boyds-hole for balance of Tax on Tobacco from June 1782 to April 1783   £   6.18. 0

for Ditto July 82 to May 1783 ....   2. 6. 6.
for Ditto to 1st October 1783 ....   26.16.10
for ....   4. 7. 6   £ 40.18.10[111]

Archer and Goodwin at Bollingbrook for Sundries ....   397. 1. 3.

Millar and Moseby at Rocketts for Surplus from October 1783 to October 1784 .... £ 73.10. 6.

Thornby and Boon at Gibsons for balance of 4/. from October 1784 to October 1785 .... £ 8.13. 9.

for Surplus Do.   14. 2. 8
for 3/. Duty Do.   30.17. 2.   £ 53.13. 7.

Watts and Cureton at Boyds for balance of Inspection money to 10th of October 1782   1. 4. 5.

for balance of 4/. duty to 1st July 1875 }   95.12.11   £ 96.17. 4

Boult and Eskridge at Coans for Surplus from October 1784 to October 1785 .... £ 80.10. 9.

Rogers and Young at Pitts Guilford etc. for balance of Surplus from October 1781 to October 1782.   19.12. 0.

for balance Do. from October 1782 to October 1783 }   3. 6.10.

for balance 6/. duty Do   71. 7. 5.

for tax 6/. hhds from October 83 to October 1784 }   37. 1. 0

---

111. The correct total is £40.8.10.

for balance of 4/.
Duty from October
84 to October 85   £ 37.12. 9.

for bal. 3/ Duty
same period   28. 4. 7.
                          _____
                          65.17.4

brot over 65.17. 4.   £131. 7. 3

Lr.

By paid in part
4/. Duty per
Treasurers books   31. 3. 5   34.13.11 £166. 1. 2.

Dunn and Booth at Poropotank for surplus
from October 1780 to Oc-
tober 1781   5. 0. 0

for balance of Tax on
Tobacco to October
1783   15. 7.10   £ 20. 7.10.

Edward and Sanford at Nominy for balance of
Tax to May 1783   £ 66. 3. 0

Stanley and Richardson at Meriwethers for 4/.
Duty from October 1787 to October 88 ....   £ 37. 5. 0

Booker and Taliaferro at Poropotank for 4/.
Duty from October 1787 to October 1788 ....   £ 20. 5. 1.

The Inspectors at Bollingbrooke for 6/. Duty
from 1st of October 1789 to 1st October 90 .... £155. 6. 2

The Inspectors at Dumfries for 6/. Duty from
1st October 1789 to 1st October 1790 .... £ 61.16. 2

The Inspectors at Manchester for 6/. Duty from
1st October 1789 to 1st October 1790 .... £714. 3. 1.

The Inspectors at Cherrystone and Naswaddox
for 4/. Duty from 1st Oc-
tober 1788 to 1st October
89   191.16. 3.

for 6/. Duty Do. Do.   310.16. 2   £502.12. 5.

The Inspectors at Lynches for 4/. Duty from 1st
October 1788 to 1st Octo-
ber 1789   17. 6. 9.

for 6/. Duty for same
time   119. 3. 7.

for 6/. Duty from 1st
October 89 to 1st Oc-
tober 90   18. 7. 8.   £154.18. 0.

The Inspectors at Meriwethers for 4/ Duty from
1st of October 1788 to 1st October 1789 .... £ 54.12. 0.

The Inspectors at Poropotank for 4/. Duty from
1st October 1788 to 1st October 1789............. £ 23.19. 9.

The Inspectors at Roys for 6/. Duty from 1st. of
October 1788 to 1st. of October 1789............. £ 89. 7. 3.

The Inspectors at Rockyridge for 4/. Duty from
1st. of October 1788 to
1st. October 1789   £445.19.11.

for 6/. Duty for
same time   146.19. 0   £592.18.11.

The Inspectors at Shockoe for 6/. Duty from 1st.
of October 1788 to the 1st. of October 1789 .... £174.18. 8.

The Inspectors at Dumfries for having failed to make return for the year 1789.

The Inspectors at Pitts Landing Guilford, etc. for failing to make returns for 1789 and 1790, and

The Inspectors at the Brickhouse, Coans, Cherrystone and Naswaddox, Cat point, Curds, Falmouth, Gibsons, Meriwethers, Nominy, Poropotank, Petersburg, Pages, Roys, Rockyridge, Suffolk, Shockoe and York for failing to make returns for the year 1790;

And for the better conducting such enquiry it is further advised that Mr. Harry Heth be appointed to exhibit the charges aforesaid against the several Delinquents in the manner prescribed by the above mentioned section of the Tobacco Law and that for his trouble in this business he shall receive a reasonable compensation; And to enable Mr. Heth to establish the said Charges It is advised that the Auditor and Solicitor be directed to furnish him with the Accounts properly stated by which the balances appear to be due from the several Inspectors.

It is advised that the account of Tunstal Quarles for rations furnished the Post at the Point of Fork amounting to eighty five pounds twelve shillings and a penny as certified by Capt. Coleman, be referred to the Auditor for settlement in the usual way.

The Governor laid before the board a letter from Mr. Thomas Newton requesting to be informed at what price the Stone formerly deposited on Cape Henry for the purpose of building a Light-house will be sold by the perch. Whereupon it is advised that Col. Newton be authorized to dispose of the above mentioned Stone for the highest price that can be obtained so that the amount be equal to twelve shillings for each Perch, the Stone to be raised from its present situation at the expence of the purchaser.

It is advised that the Auditor of Public Accounts be desired to attend at the Council Chamber on friday next in order that he may hear the Counsel of Mr. Claiborne in support of his Claim against the Commonwealth and be thereby the better enabled to give the executive such farther information on this subject as may be required of him.

It is advised that the Superintendant at the Point of Fork be authorized to contract for furnishing the Post with provisions upon the best terms he can.

All which matters so advised, the Governor Orders accordingly.

James Wood
James McClurg
Carter Braxton
Robt. Goode
Jno. H. Briggs
J. Dawson

Friday February 25th 1791

Present

The Governor

Mr. Wood   Mr. Goode
Mr. McClurg   Mr. Briggs
Mr. Braxton   Mr. Dawson

The board resumed the consideration of the Claim of Mr. William Claiborne against the Commonwealth, referred by the General Assembly to the Executive for settlement, and upon full consideration of the Vouchers adduced in support of the said Claim are of opinion that they are not sufficient to Establish any certain sum to be due thereon.

The Governor orders accordingly.

James Wood
James McClurg
Carter Braxton
Robt. Goode
J. Dawson

Tuesday March 1st 1791

Present

The Governor

Mr. Wood   Mr. Goode
Mr. McClurg   Mr. Briggs
                    Mr. Dawson

The Governor laid before the board a letter from the honorable James Mercer stating certain Doubts which had arisen on the construction of the Act of the General Assembly "for the better securing certain Debts within mentioned due and owing to the Commonwealth" and submitting to the Executive whether if it shall be their opinion that the said recited Act cannot be carried into execution according to the obvious intention of the legislature it will not be just that the sale of the Slaves ought to be postponed till the meeting of the general assembly. Whereupon it is advised that all interference of the executive in this case farther than the above recited law expressly authorizes will be improper.

The board took into consideration the 10th section of the act of the general assembly "for the better securing certain Debts within mentioned due and owing to the Commonwealth". Whereupon it is advised that the bonds to be taken by the Commissioners appointed by the above recited Act to receive and sell at public auction any Slaves that may be delivered to them by Mary Peyton administratrix of Sir John Peyton deceased Thomas Dixon and Elizabeth Dixon the surviving Executor and executrix of John Dixon deceased or either of them, Anne Fox Administratrix of John Fox or Elizabeth Whiting administratrix of Peter Beverley Whiting deceased, may be discharged by payment of securities at the following rates viz: Warrants issued for interest due on the Debts of this State at par; and other public Securities at such rates as the executive shall from time to time direct, and in order to enable such purchasers, as may not chuse to give bond, to discharge the amount of their purchases on the Day of sale, it is farther advised, that the above mentioned commissioners be empowered to receive all such facilities as may be tendered to them in prompt payment at the following rates viz Warrants for interest due on the Debts of this State at par; military and loan office Certificates and certificates for funded paper money of this State at sixteen shillings in the pound; Final settlements and loan office Certificates of the United States at eighteen shillings in the pound; Six per cent Stock of the United States at par; three per cent Ditto at ten and sixpence in the pound; Deferred Ditto at ten and six pence. It is also further advised that such of the bonds, taken by the Commissioners above mentioned, as are to be applied to the discharge of any Judgments obtained against John Dixon, or Sir John Peyton, late Sheriffs of Gloster, for any balance of the Certificate tax due from them, may be discharged by the payment of Certificates for militia Services, for impressed property, and military and loan office Certificates of this state at par.

On recommendations, It is advised that an additional Commission issue appointing Thomas Garth, George Divers, Barnard Brown, Nathaniel Garland, Tandy Key, Garland Carr, William Clark, Benjamin Harris, Christopher Hudson, James Simms, Rice Garland, Thomas Lewis and Charles Hunton gentlemen Justices of the peace for the County of Albemarle; also Commissions appointing Harwood Bacon inspector of tobacco at Hendersons warehouse in the room of Chiles Terrell who hath resigned and William Johnson additional inspector at the saw Warehouse vice the said Bacon; Also an additional Commission appointing Hartwell Cocke, Robt. Goodwyn, Robert Mabry, John Wright, Thomas Gray, Howell Edmunds, Benjamin Blunt jr. and Edwin Gray Gentlemen Justices of the peace for the County of Southampton and a Commission appointing John Taylor Coroner for the said County.

It is advised that the Solicitor General be informed that the board will on Friday next take under their consideration the situation of his office, and enquire into the cause of his frequent absences.

All which matters so advised, the Governor orders accordingly.

James Wood
James McClurg
Robt. Goode
Jno. H. Briggs
J. Dawson

Friday March 4th 1791

Present

The Governor

Mr. Wood Mr. Goode
Mr. McClurg Mr. Briggs
Mr. Dawson

The Governor informed the board that in the recess he directed the auditor to settle in the usual way, the Account of Archd. Denholm for eighty eight Day service up to the 2d of March instant, in collecting Vouchers in support of the Claims of this State against the United States. Approved.

Mr. Hardin Burnley having been elected a member of the privy Council or Council of State, vice, Thomas Madison who resigned, He appeared and took his Seat at the board; having taken the Oaths prescribed by law, before John Pendleton, a Justice of the peace for the County of Henrico.

On the application of the Directors of the public buildings It is
advised that the Auditor be directed to grant them the usual warrant
for one hundred and forty five pounds ten shillings and eight pence,
upon account, (to be paid).

Mr. Burnley is added to the Committee for visiting the public
Offices of Treasurer, Auditor and Solicitor.

On recommendation, It is advised that a Commission issue appointing Archibald Richardson, Coroner for the County of Nansemond.

All which matters so advised, the Governor orders accordingly.

> James Wood
> James McClurg
> Robt. Goode
> Jno. H. Briggs
> J. Dawson
> Hardin Burnley

Wednesday March 9th 1791

Present

The Governor

Mr. Wood	Mr. Goode
Mr. McClurg	Mr. Briggs
Mr. Braxton	Mr. Dawson

Mr. Burnley

The Governor informed the board that in the recess he issued a
commission appointing Nicholas Lewis, jr. Surveyor of Albemarle, and
required him to give bond in the penalty of two thousand pounds.
Approved.

It is advised that the account of the representatives of John Conner
deceased amounting to five pounds five shillings for the rent of a
house, for the Chancery Office, up to the 4th instant, be referred to the
Auditor for settlement and a Warrant on the Contingent fund for the
sum due. (To be paid)

John Whitlocks bond, with Joseph Yarbrough, Samuel Ward and
Robert Warding Securities, to indemnify the Commonwealth and the
United States, against a Military Certificate of which he is to obtain a
Duplicate, agreeably to an act of the last Session of the general
assembly, being laid before the board, the same is approved.

For reasons appearing to the board, It is advised that the Fine of
ten pounds imposed by the Court of Mecklenburg on Charles Burton
for assaulting and beating Wm. J. Burrus, be remitted.

The Governor laid before the board a letter from the solicitor
general desiring the direction of the Executive whether he shall issue

execution for a fine levied on Messrs. Stanley and Richardson, Inspectors at Meriwethers, by Judgment of the General Court on the 15th of November last, or whether proceedings shall be had for recovery of the Debt actually due by them. Whereupon it is advised that the Solicitor be instructed to pursue all legal means for the recovery of both the fine and the balance due from the above mentioned Inspectors.

Pursuant to an Act of the General Assembly "For reassessing the lands in the Counties of Amelia and Nottoway" It is advised that Ambrose Jeter, Gabriel Folks and John Morton gentlemen be appointed Commissioners to make a new valuation of all the Lands included in the County of Amelia before the late division thereof, and now included in the Counties of Amelia and Nottoway, in such manner that all the lands so included shall average the price of ten shillings per acre.

The Governor having laid before the board a letter from the Solicitor General requesting their particular Instructions as to the settlement of an Account according to the tenth section of the general Instructions of the Executive for the Government of his office, and certain entries thereupon to be made in the public books, It is advised that the said letter be referred to the Committee appointed to visit the public offices, and that they report thereon to the board.

The Governor laid before the board a bill of exchange, drawn by the late Board of Trade, the 21st of March 1780, on Messrs. Penet Da Costa freres and Company in favour of Simon Nathan for fifteen thousand Livres, Fournay, which has been regularly protested. Whereupon, in pursuance of a resolution of the general Assembly of the 2d of November 1787, it is advised that the Auditor be directed to settle the said bill, allowing ten per cent Damages for the first eighteen months, and five per cent afterwards, and to grant Warrants on the foreign fund for the sum due.

On consideration of the petition of George Stubblefield late Sheriff of Spotsylvania, praying that the sale of his property which is under execution for the arrearages of taxes, may be postponed for three months, on his paying Six hundred pounds; It is advised that the same be rejected.

All which matters so advised, the Governor orders accordingly.

James Wood
James McClurg
Carter Braxton
Jno. H. Briggs
J. Dawson
Hardin Burnley

Friday March 11th 1791

Present

The Governor

Mr. Wood	Mr. Briggs
Mr. McClurg	Mr. Dawson
Mr. Braxton	Mr. Burnley

The Governor informed the board that he yesterday signed an approbation of Col. Temples bond, with Anthony Singleton and Baylor Hill securities, to indemnify the Commonwealth and the United States against certain Certificates and Warrants of which the said Temple is to receive Duplicates agreeably to an Act of the last assembly. Approved.

It is advised that a warrant issue on the Contingent Fund for thirty pounds to William Pierce for his last years Salary, as Keeper of the Public building. (To be paid)

The Governor laid before the board a letter from the Directors of the James river Company requesting that they may be supplied with a sufficient sum of money or Tobacco to enable them to purchase Slaves for the carrying on the Canal. Whereupon it is advised that the Treasurer be instructed to sell to the said Directors any quantity of the public Tobacco in his hands, not exceeding two hundred hogsheads, for the highest cash price, to be charged to them on account of the delinquent shares in the said company lately purchased on public account.

The board took into consideration the letter of the Solicitor of the 8th instant together with the information of the committee to whom it was referred. Whereupon it is advised that the solicitor be informed it is understood that he is empowered by the regulations established by the executive for the government of his office, to audit and pass the accounts exhibited by individuals in discharge of such balances as appear to their Debits on the paper money books, and that with respect to the adjustment of Mr. Quarles's account, the board cannot give any particular instructions. The Solicitor must therefore govern himself by the general principles upon which similar accounts have heretofore been settled allowing the affidavit of Mr. Quarles in support of such items of his account as from their nature did not admit of his procuring the usual Vouchers.

On consideration of the petition of John Brokenbrough stating that he on the 24th. of July 1789 became security to a certain Richard Lewman for duties on rum imported on that day from Antigua, and in consequence thereof, had paid into the Solicitors office the sum of three hundred and forty pounds 6/3 military Certificates and the sum of one hundred and forty three pounds 12/6 specie; and praying to have the same refunded, the general Court having determined that

bonds taken for duties, after the 21st of July 1789 were illegal and the
bonds so taken had been delivered up by order of the executive, It is
advised that the said petition be rejected; the board having no authority
to draw on the Treasury in such cases, altho' it appears reasonable that
whatever has been thus illegally obtained ought to be refunded.

It is advised that the Directors of the public buildings be requested
to inform the Executive whether there be not an apartment unoc-
cupied in the Capitol, that would answer the purpose of an Office for
the High Court of Chancery, and save the present expence of house
rent.

All which matters so advised, the Governor orders accordingly.

James Wood
James McClurg
Carter Braxton
Jno. H. Briggs
J. Dawson
Hardin Burnley

Monday March 14th 1791

Present

The Governor

Mr. Wood   Mr. Goode
Mr. McClurg   Mr. Briggs
Mr. Braxton   Mr. Dawson
Mr. Burnley

The Governor informed the board, that in the recess, upon
application made, he remitted the Damages on the amount of a
judgment obtained against William Hubbard, as Sheriff of Charlotte for
the revenue of 1788; he having produced a statement of his account
with a receipt for the principal sum due on such judgment, together
with the legal interest thereon and costs: and that he issued a Warrant
on the Contingent Fund for the sum of thirty three shillings, to Samuel
Paine, for 44 bushels coal furnished for the use of the Executive
Approved.

On recommendations It is advised that Commissions issue appointing Richard Williams an Inspector of tobacco, at Blandford
warehouses, vice, Lessenberry Williams deceased and James Sturdiv-
ant additional inspector, vice, the said Richard Williams: and that a
Commission issue appointing William Dudley Sheriff of King and
Queen County, vice Philip Taliaferro who hath failed to give bond
according to law.

It is advised that the Treasurer be directed to fund with the Loan
Officer of the United States, as soon as possible, all the old continental

money, indents, and other securities of the United States of whatever kind, in his hands, belonging to the Commonwealth.

The Governor having informed the board that Mr. William Hay, one of the Directors of the public buildings, had told him there was a committee room which the Clerk of the General Court lately moved out of that would answer for an Office of the High Court of Chancery; It is advised that the Clerk of the said Court be directed to move into the said room, as soon as possible.

The Governor laid before the board the report of the Committee appointed to visit the offices of the Treasurer, Auditor and Solicitor General. Whereupon it is advised that the operation of the first section of the general regulations established for the government of the said offices, be suspended until the 1st. of July next; and that the Solicitor use all possible diligence in preparing Statements of the balances due on the Specie books ending in 1787, and of the Damages interest and costs entered in his temporary books, that the auditor may be enabled to complete the accounts in the books in his office.

The Governor laid before the board a letter from the superintendant of the Post at the point of Fork, inclosing several arrangmeents and statements in order to enable the executive to judge of the propriety of reducing the present expences of that post. Whereupon it is advised that after the first Day of May next the Guards and artificers be reduced to the following numbers, to wit: three soldiers and four artificers, that the superintendant be as aeconomical as is consistent with the preservation of the arms in hiring occasional labourers, that, before he proceed to sell any articles belonging to the post which may in his opinion be useless, he make out an inventory of all such articles and transmit it to the executive who will give Directions respecting the Disposal of them; and that he prepare by the 10th of April an inspection return of all the arms, ordnance and other military Stores deposited at the post in order to an accurate examination of the magazine and arsenals.

All which matters so advised, the Governor orders accordingly.

James Wood
James McClurg
Carter Braxton
Robt. Goode
Jno. H. Briggs
J. Dawson
Hardin Burnley

Friday March 18th 1791

Present

The Governor

Mr. Wood	Mr. Goode
Mr. McClurg	Mr. Briggs
Mr. Braxton	Mr. Dawson

Mr. Burnley

The Governor informed the board that in the recess, on recommendation, he issued an additional commission appointing John Wayt a Justice of the peace for the County of Rockingham; and that, upon application made, he remitted the Damages on the amount of a Judgment obtained against William Herring, as Sheriff of Rockingham, for the revenue of 1788; he having produced a statement of his account, with a receipt for the principal sum due on such judgment, together with the legal interest due thereon, and costs. Approved.

It is advised that Benjamin Hoomes be continued on the List of pensioners with his former allowance from January last.

The Board on reconsidering the subject of the petition of John Brokenbrough which was rejected on the eleventh of the present month, and taking into consideration the inconvenience which the said Brokenbrough will be subjected to by witholding from him the Certificates and warrants which he had illegally paid to the Solicitor General, It is advised that the Solicitor be instructed to repay to Mr. Brokenbrough out of any Certificates or warrants which he may hereafter receive for Duty bonds, the amount of the Certificates and Warrants which have been so illegally paid by the said Brokenbrough.

The Governor laid before the board, a letter from the honorable Cuthbert Bullitt, informing that he had been one of the persons authorized to receive the rents arising from the Bristoes lands in Prince William, which authority he was desirous of holding for the present year, in order to settle with the persons in arrears, being better acquainted with the business, than he supposes any other person can be at present; and requesting the advice of the board respecting the tobacco in the hands of Carrs executors, due to the said estate. Whereupon it is advised that a letter be written to Mr. Bullitt informing him of the destruction of the records of this board in 1781, and requesting to be informed, previous to his being advised on the subject, whether he derived his authority from any special appointment by the Legislature, or from the Executive under the power given them by the sequestration law to appoint Commissioners for british subjects.

All which matters so advised the Governor orders accordingly.

James Wood
James McClurg
Carter Braxton
Robt. Goode
Jno. H. Briggs
J. Dawson
Hardin Burnley

Wednesday March 23d 1791

Present

The Governor

Mr. Wood   Mr. Goode
Mr. McClurg   Mr. Briggs
Mr. Braxton   Mr. Dawson
          Mr. Burnley

The Governor informed the board that in the recess he granted a pardon to Negro Portige, the property of James Barnes, condemned to death, by a Court of Oyer and Terminer held in the County of Nottoway, for felony; he having been recommended as a proper object of mercy: and that he referred the Account of Dabney Minor to the Auditor of [i.e., for] settlement, amounting to fifty one pounds one and six pence for work done about the Governors garden and lot, and for tables for the General Court and the Committee rooms. Approved.

The board proceeded to the choice of a President in conformity to the Constitution or Form of Government and Mr. Wood being proposed was unanimou[s]ly elected.

It appearing that the general Government has entered into measures for the Defence of the frontiers; It is advised that the Instructions given by the Executive for the temporary Defence of the frontier Counties of this State be recalled, except so far as relates to the Counties of Russell and Wythe; and that the Governor give orders, by express, for disbanding the forces embodied in consequence of such Instructions.

On the request of the Treasurer, It is advised that a Committee be appointed to examine and see weighed, the Cut Silver Coin that shall be in the treasury the first of next month. Mr. Goode and Mr. Briggs are appointed accordingly.

It is advised that Edmund B. Lacy be appointed in addition to those already appointed to examine and burn the paper money of the State.

It is advised that Mr. William Hay be requested to have a pump fixed in the Well already dug in the Capitol Square, to be paid for out of the Contingent fund.

All which matters so advised, the Governor orders accordingly.

James Wood
James McClurg
Carter Braxton
Robt. Goode
Jno. H. Briggs
J. Dawson
Hardin Burnley

Wednesday March 30th 1791

Present

The Governor

Mr. Wood   Mr. Goode
Mr. McClurg   Mr. Briggs
Mr. Braxton   Mr. Dawson
               Mr. Burnley

The Governor informed the board that in the recess he granted a Warrant on the Contingent fund to Joseph Leiplong for twenty five pounds, upon account, for going express to Kentucky with public Dispatches: that he granted a pardon to Negro Cromwell condemned to Death by Nansemond Court of Oyer for felony; he having been recommended as a proper object of mercy; that he issued a Commission appointing James Estham Surveyor of Halifax County and required him to give bond in penalty of £2000. Approved.

On recommendation, It is advised that an additional Commission issue appointing Philip Fitzhugh, John Brown, Richard Scott Blackburn, William Downman, Charles Tyler, John Brown (B.R.) and Charles Ewell gentlemen, Justices of the peace for the County of Prince William.

It is advised that Lieutenant George Hite be continued on the pension List with an allowance [of] forty pounds per annum from January 1789, pursuant to an act of the last general assembly passed in his favour.

It being suggested that the Well already dug in the Capitol square may hereafter be found, upon laying off the square, to be in an improper place; It is advised that the pump be fixed in such part of the square as the Directors shall think best; And that the two Springs near the Capitol on the West side be put in good order.

It is advised that Samuel Todd be appointed a Collector of the revenue and Certificate taxes due from the County of Botetourt, for the year 1786.

On consideration of a letter from the Treasurer, informing that there is, remaining in the treasury, a protested bill of exchange, drawn by William Black, the 30th of November 1773, for One hundred and fifty pounds sterling, and endorsed by the late Col. Tayloe, which appears to have been left by Robert C. Nicholas, the former Treasurer, on the final adjustment of his Accounts with the Public, as public property; and requesting the Executive to direct the Steps necessary to be taken for securing the money to the Commonwealth, It is advised that the Solicitor be instructed to demand payment of the said bill as soon as possible, and, if not paid, to take legal measures for the recovery thereof.

The Governor laid before the board a letter from Mr. Newton inclosing one from Mr. McCombe making a proposal to purchase the materials formerly deposited on Cape Henry to the following purport, "As the State are not disposed to undertake to raise the Stone, I will attempt to get it up and pay for it such a price as I can afford according to their quality and quantity deducting the expence of raising." Whereupon it is advised that Mr. McCombe be allowed to make a trial to raise the abovementioned materials the expence of which if it succeed, shall be deducted from such price as shall be settled by indifferent Arbitrators if the parties cannot agree, but the State is on no account to be subject to any part of the expence of the trial should it prove unsuccessful, and that Mr. Newton be empowered to make such a contract on the part of the State.

It is advised that the treasurer be directed to borrow from any funds, money sufficient to pay the present quarters salary due to the Officers of civil Government; taking care to replace the same as soon as possible.

All which matters so advised, the Governor orders accordingly.

James Wood
James McClurg
Robt. Goode
Jno. H. Briggs
J. Dawson
Hardin Burnley

Tuesday April 5th 1791

Present

The Governor

Mr. Wood   Mr. Briggs
Mr. McClurg   Mr. Dawson
Mr. Goode   Mr. Burnley

The Governor informed the board, that in the recess, he granted a pardon to William Nicholas, who was committed by an examining Court of Chesterfield, to the District Jail of Henrico for farther trial for forgery; the Attorney General having represented that it was necessary he should be pardoned; And that, on the report of Captain Coleman, he directed the usual warrants to issue in favour of Captain Langham, for two hundred thirty five pounds seventeen shillings and six pence being the balance due the Superintendant and artificers at the Post at the Point of Fork for the last quarter; and for seventy two pounds twelve shillings, due the Guard at the post for the same time. Approved.

For reasons appearing to the board, It is advised that the fine of ten shillings imposed by Goochland Court martial on John Williams for nonattendance in March 1788, be remitted.

The Account of Mr. Pendleton for his last quarters salary as Auditor of public accounts, being examined the same is Certified for payment.

On the order of the Directors of the Lunatic hospital, It is advised that the Auditor be directed to issue a Warrant on the contingent Fund to Joseph Hornsby for two hundred pounds upon account for the use of the said hospital. (To be paid)[112]

It is advised that the sum of fifteen pounds be paid out of the Contingent fund to John Carter jr., upon account, to pay for blank books etc. purchased for the use of the Auditors office; the Auditor having granted a warrant therefor.

Upon the application of the Directors of the public buildings It is advised that the auditor be directed to grant them a warrant for one hundred and thirty five pounds, upon account. (To be paid.)

For reasons appearing to the board, It is advised that the fine of seven pounds ten shillings imposed by the Court of Hanover on Pitman Kidd for an Assault and Battery upon John Batkins, be remitted.

All which matters so advised, the Governor orders accordingly.

> James Wood
> James McClurg
> Robt. Goode
> Jno. H. Briggs
> J. Dawson
> Hardin Burnley

Wednesday April 6th 1791

Present

The Governor

Mr. Wood	Mr. Briggs
Mr. McClurg	Mr. Dawson
Mr. Goode	Mr. Burnley

---

112. "Issd. the 13 instant" is written in the margin beside this entry.

The Governor informed the board that one of the revisors of the Laws had applied to him to know whether the executive would undertake to allow them a Clerk if one should be found necessary. Whereupon it is advised that a Clerk be allowed the said Revisors, if there shall be a necessity for one: to be paid out of the Contingent fund.

It is advised that a Commission issue appointing William Bridger Collector of the taxes due from the County of Isle of Wight for the year 1790.

All which matters so advised, the Governor orders accordingly.

James Wood
James McClurg
Robt. Goode
Jno. H. Briggs
J. Dawson
Hardin Burnley

Thursday April 14th 1791

Present

The Governor

Mr. Wood   Mr. Briggs
Mr. McClurg   Mr. Dawson
Mr. Goode   Mr. Burnley

The Governor informed the board that, in the recess, he granted a pardon to Negro Bob, the property of Benjamin Hatcher, condemned to Death by the Court of Chesterfield for burglary and felony; he having been recommended as a proper object of mercy. Approved.

Upon application, It is advised that the Damages on the amount of a Judgment obtained against Benjamin Harrison, as Sheriff of Rockingham for the revenue of 1787, be remitted; he having produced a Statement of his Account with a receipt for the principal sum due on such judgment, together with the legal interest due thereon, and costs.

The President of the United States having drawn an Order on the Auditor of public Accounts, for forty thousand Dollars, to be applied towards erecting Public buildings at the permanent Seat of the Government of the United States on the bank of patowmack, It is advised that the Treasurer be directed to borrow from any funds, a sufficient sum of money to pay One thousand Dollars in part of the said order: taking care to replace the same as soon as possible.

The President of the United States having Authorized the Executive to direct such an extension of the arrangements taken by the general Government for defending the frontier, as will cover the counties of Russell and Wythe, and place them in equal security with the others, It is advised that Copies of the said arrangements be forwarded, by Express, with Instructions to the Lieutenants of Russell and Wythe to pursue the same for the defence of their Counties.

Mr. William Claiborne having produced some other proofs in support of his Claim against the public, The Board, on consideration thereof, are of Opinion that the said proofs are not so satisfactory as to Authorize the payment of his claim.

It is advised that Isabella Mercer, Mary Halbert, Larkin Chew, Charles Collins, and Ambrose Lewis be continued on the Pension List with their former allowances, from January 1790.

The Governor laid before the board an Information exhibited by Peter Saunders Lieutenant of Franklin County, against Colonel Thomas Arthurs of the Militia of the said County, arrested at the instance of the said County Lieutenant on the following charges to wit. "For forging the hand of John Gipson to a warrant to turn Conrad Harkrider out of possession in January 1788, Also for being concerned and assisting in forging an order from Sarah Graham to the Sheriff of Franklin County to pay the same to George Asberry, also for forging the hand of Thos. Prunty to certain receipt for the payment of a certain sum of money to the amount of £3.0.7½ dated the 20th January 1788, also for forging the hand of George Turnbull, esq.; also for supposed perjury in making oath before the Judges of the District Court at New London in April 1790 that Isaac Rentfro was not able to attend as a witness in his suit and Thomas Levsays, also for a charge alledged against him for bearing false witness in the suit [of] Mrs. Guthery against Hugh Innes, Also a charge of drawing a larger Sum of money out of the Treasury, when on the assembly, than he was entitled to; and for lying and not conducting himself as an officer of the Militia." On consideration whereof, It is advised, that a Court Martial be directed for the trial of the said Thomas Arthurs, to consist of the following officers, to wit: George Hairstone, Colonel of the Henry militia, as President, the Six Senior Captains, four senior Lieutenants, and two Senior Ensigns of the Franklin militia, provided they be not witnesses for or against the party accused, that a Copy of the Charges be forwarded to the president, who is to appoint the time and place of holding the said Court martial within the said County of Franklin, and that a copy of the sentence of the Court martial together with a special State of the Evidence and facts be transmitted to the Governor as soon as possible.

On consideration of a letter from Mr. Cuthbert Bullitt, of the 4th instant concerning the management of Bristoes Estate, etc., It is advised that a copy of the said letter be transmitted to Mr. Lee, and that, in the settlement with the representatives of Mr. Carr for the profits of the said Estate, he be directed to allow no more than five per Cent Commission.

All which matters so advised, the Governor orders accordingly.

> James Wood
> James McClurg
> Robt. Goode
> J. Dawson
> Hardin Burnley
> Jno. H. Briggs

Wednesday April 27th 1791

Present

The Governor

| Mr. Wood | Mr. Goode |
| Mr. McClurg | Mr. Dawson |

Mr. Burnley

The Governor informed the board that, in the recess, He directed to be paid out of the Contingent fund, Two hundred and eighty five pounds to Aug: Davis for printing the laws of the second session of Congress, One hundred and twelve pounds ten shillings to Col. William Davies for his last quarters salary, and five pounds to Joseph Clark upon Account, as an Express to the Counties of Russell and Wythe; that he remitted the damages on the following judgments, viz.

A judgment against John Mason, Sheriff of Sussex, for the revenue of 1788;

A Judgment against Thomas Barbour, Sheriff of Orange, for the revenue of 1788; and

A Judgment against Edward McGuire, Sheriff of Frederick, for the revenue of 1787, the said Sheriffs having produced statements of their Accounts with receipts for the principal sums due on such judgments, together with the legal interest due thereon, and costs: and that he gave instructions to Mr. Andrew Woodrow concerning the disposal of the public tobacco at Cressups warehouses (which instructions he read to the board the same being entered in the letter book.) Approved.

Mr. Wood informed the board, that during the indisposition of the Governor in the recess, he, as Lieutenant Governor, issued additional Commissions appointing Marquis Calames, John Grant, Charles Scott, Senior, Bartlett Collins, James M. Marshall, John Crittendon, William Henry and Robert Alexander gentlemen Justices of the peace for the County of Woodford; James Cunningham, John McCay, Robert Burnett, Henry Flesher, William Gragg, Junr., Jacob Conrod and Roger Dyer, gentlemen, Justices of the peace for the County of Pendleton; they having been recommended according to law, And that he directed the continuance of William McGuire on the pension list, pursuant to the act of the last assembly: Approved.

It is advised that a warrant issue on the Contingent Fund to the Representatives of John Conner deceased for nineteen shillings and ten pence the balance due for the rent of the Chancery office to the 21st of March last: Also a warrant on the same fund, to Edmund B. Lacy[113] for two pounds two shillings and six pence, his expences in going to Petersburg District with public Documents in evidence against certain Counterfeiters. (To be paid)

Silvester Ward's bond, with Cornelius Bogard and Jacob Westfall Securities, to indemnify the Commonwealth and the United States, against certain original Certificates of which he is to obtain Duplicates, agreeably to an act of the last Assembly, being laid before the board; the same is approved.

It being suggested that Archer and Rowlett inspectors at John Bollings warehouse are in arrears to the Commonwealth It is advised that the Solicitor be called on to inform the board why the said Inspectors were not included in the List of Delinquents reported to the Executive, and what steps, if any, have been taken to recover the said arrearages.

On application, It is advised that the Damages on the amount of a Judgment obtained against Joseph Holmes, Sheriff of Frederick, for the Certificate tax of 1786, Also the Damages on the amount of a judgment obtained against Jas. Meriwether, Sheriff of Louisa, for the Revenue of 1788, be remitted; the said Sheriffs having produced statements of their Accounts with receipts for the principal Sums due on such judgments, together with the legal Interest and costs.

Mr. Wood, Mr. Goode and Mr. Dawson are appointed a Committee to visit and examine the Offices of the Treasurer, Auditor and Solicitor, and Mr. Dawson is appointed in the room of Mr. Braxton to examine the state of the Sinking fund.

All which matters so advised, the Governor orders accordingly.

James Wood
James McClurg
Robt. Goode
J. Dawson
Hardin Burnley

Tuesday May 3d 1791

Present

The Governor

Mr. Wood   Mr. Goode
Mr. McClurg   Mr. Briggs
          Mr. Burnley

113. "Edwd. Lacy" in the clerk's index.

The Governor informed the board, that in the recess, he issued a Commission appointing James Harcum additional inspector at South Wicomico warehouse vice William Barrett deceased, that he directed the Auditor to issue a Warrant on the Contingent Fund to Archd. Blair for twenty five pounds for four months Salary as Keeper of the public Seal, and to make the usual allowance to Charles Corling, for riding Express to Petersburg, at the Instance of the attorney general; And that he directed the remission of the Damages on judgments against the following persons, viz: Lawrence Smith, Sheriff of York, for the revenue of 1784: George Gilpin, Sheriff of Fairfax, for the revenue of 1788: William Horsley, Sheriff of Amherst, for the revenue of 1787: William Royster, Sheriff of Goochland, for the revenue of 1787 and 1788: Stephen Sampson, Sheriff of Goochland, for the revenue of 1784: James Taylor, Sheriff of Caroline, for the revenue of 1788:Turner Richardson, Sheriff of Fluvanna, for the Revenue of 1786: Thomas Flournoy, Sheriff of Prince Edward, for the Revenue of 1787: and Simon Triplett, Sheriff of Loudoun, for the Certificate taxes of 1785 and 1786; and Revenue of 1786 and 1787; the said Sheriffs having produced Statements of their accounts, with receipts for the payment of the balances due thereon, together with interest and costs, prior to the first instant. Approved.

The Governor laid before the board a letter from the Governor of the State of Pennsylvania inclosing the Depositions of William Wilso and John Hillman, by which it appears, that on the 9th March last, Samuel Brady and Francis McGuire, with a body of armed men, made an attack on a party of Delaware Indians in friendship and amity with the United States of America, and murdered four of them on beaver Creek in the said State of Pennsylvania; and representing that the said Samuel Brady and Francis McGuire, the only Offenders whose names have yet been discovered, had fled from Justice into the State of Virginia, which made it necessary for him to demand the delivery of the said two above named persons, to be removed to the State of Pennsylvania as having jurisdiction of their crime, pursuant to the 2d section of the 4th article of the Constitution of the United States. Whereupon, it is advised, that a proclamation issue offering a reward of six hundred Dollars to any person or persons who shall deliver up the said Samuel Brady and Francis McGuire or three hundred Dollars for either of them, to the Executive Authority of Pennsylvania in the City of Philadelphia; and requiring all Justices of the peace, Sheriffs and Constables, and exhorting all the good people of this Commonwealth to use their best endeavors to apprehend and bring to Justice the said offenders.

It is advised that the *bonds* which may be taken for the sale of Joseph Strothers property under an act of the General Assembly "for the better securing certain Debts within mentioned, due and owing to the Commonwealth" *may* be discharged in the like securities, and at the same rates as have been, or shall be established by the executive for the discharge of the bonds taken for the Gloster sales.

All which matters so advised, the Governor orders accordingly.

The Governor notified to the board his intention to be absent, on a visit to the Point of Fork, which is ordered to be entered on the journal.

> James Wood
> James McClurg
> Robt. Goode
> Jno. H. Briggs
> Hardin Burnley

Thursday May 5th 1791

Present

Mr. Wood, who presides as Lieutenant Governor, the Governor being absent.

Mr. McClurg	Mr. Dawson
Mr. Briggs	Mr. Burnley

The Lieutenant Governor informed the board that, in the recess, he directed a remission of the Damages on the Judgments obtained against James McAllister, Sheriff of Berkeley, for the Revenue of 1787 and 1788, he having produced a statement of his accounts with receipts for the balance due on such judgments together with interest and costs, the money having been lodged prior to the first instant. Approved.

It is advised that the proclamation for apprehending Samuel Brady and Francis McGuire, be forwarded by express to the Ohio Counties.

It is advised that a warrant issue on the Contingent fund to Alexander Larry for ten pounds, upon account, as an Express to the Ohio. (To be paid)

On recommendations, It is advised that an additional Commission issue appointing James Craig gentleman a Justice of the peace for the Couty of Montgomery; Also a Commission appointing Henry Patton Sheriff of the said County.

William Preston, being commissioned Surveyor of Montgomery County; It is advised that he be required to give bond in the penalty of two thousand pounds for the faithful discharge of the duties of his office.

All which matters so advised, the Lieutenant Governor orders accordingly.

> James McClurg
> Jno. H. Briggs
> J. Dawson
> Hardin Burnley

Tuesday May 10th 1791

Present

The Governor

Mr. Wood	Mr. Briggs
Mr. McClurg	Mr. Dawson
Mr. Goode	Mr. Burnley

The Governor informed the board, that he yesterday directed a remission of the Damages on the judgments obtained against Stephen Sampson, Sheriff of Goochland, for the revenue and certificate taxes of 1785, the said Sheriff having produced Statements of his accounts with receipts for the balance due on such judgments together with interest and costs; the money having been lodged prior to the first instant. Approved.

The Governor laid before the board his report of the present state of the magazine, arsenal etc. at the Post of the Point of Fork which being read, It is advised that the consideration thereof be adjourned to Thursday next.

It is advised that a pardon issue to Caleb Hill, who was sentenced to death by the last District Court held in the City of Richmond for horsestealing; he appearing to be a proper object of mercy.

On consideration of a letter from the treasurer requesting Directions concerning the sale of the public tobacco on hand, It is advised that the crop tobacco, together with such transfer as hath not been disposed of by the Inspectors, be sold at public Sale on thursday the 9th of June next, on three months credit, the purchasers making sufficient deposits with the treasurer to ensure the punctual payment of the money at the time it shall become due; And that the Inspectors be called upon for the money in their hands arising from the Sales of the transfer tobacco in September last. It is also advised that the Directors of the James river Company be allowed, agreeable to their request, a credit at the above Sale to the amount of the balance due them on the order of the Executive the 11th of March last.

All which matters so advised, the Governor orders accordingly.

James Wood
James McClurg
Robt. Goode
Jno. H. Briggs
J. Dawson
Hardin Burnley

Thursday May 12th 1791

Present

The Governor

Mr. Wood	Mr. Briggs
Mr. McClurg	Mr. Dawson
Mr. Goode	Mr. Burnley

The Governor informed the board that he yesterday directed a remission of the Damages on the Judgment obtained against Joseph Moore, Sheriff of Rockbridge, for the revenue of 1788, the said Sheriff having produced a statement of his account, with a receipt for the balance due on such judgment together with interest and costs, prior to the first instant; and that he put into the hands of Doctor Foushee, one of the Directors of the James river Company, who was about to set off upon the business of examining the falls and contracting for clearing them, the notes for the public tobacco at Crows warehouses, which were returned by Mr. Madison as not having it in his power to dispose of them, And took his receipt for the same; he having promised to use his endeavours to pass them off in payment of the Company's contracts, upon the best terms he can, and to allow the public credit therefor. Approved.

The board resumed the consideration of the Governors report relative to the post at the point of Fork, Whereupon, it is advised, that the Articles contained in the Inventory reported by the Superintendant, be sold for money, on six months credit for all sums above three pounds, the purchasers giving bonds with sufficient Sureties, payable to the Governor and his Successors in office; that all the Clothing (after retaining six regimental coats, six vests and twelve pair of overalls) together with the horsemens caps, pistol holsters, and such parts of broken gun locks and pieces of mounting as are useless to the public, be added to the Inventory of Articles for sale, that the Superintendant give sufficient notice of the time and place of Sale, and report to the executive an accurate account of Sales, stating particularly the price at which the different articles sold. It is also advised that a ration be allowed to the Wife of Michael Jorden, a faithful old Soldier at the post, And the board approve of the donation directed by the Governor to be made to the thirteen soldiers lately discharged.

In order to expedite the business of collecting from the Auditors office and the papers of William G. Mumford late Commissary, such Vouchers as may be necessary to support the Claims of this State against the United States, It is advised that Messrs. Denholm and Vereker, who are at present engaged in that business, be authorized to employ three assistants, who shall be allowed a reasonable compensation.

The Governor laid before the board a resolution of the general assembly of the 9th and 11th of December last, referring to the Executive for final settlement, the petition of Martin Baker, praying to receive from the public a compensation for the rent of a house, taken and occupied by the State Quartermaster from some time in the month of March 1781, to the 25th of December following. Whereupon it is advised that the Auditor be directed to settle the said Bakers Claim, allowing him for six months rent of the said house, at the rate of Six thousand five hundred weight of tobacco for nine months, and grant a Warrant on the Contingent fund for the Sum due, rating the tobacco at twenty shillings per hundred.

On consideration of a letter from John Brown, Clerk of the general court, relative to the allowance made him the 22d of October last for services rendered in pursuance of the District law, and the Act amending the said law, It is advised that a Warrant issue on the contingent fund, to Mr. Brown, for two hundred and fifty seven pounds twelve shillings and three pence, in addition to the allowance made him the 22d of October last, in full for his services in preparing the causes for the District Courts, in pursuance of the District law, and for those rendered by him in the execution of the act for amending the District law.

The Governor laid before the board a letter from Col. Davies, Commissioner for settling the Continental account, complaining of the reduction of his Salary, and inclosing an Act of the State of Pennsylvania, by which it appears the allowance to their Commissioner is at the rate of eight hundred pounds per annum, that currency. Whereupon it is advised that Col. Davies's Salary be augmented to five hundred pounds per annum, commencing the first of January last.

On consideration of [a] letter from the Treasurer informing "that Mr. Prosser is desirous of purchasing about 80 hogsheads of tobacco for the purpose of paying for a Delinquent Sheriff for whom he is surety" and Mr. Prosser being willing to allow at the rate of thirteen shillings per hundred, It is advised that the treasurer be directed to furnish Mr. Prosser with that quantity of upper Potowmack tobacco, on his paying for the same at the above rates.

The Governor informed the board that in consequence of the sentiments expressed by the members of the board the other day, he had prepared a circular letter to the Justices of all those Counties wherein are any of the public warehouses, recommending to them the requring of the different Inspectors new bonds every year, which letter, being read, is approved.

All which matters so advised, the Governor orders accordingly.

James Wood
James McClurg
Robt. Goode
Jno. H. Briggs
J. Dawson
Hardin Burnley

Saturday May 14th 1791

Present

The Governor

Mr. Wood   Mr. Briggs
Mr. McClurg   Mr. Dawson
Mr. Goode   Mr. Burnley

The Governor having required the opinion of the board whether it will be proper to proceed immediately to the appointment of a public Printer in the room of Mr. John Dixon deceased It is advised that in order [to] prevent delay in printing the Acts and Journals of the General Assembly and in performing the other Duties of that Office, it will be necessary to make the appointment immediately, and that Aug: Davis be appointed, he engaging to do all Things required of his Predecessor by the Act of the Executive of the 22d of March 1787.

It is advised that Commissions issue, to take effect from and after the first of June next, appointing Abraham Penn, James Lyon, Jonathan Hanby, Daniel Carlin, William Mitchell, Samuel Clark, William Carter, William Lyon, James Armstrong, Francis Turner, William Banks and Charles Foster, Gentlemen, (the first seven of whom to be of the Quorum) Justices of the peace for the County of Patrick; and William Mitchell gentleman Sheriff of the said County.

On consideration of a letter of the 15th ultimo from Mr. John S. Wells concerning the Sherifalty of the County of Isle of Wight, It is advised that the Governor write to Mr. Wills stating the situation of that county in regard to the Sheriffs office as it appears on the Journals of the executive, and requesting him to use his endeavors to have the matter set right by the Court, and to procure a recommendation of some proper person to collect the arrearages due from the said County, Who shall have 'til the June Court 1792 to make the Collection.

All which matters so advised, the Governor orders accordingly.

James Wood
James McClurg
Robt. Goode
Jno. H. Briggs
J. Dawson
Hardin Burnley

Tuesday May 17th 1791

Present

The Governor

Mr. Wood	Mr. Briggs
Mr. McClurg	Mr. Dawson
Mr. Goode	Mr. Burnley

On consideration of the memorial of Henry Banks, praying for the settlement of a Claim of Hunter Banks and Company for sundry merchandize sold in march 1781, to David Ross the then Commercial agent, making a balance in favour of the company of seventeen hundred twenty six pounds Seven shillings specie, It is advised that the same be rejected; it appearing to the satisfaction of the board that the said Claim hath been fully paid.

The Governor laid before the board a letter from Henry Anderson informing that sundry Slaves of his, which are under mortgage to the public, to secure a debt due from him as Security for one of the Deputies of Christopher Hudson, late Sheriff of Amelia, have been seized by the present Sheriff, and advertized for Sale on the 25th. instant to satisfy sundry executions of individuals. Whereupon it is advised that Col. Everard Mead and Major Joseph Eggleston, or either of them, be requested to examine whether the Slaves thus advertized are the same mentioned in the mortgage to the public, and if they be, to forbid the sale. It is also advised that the Solicitor be directed to take the proper measures for disposing of the property mortgaged for securing the aforesaid Debt.

All which matters so advised, the Governor orders accordingly.

James Wood
James McClurg
Robt. Goode
Jno. H. Briggs
J. Dawson
Hardin Burnley

Thursday May 19th 1791

Present

The Governor

Mr. Wood	Mr. Briggs
Mr. McClurg	Mr. Dawson
Mr. Goode	Mr. Burnley

On consideration of a letter from Col. David Shepherd, of Ohio County, on the subject of the attack lately made upon a party of

Delaware Indians near the mouth of big beaver Creek, It is advised that so much of the said letter as relates to the above subject be transmitted to Governor Mifflin; and that copies of Governor Mifflins letter demanding Brady and McGuire, and of the Depositions of Willson and Hillman, on which the said demand was made, be transmitted to Col. Shepherd.

On recommendations, It is advised that additional Commissions issue appointing John Tayloe Corbin and Philip Pendelton, gentlemen, Justices of the peace for the County of King and Queen, And David Bruce, William McKinley, Robert McClure, and James Blackmore, gentlemen, Justices of the peace for the County of Ohio.

It is advised that a Warrant issue to the Directors of the James river Company for forty pounds six shillings and ten pence, to be charged to them on account of the Delinquent Shares in the said Company lately purchased on public account. (To be paid)

All which matters so advised, the Governor orders accordingly.

> James Wood
> James McClurg
> Robt. Goode
> Jno. H. Briggs
> J. Dawson
> Hardin Burnley

Tuesday May 24th 1791

Present

The Governor

Mr. Wood	Mr. Briggs
Mr. McClurg	Mr. Dawson
Mr. Goode	Mr. Burnley

The Governor laid before the board the Account of Joseph Leiplong for express hire in carrying out writs for the election of a representative to Congress in the room of Mr. Bland deceased in June 1790, and Dispatches to Kentucky in March last. Whereupon it is advised that the said Account be refered to the Auditor for settlement in the usual way, deducting the thirty pounds advanced to Mr. Leiplong upon account.

On the report of Captain Coleman, It is advised that the Claims of Edward Gullion and John McDonald for services as rangers in Jefferson from the 8th of November to the 14th December 1788, Also the claim of Ballard Smith for rations furnished the rangers of the said County for the year 1789, and the Claim of William Castor for services as a Scout in Nelson County from the 3d of April to the 2d July 1788, be referred to the Auditor for settlement in the usual way, That the Claim of William Prentis, for services in Jefferson County, be rejected, the Dates of his certificate being unintelligible; That the Claims of Ballard Smith for pay as a Captain in service in Jefferson County from the 8th of November to the 14th of December 1788, and for subsistence money, be rejected, the men in service being too few to require an officer of that rank to command them, and subsistence money not having been allowed upon any similar occasion.

All which matters so advised, the Governor orders accordingly.

> James Wood
> James McClurg
> Robt. Goode
> Jno. H. Briggs
> J. Dawson
> Hardin Burnley

Tuesday May 31st 1791

Present

The Governor

Mr. Wood	Mr. Briggs
Mr. McClurg	Mr. Dawson
Mr. Goode	Mr. Burnley

The Governor informed the board that in the recess he issued Commissions appointing Hezekiah Ellis an Inspector at Roystons warehouses, vice, John Wright deceased and Anthony Frazer additional inspector at said warehouse vice the said Ellis: approved.

Mr. Wood informed the board that, in the absence of the Governor, he referred to the Auditor for settlement in the usual way, the Account of Alexander Larry for riding express to the Ohio with public Dispatches. Approved.

Mr. John Steele and Mr. Miles Selden having been elected members of the privy Council or Council of State, They took their seats at the board, having qualified before John Pendleton and Danl. L. Hylton Justices of the peace for the County of Henrico.

On recommendations, It is advised that additional Commissions issue appointing Elias Langham and James Paine gentlemen Justices of the peace for the County of Fluvanna, James Murdaugh, Daniel Riddick, John Dorlon, John Godwin, Archibald Richardson, Willis Everitt, Henry Harrison, Joseph Holland junr., Lemuel Riddick, and James Coles gentlemen Justices of the peace for the County of Nansemond, Also a Commission appointing Rawleigh Carter Coroner for the County of Nottoway.

The Auditor being at a loss how to ascertain the distances which Mr. Leiplong lately rode express with public dispatches, The Board, in consideration of the risk and delays attending Mr. Leiplongs trip to

Kentucky, advise that he be allowed the full amount of his Account, being forty four pounds twelve shillings.

It is advised, that Captain William Barrett[114] be continued on the pension list from January 1790 with his former allowance, agreeably to an act of Assembly in his favour, that Betsey Rigg, an orphan of Benjamin Rigg late a Soldier in the Continental army, be continued with eight pounds per annum from January 1790, And that Mary Armstrong be continued with fifteen pounds per annum from the same period.

The Governor laid before the board a letter from Henry Banks inclosing a Decree of the Chancellor in favor of Hunter Banks and Company by which the Auditor is directed to grant them warrants to the amount of a thousand and sixty six pounds 13/4 with interest thereon from December 1780, and informing that he had agreed with the Attorney general that there should be reserved out of the said warrants a sufficiency to satisfy certain Debts due from him the said Banks to the commonwealth viz one hundred and seven pounds 10/6 with 5 per cent interest from the 12th of January 1785 and five pounds seventeen shillings and six pence due for duties and costs as per judgment and the further sum of two hundred and sixty pounds with interest from the first of September 1785 due for a Lot of ground purchased of the Commissioners for selling public property in Richmond, which reservation had been accordingly ordered by the Attorney as appears by his certificate on the back of the said decree; But that the Auditor insisted upon retaining out of the said Warrants a sufficient sum to produce three hundred and thirty three pounds seventeen shillings *specie* the amount of the Debt due for the Lot and one hundred and forty one pounds eight shillings and six pence of such warrants as will discharge the duties and five pounds 17/6 specie for costs, which he conceives to be unjust and therefore submits the matter to the Executive. Whereupon it is advised that the auditor be instructed to retain out of the Warrants decreed to Hunter Banks and Company only the nominal amount of the sums directed to be reserved by the Attorney General, and the further sum of two hundred pounds to secure the payment of a Debt due from the said Hunter, Banks and company, for certain Cannon received from the public during the War when their value shall be ascertained.

All which matters so advised, the Governor orders accordingly.

> James Wood
> James McClurg
> Robt. Goode
> Jno. H. Briggs
> J. Dawson
> Hardin Burnley
> Miles Selden

114. "Barret" in the clerk's index.

Saturday June 4th 1791

Present

The Governor

Mr. Wood	Mr. Dawson
Mr. McClurg	Mr. Burnley
Mr. Goode	Mr. Steele
Mr. Briggs	Mr. Selden

The Governor informed the board that in the recess he directed the remission of the Damages on the Judgment obtained against James Meriwether as Sheriff of Louisa for the revenue of 1788, the said Sheriff having produced a Statement of his account with a receipt for the payment of the balance due on such Judgment together with interest and Costs, prior to the first of May last. Approved.

The Governor laid before the board a copy of a Judgment of the General Court in November 1790, which had been put into his hands for the purpose of obtaining a remission of a Fine of five hundred pounds imposed thereby on John Standley and William Richardson, inspectors at Meriwethers Warehouses, for neglecting to account for and pay according to law the duties arising on Tobacco exported from the said Warehouses from October 1788 to October 1789, etc. Whereupon it is advised that the application for the said remission be rejected.

On consideration of the petition of Thomas Roane praying for the remission of a Fine of fifty pounds imposed on him by the District Court of King and Queen for an Assault on Robert Beverley and of the proofs now produced in support of the allegations set forth therein, It is advised that the said Fine be remitted.

On recommendation It is advised that an additional Commission issue appointing Isaac Zane, Robert S. Russell, Henry Keller, John Jorden, John Goare, John Hoop, Ebenezer Leith, Adam Shearman, Junior, Elijah Odell, John Humbough, John Burner, Alexander Hay, and Derrick Pennybacker gentlemen Justices of the peace for the County of Shenandoah.

All which matters so advised, the Governor orders accordingly.

James Wood
James McClurg
Robt. Goode
Jno. H. Briggs
J. Dawson
Hardin Burnley
John Steele
Miles Selden

Tuesday June 7th 1791

Present

The Governor

Mr. Wood   Mr. Dawson
Mr. McClurg   Mr. Burnley
Mr. Goode   Mr. Steele
Mr. Briggs   Mr. Selden

It is advised that Patty Rose be continued on the Pension List with her former allowance from January 1790.

The Governor laid before the board a letter from David Clark Collector of the taxes due for 1787 in Pittsylvania, requesting to be informed whether he is not entitled to commissions in cases of Distress, and his expences in advertizing lands for sale, etc. Whereupon it is advised that the said Letter be referred to the Attorney General for his Opinion on the several queries stated therein; And that the Attorney be requested also to inform the board whether, in his opinion, the County Courts have authority by law to make new elections of the Commissioners of the taxes at any stated periods, or at their discretion without a vacancy by resignation or otherwise.

The Governor laid before the board a letter from the Secretary at War informing that he had ordered arms and ammunition to be furnished from the magazine at Fort Pitt to Col. David Shepherd, Lieutenant of Ohio County who should account to the Executive of this State for the Disposition of the said arms and ammunition, and that the same should be charged to the State of Virginia. Whereupon it is advised that the Governor write to the Secretary at War to be informed why this state should be charged with the said arms and ammunition, when, by the Constitution of the United States, Congress are *to provide for arming the militia.*

All which matters so advised, the Governor orders accordingly.

James Wood
James McClurg
Robt. Goode
Jno. H. Briggs
J. Dawson
Hardin Burnley
John Steele
Miles Selden

Thursday June 9th 1791

Present

The Governor

Mr. Wood	Mr. Dawson
Mr. McClurg	Mr. Burnley
Mr. Goode	Mr. Steele
Mr. Briggs	Mr. Selden

It is advised that the account of Tunstal Quarles for provisions furnished the post at the point of Fork up to the 1st of May, amounting to seventy eight pounds sixteen shillings 4½ as certified by Captain Coleman, be referred to the Auditor for settlement in the usual way.

The Governor laid before the board the opinion of the Attorney general in the following words viz, "I have no doubt but that the Interest accruing on the public Debt to Hunter Banks and Company as established by the Decree of the High Court of Chancery is chargable upon the aggregate fund", Whereupon it is advised that the same be referred to the Auditor of public accounts.

It is advised that Captain Thomas Finn be continued on the pension List with his former allowance, agreeably to an Act of the last assembly in his favour.

The Governor laid before the board the account of the Solicitor for expences in forwarding Notices, Executions, etc. Whereupon it is advised that the same be referred to the auditor for examination and settlement, and a warrant on the contingent Fund for the sum due. To be paid.

The Governor laid before the board a resolution of the General Assembly referring the claim of Henry Stratton to the executive for settlement. Whereupon it is advised that the said Claim be not considered, as the resolution referring the same cannot be complied with.

For reasons appearing to the board, It is advised that the fine of Five hundred pounds imposed by the General Court on Standley and Richardson, inspectors at Meriwethers warehouse, for neglecting to account for and pay according to law the duties arising on tobacco exported from the said warehouse from October 1788 to October 1789 etc. be remitted.

All which matters so advised, the Governor orders accordingly.

James Wood
James McClurg
Robt. Goode
Jno. H. Briggs
J. Dawson
Hardin Burnley
John Steele

Saturday June 11th 1791

Present

The Governor

Mr. Wood   Mr. Dawson
Mr. McClurg   Mr. Burnley
Mr. Goode   Mr. Steele
Mr. Briggs   Mr. Selden

On consideration of a letter from Landon Carter esqr., It is advised that Branham, a negro man Slave belonging to the said Carter, under sentence of Death by the Judgment of a Court of Oyer of King George for feloniously setting fire to his Masters meathouse, be reprieved until the last Friday in July next.

It is advised that a Warrant issue on the Contingent fund, to Augustine Davis, for two hundred and sixty two pounds for printing two hundred copies of the Journal of the second session of the house of representatives and two hundred copies of the journal of the Senate of the United States, agreeably to contract. To be paid.

For reasons appearing to the board, It is advised, that the Fines imposed by the District Court, held at Suffolk in May 1790, on Anthony Murphey, Smith Shepherd, jr., William Shepherd, jun., Paul Keeling, Matthew Pallot, John Pallot, William Pallot, Thomas Thompson, William Notingham, William Deel Woodhouse and William Bishop, upon an Indictment for an assault and false imprisonment, be respectively remitted.

All which matters so advised, the Governor orders accordingly.

James Wood
James McClurg
Robt. Goode
Jno. H. Briggs
J. Dawson
Hardin Burnley
John Steele
Miles Selden

Tuesday June 14th 1791

Present

The Governor

Mr. Wood   Mr. Dawson
Mr. McClurg   Mr. Burnley
Mr. Goode   Mr. Steele
Mr. Briggs   Mr. Selden

On recommendations It is advised that an additional Commission issue appointing Francis Fitzgerald, William Irby, Robert Fitzgerald, Richard Dennis, Senr., Warning Peter Robertson, James Dupey Junr., and Hamlin Harris gentelemen Justices of the peace for the county of Nottoway, Also that a commission issue appointing James Ramsay gentn. an alderman for the Borough of Norfolk vice George Kelly, who hath resigned.

It is advised that a Commission issue appointing Wm. Hoffler, Collector of the taxes due in Norfolk County for the years 1789 and 1790.

It is advised that a Warrant issue on the Contingent Fund for fifteen pounds, to William Claiborne junr. for the expences of conveying to Col. Davies in Philadelphia, a trunk containing Vouchers in support of the Claims of this State against the United States.

The Governor laid before the board a petition of sundry inhabitants of the Counties of Chesterfield and Henrico representing that they had been deprived of the right of fishing in the falls of James river by a few individuals who have monopolized the respective fishing places; and praying that the Attorney General may be instructed to institute, on their behalf, a suit in Chancery against the Claimants of the Falls. Whereupon it is advised that the said petition be referred to the Attorney General and that he be desired to institute the proper suit or suits touching the complaint of the petitioners if, in his opinion, there be good grounds for so doing.

Edmund Pendleton, esquire, having declined accepting the office to which he was appointed by an act of the general assembly intituled "An Act to amend an Act intituled An Act concerning a new Edition of the Laws of this commonwealth, reforming certain rules of legal construction, and providing for the due publication of the laws and resolutions of each session," It is advised that James Monroe esquire be appointed to supply the vacancy occasioned by such non-acceptance.

The Governor submitted to the consideration of the board what allowance ought to be made Messrs. Denholm and Vereker[115] and their assistants in collecting and copying Vouchers in support of the Claims of this State against the United States. Whereupon it is advised that Messrs. Denholm and Vereker be allowed twelve shillings per day each, the former from the first and the latter the thirtieth of March last, Turner Richardson and Samuel Tinsley nine shillings per day each from the eleventh of May, and William Clarke nine shillings per Day from the twelfth of May, to the thirteenth of June, instant, inclusive; And that Warrants issue on the contingent fund to the aforesaid persons for the Sums due to them respectively, and for the sum of one pound eleven shillings and three pence for expences of stationary. To be paid.

The Governor laid before the board a letter from the Governor of the State of Pennsylvania demanding, in conformity to the 2d. section

115. "Veriker" in the clerk's index.

of the 4th. Article of the Constitution of the United States, the delivery of sundry persons charged with certain crimes in that State, who have fled from Justice. Whereupon it is advised that the opinion of the Attorney General be taken as to the mode proper to be pursued in the above case.

All which matters so advised, the Governor orders accordingly.

James Wood
James McClurg
Robt. Goode
Jno. H. Briggs
J. Dawson
Hardin Burnley
John Steele
Miles Selden

Friday June 17th 1791

Present

The Governor

Mr. Wood   Mr. Dawson
Mr. McClurg   Mr. Burnley
Mr. Goode   Mr. Steele
Mr. Briggs   Mr. Selden

The Governor informed the board that, in the recess, at the request of the Directors of the Marine hospital, he directed a Warrant to issue on behalf of James Herbert for one hundred and twelve pounds ten shillings due for a Lot of Land purchased for the use of the said hospital, and directed the money to be borrowed, the treasurer having certified that there was due to the Marine fund upwards of that amount, and that he issued a commission appointing Richard Noel Surveyor of Essex County and directed him to give bond in penalty of one thousand pounds for the due performance of his office. Approved.

Mr. Hornsby, treasurer of the Lunatic hospital, having applied for the balance of the late order of the Directors of the said hospital; being two hundred pounds, It is advised that he be informed that the money shall be paid so soon as the State of the Treasury will admit.

On report of Captain Coleman, It is advised, that the Claim of Alexander Ritchie jr. for his service as a Scout in Russel County from the 13th of June until the 15th of August 1789, be referred to the Auditor for settlement in the usual way.

The Governor laid before the board, information on oath that a certain James Richards and Ralph Lingo were lately hanged on a tree near the sea shore in the county of Accomack, and that there is the strongest reason to believe that the murder of the said Richards and

Lingo was committed by some persons, inhabitants of the said County, whose names are unknown. Whereupon it is advised that a proclamation issue offering a reward of three hundred Dollars for apprehending and prosecuting to conviction each, or either of the persons concerned in the murder aforesaid.

All which matters so advised, the Governor orders accordingly.

> James Wood
> James McClurg
> Robt. Goode
> Jno. H. Briggs
> J. Dawson
> Hardin Burnley
> John Steele
> Miles Selden

Monday June 20th 1791

Present

The Governor

Mr. Wood	Mr. Dawson
Mr. McClurg	Mr. Burnley
Mr. Goode	Mr. Steele
Mr. Briggs	Mr. Selden

The Governor informed the board that in the recess, he directed a warrant in favor of Col. Davies for thirty two pounds ten shillings, twelve pounds ten of which being due him for the last quarter in consequence of the augmentation of his salary, and the remaining twenty pounds, to be charged to him upon account for the contingent expences of his office; And that he issued a commission appointing William Perkins Sheriff of Buckingham he having been recommended according to law. Approved.

It appearing that there is a balance due on the foundery books, to William Ralston,[116] of one hundred and two pounds fourteen shillings and seven pence which cannot be paid from the Debts due to the said Foundery, It is advised that the Auditor be directed, on being satisfied as to the identity of the person, to grant him a Warrant for the said balance carrying an interest of five per cent: agreeably to the resolution of Assembly of the 14 and 17th of January 1786. It is also advised that Capt. Coleman be directed to receive the foundery books and papers and to write to the several persons from whom there are balances due to the said Foundery informing them that unless payment be made by the first of October next, their accounts will be transferred to the Solicitor with direction to move against them.

---

116. "Raulston" in the clerk's index.

Doubts having arisen as to the time the remission of Militia fines by an Act of the last Assembly, takes effect; It is the Opinion of the board that all Fines imposed since the adoption of the Constitution of the United States by this Commonwealth, are remitted by the said Act.

All which matters so advised the Governor orders accordingly.

The Governor notified to the board his intention to be absent which is ordered to be inserted on the journal.

> James Wood
> James McClurg
> Robt. Goode
> Jno. H. Briggs
> J. Dawson
> Hardin Burnley
> John Steele
> Miles Selden

Thursday June 30th 1791

Present

Mr. Wood who presides as Lieutenant
Governor in the absence of the Governor

Mr. McClurg	Mr. Dawson
Mr. Goode	Mr. Burnley
Mr. Briggs	Mr. Steele

Mr. Selden

The Lieutenant Governor informed the board that in the recess, on recommendations, he issued an additional commission appointing Russell Potter, Philip Pindell, John Collins and George Snider gentlemen Justices of the peace for the county of Monongalia, Also Commissions appointing Hugh McNeely Coroner and Samuel Hanway Escheater for the said County, John Gles Sheriff of Lunenburg and Jonathan Richeson Sheriff of Franklin, and that he granted a pardon to Andrew Beagle condemned to Death by the supreme Court of Kentucky District for felony, he having been recommended as a proper object of mercy. Approved.

The Lieutenant Governor laid before the board the report of a Committee appointed the 27th of April last to visit the offices of Treasurer, Auditor and Solicitor, which was read. Whereupon it is advised that the same be entered in the additional J[o]urnal, and the consideration thereof adjourned.[117]

An account of the Auditor for a Quarters salary due him this Day being examined, It is advised that the same be certified for payment. Mr. Briggs, Mr. Steele and Mr. Selden are appointed a Committee to

---

117. *See* page 352 for the additional journal entry dated 30 June 1791.

visit and examine the offices of Treasurer Auditor and Solicitor the ensuing Quarter, and Mr. McClurg, Mr. Goode and Mr. Burnley are a Committee appointed to examine the Treasurers books and accounts and certify the same according to law.

It is advised that the Treasurer be directed to borrow from any funds money sufficient to pay the present quarters salary due the officers of civil government taking care to replace the same as soon as possible.

All which matters so advised, the Lieutenant Governor orders accordingly.

> James McClurg
> Robt. Goode
> Jno. H. Briggs
> J. Dawson
> Hardin Burnley
> John Steele
> Miles Selden

Saturday July 2d 1791

Present

The Governor

Mr. Wood	Mr. Dawson
Mr. McClurg	Mr. Burnley
Mr. Goode	Mr. Steele
Mr. Briggs	Mr. Selden

On recommendation, It is advised that an additional Commission issue appointing William Davidson, William Nully, John Beal, Joseph Haynes, John Lewis, William Lewis, John Hawkins, John Smith, George Poage, Henry Walker, John Smyth (Johns Creek) and Elijah McClenechan gentlemen Justices of the peace for the County of Botetourt.

It is advised that the Solicitor General be required to attend at the Capitol on Wednesday next, when it is expected he will be prepared to deliver to the order of the executive the books and papers of his office.

All which matters so advised, the Governor orders accordingly.

> James Wood
> James McClurg
> Robt. Goode
> Jno. H. Briggs
> J. Dawson
> Hardin Burnley
> John Steele
> Miles Selden

Wednesday July 6th 1791

Present

The Governor

Mr. Wood   Mr. Dawson
Mr. McClurg   Mr. Burnley
Mr. Goode   Mr. Steele
Mr. Briggs   Mr. Selden

The Governor informed the board that in the recess, he directed the usual warrants to issue to Captain Langham for eighty eight pounds eighteen shillings and two pence for the last quarters pay due the Superintendant, the Artificers and guard at the Point of Fork, also for twenty seven pounds ten shillings due to those Artificers and guards who were discharged the 1st of May last, and two hundred and twelve pounds six shillings and eight pence for the expence of stocking 637 Muskets, as Certified by Capt. Coleman, And that, on recommendations, he issued Commissions appointing William Smith and Christopher Tompkins Coroners of King William County. Approved.

The Governor laid before the board a letter from the Sollicitor general resigning his office, Whereupon it is advised that in virtue of the powers vested in the Executive by the 5th Section of the Act for the reform of certain public boards, the said office of Solicitor be discontinued, And that the Duties thereof be for the present transfered to the auditor of public accounts who will receive from the late Solicitor all public books and papers in his possession. It is further advised that it be an instruction to the Committee appointed for the inspection of the public offices for the present quarter to prepare and report as soon as may be such arrangements as shall appear to them to be proper for conducting the business formerly assigned to the Solicitor.

The Governor laid before the board an account of Messrs. Savage and Westmore in consequence of a contract entered into with Mr. Duncan Rose late Agent for the State. Whereupon it is advised that the Auditor be directed to settle the said account allowing ten per cent on the quantity of tobacco delivered, in full for damaged tobacco, and for loss sustained by the demurrage of Vessels in consequence of the States failing to deliver the tobacco agreeable to contract, and to grant Warrants for the balance which shall appear to be due, rating the tobacco at sixteen shillings per hundred.

On consideration of a letter from the Superintendant at the Point of Fork, It is advised that he be authorized to purchase a Ton of Iron, suitable for bayonets, ramrods, etc. and that he be at liberty to comply with the presidents request to him to have a brass howetzer removed from Halifax old Town to the Point of Fork.

All which matters so advised, the Governor orders accordingly.

James McClurg
Robt. Goode
Jno. H. Briggs
Hardin Burnley except as to
the Settlement of Savage and
Westmore's account
John Steele
Miles Selden

James Wood—I Dissent from the Advice of the Board respecting the Claim of Messrs. Savage and Westmore. Because I Consider the Executive Board as an improper Tribunal to Make Allowances for Damages, in breaches of Contract between Agents of the State and Individuals. I conceive Messrs. Savage and Westmore Ought to have had Recourse to a legal Adjudication, or an Application for Redress, to the General Assembly.

J. Dawson—Well knowing the falibility of my own Judgment, and the superiority of other Gentlemen's at the board; it is always with diffidence that I differ with them in opinion; and with reluctance that I take this mode of stating that difference; but, when advices are given, which I *cannot* think right, and from the adoption of which, I am persuaded, that palpable injustice is done, and great injury may arise to the state, I hold it to be my duty to make known my disapprobation, and this consideration shall ever supercede every other.

I think with the Gentleman, who preceeded me in his dissent, that the executive board is a very improper tribunal to make compensation for damages, in breaches of contract between agents of the state and individuals, but admitting, that they may with propriety exercise this power, under the revenue law of eighty seven, I shall ever investigate with a scrutinizing eye accounts which arose as early as the year 1778, and the adjustment of which has never been urged untill this day; and shall require the most unequivocal proofs to establish them.

The claim of Messrs. Savage and Westmore comes under the above description; some of the proofs brought forward woud be inadmissible in a court of Law (where damages ought to be assertaind). I am persuaded, the whole of them do not establish the occurrence to my satisfaction. And, viewing their claim on equitable principles surely nothing can be due to them, for the payment of eight hundred and ninety eight Hogsheads of tobacco, will, I presume already be thought ample compensation for goods to the amount of £22602.12.3 ½ furnished in the year 1778; when the scale of depreciation was at 5. for one.

The Solicitor's office was established by Act of assembly; in that Act, and in others which have pass[e]d since certain powers are granted to and certain duties required from *the Solicitor General,* among many others, the power of recovering money due from Sheriffs, etc. to the commonwealth, on ten day notice, seems solely to appertain to that officer; whether then the discontinuance of that officer, will not produce an abatement of the suits of the Commonwealth, and many other suits, is a question of some difficulty, and great magnitude. I am one who think it will; and doubt of my own opinion only from the respect, which I feel for other Gentlemen's. As then great injury may arise, and but little good can by discontinuing the officer at this time; I dissent from the opinion of the board advising that measure, and think it more wise to continue, at lest a nominal Solicitor untill the meeting of the assembly, by whom the office was established, and who can best Judge of the policy of keeping it up, or puting it down.

Thursday July 7th 1791

Present

The Governor

Mr. Wood	Mr. Dawson
Mr. McClurg	Mr. Burnley
Mr. Goode	Mr. Steele
Mr. Briggs	Mr. Selden

The Governor laid before the board a letter from the Auditor of public accounts inclosing a copy of a Decision of the General Court at their last term on the cases of certain State officers claiming half pay or commutation, referred to them by the District Court of Henrico, and praying the Direction of the Executive as to the propriety of appealing from such decision, Whereupon it is the Opinion of the board that as this Decision, should it take effect, may in its operation impose a heavy burthen upon the people of this commonwealth, it will be highly proper in order to remove every doubt on the subject to obtain the opinion of the supreme Court of judicature, it is therefore advised that the Attorney General be instructed to take the necessary Steps to appeal in behalf of the Commonwealth to the Court of appeals whenever the said Decision shall become the judgment of the District Court.

Doubts having been suggested whether the discontinuance of the Solicitors office will not have the tendency to prevent the recovery of Judgments and the issuing executions etc. in behalf of the commonwealth by the Auditor to whom it is intended to assign the Duties of that office, It is advised that the Attorney General be requested to favour the board with his Opinion on the Subject as soon as convenient.

Mr. Westmore having requested that the Warrants to be issued for the balance of his Claim against the public may be put on some fund, It is advised that the Auditor be directed to issue Warrants for the balance due on said claim, expressing therein that the same will be received in discharge of the arrearages of 1786 or of any former year, agreeably to the 12th Sect. of the revenue law passed in 1787.

It is advised that Warrants issue on the Contingent Fund for six pounds three shillings and six pence to Augustine Davis for postage of public letters from January last, as per account, And three pounds to Jane West in advance for maintaining Catherine Crulls child.(To be paid)

The Governor laid before the board an Account of John Dixon amounting to twenty eight pounds two shillings and six pence for performing the Duties of public printer from the death of his father until the appointment of Mr. Davis to that office. Whereupon it is advised that the same be referred to the Auditor for settlement and the usual warrant.

It is advised that a pardon be granted to negro Branham, the property of Landon Carter, condemned to death by a Court of Oyer held for the County of King George the 2d of June, for setting fire to the meat house of his Master, he having been recommended as a proper object of mercy.

On recommendations It is advised that an additional Commission issue appointing Josiah Parker, Emanuel Wills, William Mallory, James Young, John Easson, Thomas Pierce and George Purdie Junr. gentlemen Justices of the peace for the County of Isle of Wight, Also a Commission appointing William Bridger Sheriff of the said County.

The Governor laid before the board the Opinion of the Attorney General on Governor Mifflins letter of the 4th of June 1791, to him referred, demanding sundry persons to be delivered up in conformity to the 2d Sect. of the 4th Article of the Constitution of the United States, Whereupon it is advised that a Copy of the said Opinion be transmitted to Governor Mifflin as furnishing the reasons why his demand is not complied with.

The Governor, at the request of Mr. Wood, took the opinion of the board as to the propriety of revoking the proclamation of the 3d Day of May last for apprehending Samuel Brady and Francis McGuire. Whereupon the Board are of Opinion that there appears to be no good Cause for revoking the said proclamation.

All which matters so advised, the Governor orders accordingly.

> James Wood—except as to
> the Propriety of revoking the
> Proclamation.
> James McClurg
> Robt. Goode
> J. Dawson
> Hardin Burnley
> John Steele
> Miles Selden

Saturday July 9th 1791

Present

The Governor

Mr. Wood   Mr. Dawson
Mr. McClurg   Mr. Burnley
Mr. Goode   Mr. Steele
            Mr. Selden

The Attorney General having given an Opinion that the Duties of the Solicitor cannot legally be exercised by the present Auditor, if the Solicitors office be discontinued by the Executive, and the Duties thereof transferred to the Auditor according to the advice of the sixth instant, The board under the influence of this Opinion rescind the advice above mentioned, and advise that John Pendleton esquire, the present Auditor be appointed Solicitor General.

On recommendation, It is advised that a Commission issue appointing Henry Duke Coroner for the County of Charles City.

All which matters so advised, the Governor orders accordingly.

James Wood
James McClurg
Robt. Goode
J. Dawson
Hardin Burnley
John Steele
Miles Selden

Tuesday July 12th 1791

Present

The Governor

Mr. McClurg   Mr. Dawson
Mr. Goode   Mr. Steele

On the Order of the Directors of the Lunatic hospital, It is advised that a Warrant issue on the contingent fund for fifty pounds to Richard Cole as a full compensation to himself and Guard bringing Isaac Wiseman a Lunatic from the County of Woodford. (To be paid)

On consideration of the petition of Henry Anderson concerning his property which was mortgaged for securing a Debt due from him to the commonwealth as security for one of the Deputies of Christopher Hudson, late Sheriff of Amelia; It is advised that a copy of the order of the 17th of May together with all the papers relative to the said property be sent to the present Solicitor, who is required to take immediate Steps for disposing of the Mortgaged property according to the aforesaid order; And that Mr. Mead and Mr. Eggleston be again requested to forbid the intended sale of the said property for satisfying the other Creditors of Mr. Anderson.

All which matters so advised, the Governor orders accordingly.

> James McClurg
> Robt. Goode
> J. Dawson
> John Steele

Thursday July 14th 1791

Present

The Governor

Mr. Wood	Mr. Dawson
Mr. McClurg	Mr. Steele
Mr. Goode	Mr. Selden

The Governor informed the board that in the recess he directed a Warrant to issue on the Contingent Fund to the Treasurer for twenty seven pounds six and eight pence being for scales and weights and Stationary procured for the use of his office; that, on recommendation, he issued a Commission appointing Samuel White Sheriff of Charlotte; and that he required Benoni Overstreet to give bond as Surveyor of Cumberland in penalty of one thousand pounds for the faithful discharge of his office. Approved.

It is advised that a Commission issue appointing Thomas Barbee Receiver for the Kentucky District, vice, Thomas Marshall senr. who hath resigned.

It is advised that Francis Whiting and Samuel Selden be continued on the List of Pensioners with their former allowance agreeably to an Act of the last General Assembly.

The Governor laid before the board an Account of the late Solicitor for his commission of one per cent on the moneys collected from the purchasers of Gosport lands and public boats. Whereupon it is advised that the said Account be rejected, the law having made it the Duty of the Solicitor to collect the said money.

All which matters so advised, the Governor orders accordingly.

> James Wood
> James McClurg
> Robt. Goode
> John Steele
> Miles Selden
> J. Dawson

Thursday July 21st 1791

Present

The Governor

Mr. Wood   Mr. Goode
Mr. McClurg   Mr. Steele
                Mr. Selden

The Governor informed the board that in the recess, he issued a Commission appointing George Gurley Sheriff of Southampton County; and that he granted a Warrant in favor of Ebenezer McNain[118] for thirty pounds for a Ton of iron furnished the Superintendent at the point of Fork. Approved.

For reasons appearing to the board, It is advised that the Fine of Fifty pounds imposed by the Supreme Court for the District of Kentucky on John Rodgers,[119] one of the Commissioners of the tax for Mercer County, for not taking the taxable property of Willm. Taylor and others according to law, be remitted.

On report from the Solicitor It is advised that he be directed to take the usual Steps for the removal and sale of such of the following property as may be of a moveable nature viz.

Property taken to satisfy the judgment obtained vs Robert Adams as Sheriff of Campbell, for the 1 per cent tax of 1784, to be removed to Bedford Courthouse.

Property taken to satisfy the judgments obtained vs Robert Davis as Sheriff of Rockingham, for the revenue and certificate taxes of 1786, to be removed to Staunton in Augusta.

Property taken to satisfy the judgment obtained vs David Crawford as Sheriff of Amherst for the revenue tax of 1785, to be removed to Charlottesville in Albemarle.

Property taken to satisfy the judgment obtained vs William Callaway as Sheriff of Bedford, for the revenue tax of 1785, to be removed to Lynchburg.

Property taken to satisfy the judgments obtained vs Thomas Gaskins as Sheriff of Northumberland, for the revenue and certificate taxes of 1785 and 1786, to be removed to Richmond Courthouse.

Property taken to satisfy the Judgments obtained vs Thomas Towles as Sheriff of Spotsylvania for the revenue taxes of 1786 and 1788, to be removed to Caroline Courthouse.

Property taken to satisfy the judgments obtained vs. George Rives for the revenue and certificate taxes of 1786, to be removed to Petersburg.

Property taken to satisfy the judgments obtained vs Kinchen

118. "E. McNair" in the clerk's index.
119. "Rogers" in the clerk's index.

Godwin as Sheriff of Nansemond for the revenue taxes of 1786 and 1787, and certificate tax of 1786, to be removed to Portsmouth.

Property taken to satisfy the judgment obtained vs William Leftwich, as Sheriff of Bedford for the revenue tax of 1787, to be removed to Lynchburg.

Property taken to satisfy the judgments obtained vs. Micajah Holliman as Sheriff of Southampton for the revenue taxes of 1787 and 1788, to be removed to Greensville Courthouse.

Property taken to satisfy the judgment obtained vs Charles Gwatkin, as Sheriff of Bedford, for the revenue taxes of 1788, to be removed to Lynchburg.

Property taken to satisfy the Judgment obtained vs Thomas Claiborne as Sheriff of Brunswick for the revenue taxes of 1788, to be removed to Dinwiddie Courthouse.

Property taken to satisfy the judgment obtained vs John Bernard as Sheriff of Buckingham for the revenue tax of 1788 to be removed to Cumberland Courthouse.

Property taken to satisfy the judgment obtained vs Stith Hardyman as Sheriff of Charles City for the revenue taxes of 1788, to be removed to Henrico Courthouse.

Property taken to satisfy the judgment obtained against Henry Skipwith as Sheriff of Cumberland for the revenue tax of 1788, to be removed to Powhatan Courthouse.

Property taken to satisfy the judgment obtained against James Pendleton as Sheriff of Culpeper for the revenue tax of 1788, to be removed to Fredericksburg.

Property taken to satisfy the judgment against Hugh Innes as Sheriff of Franklin, for the revenue tax of 1788, to be removed to Henry Courthouse.

Property taken to satisfy the judgment obtained against George Summers as Sheriff of Loudoun for the revenue tax of 1788, to be removed to Alexandria.

Property taken to satisfy the judgment obtained against William Nutt as Sheriff of Northumberland, for the revenue tax of 1788, to be removed to Richmond Courthouse.

And Property taken to satisfy the judgment obtained against John McMillian as Sheriff of Prince William for the revenue tax of 1788, to be removed to Alexandria.

All which matters so advised, the Governor orders accordingly.

James Wood
James McClurg
Robt. Goode
John Steele
Miles Selden

Tuesday August 2d 1791

Present

The Governor

Mr. Wood　　　　　　　　Mr. Goode
Mr. McClurg　　　　　　　Mr. Steele
Mr. Selden

The Governor informed the board that in the recess he granted receipts for five Loan office Certificates Nos. 338, 339, 340, 341 and 342 for monies paid into the Treasury the 23d of May 1780, by Pleasants and Bates, and Thomas Bates Executor of Tarlton Fleming, on account of British Subjects, according to the Sequestration law: that with the concurrence of Mr. Wood Mr. Goode and Mr. Steele, he directed the usual warrants to issue on a Draft of Col. Davies for one hundred and fifty five pounds nine shillings being for the last quarters salary due himself, and for pay due his assistants L. Cauffman, J. Hall and C. Baldwin: also on his farther Drafts for twenty seven pounds one and eight pence Pennsylvania Currency, in favor of Alexr. Benstead, and forty four and two thirds Dollars in favor of L. Cauffman for services as Clerks to the Commissioner: that on recommendations he issued additional Commissions appointing John Clark, Sackville King, John Walthol, John Irvine, John Forbes, James Clark, David Talbot, Samuel Scott, Daniel Parrow, William Jordan, Thomas M. Clark and Thomas Humphries gentlemen Justices of the peace for the County of Campbell; Robert Innes, Peter Wiatt, John Hughes, William Booth, John Seawell Junr. and Morgan Tomkies gentlemen Justices of the peace for the County of Gloster; and that he issued a Commission appointing John Custis Sheriff of Accomack. Approved.

It is advised that a Warrant issue on the Contingent Fund for fifty pounds, to the Solicitor, upon account, to defray expences in sending out notices and executions against Delinquent public Debtors. to be paid. Also a warrant on the same fund for thirty pounds to James Rind, for services as Clerk to the Revisors: to be paid.

On recommendations, It is advised that Commissions issue appointing Andrew Cowan Sheriff of Russell, John Craig Sheriff of Woodford, William Moseley Sheriff of Powhatan, Philip Taliaferro Sheriff of King and Queen. Also an additional Commission appointing James Gibson, James Scott, Samuel Robinson and Joshua Ewing gentlemen Justices of the peace for the County of Russell.

On consideration of a Letter from the Auditor, It is advised that the Committee for visiting the public Offices be requested to inspect the books of the Auditors office prior to the 1st of March 1787, which were by law committed to the hands of the late Solicitor, and report the Situation thereof to this board.

Mr. Steele and Mr. Selden are appointed a Committee pursuant to the 9th Section of the general regulations for the Government of the Offices of treasurer, auditor and Solicitor.

On consideration of a letter from the Secretary at War dated the 25th ult[im]o It is advised that Brigadier general Scott be instructed to use all necessary measures for adding efficacy to the Calls which may be made by the Commanding General of the troops of the United States for the aid of Kentucky militia.

All which matters so advised, the Governor orders accordingly.

James Wood
James McClurg
Robt. Goode
John Steele
Miles Selden

Wednesday August 3d 1791

Present

The Governor

Mr. Wood   Mr. Goode
Mr. McClurg   Mr. Steele
Mr. Selden

On recommendations, It is advised that Commissions issue appointing James Garland Sheriff of Albemarle, John Key Coroner of the said County, and Adam Clement Sheriff of Campbell.

On the application of the directors of the public buildings It is advised that the Auditor be directed to grant them the usual Warrant for one hundred and fifty pounds upon account.

It is advised that a warrant issue to Reubin Burnley for forty four and [a] half Dollars for his pay as Clerk to Col. Davies from the 20th May to 30th June last as per Draft, in his favor.

On report from Captain Coleman, It is advised, that the Abstracts of pay and rations of the Kentucky militia who were called into Service under the regulations of the 29th of December last be referred to the Auditor for settlement according to the said regulations;

that the auditor be directed to settle the account of James Wilkerson amounting to ten pounds fifteen shillings and six pence for the purchase of a boat to convey provisions to the different stations, and for tools for the use of the guards

that he settle the account of Saml. Clintin for sixty seven Days horse hire to the guards at Mouth of Kentucky, allowing at the rate of one shilling per Day;

that he settle the pay abstract of General Scott allowing him the pay of a Lt. Col. Commandant, with six rations per Day, at six pence per ration, and twelve Dollars, per month, for forage;

that he grant a warrant to John Fowler for One hundred and twenty Dollars as full compensation for pay as paymaster to the above mentioned troops, and expences in attending with their Claims for settlement, and

that he settle, in the usual way, the Claim of John Purn for services as a Scout, in Nelson County, from seventh July, to seventh of August 1788.

All which matters so advised, the Governor orders accordingly.

James Wood
James McClurg
Robt. Goode
John Steele
Miles Selden

Thursday August 4th 1791

Present

The Governor

Mr. Wood   Mr. Goode
Mr. McClurg   Mr. Steele
            Mr. Selden

It is advised that the Treasurer be directed to borrow from any funds having money, a sufficient sum to pay eighteen pounds to Mr. Fowler, in part of the allowance made him yesterday, to enable him to return to Kentucky.

The Governor laid before the board, a return of the unsold tobacco in the hands of the Agent. Whereupon, it is advised, that the Agent be directed to deliver the said tobacco to the Treasurer, whose receipt therefor shall entitle him to a credit, for the amount, on the settlement of his account with the Auditor.

All which matters so advised, the Governor orders accordingly.

James Wood
James McClurg
Robt. Goode
John Steele
Miles Selden

Friday August 5th 1791

Present

The Governor

Mr. Wood   Mr. Goode
Mr. McClurg   Mr. Steele
                Mr. Selden

On recommendations, It is advised that an additional Commission issue appointing Samuel Hancock, William Ewing, David Saunders and John Shrewsbury gentlemen Justices of the peace for the County of Bedford. Also Commissions appointing Jacob Woodson, Sheriff of Prince Edward, Isaac Hall, Sheriff of Prince George, and Anthony New, Sheriff of Caroline.

The Governor requested the opinion of the board whether it will conduce to the interest of the State to take measures for exchanging the military and other Certificates in the hands of the Agent of the Sinking Fund for continental Stock. Whereupon the board are of opinion that it does not appear to them that such evident advantage will result from such measures as to induce the adoption of them.

The Governor laid before the board the treasurers letter inclosing the Certificates of the Commissioners which have been two years returned to his office for lands purchased by them in behalf of the Commonwealth and which still remain unredeemed. Whereupon, the board taking into consideration the small amount of said Certificates, and the difficulty of procuring proper persons to sell the said Lands on commission, advise that a state thereof be laid before the general assembly.

The Governor laid before the board an account of Hunter Banks and Company with the Commonwealth. Whereupon it is advised that the auditor be directed to settle the said account charging them ninety pounds for certain Cannon and ball which they had from the foundery, and credit them with sixty three pounds ten shillings for sundries furnished the late Commercial Agent; and that after deducting the balance from the two hundred pounds ordered to be retained by the executive the 31st May last, he grant Warrants to Mr. Banks for the remainder of the said two hundred pounds.

All which matters so advised, the Governor orders accordingly.

The Governor notified to the board his intention to be absent which is ordered to be entered on the Journal.

James Wood
James McClurg
Robt. Goode
John Steele
Miles Selden

Saturday August 27th 1791

Present

The Governor

Mr. Wood   Mr. Goode
Mr. McClurg   Mr. Burnley
                    Mr. Selden

The Governor informed the Board that in the recess he directed the Auditor to settle in the usual way the account of John Adkins for going express to the Amelia Springs after Mr. Selden, as it was necessary to call a board for the appoint[ment] of a Judge in the room of Mr. Bullet deceased. Approved.

Mr. Wood informed the board that in the absence of the Governor, and with the concurrence of Mr. McClurg, Mr. Goode and Mr. Steele, he directed the continuance of Joseph and Clara Bowles, orphans of John Bowles, on the List of pensioners with their former allowance of six pounds, and increased the pension of William Musgrave,[120] orphan of James Musgrave, to ten pounds per annum from the first of January 1790; that on recommendations, he issued Commissions appointing John Boggs Sheriff of Ohio, Evan Jones Sheriff of Shenandoah, Samuel Richardson Sheriff of Fluvanna, and Samuel Love Sheriff of Loudoun. Approved.

It is advised that William Nelson jun. Esquire be appointed a Judge of the General Court, in the room of Cuthbert Bullet esqr. deceased subject to be approved or displaced by joint ballot of both houses of the general assembly, pursuant to the Constitution or Form of government.

On recommendation, It is advised that an additional Commission issue appointing James Stephenson, George Massenburg, John Brown, James Robinson, William Crawford and Robert Settelington gentlemen justices of the peace for the County of Bath.

On consideration of the report of the Committee appointed to examine the state of the auditors books prior to the first of March 1787, It is advised that the Auditor be desired to inform the board whether there be, in his office, sufficient documents to enable a statement to be made of all balances due the commonwealth on the Auditors books prior to the first of March 1787.

It is advised that the account of Joseph Clark for going express to Orange after Mr. Burnley, be referred to the Auditor for settlement in the usual way.

On recommendations, It is advised that a Commission issue appointing Benjamin Edmondson Sheriff of Charles City; Daniel Triplett Sheriff of Stafford.

The Governor laid before the board an account of Dabney Minor

120. "Wm. Musgrove" in the clerk's index.

amounting to thirty six pounds nineteen shillings and six pence for bookcases for the General Court and Chancery Court offices, and for other work done on public account. Whereupon it is advised that the auditor be decided to settle the said account and grant a warrant on the contingent fund for the sum due.

The Governor laid before the board a Draft of William Deakins jr. for three thousand Dollars being part of an order in his favour for six thousand of the forty thousand Dollars for which the President of the United States drew his Order on the Auditor of public Accounts, to be applied towards erecting the foederal buildings on the Patowmack. Whereupon it is advised that the Governor direct payment of the said three thousand Dollars in part or the whole as the state of the Treasury will admit from time to time.

All which matters so advised the Governor orders accordingly.

James Wood
James McClurg
Robt. Goode
Miles Selden

Thursday September 1st 1791

Present

The Governor

Mr. Wood   Mr. Goode
Mr. McClurg   Mr. Selden

It is advised that Elizabeth Lovell be continued on the List of pensioners with her former allowance from January 1790.

On recommendation, It is advised that a Commission issue appointing Dennis Dawley Sheriff of Princess Anne.

Daniel Hankins the present Sheriff of Pittsylvania having signified his consent to continue in office another Year; It is advised that he be continued in the said office for two years from the date of his first qualification.

For reasons appearing to the board It is advised that the Fine of ten pounds imposed on William Clark by the District Court of Washington, in October 1789, for retailing Liquors without License, be remitted.

It appearing that there is a balance on the foundery books of One pound nineteen shillings and eight pence ¾ due to Daniel L. Hylton, which cannot be paid from the Debts due to the said Foundery; It is advised that the Auditor be directed to grant him a Warrant for the sa[id] balance carrying interest agreeably to a resolution of the General Assembly of the 14th and 17th of January 1786.

Mr. Selden mentioned to the board that although the indisposition of his family occasioned his late absence from home, he did not wish the public should be at the expence of sending an express after him and therefore requested that the Auditor might be directed to give an order to the treasurer to receive from him the amount of the express hire. Whereupon it is advised that the Auditor be directed accordingly.

All which matters so advised the Governor orders accordingly.

James Wood
James McClurg
Robt. Goode
Miles Selden

Thursday September 8th 1791

Present

The Governor

Mr. Wood	Mr. Goode
Mr. McClurg	Mr. Selden

On application It is advised that the Damages on the amount of a judgment obtained against Robert Jones as Sheriff of Sussex for the revenue taxes of 1782, be remitted unto the said Sheriff; he having produced a statement of his account, with a receipt for the payment of the principal sum due on such judgment, together with interest and Costs, prior to the first of May last.

It is advised that Joseph Hodges be placed on the pension List, with twelve pounds per annum, agreeably to an Act of the last Assembly in his favour.

On recommendations It is advised that Commissions issue appointing Joseph Bell Sheriff of Augusta, John Coles Sheriff of Nansemond, and William Ward Sheriff of Pittsylvania.

On consideration of a letter from the treasurer, It is advised that he be instructed to sell the public tobacco in the treasury, on saturday the first of October next, at auction, for cash, allowing two months credit. And, to prevent confusion in the accounts, the Agent is directed, instead of returning the tobacco in his hands to the treasurer agreeably to former order, to sell the same, on the same day and on the same terms as above.

It appearing that one hundred sixty one hogsheads of tobacco, of the two hundred ordered to be sold to the Directors of the James river Company, have been rated at eleven hundred and seventy five pounds sixteen shillings and two pence ¾, It is advised as a voucher to the treasurer, that the auditor be directed to grant a Warrant for the said sum, charging the Directors therewith, on account of the delinquent shares purchased by the treasurer.

It is advised that the Auditor be directed to grant a warrant on the Contingent fund to the Administrator of William Pierce, deceased, for the balance due the said Pierce, as Keeper of the public buildings up to the time of his Death; Also a warrant on the same fund to Archd. Blair for twenty five pounds, for four months pay as Keeper of the public seal, ending the fourth instant (to be paid).

All which matters so advised, the Governor orders accordingly.

James Wood
James McClurg
Miles Selden

Thursday September 15th 1791

Present

The Governor

Mr. Wood   Mr. Burnley
Mr. McClurg   Mr. Selden

The Governor informed the board that in the recess, He, on recommendations issued Commissions appointing Isaac Hinkle Sheriff of Pendleton, George Cunningham Sheriff of Berkley, Thomas Smith junr. Coroner of Mathews, and an additional Commission appointing Jasper S. Clayton, William E. Wiatt and John Smith, gentlemen Justices of the peace for the said County of Mathews. Approved.

It is advised that a receipt be given for a Loan office Certificate (No. 349) for monies paid into the Treasury, the 23d Day of May 1780, by John Hickman, on account of Donald, Scott and Company British subjects, agreeably to the Sequestration law.

The Governor informed the board that two other Drafts of William Deakins jr., for a thousand Dollars each, had been presented for payment. Whereupon, It is advised that the whole of Mr. Deakins Drafts, to the amount of the order in his favor for six thousand Dollars, on account of the foederal buildings, be paid whenever presented.

On recommendations, It is advised that Commissions issue appointing William McConnell Sheriff of Fayette, and Samuel McAffee Sheriff of Mercer.

It is advised that a Commission issue appointing Thomas Jones jun. Notary Public of the District of Hampton, vice, Robert Brough resigned.

It is advised that a warrant issue on the Contingent fund to Joseph Leiplong for six Dollars in payment for three days detention in Kentucky for General Scotts dispatches. (To be paid)

On consideration of the petition of William Cabiness, It is advised that a Commission issue appointing him Captain of a Company of Nottoway Militia in the room of Nathan Fletcher deceased.

It is advised that a Warrant issue on the Contingent Fund, for One hundred and fifty pounds, being the balance of the Order of the Directors of the Lunatic hospital in favor of Joseph Hornsby, for the purposes of the said hospital. (To be paid)

It is advised that the Attorney General be consulted whether the Commonwealth can maintain an action on the bond given by John Ball according to the Act of May 1783 authorizing the Auditors to grant new Warrants and Certificates in certain Cases, the Original Certificate (of which the said Ball has obtained a duplicate) having been presented to the Auditor and retained by him as the law directs.

All which matters so advised, the Governor orders accordingly.

The Governor notified his intention to be absent, which is ordered to be entered on the journal.

James Wood
James McClurg
Hardin Burnley
Miles Selden

Wednesday October 5th 1791

Present

The Governor

Mr. McClurg	Mr. Burnley
Mr. Goode	Mr. Selden

The Governor informed the board that in the recess, on recommendations, he issued Commissions appointing William Wills, and Wood Tucker inspectors and Drury Dance additional Inspector at Westhill Warehouse, John Pegram and Joseph Whitehead inspectors and Daniel Pegram additional inspector at High Street Warehouse, in the Town of Petersburg; a certificate having been produced that the said Warehouses are finished and completed as the law directs; that on the report of Captain Coleman, he directed the usual Warrants to issue to Major Langham for eighty nine pounds one and eight pence for the last quarters pay due the Superintendant, Artificers and guards at the Point of Fork; and two hundred and nineteen pounds for stocking 657 Muskets: that he granted a Warrant on the Contingent Fund to the Solicitor for seventy pounds, upon Account, to defray expences in sending out notices: and that he issued a Commission appointing Edwd. Tatum Coroner of Patrick. Approved.

Mr. McClurg informed the board that in the recess, and while the Governor and President were absent, He, on recommendations, issued Commissions appointing James Rucker and Charles Johnson Inspectors and William Martin additional inspector at Lynches warehouse in Campbell, Francis Duval and John Jones inspectors and Thomas Jones additional inspector at Poropotank warehouse in Gloster County,

George Minor and Thomas Grafford jr. inspectors and Jacob Cox additional inspector at Alexandria Warehouse in Fairfax, and Christopher Haskins Sheriff for Brunswick County. Approved.

It is advised that the Treasurer be directed to pay the amount of the warrant issued to Dabney Minor the 27th of August last for thirty six pounds 19/6.

On consideration of the Cases of the following Criminals Elizabeth Hazel, condemned by the District Court held at Staunton, for murder, John Kemp, condemned by the District Court held in the City of Richmond, for forgery, and John Abbott condemned by the District Court held in Prince Edward, for horsestealing; It is advised that pardons be granted to the said Criminals; they appearing to be proper objects of mercy.

On recommendations, It is advised that Commissions issue appointing Worlick Westwood Sheriff of Elizabeth City and Rawleigh Carter Sheriff of Nottoway County.

Col. Davies having suggested that the Auditors Ledger would be of essential service in supporting the Claims of this state against the United States; It is advised that the Ledgers for paper money transactions after the year 1788 be forwarded to Col. Davies.

Mr. Burnley requested the board that the auditor might be directed to give an order to the treasurer to receive from him the amount paid to Joseph Clark for riding express to Orange requiring his attendance. Whereupon it is advised that the Auditor be directed accordingly.

All which matters so advised, the Governor orders accordingly.

James McClurg
Robt. Goode
Hardin Burnley
Miles Selden

Wednesday October 12th 1791

Present

The Governor

Mr. Wood　　　　　　Mr. Dawson
Mr. Briggs　　　　　　Mr. Burnley
Mr. Steele

The Governor informed the board that in the recess, and on recommendation, he issued a Commission appointing Frederick Jones, Sheriff of Dinwiddie County; that he granted a pardon to negro Humphry who was condemned to death by a Court of Oyer and Terminer held in the town of Fredericksburg the 10th of September for burglary; the said Humphry having been recommended by the

Court, as a proper object of mercy; and that he directed to be paid out of the contingent fund, three pounds, to Jane West, for pay due her up to the 7th instant for nursing Catherine Cruls child. Approved.

Mr. Wood informed the board that in the late recess and absence of the Governor, he, as Lieutenant Governor, issued Commissions appointing Joseph Blackwell (Son of Joseph) William Stuart, Robert Brown, Thomas Chilton, George Fitzhugh and Lawrence Ashton gentlemen Justices of the peace for the County of Fauquier, Thomas Keith Sheriff, and Joseph Blackwell (Son of Wm) Coroner, for the said County; James Buchanan, Sheriff of Rockbridge; Joseph Turner and Henry Spain inspectors and Dennis Still additional inspector of tobacco at Westbrook warehouse in Petersburg, the Court having certified that the said warehouses are built and finished according to law: and that he reprieved, John Abbott, condemned by Prince Edward District Court for horsestealing, until the last Friday in this month, to give time for transmitting a copy of the proceedings of the Court at his trial. Approved.

It is advised that a Warrant issue on the Contingent Fund to Archd. Blair, for fifteen pounds, upon account, to purchase blank books and stationary for the use of this Office. To be paid.

On application of the Directors of the public buildings It is advised that the Auditor be directed to grant them the usual warrant for twenty nine pounds, upon Account. (To be paid.)

It is advised that William Granger and Hugh Shavers, who stand condemned by the Richmond District Court to be executed on Friday next, be reprieved until Friday the 21st instant, they having requested a week longer.

It is advised that a Commission issue appointing William McGuire Notary Public for the District of Winchester.

On recommendation It is advised that an additional Commission issue appointing Littleberry Mason, Benjamin Wyche, Henry Harrison, Pleasant Hunnicutt, William Mason and Nathaniel Wyche gentlemen Justices of the peace for the County of Sussex.

It is advised that Eve Clark,[121] Sarah Stacy, Mary Rowland,[122] Susanna Rawlings Susanna Rowland and Sarah Wilkerson, be continued on the pension List with their former allowances.

The Governor laid before the board an account of the Solicitors expences in sending out notices, etc. Whereupon it is advised that the same be referred to the Auditor for settlement in the usual way.

Mr. McClurg, Mr. Goode and Mr. Briggs are appointed a Committee to examine and report a state of Mr. Heths agency in the sale of the public tobacco.

On consideration of a petition in behalf of a number of the

121. "Clarke" in the clerk's index.
122. "Mary Rowling" in the clerk's index.

religious society of people called Quakers. inhabitants of the County of Frederick, praying for the remission of Sundry fines imposed on them by the Courts martial of the said County held in 1782, 1783, and 1784, for nonattendance at General and private musters, It is advised that the fines imposed on the following persons, be remitted viz. Joseph Antrim, John Berry, Richard Barrett, Thomas Barrett, Abraham Smith, Lewis Walker, James Gawthrop, Isaac Brown, Jonathan Wright, Samuel Lupton, Isaac Lupton, David Lupton, Asa Lupton, Joseph Stur, Isaac Stur, John Parkins, Jacob Pickering, Jesse Lupton, Jacob Smith, Michael Shion, Daniel Ballinger, David Barrett, William Barrett, Amos Jollefee, Thomas Brown, Isaac Neville, John Trimble, David Ross, Abraham Branson, James Wright, Joseph Mooney, John Griffith, Nathan Wright, James Lidwell, James Purviance, Nathaniel White, John Cowgill, Joshua Cope, Lewis Neill, Messer Shepherd, James Stur, Richard Ridgway, Henry Williams, Josiah Jackson, Evan Rogers, John McCool, Jonathan Pickering, Josiah Rogers, David Berry, Jesse Hogue, and Samuel Littler, of the first battalion; John Fawcitt, Thomas Fawcitt, Jonathan Lupton, Nathan Pusey, Caleb Antrim, Richard Fawcitt, Ezekiel Cleaver, Richard Fawcitt, jun. Isaac Painter, John Smith, Robert Haines, Joshua Swain, Joseph Haines, Jesse Holloway, Anthy Moore, Robert Moore, Robert Ray, Robert Hanna, John Painter, Henry Cowgill, Samuel Berry, Joseph Warden, Isaac Parkins, Samuel Pickering, Jonathan Pickering, Joshua Lupton, Meshack Sexton, Goldsmith Chandlie, James Cowgill, Jacob McKay, David Painter, Moses McKay, Thomas Fanley, Thomas Smith, Isaac Woodrow, Jonathan Parkins, John Haines and John Lupton of the second battalion.

All which matters so advised, the Governor orders accordingly.

> James Wood
> Jno. H. Briggs
> J. Dawson
> Hardin Burnley
> John Steele

Thursday October 13th 1791

Present

The Governor

Mr. Wood	Mr. Dawson
Mr. Briggs	Mr. Burnley

Mr. Steele

The Governor informed the board that Benjamin Woodward, for whose apprehension a reward of four hundred Dollars has been offered by proclamation, was last evening brought to this City by Major

William Longstreet and Mr. Alexander McMillian, of Georgia, that Mr. Miles King of Hampton had recommended his being brought here instead of Petersburg where the proclamation required his delivery, and had furnished a boat with three Guards to assist in bringing him up, that, the Attorney General being out of town, he had consult[ed] with Mr. Marshall, and found that Woodward could not be legally committed to the Jail of this District, and in consequence thereof he wrote a letter to some of the Magistrates of the County of Dinwiddie, and Town of Petersburg, notifying them that Woodward would probably appear at Petersburg on the 14th instant for examination, and recommending to them to collect the proofs against so great an offender.

Whereupon it is advised, that the said letter be approved:

that seventy nine Dollars be allowed the apprehenders of Woodward for the expences of the Guards from Augusta to Charles Town, and the detention of them and their horses four Days at that place,

that the expences of conveying Woodward from hence to Petersburg and of two additional Guards going and returning be defrayed by the public; as also the expences of the boat and guard employed by Mr. King to bring him from Hampton, and

that the reward offered be paid upon producing to the Governor a Receipt, from the Jailor of Petersburg District, for the body of the said Woodward, or a Certificate from a Magistrate of the Corporation of Petersburg, or of the County of Dinwiddie that he was brought before him by Major Longstreet or Mr. McMillian.

On recommendation It is advised that Commissions issue appointing Dudley Street and William Spears jr. Inspectors, and William Bagby additional inspector, at Woodsons Warehouse, in Cumberland County.

On consideration of the case of Herod Voden who was condemned by the District Court of Petersburg on the 24th Ultimo, to three months imprisonment, and afterwards, until he paid and satisfied the amercement assessed upon him, It is advised that he be pardoned.

All which matters so advised, the Governor orders accordingly.

James Wood
Jno. H. Briggs
J. Dawson
Hardin Burnley
John Steele

Saturday October 15th 1791

Present

The Governor

Mr. Wood	Mr. Dawson
Mr. McClurg	Mr. Burnley
Mr. Goode	Mr. Steele
Mr. Briggs	Mr. Selden

The Governor informed the board that he yesterday directed the Auditor to make the usual allowance of Guards attending Criminals, to George Price, Samuel Bright and Thomas Kirby the Guards who brought Woodward from Hampton. to be paid out of the Contingent Fund. Approved.

It is advised that Judith Miller be continued on the Pension List with her usual allowance from January 1790.

On recommendation It is advised that a Commission issue appointing Robert Sharp jr. an additional Inspector of tobacco at Hendersons warehouse in Albemarle.

Application being made for placing on the Contingent Fund a warrant of eight pounds fourteen shillings and three pence issued by the Auditor the 19th of September last, to John Roper, for sinking a Well and building a house over it in the Richmond District Jail Yard, It is advised that the same be rejected.

It is advised that a pardon be granted to William Granger, who stands condemned to death for felony by the District Court of Richmond; he appearing to be a proper object of mercy.

On application from the Directors of the public building[s] It is advised that the Auditor be directed to grant them the usual warrant for one hundred and fifty pounds upon account. To be paid.

It is advised that Col. Davies's Draft of the 10th of August in favor of Charles Baldwin for thirty one Dollars, for services as a Clerk in his office, be paid.

It is advised that Richard Courtney and Larkin Phillips be paid twelve and six pence each for going to Petersburg as a Guard over Woodward, and thirteen shillings and nine pence for their expences in guarding him one night in Richmond.

Upon inquiry into the Situation of Luther Stoddard who is confined in the District Jail of Richmond at the suit of the Commonwealth; It is advised that he be set at liberty without the usual proceedings in Court, it appearing that his further confinement will be attended with no benefit to the public.

The Governor laid before the board a bill drawn by William Shannon, on the treasurer of Virginia, the 9th of August 1779, in favor of John Girault for three hundred and thirty one and a half Dollars which appears to be part of the paper money bills allowed in the settlement of Mr. Shannons Claim. Whereupon it is advised that the Auditor be directed to grant a Certificate for the said bill pursuant to the act of assembly "granting a sum of money to William Shannon and others" if one of the same tenor and date have not been already paid.

All which matters so advised, the Governor orders accordingly.

> James Wood
> James McClurg
> Robt. Goode
> Jno. H. Briggs
> J. Dawson
> Hardin Burnley
> John Steele

Monday October 17th 1791

Present

Beverley Randolph, Esq., Governor

Mr. Wood	Mr. Dawson
Mr. McClurg	Mr. Burnley
Mr. Goode	Mr. Steele
Mr. Briggs	Mr. Selden

The Governor laid before the board a Letter he had prepared to the General Assembly, which being read, is approved.

The Auditor and Solicitors accounts for the last quarters Salary being examined, It is advised, that the same be certified for payment.

On recommendations, It is advised that additional Commissions issue appointing James Morton, Peter Johnston, John Purnall, John Lamkin Creete, William Price jun., and Robert Kelso gentlemen, Justices of the peace for the County of Prince Edward, John Redd, William Skelton and Thomas Jameson, gentlemen, Justices of the peace for the County of Henry, Also commissions appointing, George Waller Sheriff of Henry, William Terry Sheriff of Halifax, and Woffendel Kendel Corner of King George.

It is advised that warrants issue on the Contingent Fund, to Messrs. Longstreet and McMillian, for four hundred Dollars, being the reward offered for apprehending Benjamin Woodward, also for seventy nine Dollars being for expences of the Guard from Augusta in Georgia to Charleston in South Carolina and for eight pounds thirteen shillings and five pence for boat hire and expences from Hampton to Richmond. To be paid.

All which matters so advised, the Governor orders accordingly.

James Wood
James McClurg
Robt. Goode
Jno. H. Briggs
J. Dawson
Hardin Burnley
John Steele
Miles Selden

Tuesday October 18th 1791

Present

The Governor

Mr. Wood	Mr. Dawson
Mr. McClurg	Mr. Burnley
Mr. Goode	Mr. Steele
Mr. Briggs	Mr. Selden

On recommendations, It is advised that an additional Commission issue appointing Thomas Jones, Horatio Hall, James Duncan, Julius Clarkson, Henry Coleman, Edmund Lyne, William Suddeth, Thomas McClennahan, David Marshall, and Edmund Mountjoy gentlemen Justices of the peace for the County of Bourbon; also Commissions appointing, John Gregg Sheriff of Bourbon, Thomas Roane Sheriff of Middlesex, and Edward Jackson Sheriff of Randolph.

Upon application made It is advised that the Damages on the amount of a Judgment obtained against George Rives as Sheriff of Sussex, for the Certificate tax of 1786 be remitted; the said Sheriff having produced a Statement of his account with a receipt for the principal sum due on such judgment together with the legal interest and costs, prior to the first of May last.

It is advised that a warrant issue on the Contingent Fund to Richard Towns for four pounds one shilling for Stage hire etc. of the Guards over Woodward to Petersburg and back. (To be paid)

The Governor laid before the board a report of the Committee appointed to examine the treasurers accounts, Whereupon it is advised that the same be entered in the additional journal; and that the Treasurer be furnished with a Copy thereof.[123]

Mr. Wood, Mr. McClurg, and Mr. Goode are appointed a Committee to visit and examine the Offices of Treasurer Auditor and Solicitor, the present quarter.

---

123. *See* page 355 for the additional journal entry dated 1 Oct. 1791.

All which matters so advised, the Governor orders accordingly.

James Wood
James McClurg
Robt. Goode
Jno. H. Briggs
J. Dawson
Hardin Burnley
John Steele
Miles Selden

Wednesday October 18th [i.e., 19th] 1791

Present

The Governor

Mr. McClurg
Mr. Goode
Mr. Briggs

Mr. Dawson
Mr. Burnley
Mr. Steele

Mr. Selden

It appearing to the board that Mr. Edward Archer is indebted to the commonwealth on a judgment obtained against him for duties on merchandize, that he is possessed of no property, that execution has issued against his body, which, should he be compelled to take advantage of the insolvent act, will occasion a total loss of the debt, but that he is able to give good security to pay the whole with interest by instalments if such indulgence be granted him; It is advised that, upon Mr. Archers entering into bond with such security as the executive shall approve to pay the whole amount of the judgment with interest and costs in four equal half yearly payments, the Solicitor be instructed to direct the Officer to whom the execution has been sent, to return it executed and the Defendant released by order of the Plaintiff.

On the report of Captain Coleman, It is advised that the abstract of pay and rations of the rangers called into service, in Randolph County, under the regulations of the 29th of December last, be referred to the Auditor for settlement in the usual way according to the said regulations.

All which matters so advised, the Governor orders accordingly.

James McClurg
Robt. Goode
Jno. H. Briggs
J. Dawson
Hardin Burnley
John Steele
Miles Selden

Thursday October 20th 1791

Present

The Governor

Mr. Wood	Mr. Dawson
Mr. McClurg	Mr. Burnley
Mr. Goode	Mr. Steele
Mr. Briggs	Mr. Selden

On recommendations It is advised that an additional Commission issue appointing James McDowell, gentleman, a Justice of the peace for the County of Rockbridge. Also a Commission appointing William Hutcheson gentleman Sheriff for the County of Greenbriar.

Britt Stovall gentleman being appointed Surveyor of Patrick County, It is advised that he be required to give bond in the penalty of two thousand pounds for the faithful discharge of his duty.

The Governor laid before the board an Account amounting to seven pounds ten shillings for 20 lb. powder and 40 lb. lead furnished by James Wilkerson to the rangers of Kentucky as Certified by General Scott, Whereupon, it is advised that the said Account be referred to the Auditor for Settlement and a Warrant for the sum due.

Application being made for the payment of a horse of Col. Samuel Lewis, impressed by order of General Morgan in 1781, It is advised that the same be rejected, the Executive having no authority to settle such claims.

The Committee appointed to examine the Accounts of Mr. Heths agency in the sale of public tobacco from the 20th December 1790 to the 6th instant having reported that they had accordingly compared and examined the said Accounts with his Day book and Ledger and found them to be accurate. It is advised that the said Account of Sales be laid before the General Assembly, that Mr. Heths account of expences be referred to the Auditor for settlement, who will allow him three Dollars per diem as full compensation for his expences and horse hire while traveling, and that Mr. Heth be allowed seventy five pounds for his services as Agent from the said 20th of December last.

Pursuant to an Act of the General Assembly "for the relief of persons who have been or may be injured by the destruction of the records of County Courts" It is advised that a Commission issue to George B. Poindexter, William Chamberlayne, William Hopkins, Michael Shurman, Robert Armistead, James Semple, Armistead Russel, Joseph Foster and Samuel Mark, of New Kent County, gentlemen authorizing them or any three of them to perform the Duties required by the said Act, within the County aforesaid.

The Governor laid before the board the Depositions of John Cochran and Edward Stephenson containing the following charges against James Barnett, County Lieutenant of Madison, viz. that on the

15th of March last the said Colonel Barnett required the Deponent Edward Stephenson to give him five Dollars per month for the liberty of furnishing the men to be on duty at said Stephensons house with rations, that if any of the Neighbors called for a man from the said Guard, the person calling should furnish rations at his own expence, and Stephenson should charge and draw pay for the rations of the said man, and share the profits with him the said Barnett. Whereupon, it is advised, that the said James Barnett be arrested for the misconduct aforesaid, that General Scott be directed to call a general Court Martial for the trial of the said Barnett according to law and to report the result of the proceedings herein to the Executive.

All which matters so advised, the Governor orders accordingly.

> James Wood
> James McClurg
> Robt. Goode
> Jno. H. Briggs
> J. Dawson
> Hardin Burnley
> John Steele
> Miles Selden

Monday October 24th 1791

Present

The Governor

Mr. Wood	Mr. Dawson
Mr. McClurg	Mr. Burnley
Mr. Goode	Mr. Steele
Mr. Selden	

The Governor informed the board that in the recess, he directed to be paid out of the Contingent Fund to McColl and Cunlieff, seven pounds ten shillings for two hundred Bushels of Coal furnished for the use of the General Assembly. Approved.

On recommendations, It is advised that an additional Commission issue appointing Lionel Branson and David Wilson gentlemen, Justices of the peace for the County of Hardy: Also Commissions appointing Benjamin Pope Sheriff of Nelson; Richard Allen Sheriff of Cumberland; and Jordin Richardson Sheriff of Greenesville.

William Poage, being appointed Surveyor, of Bath County, It is advised that he be required to give bond in two thousand pounds penalty for the faithfull execution of his office.

On consideration of the petition of Richard Batte and William Gray representing that in the year 1786, they imported a Cargo of Salt and entered into bond at Norfolk to secure the Duty which was then at nine pence per bushel, and proceeded to City point, the port of Delivery, where they arrived five Days after the law had passed reducing the Duty on Salt to three pence per bushel, and praying relief for the loss sustained in consequence thereof, It is advised, that the said petition be rejected, the Executive having no authority to grant relief in such cases.

It is advised that the Account of Alexander McIntire and Cornelius Washburn amounting to twelve pounds for express hire from Limestone to Point Pleasant, as certified by General Scott, be referred to the Auditor for settlement, and a Warrant for the Sum due.

On the report of Captain Coleman, It is advised that the payroll of an Ensign and twenty eight men of Captain Gilkeys Company of Nelson Rangers for services rendered in 1788, also a payroll of a Serjeant and thirty two men of Capt. Caldwells Company of rangers of said County, for services rendered in the same year, and a payroll of an Ensign Serjeant and nine men of Nelson rangers employed in 1788, be referred to the Auditor for Settlement in the usual way.

It is advised that a Warrant issue on the Contingent Fund to McColl and Cunlieff, for eleven pounds five shillings, for three hundred bushels of Coal furnished for the use of the Executive. To be paid.

The Governor laid before the board the Claims of William Long and William Dexter for services as Scouts in Russell County for the year 1790. Whereupon it is advised, that the said Claims be rejected, the services having been ordered without authority.

On the report of Captain Coleman It is advised that the abstracts of pay and rations of Monongalia Rangers employed under the regulations of the Executive the 29th of December last, be referred to the Auditor for settlement in the usual way, according to the said regulations.

The Governor laid before the board an Account of John Crittendon and Luke Cannon amounting to fifty two pounds 17/9 being the amount of a judgment and costs obtained against them in Prince William in 1786 by Lewis Lee for a Servant of his enlisted by them in the Virginia Line during the war. Whereupon it is advised that the same be rejected the Executive having no authority to allow such claims.

The Governor laid before the board a letter from the treasurer Stating that a Warrant for fifteen hundred pounds drawn by the Auditor in favor of William Deakins treasurer to the Commissioners for the foederal District being presented at his office had been paid through mistake without the usual order of the Executive for borrowing. Whereupon, it is advised that the said payment be now approved.

Thomas Sewells bond, with Bernard Todd Security, to indemnify the Commonwealth and the United States against a Certificate of which he is to obtain a Duplicate pursuant to an Act of Assembly, being laid before the board, the same is approved.

All which matters so advised, the Governor orders accordingly.

> James Wood
> James McClurg
> Robt. Goode
> J. Dawson
> Hardin Burnley
> John Steele
> Miles Selden

Wednesday October 26th 1791

Present

The Governor

Mr. Wood	Mr. Dawson
Mr. McClurg	Mr. Burnley
Mr. Goode	Mr. Steele
Mr. Briggs	Mr. Selden

The Governor informed the board that on recommendations, he, yesterday, issued commissions appointing Peter Jett, Henry Alexander Ashton, Thomas Short, John Ashton, and Charles Stuart junior, gentleman, Justices of the peace for the County of King George, and Thomas Tabb Coroner for the County of Mathews. Approved.

On recommendations, It is advised that Commissions issue appointing James Jones, Sheriff of Essex, George Savage, Sheriff of Northampton, and William Jett, an Inspector at Falmouth warehouse, vice Francis Jett, deceased.

On consideration of the petition of James McAffe praying for a settlement of Sundry bills for supplies furnished the Western Troops in 1780 and 1781, It is advised that the same be rejected; there being no law authorizing the executive to settle such Claims.

On consideration of a memorial of James Pendleton, soliciting a suspension of the execution levied on his Estate for the balance of a judgment obtained, in June 1790, against him, as Sheriff of Culpeper, for the taxes of 1788, It is advised that the same be rejected.

On the report of Captain Coleman, It is advised that the payrolls of Capt. Samuel Estills company of rangers employed in Madison County in the year 1788, Also a payroll of Ensign Thompsons Company of Lincoln Rangers employed in 1788 for the protection of the Salt Works in Jefferson County, Also a payroll of Captain William Caseys Company of Lincoln rangers for services in 1788, Also an Account for rations furnished the said Rangers by Levi Baldock, and the Claim of John Owens for Services as a Scout in Fayette County in the year 1788, be referred to the Auditor for settlement in the usual way.

The Governor laid before the board a petition of Thomas Booth, praying for permission to collect all the Old Salt pans, broken Cannon etc. belonging to the public, for the purpose of working up, and offering to pay for the same by furnishing for public use four large Stoves. Whereupon it is advised, that Mr. Booth be authorized to collect and receive any old Salt pans, broken Guns, or other old iron, belonging to the State, Shot excepted, reporting to the board, from time to time, the quantity and quality of each Article he may collect, or receive, accompanied with a Certificate relative thereto from the persons having care of any such Articles.

All which matters so advised, the Governor orders accordingly.

> James Wood
> James McClurg
> Robt. Goode
> Jno. H. Briggs
> J. Dawson
> Hardin Burnley
> Miles Selden
> John Steele

Friday October 28th 1791

Present

The Governor

Mr. Wood	Mr. Dawson
Mr. Goode	Mr. Burnley
Mr. Briggs	Mr. Steele

The Governor informed the board that he yesterday issued a Commission appointing John Rogers Coroner for the County of Northumberland and John Rochester Coroner of Westmoreland. Approved.

It is advised that Hanah Crawford, James Keeling, Mary Carver, Mary Butler and John McKenny be continued on the List of pensioners with their former allowances.

It is advised that the treasurer be directed to pay out of the Contingent fund, a Warrant issued by the Auditor the 20th instant in favor of Thomas Brend for six pounds for a record book and paper furnished for use of the general Court.

On application for the remission of the Damages on the amount of judgment obtained against William Dandridge Claiborne, as Sheriff of King William, for the revenue tax of 1788; It is advised that the same be rejected, full payment of the principal, interest, and Costs not having been made prior to the first of May as the law directs.

On report from Captain Coleman It is advised that the payroll of a detachment of Fayette Rangers for Services in 1788, be referred to the auditor for settlement in the usual way.

It appearing that executions have been issued against the body of William Stokes on judgments obtained by the Commonwealth against him for certain Duties on merchandize, and that he will be compelled to take the advantage of the insolvent Act, which will occasion a total loss of the Debt to the State, unless he can be indulged to pay the same by instalments, It is therefore advised that, upon Mr. Stokes entering into bonds with such security as the executive shall approve, to pay the whole amount of such judgments with interest and Costs in four equal half yearly payments, the Solicitor be instructed to direct the Officer to whom the executions have been sent to return them, executed and the Defendant released by order of the Executive.

All which matters so advised, the Governor orders accordingly.

> James Wood
> Robt. Goode
> Jno. H. Briggs
> J. Dawson
> Hardin Burnley
> John Steele

Saturday October 29th 1791

Present

The Governor

Mr. Wood	Mr. Dawson
Mr. Goode	Mr. Burnley
Mr. Briggs	Mr. Selden

It is advised that receipts be given for two Loan Office certificates Nos. 202 and 203 for monies paid into the Treasury the 12th of May 1780, by Nathaniel Pope, on account of British subjects, according to the Sequestration law.

On application for the remission of Damages on the judgment obtained against William Mills as Sheriff of Spotsylvania for the revenue tax of 1789, It is advised that the same be rejected.

On application for the remission of Damages on the Judgment obtained against James Barbour as Sheriff of Culpeper for the Certificate tax of 1785; It is advised that the same be rejected, the Executive having no power to remit in such cases.

All which matters so advised, the Governor orders accordingly.

> James Wood
> Robt. Goode
> Jno. H. Briggs
> J. Dawson
> Hardin Burnley
> Miles Selden

Wednesday November 2d 1791

Present

The Governor

.٧r. Wood	Mr. Burnley
Mr. Goode	Mr. Steele
Mr. Briggs	Mr. Selden

The Governor laid before the board Colonel Davies's Draft for one hundred and fifty three pounds thirteen shillings and four pence, being for his last quarters Salary as Commissioner for settling the Continental Account, for pay due James Murray for services as Clerk from the tenth of August to the thirtieth of September last, and for the contingent expences of his Office. Whereupon it is advised that the said Draft be referred to the Auditor for the usual Warrants. To be paid.

On recommendation, It is advised that a Commission issue appointing Hezekiah Davisson Coroner for the County of Harrison.

It is advised that Robert Ferguson be put on the pension List with an allowance of twelve pounds per annum agreeably to the Act of assembly in his favour.

It is advised that a Commission issue appointing Cyrus Griffin esquire to supply the vacancy in the Court of Directors for the public hospital in the City of Williamsburg, occasioned by the resignation of Joseph Prentis esquire.

On consideration of the petition of Joseph Wilson, praying that compensation may be made him for the Damages sustained by himself and his late partner William Johnson deceased by the loss of a vessel and Cargo of tobacco during the late war, owing in the first place to her detention in consequence of the State Agents failure to fulfill his contract for loading her, and afterwards to an embargos being laid upon all Vessels; It is advised that the said petition be rejected, the executive having no authority to decide in such cases.

All which matters so advised, the Governor orders accordingly.

James Wood
Robt. Goode
Jno. H. Briggs
Hardin Burnley
John Steele
Miles Selden

Friday November 4th 1791

Present

The Governor

Mr. Wood	Mr. Dawson
Mr. McClurg	Mr. Burnley
Mr. Goode	Mr. Steele
Mr. Briggs	Mr. Selden

The Governor informed the board that he yesterday issued a Commission appointing William Starling Sheriff of Mecklenburg. approved.

On recommendations It is advised that Commissions issue appointing John Cannon additional inspector of tobacco at Dumfries warehouse in Prince William; and Daniel L. Hylton, Sheriff of Henrico County.

The Governor laid before the board a Claim of Phripp and Bowdoin[124] for the hire of their Brigg Norfolk 25 Days employed in raising the Norfolk revenge Galley, and for Damage received by the said brigg in that Service. Whereupon it is advised that the same be rejected; the Executive having no authority to decide in such cases.

On consideration of the petition of John Stith praying that the sum of twenty one pound nine shillings and nine pence which he paid into the Treasury as damages on the amount of a judgment obtained against him for recruiting money put into his hands, may be refunded; It is advised that the same be rejected; the Executive having no authority to refund monies which have been paid into the treasury according to law.

The Board resumed the consideration of the allowance made to Mrs. Conner, widow of John Conner, the late Doorkeeper to this board, for cleaning out the Council Chamber and furnishing a person to act as Doorkeeper; and conceiving the indulgence already granted her, in consideration of the fidelity of her late husband, as Doorkeeper, and of his merits as a Soldier during the late war, to be as great as can, with propriety be made in her present occupation, Advise that her said allowance cease from to day; and that Mathew Pate be appointed Doorkeeper to this board, with a Salary of forty pounds per annum.

All which matters so advised, the Governor orders accordingly.

James Wood
James McClurg
Robt. Goode
Jno. H. Briggs
J. Dawson
Hardin Burnley
John Steele
Miles Selden

---

124. "Bowdon" in the clerk's index.

Wednesday November 9th 1791

Present

Mr. Wood who presides as Lieutenant Governor; the Governor
being unable to perform his duty from sickness

Mr. McClurg   Mr. Dawson
Mr. Goode   Mr. Burnley
Mr. Briggs   Mr. Steele
                 Mr. Selden

It is advised that the Claim of Reubin Eastin for subsistence money
as a Lieutenant in service in Jefferson County from the first of August
until the 14th December 1788: Also the Claim of Messrs. Hall and
Waters for Physic and attendance furnished Captain Ballard Smiths
troop of Jefferson Cavalry in service in the same year, be rejected; the
first, because it hath been unusual with the executive to allow money to
rangers in lieu of rations, and the second, because the Commanding
Officer had no authority to enter into such engagements.

It is advised that the treasurer be directed to pay out of the
Contingent fund, a Warrant issued by the Auditor, to John Carter for
fifteen pounds upon account, to purchase Stationary, Coal etc. for the
use of the Auditors Office.

The Lieutenant Governor laid before the board four bonds
entered into by Edward Archer pursuant to the Advice of the 18th
ultimo, with Thomas Blanchard and John Archer his Securities.
Whereupon it is advised that the Securities be approved, that the said
bonds be lodged with the Solicitor, and he be directed to comply with
the aforesaid Order of the 18th on the subject of Mr. Archers case.

On report from Captain Coleman, It is advised that the Claim of
John McClune for services as a ranger in Bourbon County in the year
1788; Also the Claim of Thomas Potter for services as a ranger in
Jefferson County from the 8th of November 1788 to the 8th of January
1789; Also the Claim of Joseph Parker for services as a ranger in the
said County from the 8th of November 1788 to the 14th of January
1789, be referred to the Auditor for settlement in the usual way, that
the Claims of James Fleming and David Warford for services as Spies
(or Scouts) in Jefferson County, be rejected; the times of service not
being specified; and it is presumable from the dates of the Certificates,
that the Services were performed in the year 1790, when there was no
authority from this Government for ordering out Scouts.

All which matters so advised, the Lieutenant Governor orders
accordingly.

James McClurg
Robt. Goode
Jno. H. Briggs
J. Dawson
Hardin Burnley
John Steele
Miles Selden

Saturday November 12th 1791

Present

The Governor

Mr. Wood	Mr. Dawson
Mr. Goode	Mr. Steele
Mr. Briggs	Mr. Selden

The Governor informed the board that on the eighth instant he issued a commission, on recommendation, appointing Matthew Wilson Sheriff of Botetourt. Approved.

Mr. Wood informed the board that during the recess and indisposition of the Governor, he as Lieutenant Governor, directed the auditor to settle in the usual way the Account of Tunstal Quarles amounting to ninety seven pounds nineteen shillings, as certified by Capt. Coleman, for provisions furnished the post at the point of Fork for the two last Quarters. Approved.

On recommendation, It is advised that a Commission issue appointing James Robinson Coroner for the County of Princess Anne.

The Governor laid before the board four bonds entered into by William Stokes pursuant to the advice of the twenty eighth ultimo with William Pennock his security to one of the said bonds, Wills Cowper his security to another and W and C Stokes and Company his securities to the other two. Whereupon it is advised that the Securities be approved, that the said bonds be lodged with the Solicitor and he be directed to comply with the aforesaid order of the 28th Ultimo on the subject of Stokes case.

All which matters so advised, the Governor orders accordingly.

James Wood
Robt. Goode
Jno. H. Briggs
J. Dawson
John Steele
Miles Selden

Monday November 14th 1791

Present

The Governor

Mr. Wood	Mr. Dawson
Mr. McClurg	Mr. Burnley
Mr. Goode	Mr. Steele
Mr. Briggs	Mr. Selden

On recommendations, It is advised that Commissions issue appointing Thomas Throckmorton Sheriff of Frederick and William Nevison an Alderman for the borough of Norfolk, vice John Boush deceased.

It is advised that Silby Hellion and Mary Lyon be continued on the List of pensioners with their former allowances from January 1790.

It is advised that the Treasurer be directed not to pay any further Draft of the Directors of the federal District until the farther direction of this board.

On consideration of the petition of Claude Piat praying for the remission of a fine of five hundred weight of tobacco imposed on him by the Court of Prince George County, in March 1787, for not listing his taxable property, It is advised that the same be rejected.

It is advised that the Claim of Charles White amounting to six Dollars for camp kettles furnished for the use of the Kentucky rangers called out under the regulations of the 29th December last, be referred to the auditor for settlement.

The Governor laid before the board an account of William Langhorne Executor of John S. Langhorne deceased, for the services of the said John fifty three Days in collecting Vouchers in support of the claim of this State against the united States. Whereupon it is advised that the said Claim be referred to the Auditor for settlement, allowing a Dollar per day, to be paid out of the contingent fund.

All which matters so advised, the Governor orders accordingly.

> James Wood
> James McClurg
> Robt. Goode
> Jno. H. Briggs
> J. Dawson
> Hardin Burnley
> John Steele
> Miles Selden

Thursday November 17th 1791

Present

The Governor

Mr. Wood	Mr. Dawson
Mr. McClurg	Mr. Burnley
Mr. Goode	Mr. Steele
Mr. Briggs	Mr. Selden

The Governor informed the board that in the recess he issued Commissions appointing Charles Graves and Thomas Goode inspectors and Richard Baugh additional inspector of tobacco at Johnstons warehouse in the Town of Manchester, they having been recommended according to law. Approved.

It is advised that John Waller Johnston be appointed Notary public for the District of Burmuda hundred vice David M. Randolph who hath resigned; and Moses Treadway Public Jailor for the District of Prince Edward vice John Folkes who hath resigned.

Pursuant to a resolution of the General Assembly of the 7th and 8th instant, it is advised that the Attorney General of this Commonwealth be Directed to exhibit a Bill in Chancery to foreclose the Mortgage of John Ballendine and John Reeveley, made to John Nicholas and others as trustees in behalf of this Commonwealth, for the Buckingham furnace, and the Lands and slaves therein mentioned.

The Governor laid before the board a letter from the Secretary at War of the 28th ultimo authorizing the Governor to provide for the Defence of the County of Russell, together with a resolution of the present general Assembly on the subject of providing for the Western defence. Whereupon it is advised,

that a company of men be raised for the Defence of Russell County, consisting of sixty six rank and file with the proper proportion of non commissioned Officers, to be recruited and commanded by Andrew Lewis as Captain, James Hawkins as Lieutenant, and Robert Robertson as Ensign:

that two and a half dollars per month be paid by this State to the noncommissioned officers and privates in addition to the allowance made by the general Government:

that the fifteenth of March next be the time and the Courthouse of Russell County the place of rendezvous; and that the service terminate on the first of December one thousand seven hundred and ninety two, unless the company be sooner discharged:

that Colonel Cowan be appointed to muster the men at the time of their assembling and when they shall be discharged and report on oath the actual number present at each muster:

that Joseph Kent be appointed Contractor to supply the men with rations, each ration to consist of one pound of beef or three quarters of pound of pork, one pound of bread or flour, half a gill of rum, brandy, or whiskey and one quart of salt for every hundred rations, the price of the ration to be eight Cents. And it is further advised,

that two hundred pounds of powder and eight hundred pounds of lead be furnished from the post at the point of Fork to the order of Captain Lewis for the service aforesaid.

It is advised that the treasurer be directed to pay seven thousand Dollars in part of the late Draft of the Directors of the Federal District for twenty eight thousand dollars.

It is advised that Elizabeth Southall and John Groom[125] be continued on the List of pensioners, the first with her former allowance from January 1789 and the last with his former allowance from January 1788.

---

125. "Jno. Groome" in the clerk's index.

All which matters so advised the Governor orders accordingly.

James Wood
James McClurg
Robt. Goode
Jno. H. Briggs
J. Dawson
Hardin Burnley
John Steele
Miles Selden

Saturday November 19th 1791

Present

The Governor

Mr. Wood	Mr. Dawson
Mr. McClurg	Mr. Burnley
Mr. Goode	Mr. Steele
Mr. Briggs	Mr. Selden

The Governor informed the board that he yesterday issued a Commission appointing Edmund Booker Sheriff of Amelia, he having been recommended according to law. Approved.

Upon application made, It is advised that the Damages on the amount of the Judgments obtained against William Leftwich, as Sheriff of Bedford, for the revenue and Certificate taxes of 1786, be remitted; it appearing that the balance due on the said Judgments was paid up prior to the first of May.

It is advised that the treasurer be directed to borrow from other funds money sufficient to pay off the Warrants issued or to be issued on account of the Rangers called into service under the regulations of the 29th December last.

On consideration of the petition of William McIntosh late a Soldier in the Continental army praying to be put on the pension List, It is advised that the same be rejected.

Pursuant to a resolution of the general assembly of the 1st and 5th instant It is advised that Aug. Davis be employed to print fifteen hundred copies of the laws of the last Session of Congress, at the rate of ten pounds per Sheet, provided that the same be printed on good type and paper, and compleated in time to be sent out with the Laws of the present Session of the general Assembly.

All which matters so advised, the Governor orders accordingly.

> James Wood
> James McClurg
> Robt. Goode
> Jno. H. Briggs
> J. Dawson
> Hardin Burnley
> John Steele
> Miles Selden

Wednesday November 23d 1791

Present

The Governor

Mr. Wood	Mr. Dawson
Mr. McClurg	Mr. Burnley
Mr. Goode	Mr. Steele
Mr. Briggs	Mr. Selden

The Governor informed the board that in recess he issued a commission appointing John Gunnell Coroner for Loudoun County; And that he granted a pardon to Negro Daniel, the property of John Moseley, condemned to Death by a Court of Oyer held for the County of Buckingham the 14th instant, for felony, the said Daniel having been recommended as a proper object of mercy. Approved.

On recommendation It is advised that Commissions issue appointing George Pegram and Erasmus Gill inspectors and Thomas Broadnax additional inspector at Barksdales Warehouse in the County of Dinwiddie.

The Governor laid before the board the Claim of John Bondfield of Bordeaux for payment of the freight agreed for with him by Doctor Arthur Lee of Artillery and Stores sent for this State by order of Governor Henry during the late war. Whereupon it is advised that the same be rejected, the executive having no authority to decide on such claims.

It is advised that James Gibson[126] be allowed out of the contingent Fund fifteen pounds for his trouble and expences incurred in apprehending William Smith a Criminal who escaped from this State, and bringing him from Baltimore.

On report from Captain Coleman It is advised that the abstract of pay and rations of Ohio Rangers called into service under the regula-

---

126. "Jno. Gibson" in the clerk's index.

tions of the 29th December last, be referred to the Auditor for settlement in the usual way.

On consideration of the petition of Oliver Pollock, It is advised, that the Auditor be directed to examine and report whether the bills mentioned in the said petition are part of those credited in his account heretofore settled and for which payment hath been withheld for want of the original bills with their protests.

On consideration of the Claims of William Smyly and Joseph McCullum for rations furnished the rangers in service in Nelson County in the year 1788; It is advised that the further consideration thereof be postponed; and that Capt. Coleman write to Col. Davies for copies of the necessary Documents for ascertaining whether the aforesaid Claims have been heretofore allowed.

The Governor laid before the board several Warrants which had been issued by the Auditor to a detachment of men under the command of Ensign Chapman, which appear to be improper in as much as it is expressed in the body of the said Warrants that they were granted for services in the militia agreeable to an Act of Assembly passed in November 1781 to regulate and affix the pay of the Militia heretofore called into service, whereas it appears that the service was performed in the year 1791 under the Act of the Executive of the 29th of December 1790. Whereupon it is advised that the Auditor be directed to cancel the said Warrants and to settle the payroll and ration Account of Ensign Chapman according to the abovementioned Act of the Executive and issue proper Warrants for the amount that shall appear to be due.

All which matters so advised, the Governor orders accordingly.

> James Wood
> James McClurg
> Robt. Goode
> Jno. H. Briggs
> J. Dawson
> Hardin Burnley
> John Steele
> Miles Selden

Tuesday November 29th 1791

Present

The Governor

Mr. Wood	Mr. Dawson
Mr. McClurg	Mr. Burnley
Mr. Goode	Mr. Steele
Mr. Briggs	Mr. Selden

The Governor informed the board that in the recess he issued a Commission appointing John Taylor Collector of the Revenue and Certificate taxes due from the County of Montgomery for the year 1786; and that he directed Richard Marshall to be put on the pension List agreeably to the Act of Assembly in his favor. Approved.

On recommendations, It is advised that an additional Commission issue appointing John Caruthers a justice of the peace for the County of Rockbridge; and that Commissions issue appointing Cornelius Ferree, Sheriff of Hampshire, David Edmundson and James McDowell coroners of Rockbridge, Jeduthan Haynie an inspector of tobacco at Coan Warehouse vice Richard Roul deceased and George Ashburne additional inspector at said Warehouse vice the said Haynie.

It is advised that Jesse Alexander be appointed public Jailor for the District of Richmond, Westmoreland, Lancaster and Northumberland vice John Roberts who hath resigned.

It appearing that the buildings appointed for holding the Court of the County of Hampshire are in so ruinous a condition as to be unfit for the purpose to which they were appropriated; It is advised that a proclamation issue directing that the Courts for the said County be hereafter holden in the house of Perez Drew in the Town of Romney until a new Courthouse can be erected.

It is advised that a Warrant issue on the Contingent Fund, to Aug. Davis for two pounds four shillings and seven pence, for postage of public Dispatches from the eighth of July to the 17th instant to be paid.

All which matters so advised, the Governor orders accordingly.

James Wood
James McClurg
Robt. Goode
Jno. H. Briggs
J. Dawson
Hardin Burnley
John Steele
Miles Selden

Additional Journal

Thursday January 15th 1789

Present

The Governor

Mr. Wood	Mr. Braxton
Mr. McClurg	Mr. Heth
Mr. Jones	Mr. Goode

It is advised, that the Acts of Congress of the 26th of August 1776. of the 7th of June 1785 and of the 11th of June 1788 be recorded; and they are as follows:

In Congress August 26th 1776

Whereas, in the course of the present War, some commissioned and non-commissioned officers of the Army and Navy, as also private soldiers, marines and seamen, may lose a limb, or be otherwise so disabled as to prevent their serving in the Army, or getting their livelihood, and may stand in need of relief:

Resolved, that every commissioned officer, non-commissioned officer and private Soldier, who shall lose a limb in any engagement, or be so disabled in the service of the United States of America, as to render him incapable afterwards of getting a livelihood, shall receive, during his life or the continuance of such disability one half of his monthly pay from and after the time that his pay as an officer or soldier ceases; to be paid by the Committee as hereafter mentioned:

That every commander of any ship of war or armed vessel, commissioned officer, warrant officer, marine or seaman belonging to the United States of America, who shall lose a limb in any engagement in which no prize shall be taken, or be therein otherwise so disabled as to be rendered incapable of getting a livelihood, shall receive, during his life or the continuance of such disability, the one half of his monthly pay from and after the time that his pay as an officer or marine, or seaman ceases; to be paid as hereafter mentioned. But in case a prize shall be taken at the time such loss of limb or other disability shall happen, then such sum, as he may receive out of the net profits of such prize, before a dividend is made of the same, agreeable to former orders of Congress, shall be considered as part of his half pay, and computed accordingly.

That every commissioned officer, non-commissioned officer and private soldier in the Army, and every commander, commission officer, warrant officer, marine or seaman of any of the ships of War, or armed vessels belonging to the United States of America, who shall be wounded in any engagement so as to be rendered incapable of serving in the Army or Navy, though not totally disabled from getting a livelihood, shall receive such monthly sum as shall be judged adequate by the Assembly or other representative body of the state where he belongs or resides, upon application to them for that purpose, provided the same doth not exceed his half pay.

Provided, that no commissioned officer, non-commissioned officer and private soldier in the army, commander, commission officer, warrant officer, marine or seaman of any of the ships of War or armed vessels belonging to the United States of America, who shall be wounded or disabled as aforesaid, shall be entitled to his half pay or other allowance, unless he produce to the Committee or officer appointed to receive the same in the state where he resides or belongs, or to the assembly or legislative body of such state, a certificate from the commanding officer, who was in the same engagement in which he was so wounded, or in case of his death from some other officer of the same corps, and the surgeon that attended him, or a certificate from the commander of the ship of war or armed vessel engaged in the action in which any officer, marine or Seaman received his wound, and from the Surgeon who attended him, of the name of the person so wounded, his office, rank, department, regiment, company, ship of War or armed vessel to which he belonged, his office or rank therein, the nature of his wound, and in what action or engagement he received it:

That it be recommended to the several assemblies or legislative bodies of the United States of America to appoint some person or persons in their respective states, who shall receive and examine all such certificates, as may be presented to them and register the same in a book, and also what support is adjudged by the assembly or legislative body of their state to those, whose case requires but a partial support, and also of the payment from time to time of every half pay and other allowance, and of the death of such disabled person, or ceasing of such allowance; and shall make a fair and regular report of the same quarterly to the Secretary of Congress or board of War, where a separate record shall be kept of the same:

That it be recommended to the assemblies or legislative bodies of the several states, to cause payment to be made of all such half pay or other allowances as shall be adjudged due to the persons aforenamed, on account of the United States.

Provided that all such officers and soldiers that may be entitled to the aforesaid pension, and are found to be capable of doing guard or garrison duty, shall be formed into a corps of invalids, and subject to the said duty; and all officers, marines and seamen of the navy, who shall be entitled to the pension aforesaid, and shall be found capable of doing any duty on board the navy or any department thereof, shall be liable to be so employed.

In Congress June 7th 1785

Resolved that it be, and it is hereby recommended to the several states, to make provision for officers, soldiers or seamen who have been disabled in the service of the United States, in the following manner:

1. A complete list shall be made out by such person or persons as each state shall direct, of all the officers, soldiers or seamen resident in their respective states, who have served in the Army or Navy of the United States or in the militia in the service of the United States and have been disabled in such service, so as to be incapable of military duty, or of obtaining a livelihood by labour. In this list shall be expressed the pay, age and disability of each invalid, also the regiment, corps or ship to which he belonged; and a copy of the same shall be transmitted to the office of the secretary at War, within one year after each state shall pass a law for this purpose; and a like descriptive list of the invalids resident in the respective States, shall from year to year be annually transmitted to the office of the secretary at war.

2. No officer, Soldier or Seaman, shall be considered as an invalid, or entitled to pay, unless he can produce a certificate from the commanding officer or surgeon of the regiment, ship, corps or company in which he served, or from a Physician or Surgeon of a military hospital, or other good and sufficient testimony, setting forth his disability, and that he was thus disabled while in the service of the United States.

3. That all commissioned officers within the aforesaid description, disabled in the service of the United States, so as to be wholly incapable of military duty, or of obtaining a livelihood, be allowed a yearly pension equal to half of their pay respectively: And all commissioned officers as aforesaid, who shall not have been disabled in so great a degree, be allowed a yearly pension which shall correspond with the degree of their disability compared with that of an officer wholly disabled: That all non-commissioned officers and privates, within the aforesaid description, disabled in the service of the United states, so as to be wholly incapable of military or Garrison duty, or of obtaining a livelihood by labour, be allowed a sum not exceeding five dollars per month: and all non-commissioned officers and privates as aforesaid, who shall not have been disabled in so great a degree, be allowed such a sum as shall correspond with the degree of their disability, compared with that of a noncommissioned officer or private wholly disabled.

4. That each state appoint one or more persons of suitable abilities; to examine all claimants, and to report whether the person producing a certificate, setting forth that he is an invalid, be such in fact, and if such, to what pay he is entitled; and thereupon, the persons appointed to make such enquiry, shall give to the invalid a certificate

specifying to what pay he is entitled, and transmit a copy to the person who may be appointed by the state to receive and record the same.

5. That each state be authorized to pay to the commissioned officers, non commissioned officers and privates, the sum or sums to which they shall be respectively entitled, agreeably to the before mentioned certificates, the said payments to be deducted from the respective quotas of the states for the year on which they shall be made. Provided that no officer who has accepted his commutation for half pay, shall be entered on the list of invalids, unless he shall have first returned his commutation.

6. That any state may form such invalids under the aforesaid description, as are citizens of the same, and are capable of garrison duty, into corps, to be employed in guarding military Stores, aiding the police, or otherwise as the state may direct.

7. That when invalids shall be formed into Corps, there be quarterly returns, comprehending the pay, age, disability, regiment, ship or corps to which they severally belonged, made out and signed by their commanding officer and transmitted to such person or persons as the State shall direct, that their pay may be ordered according to the said return.

8. That all invalids as well those formed into Corps, as those who are not, shall annually apply themselves to a Magistrate of the county in which they reside or may be stationed, and take the following oath, to wit; A.B. came before me, one of the justices for the county of .... in the state of .... and made oath that he was examined by .... appointed by the said State (or Commonwealth) for that purpose, obtained a certificate, (or had his certificate examined and countersigned,) setting forth that he had served in .... that he was disabled by .... and that he now lives in the .... and in the county of ....

9. That the affidavits, drawn according to the above form, and dated and attested by a magistrate, be sent by the said magistrate to the person or persons appointed by the state, to receive and record the same, and that a counter part of the affidavit be preserved by the person taking it, to be exhibited to such persons as shall be appointed by the state to pay the invalids.

In Congress June 11th 1788

Resolved, that each state shall have credit in its general account with the United States for such sums as became due to invalids before the first day of January, 1782, and which have been or shall be paid to them by the State; and for such sums as became due to invalids from the said first day of January, 1782, inclusive, to the first day of January, 1788, and which have been or shall be paid to them by any state, the state shall have credit in the existing specie requisitions of Congress; and for sums that may so become due after January, 1788, and be paid by any state, the state shall have credit in the specie requisitions of Congress which may hereafter be made.

Resolved, that no person shall be entitled to a pension as an invalid, who has not, or shall not before the expiration of six months from this time make application therefor, and produce the requisite certificates and evidence to entitle him thereto.

It is also advised, that the following letter and the resolution of the general Assembly be recorded, to wit;

Board of Treasury July 21 1788

Sir,

We have considered your letter of the 1st instant on the subject of pensions due to invalids; and as you do not appear to have seen the resolves of Congress of the 11th of June, 1788, on that subject, we now transmit them.

You wish information on two points.

1st. Whether in our opinion, the pensions of persons who were discharged from the Army in consequence of the resolve of Congress of the 23d of April, 1782, are already settled, or whether they are liable to a revision or abatement in consequence of the Act of 7th June, 1785,? And

2nd. Whether the pensions which may be settled in conformity to the act last mentioned are to commence from the time, that the pay of the claimant ceased in the Army; or from the date of his certificate?

In answer to the first we are of opinion, "that the payments under the act of April 1782, must be considered as settled and not liable to revision or abatement, so far as it respects the accounts betwixt the pensioner and the state," which we presume is what you wish to know; but if your intention is to ascertain whether the accounts of the State with the Union for pensions paid under that act, must be considered as settled, our answer is, that no credit can be given on any accounts for payments made to Invalid pensioners till the same are regularly adjusted at the treasury of the United States.

With respect to the second point, we are of opinion, "That, under the act of the 26th of August, 1776, invalid officers and soldiers acquired a right to certain pensions to be computed from the time the pay of the officer or soldier ceased in the Army." Whereever therefore no compensation has been made to invalids under the description above mentioned, we are of opinion, "that it may be made under the act of 7th June 1785; but then the account of such pension and the proof of the claimant must be conformable to the rules established in the act last mentioned, and the credit the state is entitled to, must be agreeably to the principles of the resolve of the 11th June 1788." We are Sir your obt. humble servants

(signed)   Samuel Osgood

Oliver Wolcott Esqr.   Walter Livingston
  Comptroller of Accounts for   Arthur Lee.
  the state of Connecticut

In the House of Delegates
Monday the 1st of December 1788.

Resolved, that the report of the board of treasury of the fourth of september last upon the subject of pensions comprehending a letter from the said board to Oliver Wolcott esquire, Comptroller of Accounts for the State of Massachusetts, together with a resolution of Congress directing the same to be sent to the executives of the several states for their information, be referred to the executive, to be acted upon according to the constructions therein contained: and in conformity to such explanations as may hereafter be received from Congress, or the board of treasury.

Resolved, that the Executive pay due regard to the limitation of time fixed by Congress, in their resolution of the eleventh of June last respecting pensions to persons, who have been disabled in the late War, and admit no claims contrary to the said resolution.

Teste

1788 December 4th   John Beckley Clk: h: ds.
   Agreed to by the senate
   H. Brooke C. S.

Tuesday May 25th 1790[127]

Present

The Governor

Mr. Wood	Mr. Goode
Mr. McClurg	Mr. Briggs
Mr. Braxton	Mr. Carter
	Mr. Dawson

The reports of a Committee appointed the 21st day of December 1789, under the act empowering the Executive to Superintend and arrange the offices of Treasurer, Auditor and Solicitor, having been laid before the Executive, the Board, upon due consideration thereof, advise

Sect: 1st   That the solicitor be directed to transfer to the Office of the Auditor, the Auditors specie Books ending in 1787, together with the list of balances taken therefrom; and to furnish the said Auditor as soon as may be, with an exact statement of the Costs, Interest and damages, which have accrued in the case of every delinquent sheriff, or other collector of Revenue, whose account has hitherto been, or may hereafter be settled by the solicitor.

---

127. This entry follows that of Tues. 10 Aug. 1790 in the manuscript book of the additional journal, as the Council did not direct that it be entered in the additional journal until 12 October 1790. The entries have been placed in proper chronological order here.

2nd   That the Auditor be directed, immediately upon the receipt of the abovementioned documents, to set about the compleating, as far as may be, his defective accounts against sheriffs, and other Collectors of the Revenue.

3rd   That the Auditor be directed to use his utmost exertions to keep the accounts of Sheriffs, and other Collectors of Revenue in such a state, that the solicitor may be enabled to give notices, and move for Judgment against delinquents upon certified extracts from the Auditors Books, and that for this purpose he keep a seperate day-book for transactions relating to the Revenue, which shall be Journalized and posted daily.

4th   That the Auditor be directed in opening his Annual ledger, not to transfer thither the balances of the former, nor to remove the same to the solicitor's office, as has been required by the reform law of 1786, but to close the accounts already opened in the present books, and in the new ledger to be opened this year, he shall enter all debts of what kind soever arising due *to* the Commonwealth, after the 31st of October 1790, and all Debts arising due from the Commonwealth after the 31st of December 1790, and none other, and in future his ledgers shall be perfectly annual, and comprehend only the Revenue and expenditures of the current year.

5th   The Board impressed with the necessity of obtaining an accurate register of all the certificates bearing Interest now in circulation, as well for the information of the public concerning the real state of their debt, as that any improper issue of Interest warrants, or payment of Counterfeits into the Treasury may be checked and prevented would, if they had the power, advise that the Auditor be directed to take *in* the old certificates when presented next year for drawing the Interest, erase the signature, number them on the back, and file them in his office; and to issue new certificates in their stead, with corresponding numbers. A fair numerical register of these certificates, according to their several species, should be kept both in the Auditors and Solicitors office, and after a period affixed, no certificate should be entitled to draw Interest unless its registration appeared in the face of it attested by the Auditor and Solicitor. The amounts of said registers should at the end of every Month be compared with the old Certificates filed in the Office by the Auditor and Solicitor in presence of a committee of the Executive who should certify the amount, and direct the Auditor to carry the same to the respective accounts in his Book. The Treasurer should likewise produce to the committee, such certificates bearing an Interest as may have been redeemed at the Treasury, which after an examination should be noted by the Auditor and solicitor in their respective registers and carried to account. But as this measure would exceed their authority, they advise that the Auditor be directed to number the certificates as they come in, with red Ink, erasing the old number, where the certificate shall have been numbered, and to register them in his Office, under these new numbers.

6th   It is farther advised, that the Auditor be directed in Issuing the Interest Warrants, to see that every Interest Warrant bears the number of the certificate on which it issues; and where more than one Interest Warrant issues on the same certificate that each Warrant bear the same number.

7th   That the Auditor be directed to number all other Warrants likewise, which he may issue after the 31st December [17]90, and from that period, to keep in his Office a fair numerical list of these, as well as of the Interest Warrants, above mentioned, registered daily, under their several numbers and heads, and when this regulation takes place to permit no division of any Warrant at his Office after its issue.

8th   That the Auditor be directed as soon as he has compleated his register of certificates bearing an Interest, to furnish the Treasurer with a fair copy thereof, with a Column expressing the amount of the annual Interest of each; and to supply him daily with a numerical list of all the Warrants issued at his office in the course of the day, agre[e]able to his register of Warrants.

9th   That the Auditor be directed to send up daily to this board a similar list of all Warrants issued in the course of the day for claims due from the public, other than the Interest of registered certificates to be recorded by their Clerk: And the Board will appoint once in every month, a Committee of their Body to examine the vouchers in the Auditor's Office on which they have issued.

10th That the solicitor be directed to take charge of all the paper Money books of whatever kind, and of all other Books of accounts in specie or specifics, which have not been committed to the Auditor, and to use all possible expedition in adjusting every account contained therein and carrying the several balances into a ledger, also to cause the Books and papers of the late naval officers, to be brought to his Office, and give them a carefull examination; and finally to exert strenuously the powers of his Office to recover all balances which shall appear to be due to the public, either on those, or on such as remain in the Auditors office.

11th   That the Treasurer be directed to compare all the Warrants issued after the 31st December [17]90, which shall be offered to him in payment with the list of Warrants furnished by the Auditor; and to admit none which shall not appear to have been registered by the Auditor.

12th   That the Treasurer be directed after the abovementioned period to keep his entry and receipt Books, and his list of Warrants so arranged as to be readily compared with the register of Warrants quarterly, and with the Auditors Books annually.

13th   That the Auditor be directed in his account against the Treasurer in the new ledger to charge him with those payments into the Treasury only which shall be made on accounts of debts arising due to the Commonwealth after the 31st of October 1790 each charge to be supported by a receipt from the Treasury, and to credit said accounts against the Treasurer with such sums only as shall have been certified admitted by the committee of the Executive, or the committee of the Assembly at their several examinations; the payments made into the Treasury on public account after the 31st of December 1790, should in future be checked by the entries in the Auditors accounts against the Treasurer at each examination.

14th   That the Treasurer be directed after the next Session, to state his accounts annually up to the 31st of September inclusive for the examination of the Assembly. And that the Auditor and solicitor be directed to make and certify, regular statements of the balances due to the Commonwealth on both the old and new Books, against each succeeding annual Session, to be laid before the General Assembly. These opinions of the Board, formed on the report of their Committee are sent to the officers affected by them, previous to becoming an act of the Executive; who are requested to state any objections, and suggest any alterations or additions, which in their opinion, will tend to make them more useful to the public or more practicable in the Offices.

(See the Current Journal of Oct. 12th 1790.)

Tuesday August 10th 1790

Present

The Governor

Mr. Wood   Mr. Goode
Mr. McClurg   Mr. Briggs

It is advised that the following Deed of Cession to the United States in Congress assembled, of two acres of land for the purpose of erecting a Light-house, be recorded, to wit:

To all who shall see these Presents. I Beverley Randolph Governor of the Commonwealth of Virginia send Greeting.

Whereas the General Assembly of the Commonwealth of Virginia on the thirteenth day of November One thousand seven hundred and eighty nine, passed an act intituled "An Act authorizing the Governor of the Commonwealth, to convey certain land to the United States for the purpose of building a Light-house," in these words following, to wit:

"Be it enacted by the General Assembly, that it shall and may be lawful for the Governor of this Commonwealth, and he is hereby fully authorized, for and in behalf of this Commonwealth by proper deeds and instruments in writing under his hand and the Seal of this Commonwealth, to convey, transfer, assign and make over unto the United States in Congress assembled for the use of the said United States all Interest in and right and title to, as well all the Jurisdiction which this Commonwealth possesses over so much of the Public lands, not exceeding two acres, situate lying and being in the County of *Princess Anne*, at a place commonly called the head land of Cape Henry as shall be sufficient to erect a Light-house, subject to the terms and conditions following; that is to say; that a Light House shall be erected upon the said Land, and that all charges and expences of building, and rebuilding when necessary, and keeping in good repair the said Light-house, together with the Salaries, wages or hire of the person or persons appointed by the President of the United States for the superintendance and care of the same, and all the necessary supplies, with which a Light house ought to be furnished, shall be defrayed out of the Treasury of the United States; If a light house shall not be erected within the space of seven years after the cession of the said two acres of land by this Commonwealth to the United States in Congress Assembled, or if at any time thereafter, the said Light-house shall be suffered to fall into decay, or rendered useless as to the purposes for which it is to be erected, and so continue for the aforesaid period of seven years, then and in those cases the property in the soil and Jurisdiction over the territory hereby directed to be vested in the

United States in Congress assembled, shall revert to this Commonwealth, and be considered as the property, and subject to the jurisdiction of the same, in like manner as if this Act had never been made.

Provided, that nothing in this Act contained, shall be construed to affect the right of this state to any materials heretofore placed at or near Cape Henry for the purpose of erecting a Light-house; and that the Citizens of this Commonwealth shall not, in consequence of this cession, be debarred from the Privileges they now enjoy of hauling their seines and fishing on the shores of the said land so ceded by this Act, to the United States for the purpose of building a Light house." And whereas the said General Assembly by their Resolution of November twenty eighth One thousand seven hundred and eighty nine, had constituted and appointed me the said Beverley Randolph, Governor of the said Commonwealth for one year from the third day of December then next following, which Resolution remains in full force. Now therefore Know ye, that I the said Beverley Randolph, by virtue of the Power and Authority committed to me by the Act of the said General Assembly of Virginia, before recited, and in the name and for and on behalf of the said Commonwealth, do by these presents convey, transfer, assign and make over, unto the United States in Congress Assembled, for the benefit of the said States, Virginia inclusive, all right, title and claim as well of soil as jurisdiction, which the said Commonwealth hath to two Acres of land within the limits of the said Commonwealth situate, lying and being in the County of Princess Anne at a place commonly called the head land of Cape Henry, and bounded as followeth to wit; Beginning eighty eight links to the eastward of an old chimney and running thence south eighty four degrees west four chains to a Stake, thence north six degrees east five chains, thence north eighty four degrees east four chains, and thence south six degrees west five chains to the first station by a survey made the twenty second day of July one thousand seven hundred and ninety, to and for the uses and purposes and on the Conditions of the said recited Act. In Testimony whereof I have subscribed my name and caused the seal of the Commonwealth to be affixed hereunto at Richmond this ninth day of August in the year of our Lord One thousand seven hundred and ninety and of the Commonwealth the fifteenth

Beverley Randolph

L S[128]

---

128. L. S. is an abbreviation for the Latin phrase *locus sigilli*, meaning in place of a seal.

Thursday June 30th 1791[129]

The following report of a Committee of the Executive to examine the offices of Treasurer, Auditor and Solicitor was ordered to be recorded in the Additional Journal viz.

Your Committee, conscious of their own inexperience in the business assigned them, have endeavoured to draw from the officers themselves, such information as might enable them to judge of the alterations necessary to be introduced at the several offices. Their communications are laid before the Board, as afording a ground for their ultimate decision on this subject.

It results from our enquiry, that there are two principal objects of reformation; both of which regard chiefly the Auditor's office: the one relates to the manner of keeping the revenue accounts; the other to the manner of issuing Warrants for claims due from the public, at that office.

I. In the Auditor's office, where all accounts between the public and individuals are by law directed to be kept, no complete statement of any sheriffs account is to be found. This is partly owing to the Auditors books from 1782 to 1787, which were committed first to one of the Antient Auditors and afterwards to the solicitor, having never yet been returned to that office: and partly to the costs, interest and damages accruing on any judgement, obtained against a delinquent sheriff, having never been entered in the account of such Sheriff, stated on the Auditors books. As the books ending in 1787, are now, as we are informed, posted up and a list of balances taken; and as the costs, interest and damages have been stated in the accounts hitherto kept by the solicitor with the Sheriffs in his temporary books, we presume, that the Auditor may be enabled to complete his defective accounts against Sheriffs by a direction to the Solicitor, either to furnish the Auditor with the above-mentioned list of balances, and with the account of Costs, interest and damages in the case of every delinquent sheriff, or to transfer the aforesaid books (viz the ledger ending in 1787, and his temporary books) to the Auditors office.

The same observation will apply to inspectors and other public collectors with whom accounts have been raised in the present books of the Auditor, and who have balances in the books ending in 1787, or against whom judgement has been obtained by the Solicitor.

It is considered as a very desireable thing, that in future the revenue Accounts should be so kept in the Auditors office, that the

___

129. This entry follows that of Sat. 1 Oct. 1791 in the manuscript book of the additional journal. Both dates appear to be correct, however, and thus the entries have been placed in the proper chronological order here.

Solicitor may, at any time, when it is necessary to move for judgement against a public debtor, be furnished from that office with an exact copy of his account. This will relieve him from the necessity of keeping temporary books with the Sheriffs, which may be supposed to interfere with the other various and important duties of his office, and enable him to furnish just and accurate Statements of the revenue, founded on actual receipts, when required by the Assembly.

It is supposed that this cannot be attempted, without distinguishing between past and future transactions; and therefore it is proposed, that all debts, of what kind soever, arising due to the Commonwealth previous to the first of November 1790, shall continue to be entered in the books now kept by the Auditor; and all debts arising due *from* the Commonwealth previous to the first of January 1791, shall also be entered in said books; and Warrants for claims *becoming due* before the said first of January 1791, shall continue to issue in the present manner.

The opening a new Ledger annually and transferring thereto the balances of the former, which is to be carried to the Solicitor's office as directed by the reform of 1786, is complained of by the Auditor, as increasing the trouble of the office, giving greater opportunity to error, and as being intirely useless to the Solicitor, since the balances are altered by subsequent transactions in the Auditors office before he can proceed upon them. It is proposed therefore, that the books in future to be opened at the Auditor's office shall be perfectly annual; and in those to be opened for the next year, shall be entered all debts of what kind soever arising due *to* the Commonwealth after the 31st of October 1790; and all debts arising due *from* the Commonwealth after the 31st of December 1790, and none other.

By this means the revenue, and the expenditures of the current year will appear together, free from the confusion of past, and more obscure transactions. To enable the auditor to have the Accounts of public debtors always ready for the call of the solicitor, it is further suggested that he keep a separate day book for the transactions relating to the revenue, which shall be journalized and posted daily; and that an additional Clerk, if necessary, be employed in journalizing the expenditures, which can be carried at leizure intervals into the same ledger.

II. The issue of warrants at the Auditor's office, being the foundation of all payments at the Treasury, ought to be so checked, that no improper issue shall be made, and no subsequent change in the sum take place, without certain and timely detection. For this purpose it has been proposed, that all warrants to be issued for claims, arising due *from* the commonwealth after the 31st of

December 1790, shall be countersigned by the Solicitor, and that exact registers of them according to their several Species, shall be kept in both the Auditor's and Solicitor's offices. The said Warrants ought to be numbered at the time of their issue, and registered under the same numbers, for the more easy comparison of the Warrant with the Register.

This scheme is more fully explained in the papers herewith referred, nor can we see any other objection to it, than the additional employment it gives the solicitor, who is now, he says, too much occupied to afford the necessary attention to all his duties.

An effectual check upon the issue of interest Warrants, which makes so great a part of the Annual expenditures, will be afforded by an accurate list of all the certificates bearing Interest, registered numerically under their several heads, with a column for the Annual Interest, according to the plan herewith produced. To make this register perfectly satisfactory, it should be kept both in the Auditor's and Solicitor's office; and the old certificates pre-served, to be compared with it monthly, by the Auditor and Solicitor, in presence of a Committee of the Executive, and the new certificates issued in their Stead, must correspond in number, with the Register, and shew in their face their registration attested by both the Solicitor and Auditor. This Scheme is more fully ex-plained in the papers herewith referred. If there is any objection to this compulsion of the holders to exchange their old certificates for new they might still be numbered as they come in with red ink (erasing the old number) and registered, as above, according to these new numbers.

We will add, that, in future, no division of Warrants ought to be permitted at the Auditors office after their issue; that every interest Warrant ought to bear the number of the certificate, on which it issues; and that where more than one Warrant issues on the same certificate, they ought all to bear the same number.

If the Solicitor's office is not made use of to check the ordinary issue of Warrants at the Auditors office, it is Suggested that a daily list of all Warrants issued for claims due from the Public, other than the interest of registered certificates, shall be sent up to this board, and registered in proper form by one of its clerks; and that once in every month a committee of the Executive shall examine the Vouchers in the Auditor's office on which such warrants were issued.

To enable the Treasurer to check counterfeit or altered Warrants offered for payment, it is recommended to furnish him with an exact copy of the register of Certificates bearing interest; and also with a daily return of the warrants issued, agreeable to the register preserved in the Auditor's office.

The Auditor in his Account, in the new books, against the Treasurer, shall charge him with those payments into the Treasury only, which are made on account of debts arising due to the Commonwealth after the 31st of October 1790, each charge to be supported by a receipt from the Treasury, and shall credit said Account against the Treasurer with such Sums only as shall have been certified to have been admitted by the Executive or the committee of the Assembly, at their several examinations; and the payments made into the Treasury on public account after the said 31st of December 1790, shall, in future, be checked by the entries in the Auditor's account against the Treasurer at every examination.

The Treasurer after the above mentioned period, shall keep his entry and receipt books and his list of Warrants so arranged, according to their species and numbers (or dates) as to be readily compared with the registers of Warrants quarterly, and with the Auditor's book annually.

Your committee conceive, that all the paper money books, viz. those of the Auditor, ending January 1782, those of the Commercial Agents Ross and Hay, of Thomas Smith, of Jones and Carrington, of Henry Young, of William Armistead State Agent etc. should remain, or be lodged with the Solicitor; and that he be instructed to use all possible expedition in adjusting every account contained therein, and carrying the several balances into a ledger.

The returns from the late naval officers, which we find not yet made, must also be lodged with the Solicitor, and subjected to his examination.

The Treasury accounts, after the next Session, should be stated annually for the examination of the Assembly up to the 30th of September inclusive, and regular Statements of the balances due from and to the Commonwealth both on the old, and new books, shall be made and certified by the Auditor and Solicitor, and laid before the General Assembly, at each succeeding Annual Session.

James Wood.
James McClurg.
Carter Braxton.

Saturday October 1st 1791

The following Report from the Committee appointed to examine the Treasurers Accounts was read viz.

The under written members of the Executive appointed to examine the Treasurer's accounts have carefully examined the specie, Tobacco and Bills of Credit of the 18th of March 1780 remaining in the Treasury on the thirtieth of September 1791; (on which day the Treasurer is directed to close the Annual Accounts of his Office) and find in specie the sum of three thousand five hundred and forty five pounds ½. Notes for crop Tobacco to the amount of three hundred and fifty nine Hogsheads, quantity three hundred and sixty nine thousand five hundred and thirty five pounds nett; also eight Hogsheads of light Crop, quantity seven thousand and eighty six Gro[ss]: and twenty one thousand two hundred and thirty pounds, gro[ss] transfer; making in the whole twenty five thousand seven hundred and forty two pounds nett Transfer, and amounting (at the rates of which the said Tobacco were received agreeably to law) to five thousand three hundred and fifty three pounds eleven shillings and eight pence. We find also bills of Credit of the 18th of March 1780, commonly called one for 40 money to the amount of eighty five Pounds 16/. received likewise in part of the Arrearages of Taxes.

James McClurg.
Robt. Goode.

Accounts

EDITOR'S NOTE

On 14 December 1787 the Virginia General Assembly, concerned about the size of the commonwealth's financial obligations, established a sinking fund, which it hoped would "in a few years redeem a great proportion of the public debt, and enable government greatly to reduce the present amount of taxes."[130] The governor and Council of State were directed to establish the fund (using surplus state revenues, military and other securities owned by the commonwealth, and money raised through the sale and export of tobacco) and were made responsible for its administration. The Council appointed an agent, Anthony Singleton, to oversee the new sinking fund, but required that he consult with the executive board at least once a month. The Council also decided that periodic statements of the agent's financial transactions would be recorded in their additional journal.[131]

In accord with this decision, the Council's clerk copied into the additional journal the seven accounts that follow. Each set of accounts bears the signatures of the committee of Council members chosen to review and approve the sinking fund agent's work. The first set of accounts covers the period 19 July through 31 October 1788; the second, 31 October through 31 December 1788; the third, 31 December 1788 through 30 April 1789; and the fourth, 30 April through 31 June 1789. The agent's statements appear less frequently in the additional journal after June 1789. The fifth set of accounts is dated 19 October 1789; the sixth, 12 May 1790; and the seventh, 11 May 1791.

The sinking fund lasted only five years. It was abolished by the General Assembly on 7 December 1792.

---

130. William Waller Hening, ed., *The Statutes at Large; Being a Collection of All the Laws of Virginia* . . . , 13 vols. (Richmond, 1809–1823), 12:452–454.
131. *See* H. R. McIlwaine et al., eds., *Journals of the Council of the State of Virginia*, 5 vols. (Richmond, 1931–1982), 4:355–359.

Whole amount of Specie received from the Treasury for the purpose of purchasing public Securities	13478	12	6
Amount received in Tobacco from the Treasury for the same purpose at the rates which the Tobacco was sold	1739	19	6
By which it appears that the nett sum of has been made to the State by the sinkg. Fund	63208	18	3¾
	78427	10	3¾

Note—In the above sum of £63208.18.3¾
made by the sinking Fund is included the
of £14552.3.7½ of Warrants drawn from
the Auditors for Interest on the Certificates
which have been taken in at the Treasury
for Taxes. Likewise the sum of £2831.8.1
of Interest Warrants drawn from the Auditors
on Military Certificates purchased.

There are on hand as examined by the Executive Final settlements to the amount of		27	6	9
Military Certificates	£59309.7.8			
A surplus military certificates	49.9.10	59358	17	6
Sixth years Military Interest Warrants		11	11	6
Funded Certificates		67	17	1
Loan Office Certificates		1725	—	3
Interest Warrants on do.		103	1	2
Contingent Fund Warrants		32	17	9
Indents drawn on Final settlements purchased		485	19	4
Seventh years Military Interest Warrants		148	11	10
Specie in hand		3386	9	0¾
Also Sundry public Securities likewise examined by the Executive purchased with the approbation of that board conditionally for which Advances were made to the Amount of		13079	18	1
		78427	10	3¾

Anthony Singleton
Agent of Sinking Fund

October 19th 1789

By order of the Executive, we have examined the Books of the Agent, the public securities, and the Specie in his hands, and find the above Statement to be true.

James McClurg
Carter Braxton

Amount of Specie drawn from the Treasury for the purposes of the Sinking fund	13,478	12	6
Amount of Tobo Received from the Treasury for same purpose at rates it was Sold	1,739	19	6
Nett sum of Profits appears to be	99,629	1	1½
	114,847	13	1½

Final Settlements on hand	27	6	9
Military Certificates on do	102,889	17	2
Funded Certificates on do	420	16	5
Loan Office Certificates on do	3,349	19	1¼
Indents on do	485	19	4
Interest Warrants on Military Certificates on do	5,791	9	10¼
Specie on hand	1,882	4	6
	114,847	13	1½

A Singleton Agt. S F

May 12th 1790

We have examined the Books of the Agent, The papers & Specie in his hands, and find the above Statement true.

James McClurg

Carter Braxton

May 11	To whole amount of Specie drawn from the Treasury for the purposes of the Sinking Fund	13575	13	11
	Amount received in Tobacco from the Treasury for same Purposes at rates which it sold	4449	11	7¾
	The nett sum made to the state by the sinking Fund appears to be	126094	9	3¼
		144119	14	10

11th day of May 1791.   *Cr.*

1791

May 11	By Final Settlements on hand		65	8	9
	Military Certificates do.		134478	3	3
	Funded Paper Money Certificates do.		802	16	6
	Loan office Certificates	do.	8445	15	0¼
	Crop Tobacco	do.	326	8	
	Specie for balance	do.	1	3	3¾
			144119	14	10

E[rrors] E[xcepted] Anth.y Singleton
Agent of S. Fund.

May 11th 1791.

We have examined the books of the Agent, the papers and specie in his hands, and certify the above Statement true.

Jas. McClurg.

J Dawson.

Textual Notes

Page 1, line 10: Several words appear to have been erased between the word "service" and the word "And."

Page 4, line 4: A word appears to have been erased between the word "pursued" and the word "It."

Page 6, line 19: A word between the words "employed" and "Mr." appears to have been erased. The word "by" was written over the erased word.

Page 7, line 36: The clerk inadvertently misspelled the word "Scouts" and wrote "Scouets." This error has been corrected in the printed text.

Page 19, line 9 under 18 Dec. 1788: Several words after the words "fifteen shillings" appear to have been erased. The erased words appear to have been "to be paid out of any money in the Treasury." These words were replaced with a series of dashes and ditto marks.

Page 19, line 15 under 18 Dec. 1788: The clerk originally appears to have begun the sentence with the words "On the." The word "the" appears to have been erased and the word "recommendation" written in its place.

Page 23, line 4: A word after "arrears of" appears to have been erased, and the word "taxes" was written over it.

Page 23, line 5: A word after "until the" appears to have been erased, and "10th" was written over it.

Page 23, line 7: The clerk inadvertently misspelled the name "John" and wrote "Jhon." This error has been corrected in the printed text.

Page 28, line 28: The clerk inadvertently misspelled the word "either" and wrote "eithier." This error has been corrected in the printed text.

Page 28, line 45: Two words appear to have been erased and crossed out between the words "three" and "quarters." The erased words appear to have been "and a."

Page 29, line 21: A word after the words "John Tyler" appears to have been erased. The erased word appears to have been "and."

Page 29, line 22: Several words after the word "Henry" appear to have been erased. The words "and Cuthbert Bullit" were written in place of the erased words.

Page 33, line 5: The clerk inadvertently misspelled the word "Comptroller" and wrote "Comptrollen." This error has been corrected in the printed text.

Page 34, line 28: The clerk inadvertently misspelled the word "motions" and wrote "motitions." He corrected the mistake by crossing the first "ti" out.

Page 36, line 33: Several words after the word "Treasurer" appear to have been erased and replaced with a series of dashes.

Page 36, line 40: Several words appear to have been erased after the word "John." The words "Croudson, George Travell" were written in place of the erased words.

Page 38, lines 22 and 23: A word appears to have been erased between the words "amount of the" and "Certificates." The word "military" was written in place of the erased word.

Page 38, line 23: Several words appear to have been erased between the word "have" and the word "come." The words "by any means" were inserted in place of the erased words.

Page 38, line 29: A word after the word "distinguish" appears to have been erased. The word "in" was written in place of the erased word.

Page 40, line 12: A number written before the words "Day of December" appears to have been erased. "31st" was inserted in place of the erased number.

Page 41, line 3: A word between the word "She" and the word "until" appears to have been erased. The word "reprieved" was written in place of the erased word.

Page 44, line 21: Several words at the end of the sentence following the words "his opinion thereon" appear to have been erased.

Page 45, lines 36 and 37: A word appears to have been erased between "20 privates" and the words "one Captain." The word "Frederick" was written in place of the erased word.

Page 45, line 44: The clerk inadvertently misspelled the word "advice" and wrote "advise." This error has been corrected in the printed text.

Page 46, lines 10 through 13 under 9 Feb. 1789: Several lines appear to have been erased following the words "a letter from." Written in place of the erased words was "Gabriel Fawlks esquire appointed President of a General Court martial for the trial of Col. Pauling Anderson, stating that one of the Field Officers appointed to serve as a member had failed to attend. It is advised that the said."

Page 47, line 7 under 12 Feb. 1789: The clerk inadvertently misspelled the word "Fund" and wrote "Fumd." The error has been corrected in the printed text.

Page 53, line 31: A word between the word "Negroes" and the word "belonging" appears to have been crossed out.

Page 54, line 6: A word between the word "second" and the words "of Henrico" appears to have been erased. The word "Regiment" was written in place of the erased word.

Page 56, lines 10 and 11: The clerk inadvertently misspelled the word "Lieutenant" and wrote "Leuitenant." This error has been corrected in the printed text.

Page 57, line 9: The clerk inadvertently misspelled the word "General" and wrote "Ganeral." This error has been corrected in the printed text.

Page 58, line 2: The clerk inadvertently misspelled the word "annum" and wrote "annun." This error has been corrected in the printed text.

Page 76, line 37: A word appears to have been erased between the word "of" and the word "Judgment." The word "Berkeley" was written in place of the erased word.

Page 79, lines 20 and 21: Several words appear to have been crossed out between the words "not to" and the words "against the." The crossed-out words appear to have been "go out." The words "be pursued" were written in place of the erased words.

Page 91, line 28: A word between the word "imposed" and the words "in May" appears to have been erased. A long dash was written in the text in place of the erased word.

Page 91, line 42: A word appears to have been erased between the words "President of" and the words "be informed." The erased word appears to have been "Congress." The words "the United States" were written in place of the erased word.

Page 95, line 7: Several words between the word "commission" and the word "appointing" appear to have been erased. A series of dashes was written in the text in place of the erased words.

Page 95, line 10: A word following the words "Samuel Sherwin" appears to have been erased. The erased word appears to have been "Sheriff." The word "Gentleman" was written in place of the erased word.

Page 95, line 35: A word appears to have been erased and crossed out between the word "Article" and the words "of debit."

Page 109, line 22: A word between the words "as to the" and "of conveying" appears to have been erased. The word "mode" was written in place of the erased word.

Page 114, line 27: The word after "8th of" appears to have been erased. The erased word appears to have been "April." The word "March" was written in place of the erased word.

Page 116, lines 3 and 4: Several words between the words "shillings each" and "Mr. Langhorne" appear to have been erased. The words "for copies of Vouchers furnished" were written in place of the erased words.

Page 119, line 8: A word between the word "Solicitor" and the words "fifty pounds" appears to have been erased. Dashes were written in the text in place of the erased word.

Page 131, line 20: The clerk inadvertently misspelled the word "proclamation" and wrote "ploclamation." This error has been corrected in the printed text.

Page 134, line 10 under 14 Nov. 1789: The clerk misspelled the word "Guadalupe" and wrote "Guardalupe." This error has been corrected in the printed text.

Page 142, line 8: Several words appear to have been erased between the word "Second" and the word "drawn." The word "Bills" and several dashes were written in the text in place of the erased words.

Page 143, line 30: The clerk inadvertently wrote "united," instead of the word "unite." This error has been corrected in the printed text.

Page 145, line 5 under 19 Dec. 1789: The clerk misspelled the word "point" and wrote "poimt." This error has been corrected in the printed text.

Page 156, line 15: Following the word "Donaldson" the clerk wrote the word "for" twice, then crossed out the second "for."

Page 167, line 7 under 8 Mar. 1790: A word after the words "Thomas Roane" appears to have been crossed out. The word "Sheriff" was written over it.

Page 168, line 14: The clerk wrote "ac" at the end of a line, and then wrote the word "account" at the beginning of the next line. The first "ac" was then crossed out.

Page 172, lines 16 and 17 under 25 Mar. 1790: Several words between "It is advised that" and "have three children" appear to have been erased. The words "Elizabeth Shipwash who is 45 years old and" were written in place of the erased words.

Page 175, line 11: A word following "for money" appears to have been erased. The word "or" was written in place of the erased word.

Page 184, line 5 under 15 May 1790: The clerk originally wrote "Dollar per Day day." The first "Day" was then crossed out.

Page 202, lines 4 through 6: Following the words "appearing that he has" the clerk originally wrote "done more duty." The words "done more duty" were then crossed out and "been longer in Commission as a Justice without having the Sheriffs office" was written in the text in place of the crossed-out words.

Page 237, line 24: Two words following the word "drawn" appear to have been erased and crossed out.

Page 239, lines 25 and 26: Several words between "have no" and "with such cases" appear to have been erased. The words "power to interfere" were written in the place of the erased words.

Page 241, line 9 under 20 Dec. 1790: The clerk inadvertently wrote "sixty livers" instead of "sixty livres." This error has been corrected in the printed text.

Page 282, lines 2 and 3 under 5 May 1791: A word appears to have been erased and crossed out between the word "obtained" and "against."

Page 284, line 9: A word appears to have been erased and crossed out between the word "public" and the word "tobacco."

Page 285, line 27: A word appears to have been erased and crossed out between the word "commencing" and the words "the first."

Page 310, line 3: A word appears to have been erased between the word "attending" and the word "their." The word "with" was written in place of the erased word.

Page 315, lines 21 and 22 under 15 Sept. 1791: A word appears to have been erased and crossed out between the word "Brough" and the word "resigned."

Page 315, line 28: Several words appear to have been erased following the word "Fletcher." The word "deceased" was written in place of the erased words.

Page 329, line 6: A word between the words "belonging to the" and the word

"Shot" appears to have been erased. The word "State" was written in place of the erased word.

Page 349, line 20: The clerk originally wrote "certified and admitted," then crossed out the word "and."

Page 354, lines 12 through 14: The clerk inadvertently wrote the phrase "which makes so great a part of the Annual expenditures, will be afforded by an accurate list" twice in the journal. This error has been corrected in the printed text.

Page 355, lines 1 and 2: The clerk originally wrote "against the Treasury." The word "Treasury" was then erased and the word "Treasurer" was written in its place.

Page 355, line 11: The clerk inadvertently wrote "the Treasurer at at every." This error has been corrected in the printed text.

Members of the Committee of Safety and the Council of State 1775–1791

Fifty-five Virginians served as members of the Committee of Safety or the Council of State from August 1775 through November 1791, the period covered by the five volumes in the *Journals of the Council of the State of Virginia* series published by the Virginia State Library.

The eleven-member Committee of Safety, created in August 1775 by Virginia's third revolutionary convention, functioned as the executive body of Virginia between the collapse of royal authority in 1775 and the establishment of republican government under the Constitution of 1776. Originally this committee was established to administer the colony until the meeting of the fourth convention in December 1775. In January 1776, however, that convention extended the life of the committee and chose nine of the original eleven members and two new members to constitute the Committee of Safety that governed Virginia through 5 July 1776.

The Constitution of 1776, which went into effect on 6 July, created a plural executive consisting of a governor and an eight-member advisory council, the Council of State, chosen by a joint ballot of the Senate and House of Delegates. The constitution specified no term of office for councillors, but it required the General Assembly to remove two members of the Council every third year and declared those persons ineligible to return to the executive board until three years after their removal.

The fifth convention, which had written the constitution, chose the first councillors on 29 June 1776, but stipulated that these men would serve only until the May 1777 session of the General Assembly. On 29 May 1777 the assembly reelected seven incumbent councillors and chose one new member for the board. After that, the assembly filled vacancies on the Council when they occurred and removed two members every third year as required by the constitution: the assembly removed two councillors on 17 June 1779 and on 28 May 1782 and elected new members to replace them, respectively, on 17 June 1779 and 5 June 1782. After May 1784, however, the General Assembly stopped meeting in the spring and met annually only in the autumn. Hence, starting in October 1784 the assembly held its triennial votes for the removal of councillors several months before the lame-duck councillors' terms expired. Thus, in the period for which the Council journals have been published, the members removed by votes of the General Assembly on 17 November 1784, 31 October 1787, and 12 November 1790 were not required to leave the Council until June of the following years, and, similarly, new members chosen by the General Assembly on 19 November 1784, 7 November 1787, and 26 November 1790 did not take office until each following June.

Information for the biographical sketches of the men who served on the Council of State or the Committee of Safety came both from the standard secondary sources for Virginia history and from manuscripts in the collections of the Virginia State Library and the Virginia Historical Society.

Jacquelin Ambler (1742–1798) was born on 9 August 1742, the fourth son of Richard and Elizabeth (Jacquelin) Ambler, of Yorktown. He attended the College of William and Mary and studied trade and commerce in the firm of a prominent Philadelphia merchant. His education completed, Ambler returned to Yorktown and joined his father in the mercantile business. In 1771 he was appointed sheriff of York County, and in 1774 he became naval officer for the York River district, a post he held for nearly three years. In December 1778 he was named a justice of the peace for York County.

Ambler held his first statewide office from 28 April to 23 June 1779, when he served as a commissioner of Virginia's Navy Board. The board was abolished by the General Assembly during the May 1779 session, but on 17 June 1779 the legislature chose Ambler to sit on the newly created, three-man Board of Trade. He remained in this position through May 1780, when a bill to do away with that board was introduced in the assembly. Correctly anticipating that the bill would pass (as it did on 8 July), Ambler was pleased when the assembly elected him to fill a vacancy on the Council of State. Ambler moved his family from Williamsburg to Richmond, the new state capital, within weeks of his 24 May election. He was in attendance as a member of the executive council by 20 June 1780.

Ambler remained a councillor until 13 April 1782, when he resigned to accept an appointment as interim treasurer of the commonwealth in place of George Brooke, who had died. On 28 May 1782 the General Assembly elected Ambler to the position in his own right. While treasurer, Ambler also became active in Richmond city government, serving as a member of the city's first board of aldermen from 3 July 1782 to 1 May 1783. The General Assembly reelected him to the treasurer's office each year until his death on 10 January 1798.

John Banister (1734–1788), the son of John and Wilmette Banister, of Hatcher's Run in Dinwiddie County, was born on 26 December 1734. He received his education at a private school near Wakefield, England, and was admitted to the Middle Temple in September 1753. He practiced law in Petersburg after his return to Virginia, but he also devoted much of his time to managing his fashionable and profitable Dinwiddie County estate, Battersea.

Banister's public career began in July 1765, when he was elected to the House of Burgesses from Dinwiddie County to serve in the assembly of 1766–1768. He was not returned to the short-lived assembly of May 1769, but was again a member of the House from November 1769 through May 1776. From 1774 through 1776 Banister also represented Dinwiddie at all five of Virginia's revolutionary conventions, and after independence had been declared he served in the House of Delegates from October 1776 through January 1778. Elected on 19 November 1777 a delegate to the Continental Congress, he attended Congress at Philadelphia from March through September 1778, resigning shortly thereafter. While a delegate he helped to frame the Articles of Confederation and signed the final document.

During the American Revolution, Banister served as a lieutenant colonel in the Virginia militia and county lieutenant of Dinwiddie, and he took part in the defense of Petersburg in April 1781. His Dinwiddie County constituents sent him to the House of Delegates from May 1781 through the end of the May 1782 session. On 5 June 1782 the General Assembly elected him to the Council of State. He attended his first meeting on 4 July, but thereafter was present at the board only sporadically until 17 October; early in November 1782 he submitted his resignation. He returned once more to the House, participating in the May and October sessions of 1783. In December 1783 Banister retired to Battersea and involved himself in local civic affairs, serving as the first mayor of Petersburg following the town's incorporation in 1784. He died at his home on 30 September 1788.

John Blair (1732–1800) was born in Williamsburg in 1732, the son of John and Mary (Monro) Blair. He received his collegiate education at the College of William and Mary and then studied law in England at the Middle Temple. He entered the bar upon his return to Virginia and laid the groundwork for an illustrious legal career. It was inevitable that Blair would also hold public office, as his family had long been prominent in the political affairs of the Virginia colony. His father had been a member of the House of Burgesses for many years, deputy auditor general for more than forty years, a member of the governor's

Council since 1745, and several times, as president of the Council, acting governor of the colony. Young Blair represented the College of William and Mary in the House of Burgesses in the assemblies of 1766–1768 and 1769, and in the first two sessions of the assembly of 1769–1771. He resigned before the 1771 session, as on 30 August 1770 he was appointed to replace Nathaniel Walthoe as clerk of the Council. Blair also served two terms as mayor of Williamsburg, from November 1769 to November 1770 and from November 1773 to November 1774.

Blair remained clerk of the colonial Council through 1775. In January 1776, after the collapse of the royal government in Virginia, he accepted an appointment as a judge of the admiralty court that had been created by the fourth revolutionary convention. Following the adoption of the Virginia constitution, he was elected to the Council of State on 29 June 1776. Blair was reelected to the Council the following May and served until 28 February 1778, when he resigned to become a judge of the General Court. In 1779 Blair became the chief justice of that court and a member of Virginia's first Court of Appeals. On 23 November 1780 he was elected to succeed Robert Carter Nicholas on the High Court of Chancery.

Blair was chosen in December 1786 to be one of Virginia's delegates to the Philadelphia convention of May 1787, and he was one of the three representatives from Virginia to vote for and sign the United States Constitution. He supported ratification of the Constitution at Virginia's Convention of 1788, which he attended on behalf of York County.

Blair continued to serve on the High Court of Chancery until December 1788, when he was elevated to Virginia's newly formed Supreme Court of Appeals. He served only briefly on this court, however, for on 30 September 1789 President George Washington appointed him an associate justice of the Supreme Court of the United States. Blair remained on the Supreme Court until 27 January 1796, when he resigned in failing health. He returned to Williamsburg, where he lived until his death on 31 August 1800.

Richard Bland (1710–1776) was born in Williamsburg on 6 May 1710 to Richard Bland and his second wife, Elizabeth Randolph Bland. He was educated at the College of William and Mary and may also have studied at the University of Edinburgh. A member of a prominent tidewater family, Bland quickly became an influential figure in county and colonial politics. His Prince George County constituents chose him to represent their interests in the assembly of 1742–1747 and continued to return him to the House of Burgesses through 1776. As a burgess he steadfastly defended the rights of Virginia's assembly against king and Parliament, and he articulated the colonial position on parliamentary taxation during the Stamp Act crisis in a pamphlet entitled *An Inquiry into the Rights of the British Colonies* . . . (Williamsburg, 1766).

Bland initially hoped that America's problems with Great Britain could be resolved peacefully and without separation from the mother country; he worked toward that end as a member of Virginia's committee of correspondence in 1773. He was elected to all five of Virginia's revolutionary conventions and to the Committee of Safety in 1775 and 1776. He served as a delegate to the Continental Congress during 1774 and 1775, but when reelected in August 1775 he declined to serve, excusing himself as "an Old man, almost deprived of sight." Despite his infirmity, Bland continued to participate in Virginia politics, serving in the fifth revolutionary convention and in the first session of the House of Delegates, which began on 7 October 1776, until his death on 26 October 1776.

Carter Braxton (1736–1797), the second son of George and Mary (Carter) Braxton, was born on 10 September 1736 in King and Queen County. Braxton studied for several years at the College of William and Mary but left school at the age of eighteen to marry Judith Robinson, a niece of Speaker John Robinson. Following his wife's death in 1757, Braxton left Virginia and traveled to England, where he remained for two years. Several months after his return in the fall of 1760, Braxton won election in King William County to the House of Burgesses.

Braxton served in the House of Burgesses from the assembly of 1760–1765 through the assembly of 1769–1771. In the fall of 1771 he left the House to accept an appointment as sheriff of King William County, a position he held until 1773. He resigned this post, however, to stand again for a seat in the House. Elected a burgess in July 1774, Braxton also became a member of the first four of Virginia's revolutionary conventions. On 17 August 1775 the third convention elected him to Virginia's Committee of Safety, and on 15 December the fourth convention named him a delegate to the Continental Congress. Braxton served in Congress at Philadelphia from February through August 1776. Although Braxton was more reluctant than many Virginians to declare independence from Great Britain, he supported that move once Congress made its decision, and he signed the Declaration of Independence.

Braxton returned to Virginia and served in the new House of Delegates from October 1776 through January 1778. He then retired briefly from public life to revive his sagging mercantile business. During the war he also procured needed commodities for the American army. Braxton soon returned to public service in the House of Delegates, representing King William County from May 1779 through January 1782, from May through December 1783, and from October 1785 through January 1786.

On 15 November 1785 the General Assembly elected Braxton to the Council of State in place of William Nelson, who had resigned. Braxton served on the Council until 28 May 1791, when he left in compliance with a General Assembly vote removing him from the executive board. On 12 November 1793, precisely three years after the assembly vote that removed him, Braxton was reelected to a seat on the Council. He remained an active member of the executive board until his death in Richmond on 10 October 1797.

John Howell Briggs (ca. 1755–ca. 1810), the son of Gray and Dorothea (Pleasants) Briggs, of Dinwiddie County, was born in the mid-1750s. Few records from eighteenth-century Dinwiddie County survive, and very little is known about Briggs's life. He served as an ensign in the revolutionary army under the command of Robert Bolling, and after the Revolution he purchased or inherited land in Sussex County. He represented Sussex in the House of Delegates from May 1784 through December 1789 and in the Virginia Convention of 1788, where he voted against ratification of the United States Constitution. On 28 November 1789 he was elected to the Council of State. Briggs took his seat on the Council on 21 December 1789 and served until 28 October 1793, when he resigned. He did not hold further statewide office, but did remain active in county politics. In 1800 he served as a member of the Republican committee for Sussex County. Briggs died before June 1810.

Hardin Burnley (1761–1809), the eldest son of Zachariah and Mary (Bell) Burnley, of Orange County, was born on 19 March 1761. As a young man he studied law under George Wythe in Williamsburg, and at the age of twenty-six he stood for election to the House of Delegates from his native county. He won this and several subsequent elections, serving in the House from October 1787 through December 1790. On 26 November 1790 the General Assembly elected Burnley to the Council of State in place of Thomas Madison, who had resigned. After completing his term in the House he took his seat on the executive board on 4 March 1791 and remained a member of the Council until December 1799. In his capacity as president of the Council, he acted as governor of the commonwealth from 7 to 11 December 1796. Following his resignation, Burnley appears to have retired from public life. He died on 11 March 1809 in Hanover County, after a protracted illness, at the age of forty-eight.

William Cabell (1730–1798), the eldest son of William and Elizabeth (Burks) Cabell, was born on 13 March 1730, probably near Dover in Goochland County. According to family tradition, he received his education at the College of William and Mary. As a young man he learned the art of surveying by working as an assistant in his father's business; he also began to acquire substantial landholdings throughout Albemarle County. Shortly after he turned twenty-one he became a deputy sheriff, justice of the peace, and militia officer for Albemarle County and a vestryman of Saint Anne's Parish. From May 1756 through April 1761 he also represented Albemarle in the House of Burgesses. When the General Assembly created Amherst County from southwestern Albemarle in 1761, Cabell took an active part in the organization and early government of the new polity. He served as the first presiding magistrate of the Amherst County court and as the county's first surveyor, lieutenant, and coroner. He also represented Amherst in the House from 1761 through 1776.

As the conflict between Great Britain and the American colonies mounted in the 1770s, Cabell served as chairman of Amherst County's revolutionary committee; on 17 August 1775 he was chosen a member of the Committee of Safety, to which he was reelected the following December. He attended all five of Virginia's revolutionary conventions and served as the first state senator for the district of Buckingham, Albemarle, and Amherst counties from October 1776 through March 1781. He left the Senate in 1781, but he was promptly elected to the House of Delegates from Amherst. On 12 June 1781 the assembly elected him to the Council of State. He declined this position, however, apparently preferring to remain in the House. Cabell served in the House of Delegates from May 1781 through December 1783 and from October 1787 through December 1788. He represented Amherst at the Convention of 1788 as well, where he voted against the United States Constitution. Cabell retired from state government following the assembly of 1788, although he remained active in local affairs and on the board of trustees of Hampden-Sydney College. He died at his Amherst County estate, Union Hill, on 23 March 1798.

Paul Carrington (1733–1818), the eldest of George and Anne (Mayo) Carrington's eleven children, was born on 16 March 1733 in Cumberland County. As a young man he was apprenticed to study law under Clement Read, the influential clerk of the Lunenburg County court. After receiving his law license in May 1755, Carrington practiced law before several county courts and became deputy king's attorney for the counties of Bedford, in May 1756; Mecklenburg, in April 1768; Botetourt, in May 1770; and Lunenburg, in October 1770. On 21 January 1773 he appeared before the Halifax County court and took "the usual Oaths to his Majestys Person and Government . . . and also took the Oath of a County Court Clerk." Carrington remained clerk of Halifax until his resignation on 15 August 1776. While holding these positions, he also represented Charlotte County in the House of Burgesses from the county's formation in 1765 through the final session of the House in 1776.

Carrington was chairman of the Charlotte County revolutionary committee, and he attended all five of Virginia's revolutionary conventions. On 17 August 1775 he was elected to the Committee of Safety, and he was reelected the following December. When the General Assembly organized the judicial system for the new commonwealth of Virginia, it placed Paul Carrington on the General Court. Elected to the court on 23 January 1778, he became chief justice in November 1780. As a General Court justice he also served, along with admiralty and High Court of Chancery judges, on Virginia's Court of Appeals. When the assembly reorganized the judiciary in December 1788 and created an independent Supreme Court of Appeals, it elected Carrington one of the new court's five judges. Carrington served on Virginia's Supreme Court from June 1789 until 1 January 1807, when he resigned. Carrington's public service also included attendance at the Convention of 1788, at which he supported ratification of the United States Constitution. At the end of his judicial career, Carrington retired to his Charlotte County estate, Mulberry Hill, where he died on 23 January 1818.

Charles Carter (1733–1796), born in King George County in 1733, was the son of Charles and Mary (Walker) Carter, of Cleve, and a grandson of Robert ("King") Carter. At the age of twenty-three he entered the House of Burgesses for King George County and served from the assembly of 1756–1758 through that of 1769–1771. During his first eight and a half years as a burgess, Carter represented King George County alongside his father, who died in 1764. Sometime between 1771 and 1773, Carter moved to an estate called Ludlow, in Stafford County near Fredericksburg. When Yelverton Peyton resigned from the House of Burgesses after the first session of the 1772–1774 assembly, Carter replaced him as a burgess for Stafford. He represented the county in the House through 1776.

Charles Carter, who is often confused with his cousin Charles Carter of Shirley (1732–1806), was a member of Virginia's first four revolutionary conventions. Although he was not elected to the fifth, his Stafford constituents did send him to the new House of Delegates, where he sat from October 1776 through October 1779. Carter resigned during the October 1779 session to become sheriff of Stafford County. By May 1782 he had left this position and returned to the House of Delegates, where he remained through December 1783. In 1789 Carter was chosen a state senator for the district encompassing Westmoreland, Stafford, and King George counties. He served only a few weeks, however, as on 28 November 1789 he was elected a member of the Council of State. Carter attended his first Council meeting on 2 December 1789 and served until the spring of 1791, when he left the executive board as one of the two councillors removed by vote of the General Assembly on 12 November 1790. Carter died in 1796, probably in Fredericksburg.

William Christian (ca. 1743–1786) was born early in the 1740s in Augusta County to Israel and Elizabeth (Stark) Christian. He entered the Augusta County militia in his teens, and by the age of twenty he had attained the rank of captain. For a short time he studied law under Patrick Henry, and from March 1773 through 1776 he represented the new county of Fincastle in the House of Burgesses. Christian was an avid supporter of Virginia's move toward independence and was elected by his Fincastle constituents to the first three of Virginia's revolutionary conventions. He served only at the second and third, however, as he was recruiting a regiment of Fincastle militiamen for service in Dunmore's War while the first convention was in session. In August 1775 Christian was appointed lieutenant colonel of the 1st Virginia Regiment of Foot, which became part of the Continental army in January 1776. He was promoted to colonel, but resigned his commission in the summer of 1776 to become a colonel in the Virginia militia. That fall he led a punitive expedition against the Cherokee Indians in the vicinity of the Holston River.

Christian represented Botetourt and Fincastle counties in the first Virginia Senate, from October to December 1776, and from May 1780 through December 1783 he served in the Senate for Botetourt and several new southwestern Virginia counties. Christian became a member of the Council of State on 27 November 1783 but attended only a few meetings during his two-year tenure on the board. On 17 November 1784 the General Assembly designated him as one of the councillors to be removed in the spring of 1785. Shortly after leaving the Council, Christian moved to Kentucky. He died on 9 April 1786 while leading an expedition against Indian tribes in what is today the state of Indiana.

Bartholomew Dandridge (1737–1785), the fourth child of John and Frances (Jones) Dandridge, was born in New Kent County on 25 December 1737. He entered the legal profession and established a successful practice in the county court system. At the age of thirty-five he became a burgess for New Kent County, serving in the assemblies of 1772–1774 and 1775–1776. Dandridge also represented his native county at all five of Virginia's revolutionary conventions. On 29 June 1776, the fifth revolutionary convention named him one of the first members of the Council of State. Dandridge sat on the executive board until mid-January 1778, when he resigned in order to run again for a seat in the General Assembly. He served in the House of Delegates for New Kent County in the May 1778 session but left that position when, on 30 May 1778, he was elected a judge of the General Court. Dandridge remained on the court until his death on 18 April 1785.

John Dawson (1762–1814), the son of Musgrave and Mary (Waugh) Dawson, of Caroline County, was born in 1762. Following his graduation from Harvard University in 1782, Dawson returned to

Virginia to practice law. At the age of twenty-four he was elected to represent Spotsylvania County in Virginia's House of Delegates, where he served from October 1786 through December 1789. He also attended the Convention of 1788, voting against ratification of the United States Constitution, and he represented the commonwealth at the last session of the Continental Congress, which met from November 1788 through March 1789.

On 16 December 1789, the Virginia General Assembly chose Dawson to replace Cyrus Griffin on the Council of State. Dawson remained a member of the Council until April 1797, when he resigned in order to take a seat in the United States House of Representatives. While a congressman, Dawson carried several diplomatic dispatches to France for President John Adams in 1801 and volunteered as an aide to Generals Jacob Brown and Andrew Jackson when war with Great Britain broke out in 1812. He served in Congress from 1797 until his death from tuberculosis on 30 March 1814.

Dudley Digges (1729–1790), the third son of Cole and Elizabeth (Power) Digges, was born in 1729 in York County into a family long prominent in the political affairs of the Virginia colony. He joined the militia in York County while still in his teens, and by the age of twenty-one he had risen to the rank of colonel. At twenty-three he stood for election to the House of Burgesses from York County, winning that and every subsequent election until 1776, when the House of Burgesses ceased to exist. In March 1773 Digges was chosen a member of the Virginia committee of correspondence. He attended all five of Virginia's revolutionary conventions and also served on the Virginia Committee of Safety in 1775 and 1776.

On 29 June 1776, the General Assembly chose Digges to be one of the first members of the Council of State. From April 1780 until May 1781 he was president of the Council, and, as such, acted as lieutenant governor of the commonwealth whenever Governor Thomas Jefferson was absent from the capital. He remained on the executive board until 14 May 1781, when he resigned in order to attend to pressing family and financial obligations. A year later, on 5 June 1782, the General Assembly reelected Digges to the Council, but he declined to serve. He remained active in county affairs, however, serving as sheriff of James City County from 10 March 1789 until his death on 3 June 1790.

William Fleming (1728–1795), son of Leonard and Dorothea (Saterthwaite) Fleming, was born on 7 February 1728 in Jedburgh, Scotland. Fleming served as an apprentice to a surgeon in Dumfries, Scotland, and also studied pharmacy with an eminent Scottish apothecary before enrolling as a medical student at the University of Edinburgh in 1746. There is evidence to suggest that following his medical studies Fleming worked as a surgeon either in the British navy or on an English merchant ship. Early in the 1750s his travels brought him to Virginia.

In 1755 Fleming accepted an ensign's commission in the Virginia militia, and he fought for eight years in the French and Indian War. At the war's close he settled in Staunton, where he practiced medicine. In 1768 he moved his family to an estate called Belmont in the southwestern part of Augusta County. A year later the General Assembly separated the area in which Fleming lived from Augusta and created Botetourt County. Fleming helped to establish the government of the new county and became a justice of the Botetourt County court. In June 1774 he was appointed colonel of the Botetourt militia. In October of that year he fought in Dunmore's War at the battle of Point Pleasant, where he received a serious wound from which he never fully recovered. Although his health kept him from active military duty in the Revolution, he did serve as county lieutenant of Botetourt during the war, and from May 1777 through June 1779 he sat in the General Assembly as state senator for Botetourt and several other southwestern Virginia counties. In June 1779 Governor Thomas Jefferson appointed Fleming to head a commission to settle land claims in Kentucky and to recommend locations for new forts on Virginia's frontier. Fleming spent more than eight months traveling in Kentucky, returning in mid-May 1780. While on this expedition Fleming learned that on 18 December 1779 the General Assembly had elected him a member of the Council of State. Early in June he set out for the new capital at Richmond to take his seat on the executive board.

Fleming, who is often confused with Judge William Fleming (1736–1824), served on the Council during a particularly trying period for Virginia, as in May 1781 a British army invaded the commonwealth, marched on Richmond, and forced the government to flee westward. Governor Jefferson's term expired on 2 June 1781, while government leaders were in Charlottesville. As the only councillor on hand during the first eleven days of June 1781, Fleming assumed the duties of governor until the General Assembly could reconvene in Staunton and elect a new governor. On 12 June the assembly chose Thomas Nelson, Jr., to succeed Jefferson, but Fleming continued to act as governor until Nelson arrived in Staunton on 19 June. The strain of these responsibilities proved too much for Fleming, and in an 8 September letter to the Speaker of the House of Delegates he resigned his place on the Council.

Several months later, however, Fleming reluctantly accepted an appointment as a commissioner to investigate charges of corruption and mismanagement in the government of Virginia's western territory. In this capacity, he once again traveled to the state's frontier. His last appearance in public life occurred when he represented Botetourt County in the Convention of 1788, at which he voted for ratification of the United States Constitution. Although he visited Kentucky on more than one occasion in his later years, his health declined precipitously early in the 1790s. Fleming died at Belmont in August 1795 at the age of sixty-eight.

Robert Goode (1743–1809) was born on 8 February 1743 at Whitby, the Chesterfield County estate of his parents, Robert and Mary (Turpin) Goode. Young Goode inherited Whitby upon his father's death in 1765 and became one of the wealthiest planters in the vicinity of Richmond. He was active in Chesterfield County affairs and in the mid-1770s served on the county's revolutionary committee. In 1783 Goode was elected to represent Chesterfield in the House of Delegates, where he served from May through December 1783 and again in June 1788. On 28 June 1788 the General Assembly chose him to be a member of the Council of State in place of Bolling Stark, who had died. Goode attended his first meeting of the Council on 2 July 1788 and remained on the board until the spring of 1797, when he stepped down in compliance with the assembly's vote of 29 November 1796 removing him from the Council. He died at his home in Chesterfield County on 20 April 1809.

Cyrus Griffin (1748–1810) was born on 16 July 1748 in Richmond County to LeRoy and Mary Ann (Bertrand) Griffin. He studied law at the University of Edinburgh and at the Middle Temple and returned to Virginia in 1774, settling in Lancaster County. At the age of twenty-eight he was first elected to the House of Delegates, where he represented Lancaster from May 1777 through May 1778 and again from October 1786 through January 1787. In May 1778 the General Assembly sent Griffin to the Continental Congress; he served in Congress until the spring of 1780 when he became a judge of the national Court of Appeals in Cases of Capture. Griffin presided over this court until it was abolished in 1787, then returned to Congress and served as its last president, from 22 January 1788 until the dissolution of that body on 2 March 1789.

On 27 December 1788 Griffin was chosen a member of Virginia's Council of State to replace Beverley Randolph, who had recently been elected governor. Before he took his seat on the Council, however, Congress appointed him a federal commissioner to assist in negotiating a treaty between the Creek Indians and the state of Georgia. Griffin accepted this commission, and when the negotiations were completed he returned to Richmond to take his seat on the Council. He attended his first meeting of the executive board on 29 October 1789, but on 31 October the House of Delegates decided that Griffin could not remain on the Council because the federal commission under which he had served had not yet expired. (As of December 1788, Virginia law prohibited a federal officeholder from holding a position in state government.) Griffin therefore resigned from the Council. When his federal commission ended a month later the General Assembly re-elected him to the board, but Griffin declined the appointment as he had been offered a judgeship on the United States District Court of Virginia. Griffin served in this capacity from November 1789 until his death on 14 December 1810.

Samuel Hardy (ca. 1757–1785), a son of former burgess Richard Hardy, was born in the mid-1750s in Isle of Wight County. He was educated at the College of William and Mary and on 1 October 1778 was admitted to the Virginia bar. Two days later he was chosen in a by-election to replace Josiah Parker as a delegate from Isle of Wight in the House of Delegates. Hardy served in the House during the December 1778 session and again from May 1780 through June 1781. On 12 June 1781 he was elected to the Council of State.

Hardy remained on the Council from June 1781 through November 1783, serving as president of the body from 2 December 1782 until the end of his tenure. In November 1783 he resigned to take a seat in Congress, to which he had been elected by the General Assembly the previous June. Hardy attended his first meeting of Congress in Annapolis on 26 November 1783. He remained a member of the national legislature until his death on 17 October 1785.

Benjamin Harrison (1743–1807), the only son of Nathaniel and Mary (Digges) Harrison to live to adulthood, was born in Prince George County on 13 February 1743. He was known to his contemporaries as Benjamin Harrison of Brandon to distinguish him from several other prominent Virginians of the same name, particularly Benjamin Harrison of Berkeley (1726–1791), a signer of the Declaration of Independence, and his son Benjamin (1755–1799).

Harrison received his education at the College of William and Mary and then returned to Prince George to help manage his family's estate. A supporter of the American Revolution, he served on Prince George County's revolutionary committee and on 2 July 1776 was chosen by the fifth revolutionary convention to be a member of the Council of State. Harrison served on the Council only a few months; he attended his last meeting on 8 October 1776 and resigned his position shortly thereafter. The following year he was elected to the House of Delegates from Prince George County, serving from May 1777 through December 1779 and again from May through December 1783. He does not appear to have held any other statewide office and probably retired from public life after the Revolution. He died at Brandon on 7 August 1807.

Nathaniel Harrison (1713–1791) was born in 1713, the eldest son of Nathaniel and Mary (Cary) Harrison, of Wakefield. A large landholder, he resided for a time in Stafford County, but lived the greater portion of his life at Brandon, in Prince George County. Harrison was a member of the Prince George County court and a colonel in the county militia; he also served on Prince George County's revolutionary committee. On 23 October 1776 he was elected to the Council of State in place of his son Benjamin Harrison of Brandon, who had resigned. Harrison attended his first meeting of the Council on 5 November 1776 and remained a member of the board until 16 December 1778, when he left the Council "to be a Candidate for an Employment which will not require such constant Attendance." In 1779 he was elected to the Senate from Isle of Wight, Prince George, and Surry counties, serving from May 1779 through January 1786. Harrison presided over the Senate as Speaker during the October 1779 session of the assembly in place of Archibald Cary, who did not attend. Harrison died on 1 October 1791.

William Heth (1750–1807), the eldest son of John and Mary (Mackey) Heth, was born on 19 July 1750 probably in Pennsylvania, where his father, an immigrant from northern Ireland, had settled. Several years after William's birth, the Heth family moved to Winchester, in Virginia's Shenandoah Valley. William Heth joined the Frederick County militia as a young man and served as a first lieutenant in Dunmore's War. Upon his return Heth became clerk of the Frederick County revolutionary committee, and in the summer of 1775 he joined Daniel Morgan's famous company of western Virginia riflemen as a second lieutenant.

In the American assault on Quebec, in December 1775, William Heth was wounded and captured by the British. After his release in August 1776 he continued his military career and eventually received a promotion to colonel of the 3d Virginia Regiment of Foot. He served at the siege of Charleston, South Carolina, where he was again captured and paroled. He retired from military service on 12 February 1781 and returned to his home, Curles, in Henrico County.

In January 1786 Heth replaced Edward Carrington as Virginia's commissioner responsible for obtaining reimbursement from Congress for the Virginia-financed exploration and defense of the Northwest Territory during the Revolution. On 7 November 1787 he became a member of the Council of State. Heth remained on the Council until August 1789, when President George Washington appointed him collector of ports for Bermuda Hundred. A staunch Federalist, Heth was removed from this post in 1802, during Thomas Jefferson's Republican administration. He retired from government service but remained active in the Society of the Cincinnati, serving as treasurer of the Virginia branch of that organization from 1786 until his death on 29 March 1807.

David Jameson (ca. 1723–1793) was born early in the 1720s in Saint Anne's Parish, Essex County, to James and Margaret Jameson. As a young man he settled in Yorktown, where he worked for several years as an attorney and eventually became a successful merchant. He was a civic leader in his community and a founder of the Society for the Promotion of Useful Knowledge.

A prominent Virginia merchant, Jameson signed the Nonimportation Association of June 1770, and after the American Revolution began he sat in the first state Senate that met under Virginia's Constitution of 1776, representing Elizabeth City, Warwick, and York counties from 7 October through December 1776. On 4 December 1776 he was elected to the Council of State, where he served for more than five years. With the resignation of Dudley Digges in May 1781, Jameson became senior member and president of the Council; in that capacity he served as lieutenant governor of the commonwealth on several occasions when Governors Thomas Nelson, Jr., and Benjamin Harrison were absent from the capital. He also acted as governor from 22 November 1781, when Nelson resigned, to 1 December 1781, when Harrison took office.

Jameson resigned from the Council on 30 March 1782 in order to sit in the state Senate once again. He served in the Senate for Elizabeth City, Warwick, and York counties from May 1782 through June 1783, but resigned before the October 1783 session to devote his energies to his mercantile pursuits. Jameson continued to be active in local civic affairs until his death on 10 July 1793.

Joseph Jones (1727–1805) was born in 1727 in King George County to James and Hester Jones. He studied law in England at the Inner Temple and the Middle Temple and was admitted to the English bar in 1751. Shortly thereafter Jones returned to Virginia and settled in Fredericksburg, where he practiced law. In September 1754 he became deputy king's attorney for King George County.

Jones's political career began when he stood for election to the House of Burgesses in 1771. He won his bid for an assembly seat and sat as a burgess for King George County in the assemblies of 1772–1774 and 1775–1776. His King George constituents also chose him to represent their interests at all five of Virginia's revolutionary conventions; at the fourth convention he was elected a member of the Committee of Safety.

Jones held several important positions under Virginia's new state government created by the Constitution of 1776. He served in the House of Delegates on behalf of King George County from October 1776 through June 1777, from May 1780 through March 1781, and from May 1783 through January 1785. On 23 May 1777 he was chosen a delegate to the Continental Congress, where he served from August through December 1777, and again from December 1779 through the summer of 1783. Between January 1778 and October 1779, when he was not acting as either delegate or congressman, Jones sat as a judge on the General Court. On 19 November 1784, the General Assembly selected him to fill a vacancy on the Council of State. Jones attended his first meeting of the executive board on 14 January 1785 and remained an active councillor until November 1789, when he left the Council to sit once more on the General Court. Jones took the oath of a General Court justice on 9 December 1789 and remained on that bench until his death on 26 October 1805.

Robert Lawson (1748–1805) was born on 23 January 1748 in Yorkshire, England. He emigrated to Virginia sometime before 1773, when he is known to have been practicing law in Prince Edward County. Lawson transferred his allegiance to his adopted home and supported the colonial position against Great Britain in the turbulent days before the American Revolution. He served as a member of Prince Edward County's revolutionary committee and sat in Virginia's second, third, and fourth revolutionary conventions.

The members of the fourth convention named Lawson a major in the 4th Virginia Regiment of Foot of the Continental army; several months later he was promoted to lieutenant colonel and in August 1777 to colonel. He resigned his Continental commission in December 1777, but shortly afterwards he became a brigadier general in the Virginia militia. In this capacity, he fought at the battle of Guilford Court House and in the Yorktown campaign.

Lawson sat in the House of Delegates for Prince Edward County from May through December 1778. In June 1779 he was elected to the Board of War, where he served until his resignation on 27 September of that year. He returned to the House again from May 1780 through March 1781 and from May to June 1782. On 28 June 1782, the General Assembly elected him to the Council of State.

Lawson took his seat on the executive board on 20 September 1782. He remained on the Council less than a year, however, resigning on 2 June 1783. He returned to the House for the May and October sessions of the assembly of 1783, and for the October session of the assembly of 1787 as well. Between assembly sessions from 1784 to 1788 he also served as commonwealth's attorney for Prince Edward County. In 1789 Lawson moved his family to Kentucky, where he died in April 1805.

Thomas Ludwell Lee (1730–1778), born on 13 December 1730 at Stratford Hall in Westmoreland County, was the fourth child and third son of Thomas and Hannah (Ludwell) Lee. He was educated in England, where he studied law at the Inner Temple. Upon his return to Virginia he settled in Stafford County; from 1758 through 1765 and from 1775 through 1776 he represented that county in the House of Burgesses. In 1774 Lee became a member of the Stafford County revolutionary committee, and in 1775 and 1776 he also served in Virginia's third, fourth, and fifth revolutionary conventions. He was elected to Virginia's Committee of Safety on 15 August 1775 and was reelected the following December.

Lee served in the Virginia Senate for Westmoreland, Stafford, and King George counties from October 1776 through January 1778. On 23 January he was chosen by the assembly to sit on the General Court. Lee contracted rheumatic fever shortly before the court convened, and he died on 13 April 1778 at the age of forty-seven.

Andrew Lewis (1720–1781) was born in Ireland in 1720 to John and Margaret (Lynn) Lewis. He emigrated to America with his family as a boy, and by 1732 the Lewises had located in the Valley of Virginia, near the present site of Staunton. Once grown, Andrew Lewis moved to Virginia's southwestern frontier, settling along the upper Roanoke River, near present-day Salem. There he served as leiutenant of Augusta County, and when the county of Botetourt was formed in 1769 Lewis became one of its first justices of the peace. A skillful militia leader, he fought extensively in the French and Indian War and was wounded several times, captured, and nearly killed while a prisoner. In 1768 he assisted in the negotiations that led to the Indian treaty of Fort Stanwix. When troubles with the Indians on the frontier erupted again in 1774, Lewis led an expedition of men from Virginia's southwestern counties to the Ohio River. There, at the battle of Point Pleasant, militia units under Lewis's command defeated a Shawnee Indian force in what proved to be the decisive battle of Dunmore's War. This victory earned Lewis his outstanding military reputation. On 1 March 1776 Congress appointed Lewis a brigadier general in the Continental army and placed him in command of United States forces in Williamsburg. Lewis resigned this commission in April 1777 but remained active in the state militia during most of the war.

Lewis served his colony and commonwealth in legislative and executive capacities as well. From February 1772 through May 1776 he represented Botetourt County in the House of Burgesses. He was also elected to the first four of Virginia's revolutionary conventions, although military service often interrupted his attendance. Lewis's constituents in Botetourt County returned him to the legislature for the assembly of 1780–1781, but his tenure was brief; on 24 May 1780 he was chosen a member of the Council of State. Lewis remained on the executive board until his death on 26 September 1781.

Warner Lewis (1747–1791) was born in 1747 at Warner Hall, in Gloucester County, the eldest son of Warner and Eleanor (Bowles) Lewis. He was educated at the College of William and Mary and at

Oxford University. In 1775 Lewis enlisted in the Gloucester District Battalion, and he was appointed a captain in February 1776. Later that year he was chosen a member of the Gloucester County court of commissioners, and on 23 May 1777 he received an appointment to the state's Navy Board.

Lewis remained on the Navy Board until the General Assembly abolished it in June 1779. Wishing to retain Lewis in government service, however, the assembly elected him to the Council of State on 18 June 1779. As the Council journals for this period are no longer extant (only fragmentary minutes survive), it is not possible to determine how active a councillor Lewis was. He resigned from the executive board on 4 December 1779, citing his inability "to give that attendance which the duties of the office seem to require."

Lewis disappeared from state politics until 1788, when he represented Gloucester County at the Convention of 1788 and voted for ratification of the United States Constitution. In 1789 he was chosen one of Virginia's presidential electors. Lewis died on 30 December 1791.

Thomas Lomax (1746–1811) was born on 25 January 1746 at Portobago, in Caroline County, to Lunsford and Judith (Micou) Lomax. He attended Donald Robertson's school in King and Queen County and became a prominent Rappahannock River planter. In 1774 he was chosen a member of the Caroline County revolutionary committee, and on 2 December 1776 he was appointed to the county bench. When the Virginia Constitution of 1776 went into effect, Lomax was elected to represent Hanover and Caroline counties in the state Senate, serving from October through December 1776. He also sat in the House of Delegates for Caroline from May 1778 through December 1779, and again from May through November 1781. On 30 November 1781 he was elected to the Council of State to replace John Walker, who had declined to serve.

Lomax officially remained on the Council until 17 June 1784, when the Speaker presented his letter of resignation to the House of Delegates; the last meeting Lomax had attended, however, was on 22 December 1783, after which he apparently retired from public life. Lomax died on 17 October 1811 at Portobago.

James McClurg (1746–1823), born in 1746, was the son of British naval surgeon Walter McClurg, who opened a hospital in Hampton, Virginia, for innoculation against smallpox. James was educated at the College of William and Mary and the University of Edinburgh, and then continued his study of medicine in Paris and London. At the age of twenty-six he published *Experiments Upon the Human Bile and Reflections on the Biliary Excretion* (London, 1772), which earned him an international reputation. McClurg returned to Virginia early in the

1770s, and during the American Revolution he served as a surgeon to the American navy at Hampton and, after 1777, as physician general and director of hospitals for Virginia's military forces. In December 1779 he was chosen to fill the newly created chair of medicine at the College of William and Mary. McClurg held this position until 1783, when he moved to Richmond.

There McClurg's interests turned to politics. He agreed to serve on the Council of State when elected on 22 June 1784, and he remained a councillor through May 1794, when he stepped down in compliance with a 9 November 1793 assembly vote removing him from the executive board. McClurg also represented Virginia at the Constitutional Convention of 1787, and served as mayor of Richmond from January 1801 through May 1802. He died in Richmond on 9 July 1823.

Samuel McDowell (1735–1817) was born in Pennsylvania on 27 October 1735 to John and Magdaline (Woods) McDowell. The McDowells moved to Virginia two years after Samuel's birth, settling in Augusta County where Samuel was educated by private tutors. As a young man he fought in the French and Indian War, and in 1774 he served as a captain in Dunmore's War. McDowell was also active in county politics. He was a member of the Augusta County court, and he represented the county in the House of Burgesses from February 1772 through 1776. He served on Augusta County's revolutionary committee and attended all five of Virginia's revolutionary conventions. When the Constitution of 1776 went into effect, Augusta County sent McDowell to the House of Delegates, in which he served from October 1776 through January 1778. He also represented newly formed Rockbridge County in the House from May through December 1778. During the Revolution, as a colonel in the Virginia militia, McDowell saw action at the battle of Guilford Court House and in the Yorktown campaign.

On 12 June 1781 McDowell was chosen a member of the Virginia Council of State. He remained on the Council only until October of that year, when he left to serve on a commission empowered to examine the state of public accounts in Virginia's western territory. On 4 November 1782, Governor Benjamin Harrison named McDowell an assistant judge of Kentucky's first district court. He accepted the appointment and moved permanently to Kentucky. McDowell was a prominent member of the nine Kentucky conventions held between December 1784 and July 1790, and he was the president of the 1792 convention that wrote the state's constitution. He continued on the Kentucky bench into the second decade of the nineteenth century and died near Danville, Kentucky, on 25 October 1817.

James Madison (1751–1836), the eldest child of James and Eleanor (Conway) Madison, was born on 16 March 1751 in King

George County. As a young boy he attended Donald Robertson's school in King and Queen County and received further education from a private tutor at his family's Orange County home, Montpelier. From 1769 to 1772 Madison studied at the College of New Jersey (now Princeton University). In December 1774 he was elected to the Orange County revolutionary committee, and two years later he was sent to Virginia's fifth revolutionary convention. He also served Orange County as a delegate in the first General Assembly session that met after the adoption of the Constitution of 1776.

On 15 November 1777 the General Assembly elected Madison to the Council of State. He attended his first meeting on 14 January 1778 and served on the executive board until December 1779, when he was elected a delegate to the Continental Congress. Madison served in Congress from 1780 through 1783 and from 1786 through 1788. He also sat again in the House of Delegates for Orange County from May 1784 through January 1787. In May 1787 Madison represented Virginia at the federal convention in Philadelphia, where he played an important part in the drafting of the United States Constitution. Madison forcefully advocated ratification of the Constitution in his contributions to the series of essays known as *The Federalist* and on the floor of Virginia's Convention of 1788.

Madison successfully ran for election to the first United States House of Representatives, in which he served from 1789 through 1797. During these years he was instrumental in forming the first political party system in America. Madison returned to Virginia and served in the House of Delegates in the assembly of 1799–1800, but in 1801 he was called back to national service to become secretary of state in the administration of President Thomas Jefferson. Madison held this position through Jefferson's two presidential terms, and then succeeded his friend to the presidency in 1809. He served two terms as president as well, retiring from national life to Montpelier in 1817. His last public service was as a delegate to Virginia's Convention of 1829–1830. Madison died on 28 June 1836.

Thomas Madison (1746–1798) was born in Augusta County in October 1746 to John and Agatha (Strother) Madison. As a young man he served in the militia of his native county and saw action in the French and Indian War. In 1769 he moved to the newly created county of Botetourt, where he began the practice of law and served as deputy sheriff. In 1772, when Fincastle County was carved from a portion of Botetourt, Madison also became a prominent figure in that county's affairs. He was a member of the Fincastle County revolutionary committee and signed the Fincastle resolves. He also accepted an appointment as commissary and paymaster for the western Virginia settlers' expedition against the Cherokee Indians in 1776.

Madison served as commonwealth's attorney for Botetourt

County from 1778 through 1787. His public service was not restricted to county affairs, however, as from May 1780 through March 1781 and from May through December 1782, he represented Botetourt in the House of Delegates. On 28 November 1789 the General Assembly elected him to the Council of State. He took his seat on the Council on 18 January 1790, but he attended Council meetings only sporadically. He resigned from the executive board in November 1790. Madison returned to the assembly for Botetourt in October 1793, serving through December 1796. He died in February 1798, near Cloverdale, in Botetourt County.

John Marshall (1755–1835), son of Thomas and Mary (Keith) Marshall, was born on 24 September 1755 in the vicinity of German-town, then in Prince William County. He received his early education from several local tutors and from his father, a burgess and sheriff in Fauquier County. When the movement toward revolution began in Virginia, he joined the Fauquier County militia as a lieutenant, and in September 1775 he was commissioned first lieutenant of the Culpeper District Battalion. Throughout the war he served in both the state's provincial forces and the Continental army. Marshall was released from active duty at the end of 1779, and while awaiting reassignment in the summer of 1780 he attended a series of lectures on law and natural philosophy given by George Wythe at the College of William and Mary. In August 1780 he was admitted to the bar in Fauquier County. Discharged from the army as a captain on 12 February 1781, he began his legal and political career in earnest.

Marshall represented Fauquier County in the May 1782 session of the General Assembly. He was returned to the November 1782 session as well, but on 20 November the assembly chose him to be a member of the Council of State. Marshall remained on the Council until 1 April 1784, when he resigned in the wake of a court decision that prohibited members of the Council from practicing law while serving on the executive board. Marshall preferred to concentrate on his budding legal practice, which soon earned him a statewide reputation.

Settling permanently in Richmond, Marshall took an active part in municipal affairs. In 1785 he was elected to the common hall, and he served as recorder for the city until March 1788. He also sat in the House of Delegates, from May 1784 through January 1785 for Fauquier County and from October 1787 through January 1788 for Henrico County. Elected to Virginia's Convention of 1788, Marshall firmly supported ratification of the new United States Constitution.

Although he remained active in civic affairs—representing the city of Richmond in the House of Delegates in the October 1789 session of the assembly and from November 1795 through December 1797, sitting again on the city council, and serving as acting attorney general of Virginia from October 1794 to March 1795—his ability and political philosophy propelled him toward national office. As a leading Federalist, Marshall was offered several prestigious positions in both George Washington's and John Adams's administrations. He turned them all down, however, except for a short-term appointment as U.S. minister extraordinary to France, in which capacity he became entangled in the infamous XYZ affair. Upon his return from France, he declined an offer of a place on the U.S. Supreme Court, choosing instead to run for Congress. Marshall succeeded in his bid for election to the House of Representatives, in which he served from 1799 to 1800. In May 1800 he succumbed to the entreaties of President Adams and accepted the post of secretary of state. In February 1801 Adams named Marshall chief justice of the United States. Under his direction, the power and prestige of the judicial branch of the fledgling U.S. government increased greatly.

Marshall's involvement in state politics declined markedly in his later years, although as one of Virginia's elder statesmen he attended the Convention of 1829–1830, which revised the commonwealth's constitution. He remained chief justice of the United States until his death on 6 July 1835.

George Mason (1725–1792), the son of George and Ann (Thomson) Mason, was born in 1725 in the Mason family home on Dogue's Neck, in Prince William County. His father died in an accident in 1735, and young George grew to maturity under the tutelage of his uncle John Mercer of Marlborough. Mason received his early education from private instructors and read extensively in his guardian's well-stocked library. Upon reaching his majority, Mason assumed the civic responsibilities expected of a landed gentleman. He served as a vestryman of Truro Parish (1748–1785), a trustee of the town of Alexandria (1754–1779), and a justice of the Fairfax County court (1747–1789). He sat as a burgess for Fairfax County from 1758 to 1761, but dedication to his plantation, Gunston Hall, and to his growing family, as well as occasional periods of ill health, kept him from seeking a wider involvement in colonial politics.

Great Britain's attempt to tighten her administrative control over her American dependencies following the French and Indian War aroused Mason's ire to such an extent, however, that he joined many of his fellow Virginians in protesting the Stamp Act in 1765, and several years later he helped to formulate nonimportation agreements in resistance to Parliament's Townshend Acts. As America's problems with Great Britain intensified in the 1770s, Mason emerged as one of the most articulate theorists of the colonial position. In 1774 he described America's view of her place within the British empire in a document known as the Fairfax resolves. He was active on the Fairfax County revolutionary committee and was chosen a member of the

Committee of Safety in August 1775. He represented Fairfax County at the third and fifth revolutionary conventions; ill health prevented his attendance at the fourth. He is best remembered for his contributions at the fifth convention: drafting the Virginia Declaration of Rights and writing a substantial portion of the state's first constitution. He served in the House of Delegates from 1776 through 1781 and then retired to Gunston Hall.

Mason could not be cajoled out of retirement again until the summer of 1787, when he agreed to serve as a member of the Virginia delegation to the Philadelphia convention called to discuss the problems of the Articles of Confederation. Mason believed that the articles needed revision, but he could not accept many of the provisions included in the convention's new framework for governing the thirteen states, the United States Constitution. He did not sign the document, and when he returned to Virginia he worked in both the October 1787 General Assembly session and the Convention of 1788 for rejection of the Constitution unless amendments, and especially a bill of rights, were appended. Mason lost his fight against unconditional ratification of the Constitution, and, with great bitterness, he retired again from public life. He died at Gunston Hall on 7 October 1792.

Sampson Mathews (1737–1807) was born in Augusta County in 1737 to John and Ann (Archer) Mathews. His father, an Irish immigrant, had settled in Virginia early in the 1730s. Sampson Mathews joined the Augusta militia as a young man and fought in the French and Indian War. He became one of the most prosperous merchants and landholders in the northwestern portion of the colony and served his native county as a deputy sheriff and justice of the peace. He was also present at the battle of Point Pleasant in 1774 as commissary to Colonel Andrew Lewis's troops. Mathews heartily supported Virginia's move toward independence from Britain, and in 1775 he was elected a member of the Augusta County revolutionary committee. Throughout the American Revolution he also acted as lieutenant colonel of the county militia, and he represented Augusta and several of its neighboring counties in the new state Senate from October 1776 through December 1781.

On 30 November 1781 the General Assembly appointed Mathews to the Council of State. He served faithfully on the executive board until 7 April 1788, at which time he stepped down in compliance with the 3 October 1787 assembly vote removing him from the Council. Mathews then returned to the Senate, remaining there from October 1790 through December 1791. He took an active role in the movement to form Bath County from Augusta, Botetourt, and Greenbrier counties, and became the new county's first sheriff and one of its most influential justices. He continued to direct his commercial interests and land holdings in northwestern Virginia until his death on 20 January 1807 in Staunton.

James Mercer (1736–1793) was born in Stafford County on 26 February 1736 to John Mercer of Marlborough and his first wife, Catherine Mason Mercer. After receiving his education at the College of William and Mary, Mercer served as a captain in the French and Indian War. He also became active in the land ventures of the Ohio Company, of which his father was secretary. At the age of twenty-six he was elected to the House of Burgesses from Hampshire County, which he continued to represent in the assembly from 1762 through 1776.

Mercer stepped to the forefront of Virginia politics as the colonial struggle with Great Britain intensified in the mid-1770s. He served on the Spotsylvania County revolutionary committee and also helped to bring about the first of Virginia's five colony-wide revolutionary conventions. He attended all of these meetings on behalf of Hampshire County and was elected to the Virginia Committee of Safety in 1775 and 1776. Mercer served in the House of Delegates in 1776 when the new state constitution went into effect. On 10 October the assembly chose him to sit on the Council of State, but Mercer declined the appointment. In June 1779, however, when the assembly elected him to represent Virginia in the Continental Congress, Mercer agreed. He served in Congress from November 1779 until November 1781, when he was chosen to sit on the General Court. Mercer remained a judge of the General Court until November 1789, at which time he replaced John Blair on the state's new Supreme Court of Appeals. Mercer sat on this court until his death in Richmond on 31 October 1793.

James Monroe (1758–1831), the eldest son of Spence and Elizabeth (Jones) Monroe, was born in Westmoreland County on 28 April 1758. He entered the College of William and Mary in 1774, but found it hard to concentrate on studies once the American War of Independence began. In the spring of 1776, barely eighteen years old, Monroe enlisted as a lieutenant in the 3d Virginia Regiment of Foot in the Continental army, and at the age of nineteen he was promoted to the rank of major. In December 1778 he resigned his Continental commission, hoping to raise his own regiment in the state line and become a colonel, but his command never became active. From 1780 through the end of the war he served as special assistant to Governor Thomas Jefferson, under whose direction he also studied law.

At the war's end, Monroe successfully stood for election to the House of Delegates from King George County. While attending the May 1782 session of the assembly, however, the twenty-four-year-old delegate was chosen to sit on the Council of State. Elected on 5 June, Monroe took his place on the executive board three days later and served until October 1783, when he resigned to represent Virginia in the Continental Congress from 1783 through 1786. Upon his return to Virginia, Monroe stood again for election to the House of Delegates for King George County, but was defeated. He had better luck in 1787 when he ran in Spotsylvania County. He represented Spotsylvania in the House from October 1787 through December 1788 and also in the Convention of 1788, where he joined forces with the state's Antifederalists.

Despite his opposition to ratification, Monroe accepted the Constitution and agreed to hold federal office, serving as United States senator from 1790 through 1794 and as minister to France from June 1794 through December 1796. Recalled from France toward the end of President George Washington's administration, Monroe stepped out of national politics for a short time and served as governor of Virginia from December 1799 through December 1802. He was called back to national service, however, when President Thomas Jefferson asked him to sail to France as a minister extraordinary to assist in negotiating a treaty that would settle the question of navigation rights on the Mississippi River. The final result of this mission was the Louisiana Purchase. Monroe remained in Europe from 1803 through 1807, conducting diplomatic negotiations with Great Britain and Spain for the Jefferson administration. In 1808 he ran unsuccessfully for the presidency. Returning to state politics, he sat in the House of Delegates for Albemarle County from December 1810 through January 1811 and then was again elected governor. He served only three months as Virginia's chief executive, however, as in April 1811 he accepted appointment as secretary of state in the administration of President James Madison. Monroe held this position throughout most of Madison's second term in office, although he interrupted his service in the State Department twice during the War of 1812 to act as secretary of war. In November 1816 he was elected the fifth president of the United States. President Monroe served two terms, from March 1817 to March 1825.

Monroe retired to his Loudoun County estate, Oak Hill, after leaving Washington. He did serve as first president of the Virginia Convention of 1829–1830, but ill health caused him to resign that office after only a few weeks. In 1830, following the death of his wife, Monroe moved to New York to live with his daughter. He died there on 4 July 1831.

Andrew Moore (1752–1821) was born in 1752 at Cannicello, about twenty miles south of Staunton, in Augusta County. His parents, David and Mary (Evans) Moore, had emigrated from Ireland to the Valley of Virginia shortly before his birth. After attending Augusta Academy, Moore went to Williamsburg to study law under George Wythe. He qualified for the bar in 1774, but the revolutionary war began before he could begin to practice law, and he enlisted in the 9th Virginia Regiment of Foot in the Continental army. Upon leaving the army Moore quickly became one of the leading citizens of newly formed Rockbridge County. He represented Rockbridge in the House of Delegates from May 1780 through December 1783 and from October 1785 through January 1788, and he also attended Virginia's Convention of 1788, at which he voted to ratify the United States Constitution.

On 28 June 1788 the General Assembly chose Moore to sit on the Council of State. He did not attend a meeting until 6 November 1788, however, and he served only until 2 January 1789, when he resigned in order to represent Virginia in the first federal Congress. Moore served in the House of Representatives from March 1789 until March 1797; he then returned to the Virginia assembly, representing Rockbridge County in the House of Delegates from December 1799 through January 1800 and in the Virginia Senate from December 1800 through December 1801. He served for several years as federal marshal of the western district of Virginia, but in March 1804 he returned to Congress. He sat in the House of Representatives until August 1804, when he was appointed to the U.S. Senate, where he served until 1809. In 1810 Moore was appointed U.S. marshal for Virginia, a post he held until his resignation early in 1821. He died on 24 May 1821 at his home in Lexington, Virginia.

William Nelson (1754–1813) was born in 1754, the fifth son of Elizabeth Burwell Nelson and William Nelson, Sr., a prominent Yorktown merchant and longtime member of the colonial Council. Young William attended the College of William and Mary and studied law in Williamsburg. He served in the Virginia militia during the Revolution, and at the war's end began his political and legal career.

Nelson represented James City County in the House of Delegates from May through December 1783. On 27 November 1783 he was chosen a member of the Council of State, but he did not take his seat until 6 March 1784. Nelson served on the Council until the summer of 1785, when he resigned in order to take over the law practice of Henry Tazewell, who had been appointed to the General Court. Nelson soon earned a reputation in Virginia as a distinguished legal mind. In 1789 he was appointed United States district attorney for Virginia, and in October 1790 he was named to a committee charged with revising the laws of the commonwealth. The following year Nelson was made a judge of the General Court, a position he filled until his death. In his later years he also served as professor of law at the College of William and Mary. William Nelson died on 8 March 1813.

John Page (1744–1808) was born at Rosewell, in Gloucester County, on 17 April 1744 to Mann and Alice (Grymes) Page. He received his early education from his family and at the grammar school of the Reverend William Yates, and he then attended the College of William and Mary. He served with the Gloucester County militia and at the age of twenty-eight began his political career as a burgess, representing the college at the first two sessions of the assembly of 1772–1774. In 1773 he was honored with an appointment to the governor's Council, on which both his uncle and grandfather had served. Page disagreed with Lord Dunmore on several issues put before the Council, however, and so angered the governor that he did not call Page to attend any Council meeting after May 1775. In August 1775, while still a councillor, Page was chosen a member of Virginia's Committee of Safety, to which he was reelected the following December.

When the Constitution of 1776 went into effect on 6 July, Page became a member of the new Council of State, having been elected by the fifth revolutionary convention on 29 June 1776. As president of the Council, he acted as lieutenant governor during Governor Patrick Henry's frequent and prolonged illnesses and absences from Williamsburg. Page remained on the Council until 7 April 1780, when he submitted his resignation to Governor Thomas Jefferson. Although he wished to escape public life to attend to private business, he did participate in the Yorktown campaign that ended the American Revolution, and he served in the House of Delegates for Gloucester County from 1781 to 1783, from 1785 to 1787, and in 1788. In 1789 he successfully ran for election to the United States House of Representatives, where he served until 1797. Upon his return to Virginia, Page immersed himself in state politics, serving in the House of Delegates from 1797 to 1798 and from 1800 to 1801 and taking an active part in the presidential campaign of his longtime friend Thomas Jefferson. He was also governor of Virginia from December 1802 through December 1805. In 1806 Jefferson helped him obtain a position as United States collector of loans for Virginia, a post he held until his death in Richmond on 11 October 1808.

Edmund Pendleton (1721–1803), the youngest son of Henry and Mary (Taylor) Pendleton, was born in Caroline County on 9 September 1721. His father died shortly after his birth, and at the age of fourteen Pendleton was apprenticed to Benjamin Robinson, clerk of the Caroline County court. During his apprenticeship Pendleton served as clerk of the Saint Mary's Parish vestry and of the Caroline County court-martial. At the age of twenty he was admitted to the bar.

In 1751 Pendleton became a justice of the peace for Caroline County, and the following year he was elected to the House of Burgesses, where he served until 1776. While in the House, he learned much from Speaker John Robinson, Jr., and after Robinson's death Pendleton became executor of his estate. Pendleton supported the colonial position in the disputes with Great Britain early in the 1770s and served on the Caroline County revolutionary committee and on the statewide committee of correspondence. He was one of the more conservative of Virginia's revolutionary leaders, and he played a central role in guiding the colony's move toward independence. He served as a delegate to the Continental Congress in 1774 and 1775; he attended all five of Virginia's revolutionary conventions, acting as president of the final two; and he presided over the Committee of Safety in 1775 and 1776. As president of the Committee of Safety, Pendleton was Virginia's chief executive in the interim between the collapse of royal authority and the establishment of republican government under the Constitution of 1776.

Pendleton represented Caroline County in the new House of Delegates from October 1776 through January 1778. During the October 1776 session he served as Speaker of the House. He resigned from the assembly in January 1778 to accept a seat on the newly established High Court of Chancery. In his capacity as a judge of the chancery court, he also served on the state's Court of Appeals. Pendleton represented Caroline County at the Convention of 1788, serving as president of the convention and voting for the Constitution. When the Virginia court system was reorganized in 1788 and a new Supreme Court of Appeals was established, Pendleton became this court's presiding officer. He held this position until his death on 26 October 1803.

Joseph Prentis (1754–1809), the son of William and Mary (Brooke) Prentis, was born on 24 January 1754, probably in Williamsburg. He attended the College of William and Mary and prepared himself for a career in law. At the age of twenty-two he was chosen a member of the Williamsburg revolutionary committee and a delegate from Williamsburg to the fourth revolutionary convention. The fifth convention appointed him a judge of the state's admiralty court, upon which he served until the court was superseded in December 1776. Prentis represented Williamsburg in the new House of Delegates in 1776 and then served as a delegate for York County from 1777 to 1778. On 29 May 1778 the General Assembly chose him to fill a vacancy on the Council of State. Prentis took his seat on the executive board on 7 July 1778 and attended his last meeting on 22 March 1781. He resigned shortly thereafter in order to run again for a seat in the House of Delegates. Prentis represented James City County in the House from 1781 through 1782 and York County from 1782 through 1788, presiding as Speaker from October 1786 through January 1788. On 4 January 1788 the assembly elected Prentis to the General Court. He remained a judge of the court until his death on 18 June 1809.

Beverley Randolph (1754–1797), the son of Peter and Lucy (Bolling) Randolph, of Chatsworth, in Henrico County, was born on 11 September 1754. He was graduated from the College of William and Mary in 1771 and settled in Cumberland County. He was active on the Cumberland County revolutionary committee, and he served in the county's militia at the battle of Guilford Court House and in the Yorktown campaign. In 1777 Randolph won election to the House of Delegates, where he represented Cumberland County from May 1777 through January 1778 and from May 1779 through March 1781. On 30 November 1781 he was elected to the Council of State. He served as president of the Council and acted often as lieutenant governor of the commonwealth between November 1783 and December 1788, when he became governor of Virginia. Randolph served three terms as governor, stepping down in November 1791 and retiring to his Cumberland County farm, Green Creek. He died there on 7 February 1797 at the age of forty-two.

Spencer Roane (1762–1822) was born in Essex County on 4 April 1762 to William and Elizabeth (Ball) Roane. He received his early education from private tutors and then attended the College of William and Mary, where he studied law under George Wythe. He was admitted to the bar in 1782, and in 1783 won election to the House of Delegates, where he represented Essex County from May 1783 through January 1785. On 19 November 1784 the General Assembly elected Roane to the Council of State in place of William Christian. Roane took his seat on the executive board on 2 June 1785 and served on the Council until October 1786. He resigned shortly thereafter to resume his law practice.

From June 1788 through December 1789 Roane sat in the state Senate, representing Essex and several neighboring counties. Then, at the age of twenty-seven, Roane was made a judge of the General Court. He remained on this court until 1794 when, following the resignation of Henry Tazewell, he was appointed a judge of the Supreme Court of Appeals. Roane served on the appeals court until 1822. During the last twenty-five years of his life he was also active in Virginia politics. An ardent Jeffersonian Republican, Roane founded the powerful political clique known as the Richmond Junto. He died at Warm Springs, in Bath County, on 4 September 1822.

Miles Selden (ca. 1750–1811), the third child born to Miles and Rebecca (Cary) Selden, of Pear Tree Hall, was born about 1750 in Henrico County. He was educated at the College of William and Mary and then trained as a clerk in the office of the secretary of the colony. For several years he served as clerk of the Henrico County court, and in

1782 he was elected to the Virginia Senate, where he represented Henrico, Goochland, and Louisa counties from May 1782 through January 1785. On 19 November 1784 the General Assembly elected Selden to the Council of State in place of Meriwether Smith. Selden took his seat on 9 June 1785 and remained on the executive board until April 1788, when he resigned in accord with the 31 October 1787 assembly vote that would have removed him from the Council in June. He was reelected to the Council of State by the assembly on 26 November 1790; he took his seat on 31 May 1791 and served until the spring of 1794, when he was once again removed. Selden also held the offices of sheriff and justice of the peace in Henrico County. He represented the county in the House of Delegates from June 1788 through December 1790 and December 1797 through January 1800, and in the state Senate from December 1806 through February 1810. He died on 18 May 1811.

William Short (1759–1849) was born on 30 September 1759 at Spring Garden, in Surry County, to William and Elizabeth (Skipwith) Short. He was graduated from the College of William and Mary in 1779 and received a license to practice law in 1782. Interested in foreign travel and a diplomatic career, Short sought a position as secretary to an American legation abroad. As none was available, he accepted a seat on the Council of State, to which he was elected on 6 June 1783. He attended his first meeting of the executive board on 10 June 1783 and served until August 1784, when he resigned to become secretary to the new American minister to France, Thomas Jefferson. Short served as secretary to the American legation in Paris until Jefferson's departure for the United States in 1789. He then served for a short time as chargé d'affaires in Paris and from 1792 to 1793 as minister to the Netherlands. From 1794 to 1795 he was minister to Spain, where he laid the groundwork for the Pinckney treaty of 1795. Short lived in Paris from 1795 to 1802, and then returned to the United States. In 1808 Jefferson nominated him to be minister to Russia, but the Senate refused to confirm his appointment, holding that the United States did not need a permanent minister in Saint Petersburg. Short moved to Philadelphia, where he devoted himself to business affairs. He never returned to public life, and died on 5 December 1849.

Meriwether Smith (1730–1794), the son of Francis and Lucy (Meriwether) Smith, was born in 1730 at Bathurst, in Essex County. In 1766 Smith signed the Westmoreland Association in opposition to the Stamp Act, and in 1774 he joined the Essex County revolutionary committee. He represented Essex in the House of Burgesses from July 1774 through 1776, attended all five of Virginia's revolutionary conventions, and served in the October 1776 and May 1778 sessions of

Virginia's new House of Delegates. In 1778 he was elected a delegate to the Continental Congress; he was reelected the following year, but did not attend as he was embroiled in a political controversy with the General Assembly over his accounts while a delegate in 1778. Elected again in June 1780, however, Smith sat in Congress from February through September 1781.

Smith served three times on the Council of State. He was first chosen a member of the executive board on 23 October 1776 in place of Fielding Lewis, who had declined to serve. He was not reelected in May 1777, but was chosen to serve on the Council again in November 1779. He resigned from the Council in the fall of 1780 to return to Congress and to attend the May and October 1781 sessions of the House of Delegates, but he was returned to the Council again in June 1782. He served as a councillor from 17 September 1782 until April 1785, when he resigned in accord with the General Assembly vote the previous November that would have removed him from the Council in June. Smith returned to the House of Delegates from October 1785 through December 1788 and also served in Virginia's Convention of 1788, where he voted against ratification of the United States Constitution. He died at Marigold, Essex County, on 24 January 1794.

Bolling Stark (1733–1788), the son of William and Mary (Bolling) Stark, was born in Prince George County on 20 September 1733. He represented Dinwiddie County in the House of Burgesses from May 1769 until July 1771 and was active on the Dinwiddie County revolutionary committee. He attended Virginia's fifth revolutionary convention and sat in the new House of Delegates from October 1776 through January 1778.

On 23 January 1778 the General Assembly selected Stark to sit on the Council of State. He took his seat on the executive board on 18 February 1778 and served until the fall of 1779, when he resigned. He returned to the House of Delegates, this time representing Prince George County, from May 1780 through January 1781. In January 1781 Governor Thomas Jefferson appointed Stark to the three-man Board of Auditors. He served as an auditor until December 1786, when by act of the General Assembly his position was abolished and the number of auditors reduced to two. Furious over his dismissal from the auditors' office, Stark appealed to James Madison for assistance in securing the position of collector of duties in Norfolk. Stark was not awarded the post he wanted, but on 1 December 1786 the assembly chose him to serve as a councillor once again. Stark sat on the Council of State from 4 December 1786 until his death on 25 January 1788.

John Steele (ca. 1755–1817) was born to Samuel and Sarah (Hunter) Steele near Middlebrook, in Augusta County, about 1755. In 1774 he joined the Augusta County militia and by October 1777 was an ensign in the 9th Virginia Regiment of Foot. He was wounded at the battle of Germantown, but continued to serve in the military throughout the Revolution, becoming in 1781 a first lieutenant in the 1st Virginia Regiment of Foot.

Steele's first appearance in government service was in 1788, when he represented Nelson County (now in Kentucky) at the Convention of 1788 and voted against ratification of the United States Constitution. In June 1790 President George Washington nominated him to be a lieutenant in a battalion of U.S. infantry being raised throughout the southern states. Steele declined this appointment, however, as on 26 November 1790 he was elected to the Virginia Council of State. He remained on the Council until the spring of 1797, when he left the executive board in compliance with a 29 November 1796 vote in the General Assembly removing him. In 1797 he served as a member of a commission sent to negotiate a treaty with the Cherokee Indians, and in 1798 President John Adams named him secretary of the newly created territory of Mississippi. Steele arrived in Natchez, Mississippi, in October 1798 and served as secretary until May 1802. From April through November 1801 he was also acting governor of the territory.

Steele did not return to Virginia. He became a citizen of Mississippi and served in the territorial assembly in 1804. His last public position was as a delegate from Adams County to the Mississippi constitutional convention held in 1817. Steele died in Natchez shortly after the convention ended.

John Tabb (ca. 1736–1798) was born in the mid-1730s at Clay Hill, in Amelia County, to Thomas Tabb, one of Virginia's wealthiest merchants, and Rebecca Booker Tabb. Tabb was active in public life only for a short while, during the revolutionary war period. He served in the House of Burgesses from February 1772 through the dissolution of the colonial assembly in 1776, and his Amelia County constituents elected him to all five of Virginia's revolutionary conventions. He was a member of the Committee of Safety in 1775 and 1776 and sat in the new House of Delegates in the October 1776 session and from May through December 1782, when he retired from public life. Tabb died in Amelia County in the spring of 1798.

St. George Tucker (1752–1827) was born on 29 June 1752 at Port Royal, Bermuda, to Henry and Anne (Butterfield) Tucker. He emigrated to Virginia in 1771 and enrolled in the College of William and Mary. After graduation, he was admitted to the bar and began a law practice in Williamsburg. He joined the army upon the outbreak of the American Revolution and rose to the rank of lieutenant colonel, commanding a troop of cavalry that served with Lafayette in the Yorktown campaign.

Tucker's public career began on 30 November 1781, when he was chosen by the General Assembly to be a member of the Council of State. He attended his first Council meeting on 22 January 1782 and served until 24 May; on 28 May 1782 the General Assembly removed him from the Council. Tucker returned to public life four years later when he was named a commissioner to represent Virginia at the Annapolis convention, and on 4 January 1788 he was elected a judge of the General Court. In 1789 and 1790 Tucker served on a committee charged with revising the laws of Virginia; he also succeeded George Wythe as professor of law at the College of William and Mary.

Tucker served on the General Court and as law professor until 1804, when he was elevated to Virginia's Supreme Court of Appeals. He remained on the appeals court until 1811, resigning in protest over the General Assembly's decision to double the number of days the court was to meet without increasing judicial salaries. In 1813 President James Madison appointed him a judge of the United States District Court of Virginia, a position he held for fourteen years until failing health forced him to retire. Tucker died in Nelson County on 10 November 1827.

John Walker (1744–1809) was born on 13 February 1744 at Castle Hill, in Albemarle County, to Thomas and Mildred (Thornton) Walker. He was graduated from the College of William and Mary in 1764 and became a planter on his estate, Belvoir, in Albemarle County. In 1771 he was elected to the House of Burgesses, where he represented Albemarle from 1772 through 1776. Walker was active on the Albemarle County revolutionary committee and was a member of the first through the fourth revolutionary conventions. In 1775 he traveled to Fort Pitt as part of a commission sent to conclude a treaty of peace and friendship with the Ohio Indians on Virginia's northwestern frontier, and he was named by the Continental Congress a commissioner for Indian affairs in the southern department. In 1777 he served as an aide on the staff of General George Washington.

On 17 June 1779 the General Assembly chose Walker to sit on the Council of State in place of his father, who, at his own request, had been voted off the Council. Walker served on the Council only until December 1779, when he was chosen to represent Virginia in the Continental Congress. He served in Congress from May through November 1780. In June 1781 Walker was again elected to the Council, but he declined to serve. Following the revolutionary war, he studied law and began a legal practice. He did not hold a major public office again until March 1790, when he was appointed to the United States Senate to fill the vacancy left by the death of William Grayson. He completed Grayson's term of office, serving only until November 1790.

Walker returned to his estate in Albemarle County and resumed life as a prosperous planter and lawyer. He died near Madison Mills, in Orange County, on 2 December 1809.

Thomas Walker (1715–1794) was born on 25 January 1715, the second son of Thomas and Susanna (Peachy) Walker, of King and Queen County. He is believed to have attended the College of William and Mary and to have studied medicine in Williamsburg before beginning what became a successful medical practice in Fredericksburg. Walker had an intense interest in the western region of Virginia, and in the 1740s and 1750s he was involved in extensive exploration and land speculation in the vicinity of present-day Kentucky. He represented Louisa County in the House of Burgesses from 1752 through 1754, but resigned in order to become deputy surveyor of Augusta County.

In 1755 Walker was named commissary general to George Washington's Virginia troops fighting in the French and Indian War. During the next two decades he was also active in the political life of the Virginia colony, serving in the House of Burgesses for Hampshire County from March 1756 through April 1761, for Albemarle County from November 1761 through July 1771, and for Louisa County from June 1775 through the collapse of royal government in 1776.

Walker enthusiastically supported Virginia's move toward independence in the mid-1770s, and he represented Louisa County at the first four of Virginia's revolutionary conventions. In 1775 he joined his son John on the commission sent to Fort Pitt to negotiate a treaty with the Ohio Indians, and he was named by the Continental Congress a commissioner for Indian affairs in the middle department. Walker served on the Virginia Committee of Safety from 21 January through 5 July 1776, and on 11 October 1776 the General Assembly chose him to become a member of the Council of State. He served on the executive board until 17 June 1779, when he volunteered to be one of the two councillors scheduled to be removed from the board by the General Assembly. Upon leaving the Council, he headed the Virginia commission that drew the commonwealth's boundary line with North Carolina. Walker closed his public career in 1782 by serving in the House of Delegates for Albemarle County. He died at Castle Hill on 9 November 1794.

Benjamin Waller (1716–1786) was born on 1 October 1716, the fifth child of John and Dorothy (King) Waller, then of King William County. Young Benjamin moved with his family to Newport, in Spotsylvania County, early in the 1720s but remained there only a short while. About the age of ten, he became the protégé of John Carter, the secretary of the colony. He moved with Carter to Williamsburg, where he attended the College of William and Mary. At the age of eighteen he went to work in the secretary's office under the direction of Matthew Kemp, clerk of the General Court. Waller also studied law and began a profitable practice in Williamsburg. He was awarded several county offices: deputy clerk of James City County in 1737, king's attorney for Gloucester County in 1738, and king's attorney for James City County in 1739. In December 1739 he was made clerk of James City County and, upon the death of Matthew Kemp, was appointed clerk of the General Court, one of the most powerful and lucrative positions in the colony. Waller also amassed a sizable fortune serving as a collector of debts owed to British merchants by Virginia colonists. He held these positions through the mid-1770s. In addition, Waller sat in the House of Burgesses for James City County from September 1744 through April 1761.

As a leading citizen of Williamsburg, Waller was elected to the Williamsburg revolutionary committee in 1774. In general, however, he kept a low profile in the events that led to the outbreak of war with Great Britain. Gradually, he gave up his public positions and retired to private life. In December 1778, however, he was persuaded to accept a seat on the new Council of State. He remained on the Council until he was removed by vote of the General Assembly on 17 June 1779—the same day he was elected a judge of the admiralty court. In that capacity he also sat on Virginia's first Court of Appeals, organized in August 1779.

When the capital of the commonwealth was moved to Richmond in 1781, however, Waller found it difficult to attend court sessions, owing to his old age and poor health. Complaints about his nonattendance reached him in November 1785, and he resigned his judicial posts immediately. Waller died in Williamsburg on 1 May 1786.

George Webb (1729–1792), the eldest son of George and Lucy (Foster) Webb, of New Kent County, was born on 4 July 1729. Owing to the destruction of New Kent County records, little is known about Webb's youth. At least as early as 1768 he was appointed sheriff of New Kent County, serving until about 1772. In 1775 he became a member of the Elizabeth City County revolutionary committee, and on 5 July 1776 the fifth revolutionary convention named him a commissioner of the admiralty. He served in this capacity until he was elected treasurer of Virginia in December 1776. Webb held the office until he resigned in December 1779. He also served a term as mayor of Williamsburg from November 1777 through November 1778.

On 24 May 1780 the General Assembly chose Webb to sit on the Council of State, where he remained until he was removed by vote of the General Assembly on 28 May 1782. Within a few days of his removal from the executive board, however, he accepted an offer to become receiver of continental taxes in Virginia. Webb retained this position until December 1787, when he appears to have retired from public life. He died in Goochland County on 26 September 1792.

James Wood (1741–1813) was born in Frederick County on 28 January 1741 to James and Mary (Rutherford) Wood. In 1766 he won election to the House of Burgesses for Frederick County, and shortly thereafter he became a member of the Frederick County court. In 1773 he traveled to western Florida as an agent for George Washington, and the following year he fought at the battle of Point Pleasant as captain of a Frederick County militia company. He continued to represent his native county as a burgess from 1766 through 1776.

Wood was a member of Virginia's first and fifth revolutionary conventions, and in 1775 he was appointed to a commission sent to Fort Pitt to negotiate a treaty with the Ohio Indians on Virginia's northwestern frontier. He was also named commissioner for the settlement of claims in Augusta County resulting from Dunmore's War. During the Revolution, Wood served as a colonel in both the Virginia and the Continental armies. He left the state's service in 1784 with the rank of brigadier general. Wood represented Frederick County in the May 1784 session of the House of Delegates, and on 22 June he was chosen a member of the Council of State. He served as president of the Council and acted often as lieutenant governor of the commonwealth between December 1788 and December 1796, when he was elected governor of Virginia. Wood served three terms as governor, and when he left office in December 1799 he was reelected to the Council. He stayed on the Council until the spring of 1803, when he resigned, having been chosen for removal by the General Assembly on 10 December 1802. On 7 January 1812, at the age of seventy, Wood was once again elected to the Council. He served on the executive board until his death on 16 June 1813.

INDEX

20, 46; militia in, 20; sheriff in, 63, 82, 164, 192, 213, 237, 287, 304, 337

Amelia Springs, 312

Amherst Co.: collector of vouchers in, 43; courthouse in, 76, 77, 88, 89, 204; justices of the peace in, 222; lieutenant in, 142; militia in, 142; property taken in judgment against delinquent sheriff to be sold in, 76, 77, 88, 89, 204; public warehouses in, 123, 210; sheriff in, 205, 281, 306; surveyor in, 135; tobacco inspectors in, 123, 210

Ammonet, John, 73

Ammunition, 10, 22, 86, 122, 134, 169, 213, 292

Anderson, Francis, Jr., 129

Anderson, Garland, 203

Anderson, Henry, 63, 82, 213, 237, 287, 304, 305

Anderson, James, 208

Anderson, John (Clinch River), 92

Anderson, John (criminal), 129

Anderson, John (Greenbrier Co.), 135

Anderson, Matthew (state senator), 137

Anderson, Matthew (tobacco inspector), 7, 62, 66, 179

Anderson, Mr., 199

Anderson, Natt., 6

Anderson, Paulin (Pauling), 20, 46

Anderson, Robert, 199

Anderson, Thomas (Buckingham Co.), 116

Anderson, Thomas (Louisa Co.), 130

Anderson, Thomas (Mecklenburg Co.), 212

Andrews, ———, 260

Andrews, Robert, 83, 171

Andrews, William, 63

Annapolis, Md., 151

Antelope (schooner), 42

Anthony, James, 191

Antigua, 269

Anvils, 53

Antrim, Caleb, 319

Antrim, Joseph, 319

Appeals, Court of: Attorney General instructed to take case to, 302; bookcases of, repaired, 133; clerk of, 10, 233; confirms decree of High Court of Chancery, 257; judges of, 29, 44, 136, 198

Applegate and Company, Messrs., 18

Archer, ———, 261, 280

Archer, Abraham, 137

Archer, Edward, 82, 324, 333

Archer, John, 333

Archer, John (Amelia Co.), 129

Armistead, George, 244

Armistead, Mr., 50

Armistead, Robert (New Kent Co.), 325

Armistead, Robert (Prince George Co.) 54, 87

Armistead, William, 54, 55, 64, 71, 83, 85

Armistead, William, Jr., 34

Armorer, 15, 147, 199

Arms, 10, 22, 41, 52, 68, 105, 134, 140, 292. *See also* Military, supplies; Point of Fork

Armstrong, James, 286

Armstrong, Mary, 290

Armstrong, William, 22

Arnol, John, 139

Arnold, George, 219

Arnold, John, 139

Arnold, Stephen, 139

Arthur, James, 196

Arthurs, Thomas, 278

Artificers, public, 251; account of, rejected, 68; number to be reduced, 271; pay for, 31, 69, 101, 119, 177, 197, 211, 250, 276, 300, 316; superintendent of, 31, 55, 64, 69, 71, 101, 105, 119, 177, 197, 211, 250, 284, 306; two additional to be hired, 105. *See also* Point of Fork

Asberry, George, 278

Ashburne, George, 340

Ashby, Bladen, 7

Ashby, Daniel, 115

Ashby, Stephen, 217

Donnally, Andrew, 243
Doring, Henry, 219
Dorlon, John, 289
Dorton, Mary, 24
Dorton, Moses, 220
Dorton, William, 220
Doswell, James, 159
Doswell, John, 95
Dougherty, James (Harrison Co.), 45
Dougherty, James (Monongalia Co.), 73
Douglass (Douglas), James, 153
Dowdale, James G., 224
Dowdall, Hugh, 66
Dowdall, Susanna, 66
Downman, William, 274
Dragging Canoe (Cherokee chief), 106, 108
Drake, Jeremiah, 19
Drew, Perez, 340
Drew, Thomas, 81, 82
Drinnin, William, 143
Droddy, Wm., 149
Drumgold, Alexander, 19
Drumgoold, Edmund, 120
Ducguid, George, 167
Dudley, William (King and Queen Co.), 270
Dudley, William (Warwick Co.), 195
Duke, Henry, 304
Dumfries, district of: court in, 91, 107; keeper of public jail in, 67; prisoners escape from jail in, 93; prisoners transported to jail in, 66–67, 68, 70, 141
Dumfries warehouse, 119, 178, 262, 263, 332; inspector of tobacco in, 129, 253
Dunbar, John, 60, 201
Duncan, James, 323
Dunet, William, 71
Dunlevy, George, 116
Dunlevy, James, 81
Dunn, Benja., 139
Dunn, ——— (inspector at Bowler's warehouse), 260
Dunn, ——— (inspector at Poropotank warehouse), 262

Dunscomb (Dunscombe), Andrew: accounts of, 67; as clerk to commissioner of continental accounts, 40, 65, 66, 110, 111–112, 113, 197–198, 209, 214; as commissioner of continental accounts, 3, 28, 29, 36; letter to, 80; salary of, 40, 65–66, 156, 178, 202, 209
Dupey, James, Jr., 295
Durrett, William, 181
Duval, William, 79
Duvall (Duval), Francis, 174, 316
Dyer, Roger, 279
Dymer's warehouse, 215

Eager, John, 237
Eagle (sloop), 101
Eason, Samuel, 178
Easson, John, 303
Eastern shore: Indians on, 120; public jailor on, 62
Eastin, Reubin, 333
Echkols, James, 102
Eddins, Samuel (captain), 189
Eddins, Samuel (searcher at York), 62, 187
Edgar, Thomas, 59, 195
Edgington, Joseph, 21
Edmondson, Benjamin, 312
Edmondson, James Powell, 127
Edmondson, Thomas Powell, 88
Edmunds, Howell, 266
Edmundson, Benjamin, 176
Edmundson, David, 340
Edward, ———, 262
Edwards, Jacob, 21
Eggleston, Joseph, 287, 305
Electors, presidential: appointment of, 8, 39; act concerning, to be printed, 8
Eliza (sloop), 113
Elizabeth City: collector of vouchers in, 43; coroner in, 162; escheator in, 162; justices of the peace in, 119; sheriff in, 146, 228, 317
Elizabeth River, district of: naval officer in, 54, 81
Elizabeth River Parish, 28

Nully, William, 299
Nutall, ———, 260
Nutt, William, 30, 307

OConner, Timothy, 35
Odell, Elijah, 291
O'Farrell (OFarrell), Dennis, 84
Ogle, Mary, 119, 199
Ogleby, Richard, 177
Oglesby, Jacob, 215
Ohio Co.: arms transported to, 23; assembly members from, 223; collector of vouchers in, 43; complaints concerning inadequate defense measures taken for, 235; Indian hostilities in 287; justices of the peace in, 288; lieutenant in, 45, 124, 292; militia in, 27, 45, 246; rangers in, 21, 28, 98, 124, 199, 338; scouts in, 21, 28, 98, 123, 142, 199, 223; sheriff in, 97, 199, 312
Ohio River, 91, 133, 289
Oldham, William, 206
Oliver, John, 245
Olone, Charles, 119
Onsley, Thomas, 99
Orange Co.: collector of vouchers in, 43; coroner in, 12; court of, 195; courthouse in, 204; express rider sent to, 312, 317; militia in, 195; property taken in judgment against delinquent sheriff to be sold in, 204; sheriff in, 164, 165, 226, 279
Orphans, 130, 290, 312
Orr, Alexander Dalrimple, 21
Osborn, Zenah, 234
Osborne, Abner, 23, 65
Osburn, Enock, 208
Osgood, Samuel, 345
Oster, Martin, 42, 61, 70, 168
Otey, Jno., 134
Overstreet, Benoni, 305
Overstreet, Lennah (Leanah), 206
Owen, William, Sr., 135
Owens, John, 328
Oxen, Samuel, 138

Page, Carter, 190
Page, John (Frederick Co.), 192
Page, John (Williamsburg), 15
Page's warehouse, 263
Paine, James, 289
Paine, Samuel (Boston?), 137
Paine, Samuel (Richmond), 97, 270
Painter, David, 319
Painter, George, 139
Painter, Isaac, 319
Painter, John, 319
Pallat (Pallot), John, 207
Pallat (Pallot), Matthew, 207
Pallat, William, 207
Palsley, Jacob, 234
Pankey, Stephen, 259
Paragon (schooner), 72
Parchment, Peter, 119
Pardons: conditional, 36, 70, 102; granted by Council, 7, 13, 20, 28, 84, 86, 87, 90, 99, 102, 107, 117, 129, 140, 143, 154, 156, 159, 179, 189, 199, 201, 206, 209, 212, 219, 259, 273, 274, 276, 277, 283, 317, 320, 321, 338
Parham, Lewis, 182
Parkason, Joseph, 95
Parker, Alexander, 42, 242
Parker, John, 103
Parker, Joseph, 333
Parker, Josiah (justice), 303
Parker, Josiah (naval officer), 54
Parker, Richard, 60
Parker, Thomas, 42, 86, 125, 158, 208
Parker's warehouses, 214
Parkins, Isaac, 319
Parkins, John, 319
Parkinson, Joseph, 161
Parks, William, 138
Parpoint, Charles, 163
Parrow, Daniel, 308
Parsons, Charles, 117, 219
Parsons, Isaac, 150
Parsons, Mr., 134
Parsons, William, 234
Parsons, William Ap Thomas, 119
Pasteur, William, 190

Sampson, Stephen, 78, 79, 164, 165, 183, 203, 281, 283
Sampson, William, 187
Samuels, James, 214
Sandidge, Joseph, 61, 84
Sanford,———, 262
Sanford, Daniel, 17
Sanford, Edward, 60
Sanford, Richard, 216, 234
Saunders, David, 311
Saunders, Peter, 96, 222, 278
Saunders, Robert H., 12, 26, 186
Saunders, Samuel H., 253
Savage,———, 300, 301
Savage, George, 328
Savine, Abraham, 195
Sayers, Robert, 68
Sayers, Robert (Wythe Co.), 162
Scales, 305
Scarbrough, John, 100
Schooners: charter of, 4; registers issued for, 23, 36, 42, 51, 59, 62, 72, 85, 94, 99, 110
Scott, Anderson, 112, 160
Scott, Charles (county lieutenant), 15
Scott, Charles (general), 247, 309, 315, 325, 326, 327
Scott, Charles, Sr. (justice of the peace), 279
Scott, David, 73
Scott, James (Monongalia Co.), 219
Scott, James (prisoner), 11
Scott, James (Russell Co.), 308
Scott, John, 6
Scott, Johnny, 12, 226
Scott, Joseph, 39
Scott, Samuel, 308
Scott, Walter, 83
Scott's warehouse, 143
Scouts: on the western frontier, 30; payment of, 18, 83, 117, 124, 125, 126, 138–139, 151. *See also* names of counties
Scruggs, Gross, 76, 88
Seabrook, Nicholas B., 85
Seal, public: keeper of the. *See* Blair, Archibald
Searcher, 233; at Alexandria, 60, 105, 117; books and papers of

transferred to solicitor's office, 131; at City Point, 46, 105, 145; land, 10; at Norfolk, 49, 114, 136; at Urbanna, 10; at York, 105
Searcy, Asa, 123
Seaton, Augustine (Austin), 122
Seawell, John, Jr., 308
Secretary's office, 83
Segoine (Seigoine), Louis, 91
Selden, Cary, 119
Selden, Joseph, 102
Selden, Miles, 135; appointed colonel of second regiment of Henrico militia, 54; appointed to committee to examine offices of treasurer, auditor, and solicitor, 298, 308; in attendance at Council meetings, 289–304, 305–317, 321–329, 330–340; called back to the Council, 312; offered to pay for express rider sent to retrieve him, 313–314; qualified as member of the Council, 289
Selden, Samuel, 305
Semple, James, 325
Sequestration law, 272, 308, 315, 330
Settelington, Robert, 312
Sewell, Thomas, 327
Sexton, Meshack, 319
Shackelford, Lyne, 213
Shanklin, Andrew, 221
Shannon (Shanan), William: accounts of referred to Council settlement, 18, 142, 229–230, 237, 238, 241–242, 250, 321, 322
Sharp, Robert, Jr. (Albemarle Co.), 321
Sharp, Richard, Jr. (Henrico Co.), 87, 104
Shavers, Hugh, 117, 318
Shaw, William, 200
Shearman, Adam, Jr., 291
Shearman, Joseph, 159
Shelby, Isaac (colonel), 209
Shelby, Isaac (sheriff), 219
Shelela (schooner), 62
Shelton, Abraham, 76, 77, 164
Shelton, Clough, 116
Shelton, Crispin, Jr., 181